The Origins of the Organic Movement

Philip Conford

With a Foreword by Jonathan Dimbleby

Floris Books

First published in 2001 by Floris Books

British Library CIP Data available

ISBN 0–86315–336–4

Printed in Great Britain
by Bell & Bain, Glasgow

Contents

To Betty
with love and thanks

List of abbreviations

Names printed in SMALL CAPITALS refer the reader to background notes in the Appendices.
Appendix A: Leading figures in the organic movement and the orthodox school of agriculture
Appendix B: Groups, institutions and journals

BMJ	*British Medical Journal*
BPP	British People's Party
BUF	British Union of Fascists
CCC	Council for the Church and Countryside
CSL	Church Socialist League
CT	*Church Times*
ERCI	Economic Reform Club and Institute
FJ	*Fertiliser, Feeding Stuffs and Farm Supplies Journal* [referred to in the text as *Fertiliser Journal*]
FoL	Friends of the Land
FQ	*Fascist Quarterly*
HDRA	Henry Doubleday Research Association
HL	*Health and Life*
IAOS	Irish Agricultural Organization Society
ICF	Industrial Christian Fellowship
ICI	Imperial Chemical Industries
ILP	Independent Labour Party
JMA	*Journal of the Ministry of Agriculture*
JRASE	*Journal of the Royal Agricultural Society of England*
KKK	Kibbo Kift Kin
LKG	League of the Kingdom of God
MB	*Monthly Bulletin of the ERCI*
ME	*Mother Earth*
NA	*New Age*
NB	*New Britain*
NBQ	*New Britain Quarterly*
NEW	*New English Weekly*
NFA	Natural Food Associates
NP	*New Pioneer*
NS	*New Statesman*
OWC	Order of Woodcraft Chivalry
PP	*Peoples* [sic] *Post*
RE	*Rural Economy*
RRA	Rural Reconstruction Association
SH	*Soil and Health*
SM	*Soil Magazine*
USDA	United States Department of Agriculture
VPA	Village Produce Association

Acknowledgments

The Origins of the Organic Movement is based extensively on the doctoral thesis which I submitted to the University of Reading, and I would therefore like to start by thanking my supervisors — Professor Ted Collins, Dr Jean Walsingham and Dr Ross Wordie — for the encouragement and guidance which enabled me to graduate in the summer of 2000. Dr Jeremy Burchardt, John Creasey and Heather Neo, of the Rural History Centre at Reading, also gave me much assistance and support during my years there as a part-time research student.

I have been helped over the past few years by many people who have provided either information, or access to source materials, or hospitality; in some cases all three. My grateful thanks go to Joanna Ray and her father Dr Kenneth Barlow, whose death sadly occurred as this book was being prepared for publication; Anthea Bell; Julia Byngham and Joe Potts; Giles de la Mare; Sir John Eliot Gardiner; Giles and Mary Heron; Patrick Holden; Frances Hutchinson; Mary Langman; Riccardo Ling; Fr Frank McHugh; Mrs Penelope Massingham; Fr Peter Mayhew; Adam Nott; John S. Peart-Binns; Rev David G. Peck; Dr Marjorie Reeves; Anthony Rodale; Julian Rose; the late Pamela Travers, and Dr Walter Yellowlees.

Vivian Griffiths gave me considerable help with Chapter 4, and I hope that he will feel it does reasonable justice to the role played in the early organic movement by Rudolf Steiner and his followers. Mrs Violet MacDermot and Dr Mike Tyldesley of the New Atlantis Foundation have encouraged my interest in Dmitri Mitrinovic and the various groups and movements with which he was associated. Anne Williamson of the Henry Williamson Society provided me with information about her father-in-law and enabled me to publish a piece on the organic movement in the 1999 issue of the Society's journal.

I have benefited from use of the British Library, the Rural History Centre archive at the University of Reading, the Soil Association library, the Bodleian Library, Oxford, and the Chichester branch of the West Sussex County Council library service. The Soil Association has enabled me to publish some articles on organic pioneers in its journal *Living Earth*. Some material in the book has appeared, in a different form, in *Rural*

History, whose editor Keith Snell gave me early encouragement in my writing. Part of Chapter 10, in a slightly amended form, has appeared in the *Agricultural History Review.*

I owe personal thanks to Bob Waller and his late wife Sue, who for more than a decade provided discussion of organic issues as one aspect of a most valuable friendship; to Professor Richard Sheppard and his wife Carolyn, who provided me with free lodgings in Oxford which enabled me to use the Bodleian Library during several summers, and kept me on my toes by dint of many jocular references to compost; to Simon Sykes, without whose insistence that I should escape from the claustrophobic corporatism of the further education system and cease teaching, neither the thesis nor this book could have been completed; and to Betty Boorman, for her companionship when visiting many people and many secondhand bookshops, and her readiness to learn about the curiosities of the organic family tree.

Jonathan Dimbleby, current President of the Soil Association, agreed to find time in his hectic schedule to read the manuscript and write a typically lucid foreword to it; his generosity in this is greatly appreciated. Finally, I would like to thank Christopher Moore and Christian Maclean of Floris Books for suggesting that my thesis be turned into a book, thereby ensuring that the fruit of fifteen years' reading was at least given the chance of reaching a wider public than would otherwise have been the case. I hope that their faith and patience will be rewarded.

Philip Conford
Chichester
December 2000

Foreword

Today, with the benefit of hindsight, the term 'movement' generally raises an eyebrow, a twinge of suspicion. It is a word which suggests, *inter alia,* a crusade by forces that have rejected the usual routes of debate and persuasion. The new Countryside Movement, for example, explicitly seeks to convince the public that it represents values and attitudes that transcend those expressed through the 'usual' channels of democracy by the elected representatives of the conventional political parties. We ask ourselves whether its potency in rural England at the turn of this century is a healthy rebuke to a metropolitan élite or a reactionary backlash against social and cultural progress.

We harbour such doubts because our folk memories remind us that in the early years of the last century the western world was ravaged by competing movements all claiming unique access to the Holy Grail. The Labour Movement — now quiescent if not moribund — is perhaps the only survivor of those pre-war political forces that is not viewed with retrospective distaste. The rest, associated with totalitarian or fascistic thuggery, are today disavowed as aberrations, the products of economic distress or evil demagoguery.

So where does the organic movement, which — as Philip Conford reveals — has its roots in that tumultuous era, stand in this pantheon? On the side of progress or reaction? Even to ask the question is to challenge a myth to which many supporters of the movement — to which I now belong — cling with tenacity. For us, it is self-evident on our blighted planet, where the forces of 'conventional' food production have held sway for half a century, that the organic movement is on the side of progress. How could anyone think otherwise in the face of the evidence? It is the apostles of pesticides and fertilizers that wage war on the environment who are the reactionaries, who persevere with farming methods that are self-evidently and quite rightly in terminal decline.

Yet we freely acknowledge that the organic movement does indeed hark backwards as well as looking forwards; in our mythology there was an age of innocence in which traditional — organic or quasi-organic — husbandry was not only benign in itself but driven by values to which all progressive forces would have inevitably subscribed. It is this myth that is challenged in Philip Conford's thoroughly researched and impeccably argued history. With painstaking care, he exhumes the organic movement from the murk of a largely forgotten past, dusts it down, holds it up to an impartial light, and, in this process illuminates a fascinating if disconcerting chronicle.

Many organic enthusiasts assume that the organic movement started with the revered Lady Eve Balfour and her fellow pioneers who founded the Soil Association just over half a century ago. Their belief that there is a crucial link between healthy soils and healthy plants which in turn promotes human health has become a presumption that is axiomatic for most adherents of organic farming. However, apart from that intuitive conviction, the organic movement's campaign nowadays for healthy food and a healthy environment has precious little ideological content — and the Soil Association (the leading organic body in the United Kingdom) is, in party terms, a strictly apolitical organization.

But, as Conford reveals, it was not ever thus. The roots of the organic movement go back to the years before the Second World War and are to be found entangled with some of the more eccentric, unstable and disreputable cultural and political ideas which then held sway. Conford's analysis of this intriguing phenomenon, however, is subtle and detached. Happily avoiding the temptation to deride or condemn the fellow-travellers of the early organic movement, he places their role both within the context of the economic and technological upheavals of that era and, specifically, within the framework of that miscellany of contemporary ideas and beliefs that were in constant and often self-contradictory flux during that tumultuous period.

For example, among the earliest advocates of what we would today regard as organic principles were, on the one hand, the Guild Socialists and, on the other, the Distributists, quasi-anarchists inspired by Hilaire Belloc and G.K. Chesterton, who extolled peasant life, railed against central bureaucracy, and denounced free trade. From a quite different perspective, Rudolf Steiner (the founder of the esoteric and not widely recognized doctrines of Anthroposophy) played a crucial part with his collaborators in defining the parameters of the organic debate and — within their own cosmic vision — articulating the need for a scientific basis to support the intuition of organic enthusiasts. From yet another standpoint, the work of the nutritionist, John Boyd Orr (later to become the first Director of the Food and Agricultural Organization of the United Nations) was to became a prime source of quasi-clinical evidence for the organic cause.

An eclectic range of writers and poets found themselves attracted to the organic cause: among them, H.J. Massingham, Ronald Duncan, John Middleton Murry, John Stewart Collis, Adrian Bell (the father of the BBC war reporter, later MP for Tatton, Martin Bell) and Rolf Gardiner (the father of the distinguished conductor John Eliot Gardiner, himself an organic farmer). At their most sympathetic, they saw, in Conford's felicitous phrase, that 'a sense of the sacred was a prequisite of genuine materialism' — an anachronistic notion perhaps in our secular and cynical age but reflective of values that still resonate in some parts of the modern organic movement.

But there were darker forces lurking here as well — notions that were by turns foolish and foetid. Henry Williamson, for example, became a member of Oswald Mosley's British Union of Fascists. Rolf Gardiner was a member of the English Mistery, another far-right movement. Jorian Jenks, the Soil Association's editorial secretary from 1946 until his death in 1963, not only supported the BUF but, to his own satisfaction at least, managed entirely to merge the guiding principles of organic husbandry with those of Fascism. The poet Edmund Blunden (who rather hoped that Goering would become Protector of England) and the historian Sir Arthur Bryant (who narrowly avoided internment for his Nazi sympathies) belonged to a group called 'Kinship in Husbandry' which was central to the organic movement in the forties.

It is a disconcerting narrative but by no means a cause for retrospective guilt. Indeed by exploring the lure of the organic movement for these fatuous romantics, Philip Conford has done the organic movement of today a great favour: better by far to give the dirty linen an airing than to whitewash the past.

However, there is far more to Conford's work than these salutary revelations. For example, he fully explores a range of issues that were fundamental to British agriculture and the development of the organic cause: the impact on the landscape and on rural England of the drive for agricultural efficiency; the creation of ever-larger farm units; the acceleration of mechanized means of production; the challenge of soil erosion and declining fertility; the demand for cheap food; the need for better nutrition and higher standards of health; the search for 'rural reconstruction,' and, not least, the inspiration that the British pioneers of the organic movement derived from the agriculture of Asia — or 'the Orient' as it was then quaintly described. Many of the issues which defined the terms of the organic debate in those early days are no less pertinent in our times.

The Origins of the Organic Movement may not be for the casual reader but it will be indispensable to anyone who seeks a better understanding of the origins of what has become — belatedly — one of the most compelling campaigns of the new century: a cause whose time, it appears, has finally arrived.

Jonathan Dimbleby
February 2001

1. Organic Origins

There is good news for supporters of organically-grown food: an out-standing medical scientist has lent his weight to their campaign, declaring authoritatively: 'That organic manures ... are superior to all artificial manures is now generally acknowledged.'[1]

Before the organic movement becomes too excited about this endorsement, however, I have to deflate the optimism by revealing that Dr G.V. POORE wrote the above words a century ago. Given the exponential increase in use of artificial fertilizers since the 1940s, it is understating the case to say that Poore's message did not meet with general acceptance.

In 1998 I taught at a Summer School on Ecological Agriculture held at the Agricultural University of Wageningen, in the Netherlands, and quoted Poore's opinion, asking the students to guess its date. The revelation that Poore had expressed his belief in the superiority of organic methods at the turn of the twentieth century was greeted with surprise and scepticism. Most of the students could trace the organic movement back about ten years, connecting its emergence with the food scares of the 1990s. One or two knew of Rachel Carson's *Silent Spring,* and a middle-aged Icelandic lady was aware that a branch of RUDOLF STEINER'S BIODYNAMIC MOVEMENT had been established in her country by the early 1930s. The general feeling, though, was that organic food production and an ecological approach to agriculture had emerged only since the 1960s. It is a major purpose of this book to demonstrate that a coherent ecological philosophy of agriculture had been articulated fifty years before the course at Wageningen, and that its roots can be traced back a further half-century. Along the way, some common presuppositions about the movement's political and religious affiliations will be challenged.

Certainly the organic movement must appear to most shoppers as something new. The emergence of genetically-modified crops in particular has led in Britain to a rapidly increasing demand for organic produce. More and more products on supermarket shelves advertise themselves as organic, and membership of the SOIL ASSOCIATION, Britain's chief body for promoting the organic cause, has risen rapidly over the past decade.[2]

Not only GM crops, but the salmonella scare of the late 1980s and the BSE crisis have caused concern about the way food is produced, what goes into it, and its possible effects on health. At the time of writing, discussion of GM crops is shifting to the possible environmental dangers and we are being assured that foodstuffs based on GM products cannot possibly be a health risk: an astonishingly optimistic assumption, unlikely to allay public scepticism. Other factors have contributed to unease about contemporary farming: the aesthetic implications of intensive chemical methods in arable areas, resulting in a lifeless, prairie-like landscape; the disappearance of trees, hedges, flowers and birds; the erosion of hill-lands through over-stocking with sheep for the sake of financial gain; the treatment of animals and fowls in factory-farming units; the long distances which foodstuffs travel before they reach the consumer. Even 'organic' foods may travel hundreds or perhaps thousands of miles, and Wageningen University was no doubt right to place its emphasis on 'ecological' agriculture, with organic methods one aspect of a more comprehensive environmentally-friendly approach. Criticism of food production methods has even found its way into novels: there is the tragic force-fed pig of Jane Smiley's *Moo,* and Jonathan Coe's brilliant satire *What a Carve Up!* features as one of its chief villains the cynical head of a junk-food corporation.[3]

The organic movement offers its methods as an antidote to these problems. If the public are concerned about what goes into their food, organic methods can in comparison claim freedom from contamination: no chemical fertilizers or sprays; no steroids; no genetically engineered ingredients. Expressed thus, the principles of organic farming can sound negative, based solely on rejection. Or from seeing organic farming as a contemporary trend one might swing to the other extreme and say that there is nothing special about it at all: it is simply the way that everyone had to farm before the invention of chemical fertilizers, pesticides, herbicides and factory farming units. The way then lies open for the organic movement's critics to prance on to the stage with their ritual cry of 'Luddites!' — a cliché they apply to anyone who suggests that new technology may bring dangers and that human knowledge of its possible effects is less than comprehensive.

Nevertheless, the organic philosophy is indeed at odds with the compulsory optimism enjoined on us by two recent enthusiasts for technological agriculture, since it shares with the wider environmental movement a belief in limits.[4] Frequently explicit, and always implicit, in the writings of those who created the organic movement is belief in a natural order whose laws cannot be flouted with impunity. Organic farming is not about rejection; it is about positive acceptance of the natural order and the intention to work with its laws. Fundamental to it is observing the Rule of Return, which decrees that the soil's health and fertility must be maintained by encouraging the presence of humus. Subjecting the soil to monoculture on industrial lines and trying to maintain its productiveness through chemical fertilizers can only, on this view, lead to soil exhaustion and to crops vulnerable to pests and disease. Soil requires replenishment with organic matter; it is not an inert substance, but alive, teeming with organisms, and can be killed by exploitation. To imagine that it can be kept fertile by applying chemical elements is to ignore the literally vital role played by humus, and, ultimately, to create deserts. This is the heart of the organic argument. In its extreme form it rejects altogether the use of chemical fertilizers; more moderate adherents to the organic cause have been prepared to use them for short-term purposes, or as part of a balanced process of manuring to which humus, not withstanding, is of primary importance.[5] Obeying the Rule of Return not only ensures survival of the fertile topsoil on which human life and civilization depend, but creates plants which do not need the continual application of poison sprays. Organic cultivation is about establishing a virtuous circle: the return of wastes to the soil creates humus, which encourages healthy crops whose remains, properly composted, return to enrich the soil's humus content. Not all farming before the invention of chemical fertilizers was organic, however, as the Roman *latifundia* demonstrate.

If organic *methods* have existed for centuries, the organic *movement* could begin only once an alternative to them existed. This did not happen until the nineteenth century brought the industrial production of artificial fertilizers and the rapid spread of urbanization. Between them, these processes presented a serious challenge to the practice of the Rule of Return. The crucial decade was the 1840s, during which three important events occurred which were to have far-reaching effects on British, and ultimately world, agriculture. In 1840 the German chemist JUSTUS VON LIEBIG published his monograph *Chemistry in its Application to Agriculture and Physiology,* which offered a new theory of plant nutrition. In it he argued that inorganic fertilizers could replace manure, since it was not the manure or humus which was important in itself for plant growth, but the minerals they contained. He saw his agricultural work as proof of chemistry's ability to transform an empirical activity into a science. Botanists and physiologists had neglected plant chemistry, but the processes of transformation were purely chemical and could not be understood without laboratory experiments.[6]

Liebig was not the first agricultural chemist: Sir Humphrey Davy, for instance, had lectured on the subject for ten years at the Royal Institution and in 1813 published his *Elements of Agricultural Chemistry*, which, according to Liebig's biographer William Brock, was the high point of the science before Liebig's development of organic chemistry.[7] But Liebig was influential because of his reputation in Britain and because his enthusiastic exposition of his ideas encouraged farmers to believe that a rational approach to agriculture was now possible, one which would be aware of all the necessary nutrients for a specific plant or crop. He considered agriculture to be the basis of all commerce and of the life of the state. His theories seemed for the first time to give farmers and scientists a power over the soil and a control of crops which would ensure maximum productivity. When Liebig visited Britain in 1842 he was treated like royalty, met leading agriculturalists, and was made an honorary member of the Royal Agricultural Society of England. His attempts at commercially exploiting his theories proved less successful, owing to his neglect of nitrogen's role in plant growth, and his patent fertilizer performed so badly that many farmers later resented him, criticizing his lack of practical knowledge of their calling. But even his failures provoked interest and spurred on further experimentation; Liebig's work precipitated a revolution in agriculture during the 1840s.[8]

The second important date is 1843. In that year JOHN BENNET LAWES and J.H. GILBERT — the latter had been Liebig's pupil — established the investigations at ROTHAMSTED, near Harpenden in Hertfordshire, which grew into the world-famous Experimental Station whose work came to represent so much that the organic movement disliked. Also in 1843 Lawes, who the previous year had patented a process for manufacturing superphosphates, established a fertilizer factory in Deptford, South London, which was to make him a fortune. Commercial vested interests in promoting artificial fertilizers were making their first appearance.

As a landowner with plenty of capital, and as someone who was cautious about the complexities of agricultural chemistry, Lawes was able to test his fertilizers for five years on pot plants and in field trials, ensuring that they were more successful than Liebig's and enabling him to attack Liebig in the *Journal of the Royal Agricultural Society of England* in 1847. He argued that nitrogenous manures were essential for wheat crops. Lawes' Rothamsted experiments successfully challenged a number of Liebig's theories, and the estate increasingly became a source of practical advice for farmers. A century after its founding it was the world's leading establishment for research into chemical fertilizers, and its Broadbalk field, on which, it was claimed, crops of wheat had been grown every year since 1843 with artificials but no organic manures, seemed to prove conclusively that chemical fertilizers were sufficient in themselves to maintain fertility indefinitely.

The third significant year was 1846, when the Corn Laws were repealed and Britain embarked on a policy of free trade which the pioneers of the organic movement regarded as disastrous for British agriculture. They argued that for the sake of powerful vested interests in industry, shipping and finance, Britain neglected its farming and in exchange for exporting industrial goods became dependent on overseas foodstuffs whose cultivation exhausted the soils of the countries where they were grown.

Use of artificials before the First World War was minimal in comparison with the period since 1940,[9] but warning voices, like Poore's, had been raised by 1914. Essentially these voices were prophetic: their concern about the future of agriculture was based on belief in the Rule of Return, and they found evidence for it in the example of Oriental cultivation, where soils had been kept fertile for centuries through replenishment with biological wastes. As yet, though, these voices did not amount to a coherent movement, since any such movement would need to offer scientific justification for its claim that reliance on chemical fertilizers was potentially dangerous, and provide examples of successful cultivation based on methods which, while following the basic principles of peasant farming, were developing them in the light of the latest scientific knowledge. ALBERT HOWARD'S work in India in the 1920s, discussed in detail in Chapter 3, appeared to provide just what was needed to challenge the growing orthodoxy, encouraged by vested interests, of 'the NPK mentality.'[10]

According to Howard, the role of agricultural science should be to explicate the reasons for the success of traditional methods and to find ways of improving them. Understanding the workings of the natural order would enable humanity to work with nature and realize her potential abundance. More ambitiously, it could even provide a means of reconciling science and religion, with science the servant of God's natural law. Howard drew inspiration from the Eastern image of the Wheel of Life, the 'virtuous circle' referred to earlier. This, in its full form, comprehended not just the soil and plants, but animals and human beings. The students at Wageningen who linked the rise of organic farming to food scares were correct in principle: concern about animal and human health has always been integral to the organic movement. The early organicists regarded agriculture as potentially the best form of preventive medicine. A healthy, humus-rich soil would produce healthy, disease-resistant crops, which would in turn ensure the health of the animals and human beings who consumed them; the wastes would be returned to enrich the soil. Doubts about the quality of food had been widespread in the later nineteenth century, chiefly on account of what was added to it; the early organic movement directed attention to the question of what was missing from it, criticizing 'devitalized' foods from which the nutritional value had been removed (though of course there was also a suspicious interest in the possible adverse effects of consuming food grown and sprayed with poisonous chemicals). Again, it needs to be pointed out that the organic view of health is positive, not negative. Health is not a matter of avoiding certain foods, still less of avoiding meat, nor is it the absence of illness; it is a harmonious functioning of the whole system, which can be encouraged by a diet of food grown in healthy soil.

The work in India of ROBERT MCCARRISON, described in Chapter 3, provided a source of inspiration for the fledgling organic movement. His study of the remarkably healthy Hunza tribesmen suggested that their health was attributable to a diet whose excellence stemmed from their food production methods, which scrupulously obeyed the Rule of Return. His experiments on nutrition, carried out during the 1920s, seemed to provide further scientific evidence favouring traditional cultivation.

* * *

It is notoriously difficult to identify precisely the beginning of a cultural movement, and any choice of a particular date may seem arbitrary and open to dispute. Although organic farming has in one sense existed since Adam and Eve were expelled from Eden, a movement articulating the virtues of such methods has been necessary only since the development of an alternative approach, and systematic scientific investigation of humus-based agriculture, with practical experiments, did not get under way until after the First World War. In a sense it is surprising that it began before the massive increase in application of artificial fertilizers which occurred from 1940 onwards; as late as the 1930s, advocates of artificials were regretting that farmers made insufficient use of them. Certainly the agricultural developments required by the exigencies of war spurred the organic pioneers into prolific activity, and the years from 1938 to 1947 can reasonably be regarded as the most formative in the organic movement's history. But the important strands which were pulled together at that time into a coherent philosophy had emerged a decade or two earlier, and this study will chart the emergence of the organic movement from the 1920s. More specifically, it suggests 1926 as the most suitable starting-point.

An organic view of life implies awareness of the way in which things are interconnected, with, as we have seen, the health of human beings and animals inseparable from the health of crops, which in turn is inseparable from the health and fertility of the soil. To extend the connections further, it follows that the health of the individual cannot be considered in isolation from the family, nor the health of the family in isolation from that of the wider community. In 1926 two doctors, GEORGE SCOTT WILLIAMSON and INNES PEARSE, initiated in Peckham, South London, a family health club which developed into one of the most important features of the organic movement, the PIONEER HEALTH CENTRE, described in Chapter 8. Like McCarrison, they believed that health was more than a mere absence of sickness, and wanted to create conditions to encourage it. The establishment of the Peckham Experiment is not my main reason for choosing 1926 as a starting-point, but before identifying that reason it is necessary to look at what else was happening at the time.

In India, Albert Howard had just taken charge of the Institute of Plant Industry in the State of Indore and was starting to develop the composting process which would soon be adopted in many different countries by experimental farmers; McCarrison was investigating the connection between diet and health. In Africa, the forester RICHARD ST BARBE BAKER, whose career is discussed in Chapter 3, had founded the MEN OF THE TREES and was establishing an international reputation as a conservationist. Two years earlier, the esoteric founder of Anthroposophy Rudolf Steiner had given his lectures on agriculture and, following his death in 1925, his disciple EHRENFRIED PFEIFFER had taken over the experimental work in what came to be known as 'biodynamic' cultivation. By 1928 the biodynamic movement would be established in England, running parallel in the 1930s with the work done by Howard's followers and linking with it particularly through the influence of Pfeiffer himself, as Chapter 4 will show.

Other figures later to be important members of the organic school were finding their way towards its theory and practice. On his Hampshire estate Gerard Wallop, VISCOUNT LYMINGTON, was developing ideas on agriculture which by 1928, as he recorded in his autobiography,[11] anticipated the work of Rachel Carson. In 1927 the young Wessex folk-dancing enthusiast ROLF GARDINER would take over Gore Farm near Shaftesbury in Dorset and begin the experiments in rural reconstruction whose political affiliations were to make him a controversial local figure.[12] Another estate in southern England was already a centre for similar activities: near Fordingbridge in Hampshire the doctor AUBREY WESTLAKE was running the ORDER OF WOODCRAFT CHIVALRY, with which var-

ious organicists were involved.[13] The RURAL RECONSTRUCTION ASSOCIA-
TION, which sought to influence government agricultural policy, was
formed in 1926. At Aberystwyth, R.G. STAPLEDON was preparing the way
for his major study of land-use and his gradual shift from optimistic pro-
gressivism to a more cautious awareness of technology's dangers.[14] LADY
EVE BALFOUR was farming in Suffolk, and FRIEND SYKES, was beginning
to think about animal health on his Buckinghamshire farm. In New
Zealand, JORIAN JENKS was working for the improvement of deteriorated
lands, and would return to England in 1928, starting on a path which led
him to a central position in the organic movement and to wartime imprisonment. McCarrison's interest in human health was shared by the eccentric EDGAR J. SAXON, who promoted vitality by means of nature cure and
during the 1920s established 'vitamin cafés' in London, early health food
restaurants. His journal *The Healthy Life* ran throughout the 1920s and,
reconstituted as *HEALTH AND LIFE* in 1934, would vigorously support the
organic movement, as Chapter 8 will show. At the Rowett Institute in
Aberdeen, the nutritionist JOHN BOYD ORR was carrying out the research
on dietary needs which was eventually to lead to him being appointed
first Director of the Food and Agriculture Organization of the United
Nations, and, more humbly, to make him a prime source of evidence for
the views of the organic school. In 1926 the topographer H.J. MASSING-
HAM published *Downland Man,* a major archaeological work which presented English history as a decline from a higher, more peaceful state of
civilization. Massingham's subsequent celebrations of England's rural
culture were to lead him to the heart of the organic movement. Uniting all
these figures, who would gravitate towards each other over the next fifteen years, was a concern about soil fertility, health, the state of agriculture and rural decline.

The movement's interests were inseparable from social issues, and its
development needs to be seen in the wider context of the inter-war period.
It is important to recall that only five years before 1926 one of the greatest upheavals in land ownership in British history was taking place.[15] The
result was that many farmers, hit by the repeal of the Corn Production
Act, found themselves in severe financial difficulties and tried to survive
by cutting staff and abandoning the upkeep of buildings, hedges and
drainage facilities. They fell into the power of banks and mortgage-
lenders, a fact which encouraged the organic movement's hostility to the
financial system. Farmers' neglect of their property was not the only trend
affecting the countryside's appearance; there was the rise of the motor-
car, with its associated arterial roads, suburban ribbon-development, way-
side cafés and advertisement hoardings. In 1928 the architect Clough

Williams-Ellis considered the threats to rural beauty sufficiently serious to launch a broadside against the 'octopus' whose tentacles were everywhere probing into the countryside.[16]

As the countryside became more suburban the industrialization of agriculture accelerated. A drive towards industrial methods was nothing new in itself, but the application of the internal combustion engine to the tasks of farming brought about a change so rapid that within about thirty years from 1926 the horse would almost disappear as a source of motive power on farms and the combine-harvester would drastically reduce the human labour employed. In 1925 a fixed price for sugar beet turned production of that crop in East Anglia into a large-scale industry. The following year, the Food Canning Council held its first convention, and between 1924 and 1932 the number of canning factories producing tinned food increased from eight to eighty-four.[17] The late 1920s and early 1930s saw the rapid expansion of glass-house production; cages for battery hens were pioneered in Britain around 1925 and from 1930 cages were manufactured commercially, aiding the development of large-scale production of eggs and table poultry; the pig-rearing industry was expanding rapidly at the same time.[18] We shall see in the following chapter how this industrial, specialized approach to agricultural production was encouraged from 1930 onwards by influential agriculturalists who saw it as the solution to Britain's farming crisis.

There was also a European dimension to the context of the emerging organic movement. 1926 was only five years since the Bolsheviks had established themselves firmly as Russia's new ruling power, and, remote as this may seem from the rival claims of humus and chemical fertilizers, it was an important factor in shaping the organicists' political allegiances. As opponents of what they termed 'economic orthodoxy,' the 'sound finance' which sacrificed agriculture to its vested interests, they were hostile to free trade and *laissez-faire* capitalism but could not accept State Socialism, with its bureaucracy, or atheistic, totalitarian Communism as an alternative. In contemporary terms, one might say that they were in search of a Third Way, though this had to be one which based the national economy on agriculture, not industry. Marxist criticism of capitalism might be justified, but the Marxist solution was undesirable. For the sake of social stability a different alternative had to be found. That alternative was variously identified as DISTRIBUTISM, GUILD SOCIALISM, SOCIAL CREDIT, Regional Socialism, Italian corporatism, Mosleyite Fascism, High Toryism, and home-grown fringe brands of nationalism. As if this mix were not sufficiently heady, there was a strong element of pacifism along with some Tolstoyan anarchism, and even some admiration for

Nazism, as Chapter 9 will reveal. These various nostrums shared, at least as the organic school interpreted them, a belief in the fundamental importance of agriculture to national life.

Yet it was industrial upheaval which brought about the occasion whose significance for the organic movement marks 1926 as a centrally important date in its history. In May that year the trade union movement was defeated in its attempt to improve wages and conditions through a General Strike, and DMITRI MITRINOVIC, a Serbian sage resident in Britain, called together a group of political activists, despondent at the triumph of the established economic order — or disorder, as they saw it — to consider what tactics they could now adopt in their fight for a more just and fulfilling society. The men who gathered in Mitrinovic's company were adherents of Social Credit, and former members of the Guild Socialist movement. This movement had been divided early in the 1920s over its response to Bolshevism and by the decision of one of its leading exponents, A.R. ORAGE, to adopt the Social Credit ideas of MAJOR C.H. DOUGLAS. Those who followed Orage into Social Credit were stunned when in 1922 he left Britain to study the esoteric technique of GEORGE GURDJIEFF, and the débâcle of the General Strike seemed the final blow to their morale.

The meeting took place at the Ship Restaurant in central London, and those who accepted Mitrinovic's invitation were PHILIP MAIRET, the poet Alan Porter, MAURICE RECKITT, and W.T. SYMONS. A fortnight later a second meeting was held there, with the additional presence of Albert Newsome, a contributor to the NEW AGE, and two clergymen: Egerton Swann, a Socialist who had adopted Social Credit ideas, and V.A. DEMANT. The main decision reached on that second evening appears to have been that the venue should be changed to the Chandos Restaurant in St Martin's Lane, and from June 1926 until the restaurant was destroyed in the Blitz the group which became known as the CHANDOS GROUP met there fortnightly and continued to meet, with some changes of personnel, at various West End eating-houses until the late 1960s.

What, then, is the relevance of this collection of primarily Christian thinkers to the organic movement? It lies in the fact that a few years later the Chandos Group became in effect the editorial committee of a journal called the NEW ENGLISH WEEKLY (NEW) and used the paper to promote organic husbandry, making it, in this writer's view, the single most important medium for that cause during the period of the organic movement's coalescence and formal establishment. Readers may be surprised to learn that the environmental philosophy underlying organic cultivation, sustainable use of resources, and reverence for nature, was developed within an Anglican context, but studying the *NEW* reveals that it devoted space to all the important names, issues and books, and saw the organic approach to agriculture as an integral part of the 'CHRISTIAN SOCIOLOGY' which it propounded. Chapters 10 and 11 should provide ample evidence for these claims. Today, only founder members of the Soil Association or veterans and historians of the Social Credit movement are likely to be aware of the *NEW*'s importance to British environmentalism.[19]

This book is therefore an exercise in historical retrieval of efforts which deserve to be remembered. In particular, it seeks to emphasize Philip Mairet's contribution as editor of the *NEW,* and rescue him from the obscurity which has become his lot. The poet C.H. Sisson, who contributed to the *NEW* during the 1940s, has written of Mairet's erasure from the history of the twentieth-century Church of England.[20] Lyndall Gordon's recent biography of T.S. ELIOT fails to mention Mairet despite the fact that Eliot dedicated *Notes Towards the Definition of Culture* to him 'in gratitude and admiration,' worked with him for more than a decade on the editorial board of the *NEW,* and for many years attended Chandos Group meetings.[21] The British organic movement owes Mairet an enormous amount; the *NEW* served as a forum for the views of the writers and practitioners whose activities kept the cause alive during the second half of the twentieth century.

We shall now lose sight of the Chandos Group and Mairet for much of the book, but they will return towards the end, when their significance will become clear. Along the way there will be many other figures to meet, in what might seem a bewildering network of affiliations; for this reason two Appendices are provided, one giving a brief sketch of the various people involved, and the other dealing with the organizations to which they belonged and the journals for which they wrote. Many of these will probably be unknown to readers, and some of them will cause surprise or even unease. I hope, though, that the reader who follows the various threads patiently until the whole pattern is revealed will find it as fascinating as I have found the process of discovering it.

2. Blueprint for
a New Agriculture

The drive for efficiency

In February 1941, the agricultural scientist SIR DANIEL HALL lamented in a letter to his son:

> the steady flow of books on agriculture, all written by 'litt'ry gents,' all depicting the simple life on the land before machines and artificial fertilizers came to pollute its innocent peace. All wishful thinking, but nevertheless a real hindrance to reform; one need not deny that the old world had values and virtues we have lost, but they are dead and we have got to make the new world out of living material.[1]

Hall may well have been referring to HENRY WILLIAMSON'S *The Story of a Norfolk Farm*, published the same month. Another likely target was H.J. Massingham, whose book *Chiltern Country* had appeared a couple of months previously, and whose symposium *England and the Farmer* would shortly bring together leading exponents of organic traditionalism in a concerted attack on the outlook of men like Hall — the orthodox school, as they will be referred to. Hall's response was to produce later that year *Reconstruction and the Land,* his authoritative final statement of agricultural principles and a blueprint for what he hoped would be an efficient post-war farming industry.

The landscape of arable England which we see today results from the imposition of that blueprint. Few outside agriculture or rural history will know the names of Hall or his friend C.S. ORWIN, but the implementation of the practices which they advocated has changed the face of the countryside. Hall need not have worried in 1941 about the traditionalists obstructing progress; the post-war decades saw the triumph of the progressives and their allies in commerce, industry and government.

The organic movement was concerned with much more than purely agricultural issues, but its development cannot be understood without awareness of developments in British agriculture and of official policy from the late nineteenth century onwards. There is no need here to tell this story in detail, since it can be read in various histories.[2] Briefly summarized, it is one of agriculture's long-term decline in social and economic importance after the era of 'High Farming,' a system based on mixed farming through the use of turnips, clover, and the integration of livestock husbandry with crop production; high inputs and expenditure resulted in high output and profits. High Farming came to be seen as the chief feature of a supposedly 'golden age' of agricultural prosperity, lasting from the 1840s to the 1870s. It was undermined by developments overseas, where virgin territories were starting to reveal their productivity. Advances in methods of transportation and preservation led to rapidly increasing volumes of imports into Britain, and these, combined with the consequences of the repeal of the Corn Laws in 1846 and with a series of bad seasons culminating in the disastrous harvest of 1879, instituted a period of depression from which British agriculture only began to recover slowly in the early years of the next century. It was not arable production alone which suffered: overseas dairy and meat products benefited from advances in refrigeration. Free trade was accepted as axiomatic and it was not until the First World War that farmers were able to enjoy guaranteed prices. In Lord Ernle's words:

> Food was, so to speak, the currency in which foreign nations paid
> for English manufactured goods, and its cheapness was an
> undoubted blessing to the wage-earning community.[3]

The organic school saw this exchange rather as a blessing to the manufacturers, who were able to keep down the wage bill; British agriculture was being sacrificed for the sake of trade and industry.

The Great War brought renewed prosperity, but the withdrawal of guaranteed cereal prices in 1921, only a year after they had apparently been enshrined in government policy, was regarded as a 'great betrayal.'[4] Following the Armistice many large estates were broken up and sold off, and the number of owner-occupiers increased considerably; but they soon found themselves struggling, in many cases having to let fields, buildings and drainage systems subside into dereliction. Farmers regarded agricultural wages as too high and sought labour-saving forms of production, with the result that the rural population declined.

However, this period also saw a number of positive developments. From the mid-1920s onwards there were significant advances in market gardening, in milk, egg, and fruit production, in the sugar beet industry, in canning, and in agricultural technology.[5] The 1932 Wheat Act

introduced an element of protectionism to help cereal farmers, while
Agricultural Marketing Boards were created in the early 1930s to bring
more efficient distribution and more consistent standards to the sale of
potatoes, hops, bacon and milk. From the middle of the decade the
increasing likelihood of war lent urgency to the revitalization of national
agriculture.

The Second World War ensured that farming was again of prime
importance, and by 1945 the two main political parties agreed that the
events of 1921 must not be repeated, and that farmers must be rewarded
with a high degree of security for their contribution to victory. The comprehensive and far-reaching Agriculture Act of 1947 resulted, with its
guaranteed prices and producer subsidies to aid greater efficiency.
Although its terms were altered from the mid-1950s onwards, as farmers
were accused of being 'feather-bedded,' this Act set the pattern for British
farming until the United Kingdom joined the European Economic Community in 1973.[6]

The organic school had mixed feelings about developments from the
1920s onwards. They welcomed the recognition that farmers should be
protected from the vagaries of free trade; they welcomed the development
of specialist production of nutritionally beneficial 'protective' foods like
fresh eggs, milk, fruit and vegetables; and they welcomed the importance
attached during the war to a productive countryside. In fact they saw the
war as an opportunity for Britain to re-establish farming at the heart of its
society and economy. The nation had relied too heavily on other countries
for its food and now had to learn that its very existence might depend
upon agricultural self-sufficiency. The First World War had taught the
same lesson, forgotten all too soon; the mistake must not be made again.
The renewed hostilities were a crisis demanding an end to the fudging,
piecemeal policies of the 1930s. One might almost see the organicists'
response as a kind of agricultural existentialism: they castigated Britain
for an inauthentic, parasitic existence and demanded a leap of faith
expressed in active and wholehearted commitment to her soil's neglected
productive capacities. Every available acre of ground must be made to
yield its maximum with the help of a greatly expanded rural workforce,
and perhaps those who experienced farm work for the first time would be
attracted to remain in it when the war was over. In this way, the imbalance between urban and rural in the social organism might begin to be
redressed, and the nation would be on the path to renewal.

Some of these hopes were fulfilled. The number of people involved in
agriculture increased during the war, and there was a surge of books on
farming and the countryside. The 'plough-up' campaign, inspired by Sir

George Stapledon, was an essential part of the strategy, making thousands of acres available for crop production. Urban areas found room for a host of allotment-holders, who 'dug for victory.' By 1943 the nation's food-growing capacity had been transformed in a fashion little short of miraculous, but the methods by which this had been achieved caused concern among the organic school. Wartime exigencies were also an opportunity for proponents of the industrial approach to put it to the test, with the result that between 1940 and the end of the war there was a rapid increase in the use of machinery on the land and in the use of artificial fertilizers. The war years can be seen as a turning-point in British agriculture, providing the circumstances in which a burgeoning 'agri-business' could establish its hold on farming methods and then, through the provisions of the 1947 Agriculture Act, dominate post-war policy.

At the beginning of the twenty-first century it is perhaps hard to believe that the industrial approach to farming once occupied the moral high ground, but British agriculture's wartime success was due in large measure to that approach, which could therefore be seen as having helped save the nation from disaster. Food and dollar shortages were a threat in the post-war years, and a high level of home production remained necessary. To abandon the methods which had proved so effective during the war would have seemed not merely ungrateful, but self-destructive.[7]

The organic school welcomed at least some of the features of the 1947 Act, in particular the security which guaranteed prices gave farmers. But they were unhappy about the underlying assumption that efficiency must be measured by output per man rather than by output per acre, since such a criterion implied further increases in mechanization, farm size, and the use of artificial fertilizers, chemical pesticides and weedkillers. In the organic school's view it was an industrialized standard, inappropriate for working with the natural world, and would mean a rapid decrease in the rural population with consequent undesirable cultural and social effects.

The organicists directed their protests against the 'orthodox' views of men such as Hall and Orwin, but it is important to note that these knowledgeable and influential agriculturalists were concerned that British farming should be economically viable. The organic writers at times give the impression that their orthodox opponents were hell-bent on wrecking it. During the 1930s and '40s the orthodox school argued for their remedies in many books and articles, and their voices prevailed. What they would have thought of the results half a century later can only be guessed at.

Their views provided the context in which the organic school put forward their very different approach. This chapter will examine the orthodox arguments for an industrial approach to farming, concentrating on their advocacy of mechanization, larger farm units, specialization, and increased use of chemical, or artificial, fertilizers.

Mechanization

Increased mechanization was a logical consequence of assessing efficiency in terms of output per man, but it was also seen as a means of ensuring higher wages for agricultural workers; in other words there would be fewer of them employed, but those who remained would be better paid. During the 1920s farmers regarded workers' wages as one of their heaviest financial burdens, so it was natural that they would look to machinery as one means of reducing these costs.

ASTOR and ROWNTREE, in their major survey of British agriculture in the late 1930s, adopted the same standard of efficiency, anticipating a utopian period when 'Science and the machine will gradually conquer the peasant ... greatly to the advantage of the common man.'[8] What mattered was not the number of men employed in agriculture, but the total output of the farming industry. The organicists, in contrast, believed that Britain would benefit from an increased rural population, and that replacing men by machines would accelerate rural decline.

The situation during the war years might have misled people into believing that greater use of machinery could coexist with a larger rural population, since the number of tractors and harvesters grew rapidly between 1940 and 1946, and the number of those employed in farming increased for the first time since the Edwardian era.[9] In 1942 the government established the Machinery Development Board, whose Chairman, Lord Radnor, participated that year in a radio discussion on the topic 'Machinery on the Farm.' He was proud to claim that British agriculture was the most highly mechanized in the world. His fellow panellists evidently approved of this on the grounds that mechanization would increase employment.[10] Two former Ministers of Agriculture shared this view. CHRISTOPHER ADDISON wrote in his 1939 detailed survey of Britain's farming that it was a profound mistake to suppose that large-scale farming necessarily involved a great reduction in labour;[11] while WALTER ELLIOT believed that:

> machinery can be kept the servant of man and not his master, so that everyone cheers when a new piece of machinery is brought into the district, instead of groaning that another man is being put out of work.[12]

C.S. Orwin, though, was in no doubt that technical developments and increased employment were incompatible and that it was essential to encourage the former. In the same year as the radio discussion he wrote caustically:

> By substituting horses for tractors, the demand for labour would be increased, and the return to spades and forks in place of horse-drawn implements would increase this demand still more. But the output of a dozen men with spades would be far less than that of one man on a tractor plough.[13]

As soon as the war was over, Astor and Rowntree produced a report on the need to abandon mixed farming and concentrate on specialist enterprises. They began by looking at the 70 per cent increase in output from British soils which had occurred between 1939 and 1942, attributing it to mechanization and the application of scientific research findings to farm practice. The number of tractors had tripled during the war years, and there were 50 per cent more milking machines, while combine-harvesters, binders and elevators were now commonplace.[14]

One of the chief contributors to this revolution was D.R. Bomford, Chairman of the Tractor Users' Association and a noted developer of agricultural machinery at his firm near Evesham in Worcestershire. In the mid-1930s Orwin made the Bomford family the subject of an essay in the series *Progress in English Farming Systems,* published by the Agricultural Economics Research Institute at Oxford. He noted approvingly that the landowner Benjamin Bomford was grubbing up hedges as early as the 1860s, and that his successors now envisaged the farmer of the future as an engineer and his men as mechanics, with welders preferable to carpenters. The Bomfords had lightened farm workers' toil and increased their employers' earning capacity, said Orwin, yet their methods had found few imitators.[15] At the end of the war Bomford declared: 'There is probably no farming operation to which mechanical power cannot be applied.'[16] There was no pretence that mechanization could co-exist with increased employment: Bomford made it plain that the aim of machinery was to displace hand labour.

The emphasis on an industrial criterion of efficiency in the 1947 Agriculture Act ensured that the hopes of the orthodox school would be fulfilled. The Act's stated purpose was:

> to promote a stable and efficient agricultural industry such as can produce so much of the nation's food as the Government may deem desirable at the lowest prices which allow proper remuneration for farmers and farm workers as well as an adequate return on capital.[17]

TOM WILLIAMS, the Labour Minister of Agriculture responsible for seeing the Act on to the statute book, reflected enthusiastically in his autobiography on the way in which the output of agricultural machinery, valued at £2.5m in 1938–39, had increased to £100m by 1951.[18]

Mechanization proceeded unabated during the 1950s. David Grigg has described the increase in mechanization since 1947 as 'dramatic ... only a few vegetables and soft fruit remain dependent upon hand harvesting.'[19] And the parallel increase in employment which the radio pundits predicted? In 1940 about 600,000 workers were employed in agriculture; by the late 1940s the figure was close to 800,000. Thereafter, the predictions were falsified by events: 'Since 1945 farming has lost two-thirds of its labour force.'[20] But after all, the first casualty of war is truth.

Large-scale farming units

The drive towards mechanization was inseparable from the trend towards larger farm units. According to David Grigg:

> the decline of the small farms and the increasing dominance, in terms of land occupied, of the large farm, is the principal structural change of the last 40 years.[21]

As early as 1930 C.S. Orwin was advocating the 'factory farm,' an approach pioneered in the nineteenth century by figures such as Mechi of Tiptree.[22] Orwin outlined two contrasting approaches to reconstructing agriculture. One was through encouraging smallholdings and family farms, which the organic school favoured[23]; the other was through 'continuous expansion of the size of the unit of organization and the steady absorption of the small-scale operator,' as exemplified in the progress of manufacturing industry.[24]

Orwin identified two kinds of family farmer: the continental peasant-cultivator, and the new world pioneer, keen to experiment with new machinery. He commented that it was strange that there was no policy to encourage state aid for the latter, concluding sarcastically that this was no doubt because such farmers would not help to suggest a picture of 'Merry England.' He envisaged a certain limited scope for small farmers, but denied the inevitability of English agriculture being small-scale. Fields must be enlarged to accommodate power machinery, and made regular in shape; and 'superfluous hedgerows'[25] must be removed. Orwin also believed that only large farms could offer hope of career advancement. Large-scale farming was an experiment yet to be tried, and would require machinery, technical management, and the introduction of cost accounting methods.

Orwin developed these ideas more fully in his wartime book *Speed the Plough*. A system of state purchase would assist the move towards factory farms. The farms, for instance, might be 'rolled up' to create an estate of 3,000 acres. After an interim period this unit would become attractive to capitalist farmers who were 'able to finance their equipment and to pay for management,'[26] and the entire unit would be centralized, with different specialisms represented in its different sections. Family farmers and smallholders, while socially valuable, were almost wholly uneconomic, and any policy encouraging them was merely sentimental.

Sir Daniel Hall, also writing during the war, was quite clear that the future lay with larger units, since 'a productive and progressive national agriculture cannot be built up on a small-holding basis.'[27] Although he accepted that a variety of farm sizes would be desirable, he countenanced the prospect of some units as large as 5,000 acres. Like Orwin, he believed that there were social advantages in having a strong element of small farmers in the rural population; regrettably, these advantages must be sacrificed for the sake of economic efficiency.

Astor and Rowntree, while favouring mechanization and specialization, were less convinced by the drive towards very large enterprises. In their post-war assault on mixed farming they agreed that arable farms could become larger and that there would be advantages in having farms of 1,000 acres or more, where diversified specialist departments could be interlinked. In dairy farming, though, they felt that Orwin and Hall had 'somewhat overworked' the argument about layout.[28]

The trend since they wrote, however, has clearly favoured the ideas of Orwin and Hall. Harvey attributes this to the 1947 Agriculture Act, which 'set British agriculture firmly on the path of industrialisation. Today two-thirds of UK farmland is in holdings of 250 acres or more.'[29] Grigg takes a longer-term view, pointing out that the general tendency for the past two hundred years has been for the number of smaller farms to decline and of larger farms to expand. He agrees, though, that the most dramatic changes have occurred since the Second World War. Small farmers could not survive economically and were inefficient when measured either in terms of output per £100 of labour or of total inputs. When assessed in terms of output per acre, though, smaller farms always have a higher level of productivity.[30]

Numerically, smaller farms predominated in the UK until the 1980s, and some commentators considered them a problem. JACK and FRANCES DONALDSON had supported the organic movement twenty-five years previously, but by 1972 were favouring the orthodox standard of efficiency.[31] In the late 1980s, Renée Danziger commented that the Donaldsons' arguments assumed 'that maximum farm output and minimum expenditure of both labour and capital are in themselves desirable features of the production process.'[32] This was indeed the assumption of influential figures like Orwin and Hall, and it dominated agricultural developments from 1947 onwards.

Specialization

In 1930 C.S. Orwin survyed the nation's agriculture and identified the most depressed areas as those where mixed farming predominated. The most effective resistance to the depression was demonstrated in districts with a high degree of specialist production: the success of dairying in particular was notable.[33] Those who favoured specialization claimed that it brought increased skill in labour and experience of management, larger units, greater efficiency in the use of labour and capital, and improved profitability through low production costs and the supply of a special market.[34] Those who defended mixed farming, as the organic school did, claimed that it reduced risks by spreading them, that it distributed income and labour more evenly through the year, and that it made better use of by-products: that is, that fertility could be maintained by the rotation of crops and stock without heavy reliance on artificial fertilizers.

But if, as the evidence suggested, mixed farming was more depressed than specialized enterprises, then surely the argument about security through diffusion of risk was invalid. Orwin argued that the economics of mixed farming had never been subjected to accurate cost-accounting analysis. Was it true, for instance, that low prices for beef cattle were offset by the increased corn production which resulted from the animals' manure? Orwin attached particular significance to experimental farmers whose methods suggested that dispensing with stock need not result in loss of fertility: men like F.P. Chamberlain of Crowmarsh Battle in Oxfordshire, and George Baylis of Wyfield Manor near Newbury, who in the previous century had eliminated livestock from his system and become the biggest arable farmer in England. In Orwin's view, they had disproved the two chief arguments for mixed farming: that security lies in multiplying enterprises, and that soil fertility requires animal manure. Baylis had produced the nearest thing to a factory farm yet seen in Britain, rejecting tradition and preferring to apply scientific developments. Specialization produced economies of scale and simplified procedures; mixed farming was too complex.[35]

Orwin also believed there would be advantages for distribution: mixed farmers could not efficiently market a variety of products. The costs of working capital would be reduced, since even on relatively large mixed farms there would be money locked up in machinery and plant which were not full-time employed.[36] Efficiency was much easier to assess on specialized farms, since

> the ordinary tests and controls furnished by accountancy and statistical examination, which are the life-blood of factory management, can be applied in mixed farming only with reservations and safeguards.[37]

Sir Daniel Hall identified specialization with enterprise and innovation, in contrast to the outmoded traditional attitude of 'mixed farming and safety first.' He pointed to egg production, fruit growing, and market gardening as examples. The only future for smallholdings was as units in a large-scale co-operative enterprise, where specialization would enable them to benefit from central processing and marketing. Hall envisaged what he termed 'plantation farming,' i.e. 'the specialist production of a single crop.' The method was widely used in British colonies, but Hall believed it was not applicable only in tropical countries where labour was cheap; mechanization was cheaper than labour. He wanted to see this form of large-scale cultivation developed in conjunction with large consuming firms like brewers and caterers.[38]

The case for specialization was advanced most fully just after the war, by Astor and Rowntree. The fact that mixed farms had served the nation well in wartime was irrelevant to post-war needs; in the pre-war period they had been fighting a losing battle. True, they ensured that nothing was wasted and that there was always plenty of work, but they sacrificed quality to quantity, were based on cereal growing, and relied too much on family labour and the all-round, general farm-worker. Human nature was such that nobody could do everything effectively; with rising demand for high-quality products, and rapidly increasing technical knowledge, specialized skills were vital. Ultimately, though, Astor and Rowntree based their argument on output per man as the criterion of efficiency. If this output were to improve, then a continued increase in specialization was essential.

During the 1930s economists had advanced an apparently powerful case against the viability of British farming, whose conclusion was that on purely economic grounds it would be best to buy food in the cheapest market — which was, in most instances, from abroad. Astor and Rowntree, like Hall and Orwin, were anxious to preserve British agriculture, but felt compelled to accept the economists' arguments *in so far as they were directed against the traditional forms of farming*. Only if the predominance of the mixed farm were destroyed could British agriculture be viable. Astor and Rowntree sympathized with the human tragedies involved in the decline of such farms, but could not accept the prospect of the virtual abolition of farming. Changed conditions required a changed system, not a hankering after the era of High Farming, when imports were few, labour was cheap, and artificial fertilizers were scarce. Astor and Rowntree believed that specialization based on grass was the answer to the problems of mixed farming. The small farm's defenders would be satisfied, because the family farm devoted to milk production would be essential to the new system; economists would be satisfied because public expenditure on agriculture would dwindle as its efficiency increased.

The orthodoxy of economic efficiency prevailed, the trend since 1947 having been consistent with the desires and predictions of the writers considered above. In 1941, 25.3% of all agricultural holdings were classified as mixed farms, but since 1980 the classification system adopted for farms has had no category for mixed farming. Because the 1947 Act established favourable prices for cereals, many farmers in eastern counties of England have specialized in them, being enabled to do so by advances in mechanization and the breeding of high-yield varieties. The production of relatively cheap cereals has in turn reduced the need for traditional fodder crops. Fodder roots have declined in acreage because herbicides have made cleaning crops unnecessary. Whereas crop rotations were used as a means of protection against plant disease, the use of fungicides and insecticides has superseded the traditional practice. The high cost of mechanization has deterred the production of a variety of crops. Farmers have largely withdrawn from pig and poultry farming, which are now more accurately categorized as forms of industry.[39] All of this is part of a much longer process, but the pace of change accelerated considerably from 1940 onwards.

Central to all these developments is the role of chemical, or artificial, fertilizers, which:

> alone are perfectly capable of maintaining long-term soil fertility. Consequently there is no longer any need to keep livestock to provide manure ... The chemical revolution undermined the biological fundamentals of mixed farming.[40]

We must now look at the importance of artificials to the agricultural orthodoxy which has determined policy since 1947.

Artificial fertilizers

The word 'artificial' has negative associations, and the orthodox school felt that their organic opponents, in using it to describe chemical fertilizers, were loading their arguments with an unjustified bias. DONALD P. HOPKINS, a scientist employed by the fertilizer industry, was a tireless opponent of the organic school: a one-man rebuttal unit who, with terrier-like thoroughness, read their books and articles in order to refute their arguments. He deplored the prefacing of the word 'fertilizers' with 'chemical' and, even worse, 'artificial,' since the former suggested 'something acid or caustic or at any rate harsh,' and the latter was 'a hopelessly degraded word to-day, suggesting something pretentious and inadequate.' The trouble was that fertilizers and manures were regarded as serving the same purpose, which meant that the former had to be distinguished from the latter and ended up being associated with undesirable qualities. Hopkins suggested that manure's purpose was to add humus to the soil, whereas fertilizers were concentrated materials supplying simple plant nutrients. If this difference was appreciated, there would be no need to distinguish manures, naturally produced, from 'artificial' fertilizers. This would not only deprive 'the extremist literature of the humus school'[41] of its moral superiority, but would cut the ground from under it: if chemical fertilizers were not intended to create humus there was little point in condemning them because they failed to do so.

Sir Daniel Hall was another authority on fertilizers and manures who wanted the terminology revised. Farmyard manure should be regarded as the typical 'manure,' marl and chalk as 'soil improvers,' and substances supplying specific elements in the nutrition of a plant as 'fertilizers.' He cast doubt on the notion of any clear division between 'natural' and 'artificial' manures, concluding that the best distinction was between bulky organic materials on the one hand, and more concentrated, mainly inorganic, compounds on the other.[42] Hopkins suggested a more complex classification, distinguishing between raw minerals, processed minerals, raw organic and processed organic. But he was unhappy even about the division into mineral and organic: gasworks ammonia, for instance, was originally organic, though the process of change in the coal-product took many centuries.[43]

It seems, then, that the response of the orthodox school to the criticisms of their organic opponents was to deny that any such things as artificial fertilizers existed. The organic writers were quite sure that they did. Lady Eve Balfour, in the first edition of *The Living Soil,* did not define them, an omission rectified in the second edition.

The nearest definition is, 'manufactured synthetic inorganic chemicals,' or more simply still, 'fertilizers not derived from *living* matter.' Quite definitely the term does not include such organic products as chalk, guano, pure bone or fish meal, etc.[44]

Jorian Jenks regarded 'artificial' as synonymous with 'chemical,' looking at the issue from a philosophical perspective. Chemical fertilizers were 'artificials' because they were the product of theories, developed under laboratory conditions, which interpreted biological processes as chemical mechanisms. Chemistry breaks down natural substances into their constituent elements and reassembles them by a process of synthesis into new combinations, operating mathematically. Jenks refused to accept that fertilizers produced by such means could be considered natural:

The materials handled by the chemist are, of course, derived from Nature, but the materials he produces by fragmentation and synthesis are not found in organic (i.e. living) Nature, though they may closely resemble natural substances and indeed be of identical chemical composition.[45]

Whatever the disagreements about the nature of artificial fertilizers, there is at least consensus as to the decade when the development and study of these substances began. In 1840 the German chemist Justus von Liebig published his monograph *Chemistry in its Application to Agriculture and Physiology,* a report to the British Association which was to lay the foundations of agricultural chemistry, and in particular the study of fertilizers and manures.[46] Liebig's theory of plant nutrition overturned the majority view of the time, that plants drew their carbon and other elements entirely from the humus in the soil. He argued that crops rose and fell exactly in proportion to the amount of mineral substances given to the soil in manure. If you analysed the ashes of crops, and then analysed the soil, adding to it the chemical and mineral salts it lacked, good crops could be ensured.

According to Hall,[47] Liebig made little original contribution to agricultural chemistry, but his reputation ensured that his theories aroused interest and gave impetus to experimental investigation; about fifty British students carried on his work. The most noted experiments were undertaken — and are still being undertaken — by the Rothamsted Experimental Station in Hertfordshire: 'the Mecca of the orthodox,' as Sir Albert Howard ironically dubbed it.[48]

Rothamsted was an object of hostility and derision for the organic school, who blithely ignored its worldwide reputation and the scientific achievements of its distinguished Directors: Sir Daniel Hall, SIR JOHN RUSSELL, and SIR WILLIAM OGG. Donald Hopkins was particularly irritated by the cavalier fashion in which the 'humus extremists' were prepared to sweep away the work of men like Hall and Russell, and of Rothamsted's founder John Bennet Lawes.[49]

Rothamsted became the headquarters of what the organic school termed 'the NPK mentality,' that is, the belief that the major plant nutrients are nitrogen, phosphorus and potassium; that they are available to plants only in soluble form, and that if there is sufficient NPK and lime the other dozen or so elements which plants require will be adequately supplied from natural sources. Such an outlook was considered adequate to problems of plant growth only because the 'laboratory hermit' — to introduce another figure in the organic demonology — ignored all the complexities found in the farmer's field.

The most controversial Rothamsted experiment was that of the 'Broadbalk' field, begun by Lawes and Gilbert in 1843 and still continuing today. It was of crucial significance in the artificials-vs.-humus debate. Lawes decided to grow wheat on the field indefinitely to see what would happen; he divided it into plots, one of which was kept without manure or fertilizer of any kind and another of which was treated with farmyard manure. The rest were treated with various combinations of artificials but no dung. A century later the Station's retiring Director, Sir John Russell, said that the Broadbalk experiments had completely disproved the prophets of doom who had predicted that the soil would become sterile.

> Many farmers to-day are anxious because they can no longer make good farmyard manure, but must rely more on artificials, and grow cereals more often. Will they injure the soil? The Broadbalk results show that, apart from disease, the yield of wheat can be kept up indefinitely by proper artificials.[50]

At the centenary celebrations in July 1943 the Minister of Agriculture, R.S. Hudson, praised the work of Lawes and Gilbert, particularly their discovery of the fertilizing value of superphosphates, which led to the founding of the fertilizer industry and:

> established the main principles of agricultural science upon which our modern knowledge is based ... Their work ... has perhaps had a greater effect on British agriculture — and indeed on world agriculture — than any other agricultural research work before or since.[51]

Rothamsted did not deny that certain crops, including potatoes and root crops, required manure. But for the orthodox school the significance of the Broadbalk results lay in the implication that, for corn at least, artificials alone could ensure continued productivity from the same plot of land.

For over seventy years superphosphate was the only manufactured fertilizer in use; of the nitrogenous fertilizers, nitrate of soda was extracted from deposits in Chile and sulphate of ammonia was a by-product of the gas industry. The First World War gave impetus to the study of nitrification, and Russell worked on the Nitrogen Committee, seeking economies in nitrogen manufacture in order to increase production of high explosives. After Germany's defeat, British chemists learned the nature of the catalysts used by German chemists to synthesize ammonium nitrate. Sir Alfred Mond set up the factory on Teesside which became Imperial Chemical Industries, and another leading institution in the organic demonology was established.[52]

Despite advances in fertilizer production, application of chemical fertilizer was still low in the 1930s. The quality of artificials was often poor, and they could be unpleasant to deal with. The inherent caution of farmers made them sceptical of artificials even when the quality did improve; also, there was a shortage of detail about results. No systematic study of yields was made until 1941, when E.M. Crowther of Rothamsted assembled results from the United Kingdom and Western Europe. His conclusions helped to boost the use of artificials.

Crowther had recommended systematic experimentation a decade previously. Rejecting claims that there was an over-production of fertilizers, he reminded his audience at the British Association to remember that 'the average rate of fertilizer consumption is still very low, even in countries of relatively highly developed agriculture.'[53] Since farmers would use artificials only if a direct economic advantage could be demonstrated, there needed to be efficient co-operation between farmers, advisers and research workers to ensure adequate information.

Sir Frederick Keeble similarly regretted the under-use of artificials, though cynics might have suspected a connection between this regret and the fact that the book in which he expressed it was largely the work of staff at ICI's Jealott's Hill research station. He said that the work done there clearly demonstrated how fertilizers could increase food production and augment the land's fertility, referring disapprovingly to the findings of a recent survey of 300 Hertfordshire farms, which showed that more than a quarter of them used no fertilizers whatsoever.[54] To rectify this situation would benefit everyone: the British population, whose bill for

imported foods would be substantially reduced; the farmers, whose profits would increase; and, coincidentally, the fertilizer companies. The
Ministry of Agriculture's official journal reiterated the message during
the 1930s.[55]

Profit From Fertilizers, a book first published in 1936, encouraged
farmers to realize that artificials could amply repay expenditure. The editor, H.C. Long, encouraged farmers to risk spending money in order to
increase profits. By 1944, when the second edition appeared, he was able
to report that 'almost all farmers are using inorganic fertilizers as never
before.'[56] The statistics support this: annual expenditure on lime and artificials increased from £8m. in 1937–38 to £51m. in 1950–51.[57] Fertilizer
consumption increased dramatically from 1940 onwards.

> Encouraged by subsidised prices and propaganda from the Min-
> istry of Agriculture, farmers who had hardly considered the use of
> artificials before became converts. By 1943–44 three times as
> much nitrogen was being used as in 1938–39, twice as much phos-
> phate, and 50 per cent more potash.[58]

To all intents and purposes the use of artificials became compulsory, and
the end of the war made little difference. In July 1946 the Minister of
Agriculture, Tom Williams, addressed the Fertilizer Manufacturers'
Association and reassured the assembled company that there would be no
decline in demand for their products, since:

> the Government's long-term policy for agriculture means that food
> production must be continued at a high level. It follows that ... the
> Government would view with considerable anxiety any marked
> tendency for the present level of fertiliser consumption to
> decline.[59]

The Labour Government's stated policy was to continue to increase net
agricultural output so that by 1952 it would be 50 per cent above pre-war
levels and 15 per cent above the wartime peak of 1943–44. The 1947 Act
provided subsidies for fertilizers, particularly nitrates and phosphates,
and the newly-established National Agricultural Advisory Service was
ready to initiate improvements in husbandry if farmers proved recalci-
trant. The authoritative voice of Sir James Scott Watson, in a paper to the
Farmers' Club in January 1950, argued for greater use of nitrogenous
fertilizers. These calls for increased use of artificials continued despite
the fact that, according to the trade press, 'British farmers are among the
highest users of fertilizers on a *pro rata* or per acre basis.'[60]

The fertilizer industry drummed home the message that the nation and indeed the world could be fed only through the more liberal use of fertilizers. Fisons presented themselves as concerned conservationists in a 1945 advertisement lamenting that native farmers in the tropics wasted the earth's surface because they lacked Fisons fertilizers to raise their soils to an 'infinitely higher level'[61] than was possible with farmyard manure. In the same year, ICI produced a series of advertisements disparaging ancient or traditional ideas of fertility. At the top of each would be a mythological symbol: the Egyptian Key of Abundance, the pine cone, the bull, the rain-god or the sun. Then the ignorance of the past would be contrasted with the enlightenment of the present: the pine 'was thought to be the home of the tree spirit'; early man 'did not know' that human life depended on the soil's fertility; by drawing a rain-god's symbol on their cheeks 'the Indians believed that they could make rain.' Each advertisement concluded with the proud boast that myth and superstition had now been vanquished by science: 'To-day science holds the key to the mysteries of growth'; 'Instead of magic there is science'; 'Science has found surer ways of keeping the earth fertile.' The concluding sentence in each case was: 'To-day the symbol of fertility is ICI.'[62] These advertisements, backed by a government policy which identified good husbandry with the use of artificials, had their effect, particularly where nitrogen fertilizers were concerned. In 1945 about 100,000 tonnes of them were used; by 1980 the figure was close to 1,300,000.[63]

Despite the fact that the tide in the 1940s was flowing strongly in favour of artificials, their advocates felt obliged to answer the criticisms made by the organic school. The case of Broadbalk notwithstanding, many supporters of artificials thought that artificials alone were insufficient to maintain soil fertility, and they paid tribute to the need for organic matter in the soil. The favourite phrase was 'balanced manuring.' In 1948, Fisons produced a series of advertisements entitled 'Facts About Balanced Manuring'; they conceded that organic matter was one of the elements necessary for effective use of fertilizers, but emphasized that farmyard manure was inadequate to supply all the plant foods necessary for growth.[64]

The contemporary organic movement tends to believe that the ideas of its founders were ignored,[65] but this was not so. The fertilizer industry went to considerable lengths to discredit their views and present them as extremists. An ICI advertisement referred to 'extremists' who 'suggest that modern farming methods are in danger of turning our green and pleasant England into a dust-bowl ...' The scientist F.E. Corrie tried to harmonize the opposing points of view by arguing that only extremists believed the organic approach incompatible with using artificials. While assuring the organic school that everyone realized the importance of organic matter, he argued that there was no harm at all in using artificials with due care. Such care could be assured only if there were a proper advisory service and efficient salesmanship.[66]

The most thorough analysis of the humus-vs.-artificials debate during this period was provided by Donald P. Hopkins, and it is hard to believe that Hopkins would have written as much as he did if the fertilizer industry had not been bothered by the attacks of the organic school. Like other supporters of artificials, he saw no reason why recognizing the importance of humus, which he did, should imply opposition to chemicals; the two were complementary. He discerned a 'totalitarian' tendency in the organic outlook, and appealed to the work of Rothamsted, whose experiments had been carefully conducted for more than half a century. Its case had been built up patiently by scientific research, 'by solid unemotional argument and deduction, by unexaggerated exposition in the appropriate scientific journals.' This contrasted with the organic school's blitz of criticism and populist denunciations. Indulging in rhetoric himself, Hopkins foresaw a time not far away when 'those who make, distribute, or recommend artificial fertilisers will have to keep their affairs a close secret.' In a speech to the 1948 AGM of the Horticultural Fertilisers Association, he told the audience: 'If we believe in ourselves, in the goods that we manufacture and distribute, then we should defend them whenever they are attacked.'[67] He was not, in fact, an impartial observer of this issue, and in his book on the controversy he admitted that fertilizers were manufactured for sale, whereas no primary commercial transaction was made in the operation of preparing manures on the farm.[68] Hopkins did not deny the necessity of humus, and believed that the organic school had performed a valuable service in emphasizing its importance. Nevertheless, he was employed to promote the interests of the artificial fertilizer industry, and artificials, pesticides and herbicides have been the means by which industrialized agriculture has operated since the 1940s.

David Grigg, an authoritative contemporary commentator on agricultural development, shares the orthodox school's technological optimism. 'In the space of forty years the entire basis of mixed farming has been undermined,' he says; pesticides can control disease, artificials have replaced farmyard manure, herbicides dispose of weeds, and so 'the problems of famine and hunger [in the West] have been overcome.'[69]

Organic criticisms

Has agri-business then been a success? In terms of efficiency judged solely by the criterion of output per man it undoubtedly has, and productivity per acre, animal and bird has increased in absolute terms as well.[70] Blaxter and Robertson, the descendants of Hall and Orwin — or, for that matter, of Swift's projectors in the third voyage of *Gulliver's Travels* — declare proudly that:

> the scientists of the modern agricultural revolution in the United Kingdom did deliver what was required. If a sound policy for world agriculture can be developed there is no doubt that the science of tomorrow is even better fitted to facilitate its implementation.[71]

They admit that there are problems, but more funds will sort them out, since 'it is *necessary* [my italics] to subscribe to ... "technological optimism".'[72] Those who want to return to simpler farming methods are refusing to accept that high energy costs are here to stay. Mechanization has increased speed and flexibility of working, and reduced the number of agricultural workers.

Contemporary supporters of organic farming believe that agriculture's development since the 1940s has fully justified the fears of the movement's founders.[73] The organic school argued that industrial farming would lead to a depopulated and aesthetically displeasing countryside. Their philosophy led them to believe that a national organism without a strong rural population was unbalanced and unhealthy, and that nothing ugly could be truly efficient. They argued that a purely financial concept of 'economy' was inadequate: since everything in a society has its effect on everything else, the financial advantages of industrialized agriculture would be counterbalanced by various social disadvantages. Even in purely monetary terms Orwin's favoured accounting methods were inadequate to deal with the hidden costs of 'factory' farms. The organic school interpreted the inevitable crop diseases and infestations of pests as warnings that progressive methods were misconceived, but the industrial farmer would ignore them and treat the problems with pesticides likely to have unintended and unpredictable consequences.[74] Hens and animals, judged by a purely economic or technical standard of efficiency, would be regarded as machines and kept disease-free only by medication. Human health would be increasingly at risk from foodstuffs produced by such methods.

If the orthodox school appear optimistic, their organic opponents may seem pessimists in contrast. It would be more accurate, though, to describe them as cautious, respecting what Sir George Stapledon termed 'the law of Operative Ignorance.'[75] In a message to the 1956 meeting of the Grassland Society he wrote:

> Today technology has begun to run riot and amazingly enough perhaps nowhere more so than on the most progressive farm. The red lights ... are there for those who can to discern them ... My own belief is that these dangers will become ... of much greater significance in the biological fields than even in those of physics and engineering ... Man in putting all his money on narrow specialization and on the newly dawned age of technology has backed a wild horse which given its head is bound to get out of control.[76]

In part, the organic school's caution could be attributed to a capacity to see where the logic of the orthodox school might lead. Chiefly though, their opposition to industrial agriculture was rooted in a belief in a natural order whose limits could not be exceeded with impunity. Writers like Hall and Orwin had an essentially mechanistic view of natural processes, the organic school alleged. They appeared to believe that the soil was an inert material to be goaded by chemical whips and spurs into ever-increasing productivity. They wanted to take from the land without giving back the life it needed in the form of humus. Such an attitude broke a God-given law of life, the Rule of Return. The organic criticism of orthodoxy was essentially prophetic: it predicted problems and ultimate disaster for any agricultural system which flew in the face of the natural order; it read the signs of the times and called for a return to God's ways.

We started this chapter with Sir Daniel Hall complaining about the nostalgia of 'litt'ry gents' for pre-industrial farming. We can finish it by quoting from a letter he wrote to Orwin in 1942:

> These men who want to go back to the old farming have something real at the back of their minds. They are full of the evils that industrialism brought to the common man — how the factory bred the slum. They see industrialism coming to farming, which they want to preserve as an *enclave* in an otherwise wage-slave world. I conclude it is an argument worth dealing with.[77]

Even Hall, then, conceded that there was more than just nostalgia to the concerns of the organic school. But between him, Orwin, Astor and ICI on the one hand, and the contributors to Massingham's *England and*

the Farmer on the other, there was a gulf fixed. The orthodox agriculturalists, devotees of the Victorian cult of progress through technical
advance, believed that Britain's agriculture could survive only by rejecting the traditional principles of farming. The organic writers believed that
only a return to traditional principles could assure a productive and secure
future. This paradox was only apparent: if the natural world exhibited the
signs of a God-given order, then the laws according to which it operated
would always be the same. Instead of rejecting traditional methods
because they belonged to the past, as Hall and Orwin were keen to do,
agriculturalists should be prepared to learn from them. Rather than imagine a future of vast chemical factory farms, the organic school preferred
to study the practice of cultivators untouched by western science. The following chapter examines the influence on the organic movement of lessons learned from Asia and Africa.

3. Shangri-La and Three Servants of Empire

Looking to the Orient

One of the best-sellers of the 1930s was James Hilton's novel *Lost Horizon,* first published in 1933 and later turned into a film. A plane crash-lands somewhere in the mountain ranges of Tibet; the passengers are providentially rescued by denizens of the hidden valley of Shangri-La, and given hospitality in the lamasery, a place of culture and tranquillity. Its High Lama is a man whose great age is the result of practising methods which slacken the tempo of life. With a tide of chaos rising in the world beyond the mountains, he offers Shangri-La as an enclave of sanity and survival; the Dark Ages had been 'full of flickering lanterns,' but the forthcoming age of desolation would 'cover the world in a single pall; there will be neither escape nor sanctuary, save such as are too secret to be found or too humble to be noticed. And Shangri-La may hope to be both of these.'[1]

The organic movement had its own Shangri-La, though it differed from Hilton's in a number of respects: its civilization had not been established by a European; it was not a centre of learning, and, most importantly, it was not fictional. Although remote, it was not as inaccessible as the novelist's valley, and had been studied by various western observers. But the organic school regarded it as an example of sanity for the industrial world: it was an oasis of physical health and equable temperaments, free from the injustices, exploitation and war created by trade and finance, and demonstrating the true wealth which results from living in harmony with the natural order. The place in question was the valley of India's northwest frontier where dwelt the Hunza tribesmen, central characters in the organic mythology.[2]

We saw in the previous chapter how the orthodox school of agriculture in Britain rejected traditional practices. The implication was that past agriculture could offer little of relevance to the new prospects being opened up by chemistry and technology. The organic school took a diametrically opposed view, encapsulated in the testimony of Sir Albert Howard: 'my best teachers were the peasants of India themselves.'[3] It was ironic that the British Empire, based on trade and industrial superiority, should have produced, in three of its distinguished representatives, critics of the very principles which sustained it. This chapter examines the careers and ideas of Sir Robert McCarrison, Sir Albert Howard and Richard St Barbe Baker, who believed that humanity's survival would depend, not on a fantasy of technological domination of nature, but on learning from proven practices which had enabled so-called primitive peoples to survive for many centuries. Underlying those practices was the Rule of Return, an eternal feature of the natural order.

The peasants of Asia did not understand the scientific principles on which their practices were based, but they knew that the practices worked. The task of western scientists was to make the scientific basis explicit and use that knowledge to improve methods of cultivation. LADY LOUISE HOWARD (*née* Louise Matthaei) described her husband's success in doing so as 'one of the most signal and successful instances of the marriage of Western knowledge to Eastern wisdom.'[4]

The Eastern wisdom which Lady Howard valued had been noted by Victor Hugo in his digression on the Parisian sewage system in *Les Misérables;* such a system was doubly wasteful, with the soil impoverished and the water infected. A 'restitution of mire to the land'[5] was required; the alternative was to squander potentially precious fertility.

> Thanks to human fertilisation, the earth in China is as young as in the days of Abraham ... All the human and animal manure which the world loses, restored to the land, instead of being thrown into the water, would suffice to nourish the world.[6]

Hugo identified Chinese soil as a supreme example of the blessings which follow obedience to the Rule of Return. His view was shared by Howard, who never visited the Far East to see their practice for himself, but knew the work of the American soil scientist, FRANKLIN H. KING, who had done so.

King resigned from his position as Chief of the Division of Soil Management at the United States Department of Agriculture to fulfil a longstanding ambition and study the native agriculture of China, Japan and Korea. The record of his visit, made in 1907, was published in America in 1911 as *Farmers of Forty Centuries* and eventually appeared in Britain in 1927, becoming a classic text in the organic canon. King did not quote Hugo, but shared the Frenchman's view that Oriental agriculture is a form of alchemy:

No Chinese peasant [wrote Hugo] goes to the city without carrying back, at the two ends of his bamboo, two buckets full of what
we call filth ... To employ the city to enrich the plain would be a
sure success. If our gold is filth, on the other hand, our filth is
gold.[7]

King expresses the same idea rather more scientifically:

Human waste must be disposed of. We turn it into the sea. They
return it to the soil. Doing so, they save for plant feeding more
than a ton of phosphorus ... and more than two tons of potassium
... per day for each million of adult population.[8]

The title of King's book is in itself a shaft aimed at the school of progressive orthodoxy. Can there be anything fundamentally wrong, it
implies, with methods which have sustained people for 4,000 years?
American agriculture was inefficient in comparison:

Complete a square on the lines drawn from Chicago southward to
the Gulf and westward across Kansas, and there will be enclosed
an area greater than the cultivated fields of China, Korea and
Japan, from which five times our present population are fed.[9]

The Oriental farmers achieved this firstly through taking a long-term
view and allowing plenty of time for transforming organic matter, and
through awareness that survival depended on increasing soil fertility. That
in turn was achieved through obeying the Rule of Return: a refusal to
waste anything, which ensured that every possible material, including
human wastes, was composted and used to enrich the earth. King did not
deny that this process was laborious, but he did deny that it was a sign of
ignorance. Such methods had been verified by hard experience, and the
peoples who employed them were evidently fit, healthy and content.
  King was impressed by many other aspects of Far Eastern methods,
and believed that this supposedly backward peasantry could teach the
West important lessons:

In selecting rice as their staple crop; in developing and maintaining their systems of combined irrigation and drainage, notwithstanding they have a large summer rainfall; in their systems of
multiple cropping; in their extensive and persistent use of legumes;
in their rotations for green manure to maintain the humus of their
soils and for composting; and in the almost religious fidelity with
which they have returned to their fields every form of waste which

can replace plant food removed by the crops, these nations have demonstrated a grasp of essentials and of fundamental principles which may well cause western nations to pause and reflect.[10]

King had intended to include as an epilogue to the book a 'Message of China and Japan to the World'; he died before it could be written, though its title remains rather poignantly at the end of the List of Contents. Dr L.H. Bailey, in his Preface, opined that the message would have been that 'The first condition of farming is to maintain fertility,' a truth the North Americans were in danger of ignoring. They prided themselves on their agricultural wealth and weight of exports, 'but this wealth is great because our soil is fertile and new, and in large acreage for every person.'[11] They were extremely wasteful, tolerating degrees of field erosion in the southern states which would never be accepted in the Far East.[12] Things had been too easy for them, and they had not yet needed to learn how to farm well.

The Hunzas too knew the secret of good farming, using the methods which King praised. DR G.T. WRENCH, who made the pilgrimage to their remote valley, speculated that perhaps 'it was in their country of the lofty hills that in the distant past this form of compost-culture first came into being in Asia.'[13] Here was to be found not merely the wisdom of the East, but something almost literally timeless, protected from the outside world like the lamasery of Shangri-La. The Hunza seemed to be:

> an erratic block of an ancient world, still perhaps with its peculiar knowledge and traditions, and preserved in that profound cleft of theirs from the decay of time ... Everything suggests that in its remoteness it may preserve from the distant past, things that the modern world has forgotten and does not any longer understand. And among those things are perfect physique and health.[14]

Sir Robert McCarrison

The health and physique of the Hunza tribesmen were so remarkable that they inspired the work of one of the organic movement's most influential writers, the nutritionist Major-General Robert (later Sir Robert) McCarrison. His revolutionary contribution to medicine was to shift attention from the causes and cure of sickness to the conditions which make for health.[15]

Since the organic movement tends to attract charges of obscurantism it is worth emphasizing that McCarrison was a highly distinguished scientist who received many international academic honours, as well as being awarded the Kaiser-i-Hind Gold Medal for public service in India. When Lord Linlithgow, Chairman of the Royal Commission on Agriculture, visited the sub-continent in 1926 he insisted on seeing McCarrison's work, and the Commission recognized its importance. This was a welcome compliment, since McCarrison's research was criticized by some of his scientific colleagues, and he funded a good deal of it out of his own pocket.[16]

McCarrison was led to his interest in the causes of health through studying the fighting men of India: Sikhs, Pathans and Hunzas. What made the men of these tribes such magnificent physical beings? Wrench believed that it was McCarrison's 'intellectual passion for wholeness'[17] which led him to posit nutrition as the answer to the mystery. Research into malnutrition had previously concentrated on the way in which faulty food affected particular parts of the body; McCarrison began to concentrate on the idea of health as a positive quality rather than as the absence of illness. Of the three tribes referred to, the Hunzas were supreme. Towards the end of the nineteenth century the mountaineer General Bruce had noted their exceptional stamina as porters, and a later explorer commented on their agility, lack of nerves, and cheerful manners. McCarrison spent seven years among the Hunzas and found that the treatment he was required to undertake was either for accidental ills or for maladies which had nothing to do with food supply. Certain complaints common in Europe, were unknown.[18] In his seven years among them he saw no heart disease, cancer, appendicitis, peptic ulcer, diabetes or multiple sclerosis. McCarrison concluded that the Hunzas' remarkable health was the result of their diet and methods of cultivation.

The Hunzas consumed 'wholemeal grains, vegetables, fruit, plenty of milk, butter, and not much meat or alcohol.'[19] Not only was human ill-health rare among them, but their farming was remarkably free of plant disease. Their agricultural practice demonstrated both physical strength and intelligence. They were famed for the size and effectiveness of the Berber irrigation conduit, and their use of aqueducts ensured that the soil was to some extent renewed by the black glacier-ground sand contained in the water. The most important feature of Hunza cultivation was fidelity to the Rule of Return. The Hunzas claimed to have received culture from the Tibetan inhabitants of Baltistan, and their cheerful temperament was shared by Tibetans, Chinese, Koreans and Japanese. Perhaps the clue to the health and contentedness of all these peoples was their observance of the Rule of Return.

> The men of Hunza ... follow the Chinese custom. They have flat
> fields. They spread out the compost evenly like butter upon bread.
> They follow, in a word, the garden culture of the immemorial East,
> and ... it may perhaps be that in the distant past this form of com-
> post-culture first came into being in Asia.[20]

The region of the Hunzas could be regarded as in effect a laboratory, housing an extremely long-term nutritional experiment, but it did not fulfil the demands of Western scientific method. McCarrison undertook a sequence of experiments with rats, despite a shortage of funds and initial obstructiveness from officialdom. By 1927 he had tested nearly 2,500 rats, feeding them on various faulty foods and comparing their health, condition and longevity with a control group of well-fed stock rats. The mortality rate of the ill-fed creatures was thirty times greater than that of the control group. One experiment which seemed especially significant was that in which one group of rats was fed on a Sikh diet, and another on a diet common to the poorer classes in England: white bread, sweet tea, boiled vegetables, tinned meat, jam and margarine. The former group flourished physically and co-existed harmoniously; the latter became stunted and ill-proportioned, their coats lacked gloss, they were nervous and aggressive, and they suffered greater incidence of disease, particularly pulmonary and gastro-intestinal — ailments common among the poorer British.[21]

McCarrison carried out experiments with other animals and with birds, noting a number of instances which strongly suggested that vitamin deficiency caused particular illnesses.[22] Since it was known that faulty feeding could cause various morbid states in domestic animals, it was reasonable to hypothesize that many human illnesses resulted from poor nutrition. If this were so, it followed that the diet of a large proportion of the European population was inadequate and needed changing. The case of the Danish diet during the First World War supported this view: rationing enforced changes which within a year were followed by a dramatic decline in the death-rate.[23] The new diet meant a reduction in the amount of meat and alcohol consumed, and an emphasis on porridge, vegetables, fruit, butter and milk; in other words, it strongly resembled a Hunza diet. Evidently westerners were more ignorant about nutrition than were the 'primitive' Indian tribesmen.

The Hunzas obeyed natural law in the form of the 'Wheel of Health,' the cycle by which wastes nourish the soil, creating healthy plants, which create healthy animals and humans, whose wastes, properly treated, further nourish the soil. McCarrison believed this cycle to be both scientifically demonstrable and and aesthetically satisfying, quoting the words of Robert Bridges:

> From Universal Mind the first-born atoms draw
> their function, whose rich chemistry the plants transmute
> to make organic life, whereon animals feed
> to fashion sight and sensé and give service to man,
> who sprung from them is conscient in his last degree
> of ministry unto God, the Universal Mind,
> whither all effect returneth whence it first began.[24]

In 1935 McCarrison returned to England, and the following year delivered the Cantor Lectures at the Royal Society of Arts; his thesis was that 'the greatest single factor in the acquisition and maintenance of good health is perfectly constituted food.'[25] By that time he had been in contact for about ten years with Drs George Scott Williamson and Innes Pearse, who saw in his work an answer to the problems of poor health and nutrition in Britain. Their work at the Pioneer Health Centre in South London is considered in Chapter 8. McCarrison also influenced LIONEL PICTON, who was responsible in 1939 for launching the MEDICAL TESTAMENT at Crewe, on which occasion McCarrison was one of the guest speakers. The other was Sir Albert Howard, who had returned to England in 1931 after a quarter of a century in India, having reached similar conclusions about the relation of agricultural methods to health.

Sir Albert Howard

Howard's family background is of great significance to his later views. His father was a Shropshire farmer who followed the traditional principles of mixed farming. Howard had practical experience of farming during childhood and this made him hostile, as a scientist, to what he termed 'the laboratory hermit.'[26] In later life he maintained that only those with experience of farming in their early years were fit to judge agricultural practices.[27] But it would be wrong to conclude from this that he was in any way an amateur as a scientist. He was outstandingly able, and his opposition to chemical fertilizers did not stem from ignorance of chemistry; at the Royal College of Science, Kensington, to which he went in 1893, he had an associateship in Chemistry with first-class distinction. At Cambridge he took a First in Natural Science and in 1897 was first in all England in the Agricultural Diploma. His farming background had given him respect for practitioners, and he was always prepared to learn from the people he had been appointed to teach. His first post, as a lecturer in agricultural science at Harrison College, Barbados, made him aware of the gulf between laboratory work and the needs of the cultivators whom he was advising. This was followed by three years at Wye College in Kent, but according to Sir John Russell this was not a particularly happy period for him.[28] Perhaps Howard's respect for indigenous West Indian cultivation had already made him sceptical about the 'orthodoxy' at Wye, where Russell had been appointed lecturer in Chemistry the previous year and A.D. Hall had just resigned as Principal to become Director of Rothamsted. Howard took over Hall's work on hops and reversed the practices of leading hop-growers, who had eliminated the male plant. Howard discovered that pollination both accelerated growth and strengthened resistance to greenfly and mildew, concluding from this that established practice was 'a wide departure from natural law. My suggestion amounted to a demand that Nature no longer be defied. It was for this reason highly successful.' This success gave him 'a glimpse of the way Nature regulates her kingdom; it also did much to strengthen [his] conviction that the most promising method of dealing with plant diseases lay in prevention.'[29]

In 1905 Howard went to India as Economic Botanist at the Agricultural Research Institute about to be founded at Pusa by Lord Curzon. He seized 75 acres of land not yet allocated and spent five years learning to grow the crops it was his duty to improve through plant-breeding. His teachers, he said many years later, were the peasants themselves, whose methods had stood the test of time[30] and produced remarkably pest-free crops. He did not idealize the Indian cultivators, but he believed that any approach to farming which had enabled peoples to survive in difficult circumstances must have a good deal to recommend it. Later he claimed that:

> by 1910 I had learnt how to grow healthy crops, practically free from disease, without the slightest help from ... all the ... expensive paraphernalia of the modern experiment station.[31]

At Pusa, Howard developed new types of tobacco, linseed and wheat. Pusa wheats were rust-resistant and spectacularly successful, being marketed worldwide and regularly winning prizes. Howard's practical abilities were further demonstrated by his improvement of packaging and transportation methods. He also experimented with cattle, testing the health of the oxen by feeding them from healthy soil, and finding that they developed a high degree of immunity to disease. He concluded that 'the foundations of all good cultivation lie not so much in the plant as in the soil itself.'[32]

By 1918 Howard believed that the health of the soil, plant and animal were linked to each other, that fertile soil held the key to increased crop yield, and that manure was the key to soil fertility. Since there was a shortage of farmyard manure, Howard, who knew King's work on Oriental farming, decided that Chinese methods of composting must be adapted to Indian conditions. The chief obstacle was the official tendency to compartmentalize. It took Howard six years to overcome the bureaucratic problems involved, but in 1924 he was finally granted the freedom he required. He was appointed first Director of the Institute of Plant Industry in the State of Indore, an establishment which he planned and organized on his chosen lines. The two essential features of the work there were 'the study of the whole crop within its environment, and the care and attention paid to the duty of conveying results to those to be served.'[33] Howard also adopted progressive policies in his treatment of the workers, providing certificates of efficiency, medical services, rest periods, shorter hours and prompt payment.[34] Within five years the Institute was noted for its commercial success in developing ploughs and tools, for the health of its cattle, and for the standard of its crops, particularly cotton, grown on land which had been rapidly redeemed from dereliction. Post-graduate training was undertaken and demonstration farms were established in various districts. The Institute was a major agency of advancement in Central India during a period of determination to develop the Empire's agriculture through applying scientific knowledge. Above all, the Institute developed what came to be known as the INDORE PROCESS of composting. Howard developed it slowly, constantly testing its results in the field. By the time he left Indore the Institute annually produced 1,000 tons of compost, and the land stood out 'like a green jewel'[35] from the surrounding countryside.

It must be emphasized that Howard's remarkable success was the result of teamwork. The year he took up his post in India, Howard married another gifted scientist, GABRIELLE MATTHAEI, a Fellow of Newnham College whose research into vegetable assimilation resulted in notable papers presented to the Royal Society.[36] Her achievements at Pusa led to her appointment in 1913 as Second Imperial Economic Botanist to the Government of India, and in the 1920s she was active in establishing the Indian Science Congress, being President of its Botanical and Agricultural Sections. The Howards became known as 'the Sidney and Beatrice Webb of India,' exhibiting a comradeship so close that observers said it was impossible to distinguish the contribution of either one of them to the papers and books which they published: more than one hundred items in all. However, Gabrielle's sister Louise — later to become Howard's second wife — believed that she made one particularly important suggestion in an engagement letter to Albert, encouraging him to take a holistic view of the plant 'as a live thing, knowing no divisions of science.'[37] Such an approach was fundamental to the organic philosophy.

Just as McCarrison decided to study the conditions that make for human health, so Howard became interested in those plants which survived attacks by bacterium, virus, fungus or parasite, rather than in those which succumbed. For the conception of susceptibility Howard substituted the conception of resistance, concluding that the soil was a major factor in determining a plant's power of disease-resistance.

Louise Howard summarized the essence of Sir Albert's ideas as follows:

> A fertile soil, that is, a soil teeming with healthy life in the shape of abundant microflora and microfauna, will bear healthy plants, and these, when consumed by animals and man, will confer health on animals and man. But an infertile soil, that is, one lacking sufficient microbial, fungous, and other life, will pass on some form of deficiency to the plant, and such plant, in turn, will pass on some form of deficiency to animal and man.[38]

Howard's ideas on plant disease led him to experiment with cattle to see if the same principles would apply, and he obtained six pairs of oxen, animals with which he was familiar from his youth on the family farm. These were given fresh fodder, silage and grain from fertile soil, and were carefully housed and groomed — but they were not inoculated against infectious diseases. Howard deliberately brought them into contact with diseased stock, ensuring that they used common pastures and had direct contact with animals suffering from foot-and-mouth. The experiment was repeated annually for more than a decade, but no infection of the healthy cattle ever occurred. When Howard read McCarrison's reports from the valley of the Hunzas he saw them as further confirmation of the resistance theory: a healthy, humus-rich soil was the key to the health of plant, animal and man.

Gabrielle Howard died suddenly in August 1930 at Geneva, where she was visiting her sister Louise. Howard could not face the prospect of further work in India without Gabrielle, resigned his post, and married Louise. Before returning to England in 1931 he wrote, with his colleague the chemist Yeshwant D. Wad, what he intended to be his last contribution to agricultural science, *The Waste Products of Agriculture*.[39] Far from marking the conclusion of Howard's scientific work, it opened a new and relentlessly active stage in his life. During the 1930s the Indore Process was adopted by cultivators in various parts of the world, and Howard travelled widely to advise on the establishment of particular schemes. The Process had originally been devised for Indian cotton growers, but the Superintendent of the Governor's estates in Bengal used it for improving the rice crop, while in the northern area of that province J.C. Watson used it on his tea estate from 1934 onwards. In 1937 Howard toured the tea districts of India and Ceylon, and the following year studied the rubber estates. The official response to his ideas was for some years unenthusiastic, but he hoped that pioneering estate-owners would convince Indian government authorities that the problems of cotton production were better dealt with by soil improvement than by plant breeding and pest control.[40]

The Waste Products of Agriculture rapidly aroused interest in Africa, where the Kenyan estate-owner and coffee producer Major Grogan was the first to institute the Indore Process and was fortunate enough to have Howard's personal advice in doing so. Further south, the Rhodesian estate-owner Captain J.M. Moubray became one of Howard's most fervent supporters.[41] He had made compost for many years, but found that the Indore Process produced spectacular results for a variety of crops including hemp and oranges. In particular he noted the contrasting state of two orange groves in the valley where he lived: one, treated with chemicals, given little organic waste and cultivated cleanly, was almost finished, the trees full of dead wood and their crop uneconomic; the other, where cover-crops were grown, weeds permitted and organic matter added, was cropping heavily, its trees full of fresh growth and their foliage a healthy deep green. Moubray asked rhetorically of Donald P. Hopkins, scourge of the organic school, which system of culture he would adopt if he decided to become an orange-grower.[42] Moubray believed that a purely economic approach flew in the face of the natural order:

> The so-called 'law of diminishing returns' is seen to apply only to those who do not really understand the soil and treat it as Nature meant it to be treated ... The present system ... must be exchanged for real soil-building according to Nature's methods.[43]

Further south still were two other important figures who successfully adopted the Indore Process. G.C. Dymond, Chief Chemist to the South African Sugar Company in Natal, cured viral problems in sugar cane by manuring with compost made from a variation of Howard's methods. Dymond attributed the popularity of artificials to the fact that they were easy to purchase and apply. Howard's critics, though, turned the former fact into an argument against the possibility of the Indore Process' widespread adoption: how were sufficient amounts of compost to be produced, particularly in urban areas? It seemed that the Orange Free State in South Africa was providing an answer.

Early in 1939 J.P.J. van Vuren was appointed Agricultural Extension Officer at Ficksburg, establishing the first experimental compost pit in May that year. He was determined to apply Howard's principles to making municipal compost, from nightsoil and all other available wastes, using scientific methods based on the Indore Process to create an improved, more hygienic version of Oriental techniques. He overcame the various problems and in 1942 was appointed co-ordinating officer of a national campaign. By 1949 half a million cubic yards of compost annually were being produced in South Africa.[44] Here was a way in which the serious problem of soil erosion in Southern Africa might be tackled.

Elsewhere in the Empire Howard's methods were adapted to a variety of conditions. J.W. Scharff, Chief Officer of Health at Singapore, heard Howard lecture at the London School of Tropical Medicine in 1937 and on his return to Malaya established several municipal composting systems. A number of plantation-owners in the coconut and rubber trades also used composting, proving to Howard's satisfaction that compost and livestock were essential to successful plantation industries. Scharff also provided evidence to support McCarrison's ideas. Between January 1940 and the fall of Singapore to the Japanese early in 1942 Scharff carried out a nutritional experiment with the assistance of his department's Tamil labour force. The labourers were given vegetable and fruit allotments on the condition that they cultivated them with compost and used the produce only for themselves and their families. They were taught how to grow, cook and prepare the food, and soon became enthusiastic gardeners once they saw how well the plants grew in humus-rich soil. Scharff observed that by the end of the first year there was a remarkable improvement in stamina and health among the Tamils, with debility and sickness disappearing not just from among the labourers but their families too. The health of those

> who had been served consistently with healthy food grown on fertile soil, was outstandingly better than it was amongst those similarly placed, but not enjoying the benefits of such health-yielding produce. An oasis of good health had become established, founded upon a diet of compost-grown food.[45]

It was possible, in other words, to re-create something approximating to the Shangri-La of the Hunza valley. Ironically, Scharff was prevented from collating a statistical record of the benefits of the Tamils' regimen by the invasion of a nation which traditionally practised the methods he had introduced, and the experiment was destroyed.

Howard also had admirers outside the Empire. Señor Don Mariano Montealegre of Costa Rica helped ensure the translation of much of Howard's work into Spanish, making it known in Latin America.[46] He later became Minister of Agriculture and Lands and was responsible for the coffee industry, which he believed the Indore Process had saved from extinction.

Howard's critics did not deny the successes of the Indore Process, but they argued that its effectiveness depended on a hot climate, cheap labour and large amounts of organic waste; the creation of humus through composting could not therefore be the answer to British agriculture's problems. Nevertheless, Howard attracted some successful followers in the home country, as Chapter 5 will demonstrate.

Out of Africa

Richard St Barbe Baker

We have seen that Howard paid tribute to the Indian peasant farmers as his best teachers, and that he believed Chinese agriculture to be superior to Indian. But there was a greater farmer still: Nature herself, whose work in the forests provided the supreme example of soil enrichment.[47] Howard believed that:

> The destruction of trees and forests is ... most injurious to the land, for not only are the physical effects harmful — the anchoring roots and the sheltering leaf canopy being alike removed — but the necessary circulation of minerals is put out of action. It is at least possible that the present mineral poverty of certain tracts of the earth's surface ... is due to the destruction over wide areas and for long periods of all forest growth, both by the wasteful practices of indigenous tribes and latterly sometimes by exploiting Western interests.[48]

By the time Howard wrote these words, in the mid-1940s, he had become involved with the Men of the Trees organization. Its founder and driving force was Richard St Barbe Baker, whose experiences serving the British Empire during the 1920s were to be almost as important to the organic movement as those of McCarrison and Howard. Baker spent most of the decade in Africa, but he too sought the simple beauty of Shangri-La.[49]

St Barbe Baker's life was one of astonishing vigour and expertise, linking the pre-1914 world of the Canadian prairies with the establishment of the Findhorn Community. It demonstrates the close relationship between the organic movement and religious faith, for its defining moment occurred when Baker as a small child underwent a mystical experience which could only be regarded as a 'vocation' in the true sense of that word: a calling by a greater power. Among the trees near his Hampshire home he felt himself overwhelmed by the overpowering beauty of the forest, his heart brimming with 'a sense of unspeakable thankfulness' as he 'tasted immortality' and experienced 're-birth.'[50] In his autobiography he said that his gratitude for the experience, which made him in love with life, could be best expressed by the metrical version of the Twenty-third Psalm:

> Goodness and Mercy all my life,
> Shall surely follow me:
> And in God's house for evermore,
> My dwelling-place shall be.[51]

St Barbe Baker's father, a forester, was also an evangelist, and Baker himself went to Canada as a missionary, joining a group of students at Emmanuel College, Saskatchewan University, whose task was to take the Word to the settlers of the prairies beyond the railways. During the three or four years he spent there he was a bronco-buster and traded with Indians; in 1910 he saw deserts in the making where trees had been chopped down and the soil was drifting. He responded by encouraging tree-planting around homesteads and for shelter-belts, and helped develop nurseries on the university farm.

He returned to England to study Divinity at Ridley Hall, Cambridge, and was there when the First World War broke out. After a crisis of conscience he volunteered, spending the war as an artillery officer, and returning to Cambridge in 1919. By now the object of his missionary zeal had changed, and he sat for the Diploma in Forestry. He was in his early thirties, and the remaining sixty years of his long and active life would be devoted to the planting and care of trees.[52]

The Colonial Office assigned him to Kenya in November 1920. In the highlands of that country there was no ideal society such as McCarrison had discovered in north-west India, but a landscape scarred by centuries of irresponsible farming. Arab husbandmen had invaded the forests, removing the trees which protected the soil, and their herds of goats prevented the tree cover from returning. Now they were succeeded by European colonizers, whose

> giant steam engines [used] prodigious quantities of wood. Indian fuel contractors were kept busy felling wide areas of beautiful and valuable trees, such as cedars and olives, and destroying a delectable land that had survived centuries of nomadic farming through crop rotation. Into the cleared land came thousands of white invaders ... with tractors and ploughs to hasten destruction with fertilizers and monoculture.[53]

St Barbe Baker's account of his response to the situation contrasts the dynamism of the colonial administrator with native fatalism. The tribal chiefs and elders saw the existence of trees as *'shavri ya mungu* — God's business,' and the young warriors were evidently more interested in dancing than in tree planting. Baker suggested that a 'Dance of the Trees' might be instituted, along the lines of the ritual dances for bean planting and corn reaping, and three weeks later three thousand warriors came to his camp, taking their place in front of the sacred solitary tree which had been left standing as a home for the spirits of all the trees which had been felled. Baker called for volunteers to plant trees and protect the native forests: thus was born the Men of the Trees movement, which still exists today under the more politically correct and bureaucratic name of the International Tree Foundation. The native volunteers planted thousands of seedlings from the colonial nurseries, and helped to establish a more varied bank of young trees. Baker convinced the tribesmen that to re-establish forests was the only way to ensure a future, and he commented that the young men who helped him develop nurseries were brought up in a tradition of mixed farming and grew healthy crops without using chemical fertilizers. His portrayal of colonial power does not present British administrators as invariably energetic and wise: he criticizes his superior officer in Kenya for thoughtlessly serving 'a régime which had done virtually nothing to protect the soil, forests or wild life,'[54] and he frequently found himself frustrated by officialdom in his efforts to develop nurseries and scientific resources.

In 1924 St Barbe Baker became Assistant Conservator of Forests in Nigeria, responsible for an area the size of France, which included one of the best remaining forests in tropical Africa, a rain forest full of splendid mahogany trees. He noted that the prized Guarea mahoganies were never found in single stands, again drawing conclusions from this about the dangers of monoculture. He saw a forest as the perfect farming system, manuring itself, working quietly and efficiently with no need for pesticides and weed-killers. Nature's rhythm was perfectly balanced; there were no sanitary problems, for she was 'the supreme chemist.'[55] The humus-rich forest soil acted as a sponge, a huge reservoir which prevented flooding and released its water in the form of springs. But despite his reverence for the forest, Baker was issuing permits to fell huge amounts of mahogany while having virtually no funds for reafforestation and proper management. A purely economic approach to profit-making had been adopted in Northern Nigeria, with fast-growing exotic trees being planted for the sake of rapid timber production, regardless of ecological suitability.

Just as King, McCarrison and Howard believed that westerners could learn from the practices of Asian farmers, so Baker believed they could learn from what the African forests revealed. In both cases survival through the centuries had been achieved by balance and variety. Forestry as an economic science could be successful only if it aimed to approximate the conditions of the natural forests which Baker studied all over Africa during the mid-1920s. Nomadic farming had destroyed the balance, but Western silviculture, when not driven by the profit motive, could show the way to recovery and save tribal populations from suicide. Towards the end of his life Baker summed up his philosophy in terms of obedience to the natural order: 'The fate of an individual or a nation will always be determined by the degree of his or its harmony with the forces and laws of Nature and the universe.'[56]

Given St Barbe Baker's attitude to the natural world, it was inevitable that he would become involved with the organic movement. In 1936 he established the journal of the Men of the Trees, simply entitled *TREES*, to which several important members of the organic school contributed, and the first Men of the Trees Summer School was held in 1938, the speakers including Sir Albert Howard and Rolf Gardiner.[57]

Baker found in Africa a world where the effects of the Fall on humanity's relationship to the earth were further advanced than in the land of the Hunzas, to the extent that survival itself might become problematic. He was aware of the threat to water supplies, which today is recognized as one of the severest resource shortages facing the world: the forest was 'the mother of the rivers,' and to destroy the forest was to endanger the very source of life. To carry on 'skinning the earth alive in ... greed and folly'[58] was self-destructive. Instead of an industrial economy, a sylvan economy was essential. At the end of his autobiography Baker offers his dream of world unity and rural regeneration, one combining the potent symbols of Eden and Shangri-La:

I picture village communities of the future living in valleys protected by sheltering trees on the high ground. They will have fruit
and nut orchards and live free from disease and enjoy leisure, liberty and justice for all, living with a sense of their oneness with
the earth and with all living things ... then with St Francis of
Assisi we shall be able to say: 'Praise be, my Lord, for our Sister,
Mother Earth, which does sustain and keep us and bringeth forth
divers fruits and flowers of many colours and grass.'[59]

* * *

The relationship between the organic movement and what we today term
'the Third World' is paradoxical and ambivalent. F.H. King sought the
key to his country's agricultural security in the ancient methods of peasant farmers. The young Albert Howard knew that the dissemination of
knowledge to West Indian cultivators could not be just a one-way process,
because established practice must have something to teach those whose
mission was to improve it. Robert McCarrison, too, rejected any naive
assumptions about the superiority of Western progress over Asian tradition. Howard, McCarrison and St Barbe Baker all had to contend with
obstructive officialdom, yet ultimately it was the institutions of Empire
which enabled them to make their discoveries and initiate their projects.

It is hard to avoid the sense of a certain romanticism in the writings of
King and Wrench in particular, tinged with a melancholy reminiscent of
the novels of Pierre Loti,[60] as European civilization touches a delicate and
ancient culture which is irrevocably changed by the contact. But taking
the picture as a whole there is no doubt that a fallen world is being
described: even the Hunzas are suffering under the curse laid on Adam,
tilling the earth by the sweat of their brows. St Barbe Baker's account of
Africa tells of a landscape ruined by human thoughtlessness. Only a rem-
nant of natives are concerned about their future, and short-sighted officialdom obstructs the possibility of renewal; but the tribesmen are ready
to be aroused from their apathy by the inspiration of a westerner's scientific and practical knowledge. Baker's combination of scientific skill and
religious reverence anticipates the contemporary work in East Africa of
Wangari Maathai and the Green Belt Movement.[61]

McCarrison, Wrench, the Howards and St Barbe Baker were all, objec-
tively speaking, the servants of imperialism through their professional
and official status as representatives of colonial power. One could argue,
though, that to some extent they 'went native,' in that they believed traditional native culture could offer valuable lessons to the industrial nations.
Louise Howard recorded that her sister Gabrielle had been 'intensely

attached to India,'[62] and Albert Howard used the Eastern image of the Wheel of Life to demonstrate the essence of the humus theory. St Barbe Baker ended up rejecting the whole idea of 'progress' based on industrialism, militarism and exploitation of natural resources. By the mid-1930s McCarrison, Howard and Baker were once more based in England, and the conclusions they drew from their colonial experiences would prove central to the critique of English society and Western civilization which the emerging organic movement was to formulate during the next fifteen years.

4. Rudolf Steiner and Biodynamic Cultivation

So if we want to work with chamomile as we did with yarrow, we must pick its beautiful, delicate, white-and-yellow flower heads and treat them just like we did the yarrow umbals; but we must stuff them into cattle intestines rather than in a bladder ... In this case, since we want [the chamomile] to be worked on by a vitality that is as closely related to the earthy element as possible, we need to take these precious little sausages ... and again let them spend the entire winter under ground. They should be placed not too deeply in soil that is as rich as possible in humus. We should also try to choose a spot that will remain covered with snow for a long time, and where this snow will be shone upon by the Sun as much as possible, so that the cosmic-astral influences will work down into the soil where the sausages are buried. Then, when spring comes, dig up the sausages and store them or add their contents to your manure ... You will find that your manure ... has the ability to enliven the soil so that plant growth is extraordinarily stimulated. Above all, you will get healthier plants — really much healthier plants — if you fertilize this way.

To our modern way of thinking, this all sounds quite insane. I am well aware of that.[1]

Rudolf Steiner dispensed the above advice on pest control and fertilization in 1924, to a group of farmers and landowners gathered on the estate of a Count Keyserlingk at Koberwitz in Silesia. There was more in the same vein: how to put manure into cow horns and bury them for an entire winter so that the manure could capture the Earth's etherizing and astralizing rays and be transformed into a powerful fertilizing force; how to sew up dandelion heads in a bovine mesentery in order to attract silicic acid, and to fill the bladder of a red stag with yarrow; how to encourage plant growth by sowing according to the phases of the moon; how different plants influence different parts of an animal's anatomy; how to catch insects according to whether the constellation was in Aquarius or Cancer. The phrase 'all muck and magic,' so often directed against the organicmovement, seems to have some justification where Steiner's ideas are concerned.

A theory of agriculture based on the influence of astral and zodiacal forces could attempt to justify itself only by the bold expedient of challenging the assumptions of established scientific method and arguing, as Steiner did, that it was modern science rather than his own method which was 'quite insane.' Sir Albert Howard was not averse to personifying Nature, but he was uncompromisingly sceptical about Steiner's biodynamic cultivation.[2] Nevertheless, there were certain similarities between the principles on which the Indore Process was based and those which underlay biodynamic cultivation. Steiner's ideas influenced some members of the mainstream organic movement, and his chief disciple, Ehrenfried Pfeiffer, was closely connected with it.[3]

One major similarity between Howard's views and those of Steiner was the importance which both men attached to the traditional knowledge of peasant farmers. Steiner believed that European civilization had:

> lost the knowledge of what it takes to continue to care for the natural world. The most important things are no longer known.
> Because of certain healthy instincts, things are continued, but these instincts are gradually disappearing; the traditions are vanishing.'[4]

Steiner had experienced the traditional agriculture in his early life. He said that his own ideas on cultivation had 'grown out of a peasant's skull,' and that:

> [he] would much rather listen to the experiences of people who work directly on the fields, than to all the ahrimanic statistics we get from science ... it is just in this area of practicality, of practical implementation, that I have always found science to be extremely stupid. Thus, in order to make this science more intelligent, we in Dornach are trying to bring some 'peasant stupidity' into it. Then this stupidity will become wisdom in the eyes of God.[5]

A spiritual science

The influence of the East — or more accurately, of a European response to Eastern religious philosophy — played a significant part in Steiner's intellectual development and, indirectly, a part in the development of biodynamic cultivation. His early career, though, was dedicated to the study of western science and philosophy, at which he excelled.[6] In 1879 he became a student at the Vienna Polytechnic, specializing in mathematics, physics, biology and chemistry, with Franz Brentano as his Philosophy teacher. Steiner was so passionately devoted to Goethe's scientific writings that at 21 he was appointed to the team of scholars editing the complete works. During the next fifteen years he produced major studies of Goethe's aesthetics and epistemology, seeing in his quest for a new interpretation of the organic sciences a basis for refuting materialism, and describing him as 'the Copernicus and the Kepler of the organic world.'[7] He spent from 1890 to 1897 at the Goethe-Schiller archives in Weimar, and during this period met such noted philosophers as Nietzsche and Haeckel.

Goethe's importance for Steiner lay in his attempt to find what would today be termed a 'holistic' theory of plant life, to replace the inadequate analytical approach which broke everything into its constituent parts and then found itself unable to explain life and growth. Steiner believed that methods appropriate for physics were illegitimate when applied to living things, imposing 'an alien set of laws. And so by denying to the organic world its essential nature you fail to recognize it for what it is.' Towards the end of the nineteenth century and early in the twentieth various attempts were made to develop some form of 'vitalist' philosophy which could refute the pretensions of materialism in the life sciences: the work of Bergson, Driesch and Smuts is probably the best-known among these. Steiner's work was a part of this wider movement, seeking to develop a theory of knowledge which could be rigorously applied to biological research. Yet there were paradoxes in Steiner's writings: he greatly admired the philosopher of evolutionary theory Ernst Haeckel, whose work might be regarded as the apogee of the very materialism which Steiner opposed. Steiner's support for Haeckel's ideas stemmed from his conviction that the idea of the evolution of life was correct and that in some form it must be accepted. He found Haeckel's theory inspiring but Haeckel himself an inadequate expositor of its implications. Properly conceived, it was capable of leading to 'the loftiest spiritualistic conclusions'; indeed, there was 'no better foundation for occultism than Haeckel's theory.'[8]

After his move from Weimar to Berlin in 1897, Steiner became involved with the esoteric doctrines of Theosophy. A syncretic set of ideas derived from Eastern religious philosophy, Theosophy and its influence on Europeans have been analysed with wit and in detail by Peter Washington.[9] It played a part in the emergence of the organic movement through its effect on Steiner and, less directly, through A.R. Orage, a Theosophist as a young man who towards the end of his life established the *New English Weekly*.[10]

Steiner was working in Berlin as a lecturer when he was invited to speak, in September 1900, at two meetings given in the Theosophical Library. Such was their success that in 1902 he joined the Theosophical Society, becoming Secretary General of its German branch. He was an active member for ten years, but there were fundamental differences between his outlook and that of the Society's dominant figures, Helena Blavatsky and Annie Besant. He would not accept occult doctrines without subjecting them to scientific investigation, and he believed that the life of Christ was of unique significance, refusing to recognize the young Krishnamurti as Christ's reincarnation.

> [Steiner] was convinced that there was nothing in the riches of the traditional wisdom of Asia that could give it the power to overcome the scientific materialism that sets the intellectual tone for the civilized world today. The power to do this resides in the mind of the West itself.[11]

The decade Steiner spent in the Theosophical Society saw the beginning of his conviction of the presence of etheric formative forces, which later became centrally important to his agricultural researches.

Steiner broke away to found his own school of Anthroposophy, formally instituted as a Society in February 1913. He had another dozen years to live, and filled them with activity: lectures all over Europe; courses for doctors and teachers; the establishment of The Christian Community; the design and building of the Goetheanum, a centre for mystery plays and anthroposophical activities at Dornach in Switzerland; the establishment of the first Waldorf School; courses in eurhythmy; addresses to factory workers, and, always, the exposition of his ideas through books. Steiner's philosophy had implications for all areas of social life.[12]

In 1921 Steiner established a research laboratory at Dornach. From investigating the forces active in living organisms he drew conclusions with implications for agriculture, medicine and the art of healing, and he soon found himself approached by farmers and scientists concerned about the degeneration of seed stocks and cultivated plants, and the increase in animal diseases.[13] Scientists from the Weleda drug company went to Steiner to express their anxiety about sterility and foot-and-mouth disease among cattle. These concerns were drawn together by Count Carl von Keyserlingk — not to be confused with the religious philosopher Count Keyserling of Darmstadt — who in June 1924 made his estate available for a course which Steiner delivered to a selected group of practical farmers, gardeners, doctors, scientists and students of Anthroposophy who

> had experienced something of the co-ordinating value of Dr
> Steiner's teaching and had confidence that in the sphere of agricul-
> ture it would provide a broader outlook and a sane foundation for
> practice.[14]

Steiner delivered eight lectures and held four discussions; the transcripts were given the title *Spiritual Foundations for the Renewal of Agriculture,* and a new translation of them, complete with photographs of Steiner's notes, was issued in 1993. The reader will notice that Steiner articulated the principles of biodynamic cultivation at the same time that, in the Indian State of Indore, Albert Howard was seeking to establish the Institute of Plant Industry; both men were looking to re-establish agriculture on a more sound basis.

Steiner's biographer Hemleben comments on the remarkable fact that a 'spiritual scientist and initiate'[15] should be respectfully listened to by an audience of practitioners, attributing it to Steiner's peasant background. However, the audience were of course already sympathetic to, or active adherents of, his spiritual science. Another possible explanation is that his practical suggestions have a good deal in common with mainstream organic ideas, which do not depend on a complex esoteric system and can therefore appeal to cultivators unhappy about the results of orthodox agriculture. The Rule of Return has a rationale which is independent of any theory of cosmic influences. Steinerians might reply that to remove the idea of cosmic influences is to remove the heart of the theory. We shall return to this issue of 'secularization' in a while, but there is no doubt that Steiner's agricultural theory was based on the idea of a correspondence between earth and the heavens. He identified two sorts of force at work in nature: the 'terrestrial,' which work from within outwards, and the 'cosmic,' emitted by heavenly bodies, which affect plants and animals from outside. These latter forces influence the form and quality of living things, and the art, or science, of the agriculturalist is to help nature make full use of them: hence the importance of astrological and lunar phases, and of silica, which 'acts as carrier for the cosmic forces.'[16] Planetary rhythms affect the life-span and quality of the plants they influence, and even the chemical elements have their own distinctive spiritual nature. A particular type of soil cannot be brought to full fertility unless its planetary affinity is known and the manuring undertaken with the aid of herbal preparations which act dynamically as regulators. Steiner analysed the relation of pests and plant diseases to the influence of the planets, of weeds to the moon, and of animals to the signs of the Zodiac. There is a constant interchange of above and below, and a farmer can be effective only if he is in harmony with the visible and invisible structures of plant, animal and human.

Against specialized farming, Steiner argued that a farm should be developed 'as an organism with its own foundation, self-inclosed as a living unity and totality.'[17] Balance and interconnectedness are vital features of an organism, and he stressed the importance of having soil, plants, insects, animals, woodland and birds in the correct proportion to each other. Steiner saw in mixed farming the only viable form of agriculture.

Steiner emphasized the importance of the Rule of Return, and opposed artificial fertilizers ('mineral fertilizers,' as he called them), arguing that they were unnecessary if the soil were properly cared for; he optimistically predicted that artificials would simply disappear again, reliance on them being the result of a short-term outlook:

> Everything is being mechanized and mineralized nowadays, but
> the fact is that what is mineral should work only in the way it does
> in nature. Unless you incorporate it into something else, you
> shouldn't introduce anything that is mineral or totally lifeless into
> the living soil.[18]

Like McCarrison and Howard he perceived a connection between methods of cultivation and the health of those who consumed the produce, saying that use of artificials 'gradually reduces the nutritive value of whatever is grown on the fields where [they are] used.'[19] He opposed the incarceration of animals in stalls, where they would be unable to seek out the cosmic forces they needed for their health; and he may even have anticipated the outbreak of BSE, predicting the risks attached to feeding animal protein to cattle.[20]

The biodynamic movement

During Steiner's visit to Keyserlingk's estate an Experimental Circle was formed, whose purpose was to give practical effect to the ideas put forward. In less than a year Steiner was dead, but the movement he founded spread rapidly and was established in England before the end of the 1920s. Despite the esoteric theories on which the practice was based, the Group was clear from the start that the methods and effects of the preparations were for *all* farmers, and not the possession of an élite. Steiner thought it imperative to carry the blessings of the preparations 'to the largest possible areas over the entire Earth, so that the Earth may be healed and the nutritive quality of its produce improved in every respect.'[21]

There was therefore a duality in the movement: on the one hand, an esoteric set of doctrines studied by a small group of Anthroposophists, and on the other a set of practices which any farmer could adopt regardless of his beliefs. Steiner's chief agricultural disciple, Ehrenfried Pfeiffer, believed that anyone who adopted biodynamic practice would tend to be drawn towards the theories, developing a perspective on biological processes different from that of the more materialistic chemical farmer. Nevertheless, the practice was based on the theories, and Pfeiffer saw the work of the Natural Science Section at Dornach as 'the source, the creative, fructifying element' of the biodynamic movement.[22]

Biodynamic farms have been described as 'organic-plus,' the 'plus' consisting of specially prepared composts and treatment of the soil 'with homoeopathic doses of cow-horn-based sprays to enhance its fertility.'[23] Howard's scepticism about Steiner's methods was in effect a denial of the value of the 'plus.' Whereas Steiner drew conclusions deductively from a complex theory of cosmic correspondences, Howard's mode of thought was essentially inductive, working from observation of practice to a theory of cultivation and health which was then tested by systematic experiment. If biodynamic methods produced a fertile soil and healthy crops and animals, this could be explained by reference to the Rule of Return rather than by invoking astrological and lunar phases.

Since Howard and his followers saw no need to subscribe to the esoteric theories underpinning biodynamic methods, one could argue that there was a fundamental difference between Howard and Steiner, but in practice the two approaches had more in common with each other than either did with orthodox agriculture, as is suggested by the fact that

Howard's prominent disciples, LORD NORTHBOURNE and ROY WILSON used both the Indore Process and biodynamic methods on their estates. There were in fact a number of practitioners with a foot in both camps, one of the most influential being Ehrenfried Pfeiffer.[24]

Ehrenfried Pfeiffer

Around 1920 Ehrenfried Pfeiffer attended lectures by Steiner and was attracted by the idea that etheric and creative forces manifest themselves in nature; he believed that if one could learn how to handle these forces sensitively they could be applied to solve the problems of everyday life. Steiner advised him to study inorganic chemistry, which he did, also becoming a student of Anthroposophy. Pfeiffer worked with Steiner on the experiments preceding the 1924 Agriculture Course, and after Steiner's death he established at Dornach the laboratory for biochemical research. Here was developed the technique of 'sensitive crystallization,' a method by which copper chloride crystallizes in a thin layer resembling 'ice flowers,' showing typical forms according to the substance added to it. The biodynamic experimenters used it to identify subtle variations in the quality of foods or composts, and by the mid-1930s it had been praised for its value to medical research.[25] In 1939 Pfeiffer gave a report on it to the World Cancer Conference, and his work on the early diagnosis of cancer won him an honorary Doctorate. The EARL OF PORTSMOUTH recalled in his autobiography Pfeiffer lecturing on crystallization of plant juices, and diagnosing human illness from slides of crystallized blood; as a result Portsmouth grew sympathetic to the idea of cosmic influences affecting plants and humans.[26]

Despite his youth, Pfeiffer became the leading figure in the rapid spread of biodynamic cultivation which occurred during the late 1920s. In 1927 he was invited to take over the 800-acre Loverendale Estate at Walcheren in the Netherlands, which became the largest biodynamic enterprise in Europe. He developed the estate as an organism complete in itself and succeeded in supplying 700 families with most of the food they needed. Portsmouth — Viscount Lymington as he was then — visited Walcheren every year from 1935 to 1939, on at least one occasion with Sir Albert Howard, and described in his autobiography the estate's absorbing interest. Portsmouth praised the quality of the vegetables, bread and fruit, but also emphasized Pfeiffer's economic skills:

> He could work out the value of a dung heap to the last penny in
> the agricultural terms of the professional valuer. Nor did he
> despise making use of machinery in the most efficient way.[27]

This would explain why Pfeiffer was also much in demand as an agricultural consultant.

Pfeiffer visited the United States for the first time in 1933, and several other visits followed until in 1938 he settled there permanently. The biodynamic movement had been established in North America by 1927, when the Anthroposophists Elise Stolting and Gladys Barnett bought Threefold Farm, New York State; but Pfeiffer began to turn the biodynamic movement in a more secular direction, wanting to offer scientific justification for organic and biodynamic methods.

> He sought to obviate any impression that there existed unproven
> and misunderstood assertions or assumptions, such as can easily
> persist in a movement which originates in old traditions and in
> spiritual knowledge which is not accessible to all.[28]

The work on crystallization was central to this task, but other forms of observation proved persuasive as well. Pfeiffer was asked to investigate disease and wastage in some Florida orange groves, and found that the groves were being treated monoculturally, with heavy inputs of pesticides and chemical fertilizers. His response was to spend a considerable time studying nearby virgin woods and swamps to see where wild oranges were growing well. Having built up a theory of plant association he returned and advised the cultivators to cut down a proportion of their trees per acre 'and plant instead the wild trees and shrubs with which the orange flourished naturally in ecological association.'[29] Most of the planters rejected the advice, arguing that reduction of trees meant a reduction of crop, but those who followed it benefited. This story fits well into the organic mythology in the morals that it offers: respect for the natural order as revealed particularly by the wilderness brings economic benefit to those who are not fixated on short-term gains; true science goes out from the laboratory and studies the ecological context, observing rather than trying to dominate; variety is more productive than monoculture; industrial products bring disease and waste.

We shall return to Pfeiffer's work in the United States in Chapter 6, but what of his influence in Britain? Evidently he was the 'acceptable,' exoteric form of Steinerism for the mainstream organic movement. The visits of Portsmouth and Howard to Walcheren have already been mentioned, and shortly before the Second World War Lord Northbourne organized a summer camp and school at his Kent estate at which Pfeiffer spoke. In 1947 FABER AND FABER published two of Pfeiffer's books: *Soil Fertility* had an introduction by Lady Balfour, and Sir George Stapledon contributed a foreword to *The Earth's Face*. The latter book is a treatise on ecological landscape management, free of the esoteric detail found in Steiner's Agriculture Course; but it would be more accurate to describe it as 'exoteric' rather than 'secular,' for the sense of the sacred is explicitly invoked in the chapter on agricultural history. Pfeiffer points out the close links in ancient and traditional societies between cultivation and religion, and shows himself typical of the mainstream organic movement in attacking the modern, secular god of 'Economy,' blaming its rise to power in Anglo-American civilization on the growth of Puritanism with its accompanying veneration of trade:

> Then the scientific world-conception which blotted out the religious consciousness of many people gave rise to the demon of profit-making.[30]

Successful farming was possible, Pfeiffer believed, only where the farmer had the right spiritual attitude towards the land he cultivated. Lady Balfour agreed, arguing in her introduction to *Soil Fertility* that the truly scientific mind was open and humble:

> It is the unscientific mind ... that instantly dismisses as superstition, magic, or even as non-existent, happenings brought about through the operation of some natural law which we do not yet understand.[31]

Portsmouth identified Pfeiffer's work as one of the main reasons for the organic movement's coalescence. A group of fellow spirits, among them Gardiner, Howard, McCarrison, Northbourne, Pfeiffer, Stapledon and Wilson, met at Portsmouth's Hampshire estate in July 1938 to discuss whether the work of Howard and Pfeiffer was susceptible to a rigorous scientific evaluation which would compare its results with those achieved by using artificials. Lady Balfour's experiment at Haughley in Suffolk, later taken over by the Soil Association, was an indirect result of this informal weekend conference.[32]

A dozen years later, Pfeiffer attended a European Husbandry Meeting held in Britain and organized by the KINSHIP IN HUSBANDRY GROUP.[33] Rolf Gardiner described Pfeiffer's advice as:

> penetrating and wise. Seldom was there a man who knew the peculiarities of the working soils of different European countries and who had then become a practical commercial farmer in the United States who could look at the whole earth with such earned authority.[34]

In a memorial tribute, Gardiner recalled Pfeiffer speaking at his Springhead estate in Dorset, under an acacia tree, addressing a meeting of the husbandry conference. Richard St Barbe Baker was another of the speakers.[35]

However, it was not Pfeiffer who introduced biodynamic cultivation to the United Kingdom: that honour went to CARL ALEXANDER MIER.[36] Mier spent the first half of the 1920s studying agriculture, receiving his diploma in 1926. He never knew Steiner, but met Count Keyserlingk and was a convert to Anthroposophy, becoming his scientific advisor. His doctorate, awarded by the University of Berlin in 1928, was on the effect of dietary variation on rabbits. That year an Anthroposophical World Conference was held in London, and the organizer and secretary of the British branch, Daniel L. Dunlop, asked Keyserlingk if he could send someone to represent the agricultural movement; the Count, who spoke no English, sent Mier, and it appears that his lecture was one of the conference's successes, for he was invited to start the new agricultural work in Britain.

According to Rom Landau, writing in the mid-1930s, Anthroposophy had entered quite deeply into English life, but Britain was the last European country to follow up Steiner's ideas on agriculture, since the British farmer's conservatism made him 'one of the last to adopt the method of chemical cultivation.'[37] By 1929, though, the British biodynamic movement was taking shape. Mier spent some time in Yorkshire with MAURICE WOOD, who began using Steiner's methods in 1928. Originally a poultry farmer, Wood 'learnt his first lessons in the danger of applying mechanical methods in the realm of life,'[38] and changed his policy to create a more balanced holding, moving in the opposite direction from that being urged by Orwin and company. He was later to be one of the Soil Association's founder members.

By the autumn of 1929 Mier and his family were living at Bray in Berkshire at the home of Marna Pease. After further moves they eventually settled in 1933 at the recently-purchased Broome Farm, near Clent in Worcestershire, which belonged to David Clement and was a centre of biodynamic experimentation and the Association's office for more than half a century. This ran in tandem with the curative education work being undertaken close by, and when the Second World War broke out the Biodynamic Agricultural Association was sufficiently well-established and well connected to be able to send a memorandum on UK food production to the Minister of Agriculture.[39]

Was there any likelihood that a Minister of Agriculture would take notice of cultivators who based their methods on an esoteric theory of cosmic forces? The possibility is not as far-fetched as it may appear, since the Public Relations Officer for the Ministry of Agriculture during the first two years of the war was the journalist LAURENCE EASTERBROOK, whose support for organic methods resulted from contact with the biodynamic movement.

Laurence Easterbrook

Easterbrook had read some of Steiner's writings before 1914 but it was not until nearly twenty years later that he really felt his influence. On demobilization at the end of the First World War he set about learning to farm, and articles which he contributed to the national press led to Lloyd George asking him to help produce a land policy for the Liberal Party. From there he went on to be agricultural correspondent for the *Daily Telegraph* and the *News Chronicle*. He was also a practical farmer near Midhurst, in Sussex. In the 1930s he visited, in his capacity as a journalist, Marna Pease, and through her went to see Carl Mier at Clent. Years later he described how Mier had brought Steiner's teachings to life for him, so that 'Demeter, the sweet mother, trod those English fields beside us.' What he termed a 'hunch' about the rightness of Steiner's ideas began to appeal to his common sense, a common sense firmly based on a belief in a Mind which had designed nature with 'amazing skill and forethought' and established a 'natural order of living things.' Easterbrook defined an organic farmer simply as 'one who has learnt a little of how Nature goes to work to achieve her ends and endeavours to fit his farming into her broad principles that science increasingly reveals to us.' His article contained none of Steiner's esoteric terminology; it was couched in language acceptable to any of the mainstream organic school and was based on a sense of experiment: he did not rule out occasional use of artificials for specific short-term purposes. Organic farming was for him a determination to avoid 'the sin of arrogance.'[40]

Easterbrook wore his esoteric philosophy lightly enough to represent the voice of official farming policy during the rapid expansion of agriculture early in the war; to edit the 1943 publication *The Future of Farming,* whose contributors included the Minister of Agriculture R.S. Hudson, Sir George Stapledon, and Sir John Russell of Rothamsted; and to write the post-war guide to *British Agriculture* (1950) for the British Council. He was an excellent example of the combination of earth and spirit so typical of the early organic movement. His autobiographical essay *How To Be Happy though Civilised* was published in 1970 by the Spiritualist Association of Great Britain, and included the text of a lecture he had given to the Association in which he sardonically revealed that in later life he had discarded the teachings of the Church of England in favour of the teachings of Christ. He is presumably the only PRO for the Ministry of Agriculture to publish a pamphlet on reincarnation.[41] Easterbrook was very much a part of the mainstream organic movement, being a founder member of the Soil Association and serving uninterruptedly on its Council from 1946 right through to the 1960s.

Another link between the biodynamic movement and the higher echelons of government was provided by C. ALMA BAKER, who serves as further evidence that there need be no disjunction between adherence to Steiner's esoteric philosophy and success in worldly practical matters. Born in New Zealand, he owned cattle stations there and in Australia, and rubber estates and tin mines in Malaya; during the First World War he founded the Australian and Malayan Battleplane Squadrons, for which he was awarded the CBE. According to Vivian Griffiths[42] his 1940 book *The Labouring Earth* was co-written with Ben Suzmann, an agricultural journalist on the *New Statesman,* so that paper's judgement, recorded on the 1942 reprint's dust-jacket, that the book was 'challenging and highly readable' does not perhaps carry great weight; more persuasive was the enthusiasm of *The Times,* the *Yorkshire Post, The Field* and *Country Life,* which was a tribute to Baker's international renown as an agriculturalist. More significant still is the introduction, written by Lord Addison, who particularly recommended the chapter 'A Personal Belief,' which included a plea for 'a definite enquiry into the truths of astrology so far as they affect plant growth.' Although sceptical of such ideas he nonetheless found that Baker's book unsettled his established patterns of thought and that it mounted a serious challenge to 'much of what is called Progress.'[43] Baker's belief in astrological influences did not stand in the way of practical suggestions for post-war agricultural policy, and Addison praised the final chapters for:

> [their] intimate understanding of the work of the Government
> machine and [their] specific proposals for the researches required,
> for farmers' education, and for the institution of an 'Imperial
> Bureau' whereby international co-operation may be secured.[44]

The book reads today as an excellent introduction to many of the agricultural issues at the start of the Second World War, and to some major themes and figures of the organic movement. The religious basis of its viewpoint is evident on its title page, with its quotations from Ecclesiastes ('the profit of the earth is for all') and Ruskin ('God has lent us the earth for our life; it is a great entail'). Baker introduces the idea of natural law on the first page of the preface, and refers to the 'Supreme Architect' during a discussion of the ecological function of forests and rivers.

The ultimate cause of soil exhaustion and erosion was secularism; agriculture must become once again 'the most sacred' of all human tasks.[45]

Finally, in this necessarily brief survey of Steiner's influence, a word about gardening. Baker had pointed to the achievements of Marna Pease as a possible solution to the problems of fruit production being investigated by Rothamsted scientists. Her home at Bray became the first centre for biodynamic cultivation in Britain after Mier lectured in London. As well as fruit and vegetables she had a large apiary and a herb garden, and after a decade of experimental work was growing, under ordinary conditions, crops that were 'perfectly healthy, continuously free from the worst forms of diseases that worry growers, and entirely free from contamination by any form of mineral poison.' The tomatoes in particular were 'some of the finest fruit it has been [the writer's] privilege to handle.'[46] Another plot managed on biodynamic lines was that of Miss MAYE BRUCE of Sapperton in Gloucestershire, who after a period serving on the Experimental Circle of biodynamic cultivation developed her own 'Quick Return' compost system derived from her knowledge of Mier's work. It 'evolved on the foundation of herbal treatment for compost heaps,' a treatment first recommended by Steiner. Miss Bruce 'built up a rich envelope of humus over the thin soil on the Cotswold rock,'[47] creating a showpiece kitchen garden. She became a founder member of the Soil Association, contributing an article on her methods to the second issue of *Mother Earth*. Her compost heap was for her a place of miracles, due to 'the powers of Radiation ... In the compost heap we have a great co-operation, all parts working together in harmony to the glory of God.'[48]

The example of biodynamic methods played a part in the early career of LAWRENCE HILLS, probably the best-known of all organic gardeners through his establishment of the HENRY DOUBLEDAY RESEARCH ASSOCIATION (HDRA) and the gardening experiment which, now based at Ryton, near Coventry, has become one of the world's most noted centres for organic methods. In his autobiography *Fighting Like the Flowers* Hills recorded that during the Second World War — by which time he was an experienced nurseryman specializing in alpines — he read a copy of a journal published by the Biodynamic Association (presumably *Star and Furrow)* and saw in it an advertisement for Maurice Wood's Yorkshire farm. Posted to a dismal RAF station in the east of England, Hills wrote to Wood and asked if he could visit on his next 48-hour pass. 'I spent a delightful weekend walking over the farm, feeling for the first time the springiness of the living soil of the first organic pastures I had ever trod'[49] It was not until he corresponded with Sir Albert Howard, though, that Hills committed himself to the organic movement. This story will be told

in the next chapter, as will that of Roy Wilson's Iceni Nurseries at Surfleet in Lincolnshire, a highly successful market gardening business
which Carl Mier visited in 1937 and which made considerable use of
Howard's Indore Process.

* * *

To try to determine the influence of Steiner's followers on the mainstream
organic movement is a task deserving a study in its own right, and my
conclusions here can only be provisional. There is no doubt that there was
an influence; as we have seen, some of the most noted figures in the
organic movement were impressed by or actually experimented with biodynamic methods; Pfeiffer was closely associated with the Kinship in
Husbandry, and Steinerians were actively involved with the Soil Association. It would be interesting to know whether the experiments were felt
to have established the superiority of biodynamic methods to the Indore
Process and, if so, whether this was specifically the result of the various
preparations added to the compost or whether other factors might have
played a part. Certainly there were senior figures in the Soil Association
who took an interest in biodynamic cultivation; Vivian Griffiths[50] says
that Jorian Jenks, its first Editorial Secretary, visited David Clement at
Broome Farm during the 1950s, and that his successor Robert Waller
once said to Clement: 'We have the technical knowledge of organic husbandry; you have the poetry.' In 1959 several Soil Association members
joined a 'very happy and memorable'[51] tour of Denmark organized by the
Biodynamic Agricultural Association. However, looking at the Index for
the first fifteen years of *Mother Earth*, one is struck by how few references there are to biodynamic cultivation. Carl Mier, writing in the Spring
1956 issue of *Star and Furrow*, gave the impression of feeling somewhat
neglected by the pragmatists of the Soil Association, complaining that
'fundamental principles and issues have been lost sight of,' and arguing
that the biodynamic approach could 'make a vital contribution to the
understanding of the theory which lies behind organic practice.'[52] The
New English Weekly, the most important journal in the organic movement's formative period, rarely referred to biodynamic cultivation, but its
editor Philip Mairet was familiar with Steiner's work, and one of Mairet's
gurus, Dmitri Mitrinovic, greatly admired and even envied Steiner.[53]

Was an esoteric theory of astral correspondences necessary? Neither
Howard nor Stapledon thought so. Another keen advocate of organic
methods, H.J. Massingham, provided a satirical account of Steinerian
composting in *This Plot of Earth*, wondering whether the 'acolytes' who
ministered to the occult influences did so 'with appropriate incantations

and invocations,' and describing their methods as 'an elaborate and pantheistic cultism ... a white witchcraft [which] tends to frighten people
away from its eccentricity.'[54] In other words, Massingham considered the
biodynamic movement potentially damaging to the wider organic movement. Why not apply Occam's Razor and simply say that God had made
the natural world in such a way that humanity had to obey the Rule of
Return in order to survive? This was the view held by Howard and the
general run of his disciples. Or, to put it another way, the difference
between Steiner's methods and those of Howard was the difference
between deductive and inductive approaches to cultivation. From a theory of cosmic correspondences Steiner drew conclusions about the best
way to grow things; Howard's conclusions were drawn from observation
and experiment.

Without ignoring Steiner's considerable influence, it is highly probable that a movement for organic husbandry would have existed in Britain
even if biodynamic methods had never been developed. It is hard to imagine, though, that the movement would have spread in the way it did if
Howard had never developed the Indore Process. The following chapter
examines the widespread influence of that Process.

5. The Great Humus Controversy

Howard's disciples

A Meeting of the Farmers' Club was held at the Royal Society of Arts (John Street, Adelphi, W.C.2) on Monday, February 1st, 1937, Mr. J.F. BLACKSHAW, O.B.E., Chairman of the Club, presiding.[1]

This bland official report obscures one of the great dramatic confrontations of the early organic movement. Although one can read the transcript in Part 1 of the 1937 volume of the *Journal of the Farmers' Club*, how much more exciting it would have been to attend Sir Albert Howard's lecture on 'The Restoration and Maintenance of Fertility,' and hear him respond to the objections raised by members of the audience who represented the voice of orthodoxy.

The occasion offered a microcosm of the humus-vs.-artificials debate. Professor R.G. Stapledon proposed the vote of thanks and was seconded by the Wiltshire farmer A.J. Hosier, a pioneer of dairy farming methods. The audience included notable sympathizers with the organic cause like Christopher Turnor of Lincolnshire and Baron de Rutzen of West Wales. The big guns on the other side were Dr E.M. Crowther of Rothamsted, the agricultural chemist Dr J.A. Voelcker, and Dr S.J. Watson of ICI's Jealott's Hill Research Station. Howard dealt with them ruthlessly, claiming to 'have learned more from the diseases of plants and animals than I have from all the professors at Cambridge, Rothamsted and other places who gave me my preliminary training.' Watson expressed his admiration for Howard's work on the value of waste products in improving fertility, but doubted whether use of organic matter improved the health value of the crops grown. Crowther accused Howard of speaking in vague and general terms, disputing with him particularly as to the effect of artificials on the earthworm population. Howard retorted that Crowther had been 'very superficial,' everything he said on the topic being 'entirely

unsound.' We saw in an earlier chapter that Howard's chief aim was
always to help the practical farmer; this emphasis on economic survival
struck Crowther as reluctance to submit the Indore Process to the rigours
of scientific evidence. Howard had given no precise meaning to terms like
'soil fertility' and 'quality of crops'; he 'scorned field experiments and
appealed only to commercial success for his evidence.' Howard was a
man in a hurry, who admired above all the 'rare combination of science
and practice' which he recognized in Stapledon and Hosier. The methods
they had pioneered in their treatment of grassland would ensure a valuable reserve of fertility for producing arable crops in time of war. 'There
is no time lag between a *real* discovery,' he said, 'and its practical application on the part of the tillers of soil anywhere,' contrasting 'the live
wires who cultivate the soil' with the plodding conventional methods of
Experimental Stations: 'randomised small plots, followed by statistical
interpretation of the results.'[2] His experience was that farmers of any
kind, whether Indian peasants or English estate-owners, quickly adopted
proposals which appealed to them. In little more than five years since *The
Waste Products of Agriculture* appeared, farmers in ten different English
counties had adopted the Indore Process and were producing a volume of
compost considerably greater than anticipated. Howard did not deny that
there were problems, but it was precisely the role of the agricultural scientist to overcome problems. Howard concluded his response to the discussion with the following challenge:

> The question of fertility will turn on the results of the work now in
> progress. This has been much more successful than I anticipated.
> When the facts, not only in this country but in other countries, are
> brought together and published, I shall have a complete answer to
> everything that has been said to-night belittling the various matters
> I have brought forward. I am going to rely on the one unanswer-
> able argument — success — not on my own opinion or on other
> people's opinion. My reply is going to be written on the land.[3]

His reply was already being written on the land. One of the most
notable 'writers' was Friend Sykes of Chute, near Andover, who transformed the thin soil of his upland estate through applying the Indore
Process.[4] Sykes and his brothers had farmed in Buckinghamshire, winning many prizes for animal breeding. However, when the University of
Reading asked them to submit their dairy cattle to the newly instituted
Tuberculin Test they discovered that two-thirds of the herd reacted. What,
Sykes wondered, was the condition of other, non-prizewinning herds? As
a racehorse breeder, he was familiar with the saying "'50 per cent of the

pedigree goes in at the mouth".' The brothers concluded that there was something wrong with their feeding system, deciding to disperse their herd and replace it with cattle which they would feed without concentrated cakes, aiming not for the highest possible milk production but for healthy cattle with a good constitution. Another event at about the same time confirmed Sykes in his belief that correct feeding was the key to health. A valuable thoroughbred mare contracted contagious abortion and he was advised to destroy her. Instead he kept her in a large paddock where artificials had never been applied and fed her for two years on almost nothing but grass. She was cured, and went on to breed four colts. 'Here was my first attempt,' wrote Sykes, 'to cure an allegedly incurable disease by giving the creature ... Nature's food from humus-filled land.'[5]

Sykes took over the run-down Chantry estate in 1936 because he believed that chalk uplands produced superior thoroughbred horses. After early problems with costly animal diseases he decided to plough up the whole 750 acres. He avoided all factory compounds and concentrates and refused to apply any artificials, preferring to adapt Howard's methods to the conditions he faced. By 1945 he had almost completely rid the farm of disease and had established a herd of tubercle-free cattle. He went on to achieve many successes with his racehorses[6]; he grew wheat which was in demand with J.B. Priestley and Yehudi Menuhin, among other luminaries, and he contributed to the development of agricultural machinery through his design of the Rapier muck-shifter.[7] His experience demonstrated not just that organic methods made the land more fertile, the stock healthier and the crops and seeds disease-resistant, but that the whole virtuous circle would also be profitable. Organic farming was 'economic' in both senses of the term: it could save money, and help the farmer achieve self-sufficiency.

Howard was convinced that the Chantry Estate was a stronger argument for organic farming than any attempt at a scientific experiment such as Lady Balfour's work at Haughley, which the Soil Association took over. He insisted that Sykes should write the story of his first decade at Chantry, and since he was, in Sykes' experience, a hard man to refuse, the result was *Humus and the Farmer,* published by Faber in 1946. In it Sykes argued that a British farming system based on compost would not only be immensely productive, but would create a population 'healthy, robust, and practically disease-free': a nation of Hunzas, in other words. He was aware, though, of the power of those vested interests which for the sake of profit fostered the delusion that 'the refertilization of land is a chemical and not a biological process.'[8] How could that delusion be dispelled? Sykes agreed with Howard that disease was the spur to a better future: the spread of plant and animal disease would force humanity to return to creating humus-rich soils, and the nation would accept the justice of Howard's strictures on modern farming. Insecticides would be unable to cope with the problems of plant disease; insect pests were already developing resistance to DDT and fumigation, and Nature's balance was being upset, with unpredictable results. Sykes personified Nature as a power capable of consciously resisting human depradations: 'The first thing that Nature does when she has been treated with poison is to battle against it and try to breed a resistant strain of the form of life that is being attacked.'[9] Pests were a sign that the soil in which the plant grew was itself depleted and unhealthy, as would invariably be the case if humanity ignored the inter-relations of the natural order:

> All [the] processes of living existence are necessary for each and every one of us. This is the discipline of Nature. Nature has been described as a vast spontaneous universe moving in its own right according to its own order.[10]

Writing on the importance of afforestation, Sykes referred explicitly to the Law-Giver responsible for Nature's order when he said: 'Of all the glorious creations of the Almighty perhaps trees can claim pride of place.' Supreme among the Almighty's laws was the Rule of Return.[11]

Another of Howard's disciples, NEWMAN TURNER, who farmed near Bridgewater in Somerset, actually gave God a place in the index of his book *Fertility Farming*. His philosophy of farming was based on the belief that humanity has no right of possession over the resources of life, whether physical or spiritual:

> We are but the tenants of life, having on loan the physical from the earth and the spiritual from God. What happens to our spiritual being and its inspiration remains to be discovered after we lay down the physical life. But our duties regarding the physical body and its means of natural sustenance are clear to all. It must be returned, together with all organic matter derived from the earth, back to the earth.[12]

Another of Howard's followers expressed a similar faith. Howard had offered an agricultural 'testament'; Roy Wilson, the Fenland market gardener, presented, in his tract *I Believe*, an organic creed which derived from his success in creating the fertile and commercially noted Iceni Nurseries from an unpromising, run-down estate at Surfleet in Lincolnshire.[13] During the 1920s Wilson ran a mixed farm at Littleport in Cambridgeshire on orthodox lines, becoming sceptical about agricultural

science when he found that after four or five years during which the soil
had improved tremendously, its chemical analysis remained almost
unchanged. He bought the Surfleet estate in 1931, to demonstrate that
restoring poorly farmed land could be a commercial proposition, and ran
300 acres of it as an experiment in increasing fertility through the intensive approach of the European peasantry. In 1935 he went to hear Howard
address the Cambridge University School of Agriculture; Howard subsequently visited Surfleet to help supervise the inception of the Indore
Process, and in 1937 C.A. Mier visited the estate. According to George
Godwin, a 'chance meeting' with Viscount Lymington in 1935 led to Wilson visiting Lymington's Hampshire estate for an agricultural conference;
the quasi-fascist group the ENGLISH ARRAY may have brought them
together.[14] By 1939 the Iceni Nurseries were at their height, with two
London retail outlets to which they regularly delivered organically-grown
produce direct from Surfleet. Wilson won prizes from the Royal Horticultural Society and the Lincolnshire Agricultural Society, but his inten-
tions went beyond commercial success. *I Believe,* first published in 1941
and slightly revised in 1948, presented the diagnosis of industrial civilization's ills which was developed more fully by other members of the
organic movement: the misuse of money and consequent exploitation of
the soil; loss of craftsmanship; unhealthy food, and the cultural degeneration which results from an imbalance between urban and rural. Recognizing the land as the source of real wealth would lead to a change in
social policies which would start to rectify these evils. Wilson concluded
in the pamphlet's revised edition that his earlier suggestions for reform
had been too materialistic. He now realized that 'unless one attempted to
see life in its wholeness, no suggestions could help to cure our troubles.'[15]

> If man consciously tries to work with nature, he becomes immedi-
> ately aware of his responsibility to his soil, his plants and his ani-
> mals, and above all to his fellow beings, who are going to
> consume and live upon the food which he produces. His duty to
> his neighbour becomes clear, and that is probably the first and
> surest step towards the appreciation of a Divine purpose in life.[16]

Wilson was one of Lady Balfour's sources of information when she wrote
The Living Soil, and served for several years on the Soil Association's
Advisory Panel. Before examining the Association's origins, though, we
must return to the Farmers' Club to consider the ideas of another
landowner who adopted the Indore Process.

Shortly before his death in 1939 SIR BERNARD GREENWELL addressed
the Club on the subject of *Soil Fertility — The Farm's Capital.* Howard

himself proposed the vote of thanks, and the audience included VISCOUNT
BLEDISLOE and G.T. Wrench. On his Surrey estate, Greenwell had
reformed the manure heap through manufacturing humus by composting
pulverized town wastes with ordinary dung. Howard had visited the estate
and found that 'In every case the crops grown with humus ... were definitely better than those raised with farmyard manure.'[17] Greenwell had the
pulverized refuse delivered to him from the London Borough of Southwark, which, after removing items like bottles and tins from its collected
rubbish crushed it fine and sold it to farmers.

Using town wastes to supply humus was one of Howard's favourite
projects. One of the main obstacles to widespread composting was the
lack of organic wastes in any society using water-borne sewage systems;
towns were parasitic upon the countryside, failing to observe the Rule of
Return. Nothing on a scale comparable to South African initiatives
existed in Britain, but there were some schemes in boroughs apart from
Southwark. One at Maidenhead in Berkshire influenced John L. Davies,
Chief Engineer at Leatherhead, Surrey, and in 1936 the Urban District
Council there instituted a composting process which by the late 1940s
was selling 300 tons a year to local ratepayers and the rest to farmers and
gardeners via a firm of agricultural contractors.[18] In Dumfries the Chief
Engineer J.C. Wylie organized another successful scheme; he dedicated
his book *Fertility From Town Wastes* (1955) to Lady Howard, and
Lawrence Hills read the manuscript for Faber. Lady Balfour visited Wylie
in 1949 and recorded her impressions of the Dumfries scheme in *Mother
Earth*.[19] Wylie believed that a holistic outlook would show how agriculture's problems were linked to those of towns and cities, to the advantage
of both rural and urban.[20]

Two other observations by Greenwell in his Farmers' Club address
require digressions. Like Friend Sykes, he believed the process of sub-
soiling to be essential to increased fertility, one reason being that it
increased the earthworm population. Earthworms, Greenwell said, carried out a lot of deep cultivation by aerating the soil, and acted as scav-
engers. In his experience they disappeared from grassland treated with
artificials. In 1945 Faber reissued Darwin's study of earthworms, with an
introduction by Howard, who recalled how on the Cambridge University
Diploma in Agriculture in 1896–97 there had been no reference to the
role of earthworms in increasing soil fertility, or to Darwin's work.[21] In
the United States, though, Dr George S. Oliver had been undertaking
extensive studies of the earthworm since the 1920s, his work and conclusions being summarized by his friend Thomas J. Barrett in *Harnessing
the Earthworm*, a Faber book with a title made in heaven and an intro-

duction by Lady Balfour. For Barrett, the earthworm was 'the most important animal in the world,'[22] for through 'harnessing' it mankind could build topsoil more rapidly than nature, thereby increasing soil fertility and crop yields.

The third digression concerns the biological relationship known as 'mycorrhizal association.' When Greenwell spoke it was still in the early stages of investigation, but the organic school were interested in it because the presence of humus in the soil appeared to encourage it, with beneficial results for the health of crops. During the inter-war period M.C. RAYNER and W. Neilson-Jones investigated its ecological significance on Forestry Commission land at Wareham in Dorset. The term refers to the relationship between the roots of plants and fungus mycelium — 'the system of branched or unbranched, colourless or coloured tubes or hyphae [filaments] that make up the body of a fungus.'[23] Rayner and Neilson-Jones believed that their experiments provided evidence for the positive effects of certain organic composts on the formation of mycorrhiza. Howard and Lady Balfour were interested in the work at Wareham because the Indore Process had been particularly successful in regenerating tea plantations, and tea shrubs, like the conifers studied at Wareham, were plants whose roots associated with fungi. It had been assumed that humus acted indirectly on plants by forming salts in the soil, but the Wareham experiments suggested that its action was more direct, the mycorrhizal association being a living bridge which connected a humus-rich soil and its crop. Howard thought it probable that the digestion products of the soil fungi were

> at the root of disease resistance and quality ... If this is the case it would follow that on the efficiency of this mycorrhizal association the health and wellbeing of mankind must depend.[24]

Organic material, it seemed, stimulated the action of fungi and thus the health of the plant; where humus was lacking, plants tended to suffer lack of nutrition. Not all plants form mycorrhizal associations. The organic school thought that the Wareham experiments suggested the more general importance of vigorous fungal activity in the soil, and that such activity depended on 'maintenance of correct biological balance brought about otherwise than by increased supply of mineral nutrients.'[25]

Lady Balfour and the Soil Association

Howard's most influential British convert was Lady Eve Balfour, first President of the Soil Association, and author of the highly successful book *The Living Soil,* first published in 1943 and into its eighth edition five years later.[26] Niece of the Prime Minister Sir Arthur Balfour, she knew her vocation as a farmer from the age of twelve, taking the Agricultural Diploma at the University of Reading in 1917. Two years later she and her elder sister began farming at Haughley in Suffolk, learning the hard way during the depression of the 1920s. In 1938 she read Viscount Lymington's polemic *Famine in England* and as a result became aware of the questions relating to nutrition, health, and treatment of the soil. She met Howard the same year and began a thorough study of the issues which he and Lymington discussed, through them coming into contact with Lionel Picton and G.T. Wrench. In her own words:

> Nowhere had a long-term, comparative, controlled ecological experiment been undertaken to test the theories put forward, by Howard and others ... I was deeply impressed with the urgent need for the establishment of some such test.[27]

Lady Eve was owner-occupier of New Bells Farm, and tenant of the neighbouring Walnut Tree Farm. Alice Debenham, her landlord, supported her desire to establish the experiment; she set up the Haughley Research Trust and made to it the gift of her farm. Her sister knew one of the directors of Faber and Faber, and through her Lady Eve met RICHARD DE LA MARE, who, as editor of the firm's agriculture and horticulture lists, was supporting the organic cause. When Faber published *The Living Soil* the response from others thinking and working along similar lines was so great that creation of a formal organization to pool their experiences became inevitable. The Soil Association's founders met in June 1945, united in their concern for the health of the soil but with many conflicting opinions on how best to fight for it. Several months passed before an agreed Constitution could be framed, and the Association formally registered in May 1946. Its aims were:

1. To bring together all those working for a fuller understanding of the vital relationships between soil, plant, animal and man.
2. To initiate, co-ordinate and assist research in this field.
3. To collect and distribute the knowledge gained so as to create a body of informed public opinion.[28]

Lady Balfour identified the common ground uniting the founders as follows:

1. The conception of the soil as a living entity.
2. The recognition that human activities must conform to Nature's fixed biological laws if they are not to end in self-destruction.
3. Desire to promote research to interpret more fully what these laws are and how they work.
4. A determination to resist attempts to disregard these laws ... from whatever quarter, and with whatever motives such attempts are made.
5. The belief that this can be best achieved by using all possible means to disseminate information concerning proved knowledge and in this way to expose exploitation, particularly the exploitation of ignorance.[29]

Here we can see clearly the fundamental importance of belief in a natural order, and Lady Balfour demonstrated in *The Living Soil* that this belief was rooted in her Christian faith.

Lady Balfour shared with the other organic pioneers a concern to encourage an attitude to the natural world which would have social implications. She advocated some form of public ownership of land; a National Food Service; a merger of the Ministries of Health, Agriculture and Food; more rural-urban integration; greater emphasis on agriculture in education; and a 'spiritual and moral revival involving the adoption of a different standard of values,'[30] in which land-work would play an essential role. The war had brought the question of values to the fore: military victory was not enough; there must also be spiritual victory.

> The false idols of comfort and money, must be dethroned, and the Christian God of service put in their place. Service to God, service to our soil, service to each other, and, through each other, to the community and the world.[31]

The front covers of *Mother Earth* periodically reinforced the message during its first decade, displaying quotations from the Bible, Alexander Pope and Archbishop TEMPLE.[32]

Almost all the important figures in the organic movement were Soil Association members. Its first Council included Sir Bernard Greenwell's son Sir Peter, Richard de la Mare, Scott Williamson and Innes Pearse of the Pioneer Health Centre, and LORD SEMPILL. On its first Advisory Panel were Laurence Easterbrook, M.C. Rayner, Friend Sykes and Roy Wilson. In subsequent years KENNETH BARLOW, Rolf Gardiner,

H.J. Massingham, Lord Portsmouth, Lionel Picton, Richard St Barbe Baker, Maye Bruce, Newman Turner and Lady Howard were members either of the Council or the Panel. Two names are conspicuous by their absence: Sir Albert Howard and Sir George Stapledon. Howard believed that the decision to take over the experiment at Haughley was mistaken, since it could not be made scientifically watertight without huge financial costs. Stapledon was a member of the Association's Scientific Management Committee, which appointed independent observers of the Haughley experiment.[33]

Howard's scepticism was probably justified, as the results at Haughley do not appear to have been at all conclusive, and in any case there was a sense in which the experiment was established in the hope that a particular set of results would emerge. It was eventually abandoned, its story being added to the 1975 re-issue of *The Living Soil*.[34] The Association was more effective in its purpose of gathering and disseminating information on organic methods; by 1957 there were about 3,500 members from over 50 countries throughout the world.

Howard also influenced gardeners, notably Lawrence Hills. Hills' work for a Kent nursery in the 1930s had brought him into the company of

> gardeners who had gone on learning through their long lives, in the days when nicotine soap wash was the favourite insecticide and manure from the home farm the only fertilizer. They were organic gardeners from conservatism, the need to economize on materials rather than labour, and because they were observant men who had trained in an age without chemicals.[35]

As we saw earlier, Hills visited the biodynamic farmer Maurice Wood during his wartime service in the RAF, but he dated his entry into the organic movement from the day he received a letter from Sir Albert Howard. Having responsibility for the bucket sanitation of 200 men at the station where he was posted, he bought Howard and Wad's *The Waste Products of Agriculture* and subsequently wrote to Howard with various questions. Howard's reply ran to nine pages, and Hills was won to the cause of humus. In his autobiography he explained:

> An aspect of the greatness of Sir Albert Howard is shown by the fact that he took the time to write that long letter in his own handwriting ... to an unknown man in the RAF who asked a complicated question.[36]

Hills made another important contact during the war: he approached

Faber offering to write a book on his specialism, alpines, and this led to a lifelong friendship with Richard de la Mare. Hills became a reader for Faber, work he undertook for twenty-five years.

The origin of the Henry Doubleday Research Association (HDRA) was Hills' interest in comfrey. He became fascinated by the figure of Henry Doubleday, an Essex smallholder who introduced Russian comfrey into Britain in the 1870s and as a result was awarded a Fellowship of the Royal Society. For Doubleday, as later for Hills, comfrey was a plant of unique value, as a fodder crop, a green manure, and medicinally for humans. From the research station which Hills founded in Essex in the mid-1950s has grown one of Europe's largest centres for organic cultivation. His reputation was not confined to the organic movement: he was gardening correspondent for the *Observer* for several years. This was a useful platform for spreading the message.

Howard influenced other gardeners. Ben Easey recommended variations of the Indore Process, as did the Surrey commercial gardener J.L.H. Chase.[37] But perhaps Howard's most devoted horticultural disciple was F.C. KING, head gardener at Levens Hall in Westmorland, to whose book *Gardening with Compost* Howard contributed both an introduction and a closing chapter. Howard described the Levens Hall gardens as 'a place of pilgrimage,' producing excellent fruit and vegetables, and inspiring other gardeners to give up artificial fertilizers and poison sprays. King's belief in organic methods stemmed from faith in a personified female Nature, 'the supreme gardener,' 'one and indivisible,' departure from whose laws was 'fraught with peril.'[38] Ignoring the law of return, science was going against the unending round of Nature:

> It is no wonder that failures are so common in a system so
> divorced from that which Mother Earth has chosen to follow. Yet
> in his perversity man is wont to rail against the very principles of
> Nature he daily frustrates and obstructs; he ignores the fact that his
> interruption of Nature's round cannot but bring in its train serious
> consequences.[39]

In his early seventies when the Second World War ended, Howard had no intention of retiring from the fray. Having quarrelled with the Soil Association's founders over its scientific strategy, he established the journal *SOIL AND HEALTH*, which ran from February 1946 to Spring 1948, its final issue being a Memorial Number celebrating his career and influence. *Soil and Health* was in effect a continuation of the *News Letter on Compost,* which had been issued since 1941 by the Panel Committee of the Cheshire doctors responsible for the *Medical Testament;* it was edited by Lionel Picton. *Soil and Health*'s first issue announced that its objects in its new incarnation would be, as before:

> to publish all information pertinent to the spread of ideas on the restoration of our soils to adequate fertility and on the connection between a fertile soil and improved standards of health in crops, animals and man.[40]

These objects were to all intents and purposes those of the Soil Association, and there was little significant difference between the contents of Howard's journal and those of *Mother Earth;* indeed, many names appear in both. Although its cover design of white cliffs and rural landscape was quintessentially English, the journal gave a lot of coverage to worldwide developments, and printed articles by humus pioneers in New Zealand, South Africa, Bengal and Costa Rica. Howard wrote a piece called 'The Living Pharaohs' on the Watussi tribe of Rwanda, an African equivalent of the Hunzas, offering them as an object-lesson in how to maintain health and avoid spending millions on a government-funded health service. He also monitored the debate on the quality of bread.[41]

Soil and Health provides evidence of the distinctively Christian strain in the organic movement. It refers a number of times to *The Cross and the Plough,* journal of the Catholic Land Association, and it reprinted an article from it by Cecil Bachelor, containing the prophetic utterance: 'Industry has neither Soul nor Soil: it sacrifices all to its gods — Power and Money! Nature is long suffering, but she repays!'[42] Howard's methods were practised at various Catholic institutions: Campion House at Osterley, Middlesex; the Holy Ghost Missionary College, Co. Dublin; and St Columba's College, near Dublin city. Guy Clutton-Brock wrote to the journal declaring that:

> as a Christian I understand something of the necessity for obedience to the laws by which the world is governed. I am therefore profoundly interested in what your journal stands for.[43]

The last word in the Memorial Number came from an anonymous Catholic priest, who expressed admiration for Howard's cause and the manner in which he had conducted it.[44]

Howard's death in 1947 was sudden and unexpected, but it served to reunite his widow with the Soil Association. Lady Louise Howard served the Association until her death in 1969.

Other initiatives

Another internecine rival, though, maintained a civil war with the Soil Association until the early 1950s, describing its supporters as 'feeble-minded.'[45] This was Dr SIEGFRIED MARIAN, an Austrian industrial chemist whose contribution to the organic movement seems now to have been almost completely forgotten. He founded and edited his own SOIL MAGAZINE to promote both an organic approach to the soil and the virtues of his product 'Actumus,' a highly concentrated and soluble blend of humus with charcoal. Lady Balfour visited Marian when touring the West Country in the autumn of 1948, and was impressed by his work at Dartington Hall, where he was preparing several hundred acres for reafforestation and using the surface humus of the cleared site as part of a composting system with other natural products. Lady Balfour herself experimented with 'Actumus,' keeping an open mind on Marian's claims, though, like other experimenters, she found evidence that it did encourage earthworms.[46]

Marian had undertaken research work at the Institute for Analytical Chemistry in Vienna, where his professor believed that using ammonia salts as fertilizers would eventually destroy the soil. Marian was so disturbed by this thought that he discovered his vocation, to know:

> how the mechanism of life functioned. Life had existed for so long
> without fertilizers. There must, therefore, be a reaction, or a chain
> of reactions, perpetuating life. I knew that my grandfather had
> spread carefully prepared animal manures. What is the mechanism
> of their fertilizing action? How do forests exist without any
> manurial action at all? Here was a set of questions which I had to
> answer first before I could dare a suicide attack on the sellers of
> artificial fertilizers, especially on those who were selling one and
> the same ammonia salts for fertilizers and explosives.[47]

Marian believed in the importance of what he termed the 'bio-energetical' dimension of soil fertility, something which, he maintained, could be measured using established scientific techniques to determine the soil's surface energy and surface tension. Such experiments established, in measurable fashion, that humus increased soil fertility:

> Extensive cropping of soil on organic lines cannot lead to exhaustion,
> but to measurable increase of bio-energy and fertility. Soil exhaustion
> is only possible by intensive cultivation with chemical salts, which
> gradually reduce the energy level until it is completely destroyed.[48]

Like Howard, he attacked the Rothamsted experiments, describing the Research Station as a 'dummy' ritually appealed to whenever anyone raised doubts about artificials. He also attacked Lady Balfour,[49] but this was essentially a family quarrel; the Soil Association, to which Marian belonged in its early days, and *Soil Magazine* agreed on fundamentals.

Marian's rigorous training as an analytical chemist did not prevent the journal's perspective from being overtly spiritual. The July 1949 issue declared on its front cover, 'The Laws of Nature are the Thoughts of God,' and an editorial called for a restoration of religion, since all religions were 'based on a natural order, meaning to give us the lead how to live in peace and happiness to the will of the Creator.'[50] One correspondent, evidently of a biodynamic persuasion, praised Marian for:

> [being the first] to produce a scientific thesis which does not collide with religion ... All that lives relies on the connection between the life creating factor in our earth, our bodies and plants, conncecting with the incessant energy sent to us from above ... Man is thus obliged to care for the earthy part of life while God is sending us the cosmic part. Do you agree?[51]

Marian's answer was an emphatic 'YES.' A certain H.H. Bennett wrote an article on the Bible as a gardener's handbook,[52] and frequent contributions by DION BYNGHAM, who became Assistant Editor after Marian's death in 1952, guaranteed a strongly mystical element.

Byngham reviewed at length two books by PHILIP OYLER, a member of the Kinship in Husbandry who at one time had managed Aubrey Westlake's estate. In 1950 Oyler wrote *The Generous Earth,* praising the peasant culture of the Dordogne, which he presented as another example of the superiority of traditional husbandry based on the Rule of Return. Oyler celebrated the productiveness of the French farmers, mocking the idea that one should pity the poor peasant: these peasants enjoyed a luxurious standard of living that made them objects of either envy or emulation for other Frenchman.[53] Their benefits were not gastronomic only: they enjoyed life, had time for fetes, co-operated with each other, and, as Lady Balfour suggested in her own review of the book, brought 'true conservatism and true socialism together.'[54] Oyler saw all these things as benefits of a right approach to the earth, 'accord[ing] in externals with the practice of Christian principles.' This was in contrast with the prodigality of the Anglo-Saxon races, who behaved 'as if we were entitled to do whatever we choose with any plot of this earth, as though it was our own making (and not the Creator's).' Oyler believed that 'A nation's love of God can be guaged by its love and respect for the land (agriculture being the basis of all culture) and by its attitude to work.'[55]

Oyler's subsequent book, *Feeding Ourselves,* examined the psychological reasons for Britain's refusal to follow the example of the Dordogne peasants, preferring to rely heavily on exporting industrial goods in order to import foodstuffs. The British had flouted Providence and needed to turn their hearts 'back to God and away from scientific materialism.' Radical social changes were required, one of them being widespread distribution of land to increase individual ownership — a policy which HILAIRE BELLOC and G.K. CHESTERTON had advocated twenty or thirty years previously, and which Oyler described as 'a revolutionary step ... in order to reach an external state that will conform with the teaching in the Gospels.' There was no place in a Christian society for large estates, big business or state planning, since 'Human theories are always at variance with divine order.' Oyler did not believe that the peasants who lived in obedience to the divine order were saints, but they never denied God, 'for they have to wait upon Him for benefits conferred, whether it suits them or not to do so.'[56]

The Generous Earth had an introduction by Lord Northbourne, and we can bring this chapter to a close by looking at the ideas of this important figure. Northbourne is particularly significant, since he was apparently the first person to use the term 'organic' in application to farming.[57]

After serving in the 1914–18 war, Walter Northbourne took a degree in Agriculture at Oxford and taught there during the 1920s. In 1932 he succeeded to the family estate near Deal in Kent, and eight years later wrote an influential book, *Look to the Land,* in which he elaborated the idea of the farm as an 'organic whole,' one where there is a 'biological completeness' based on a 'cycle of conversion of vegetable products.'[58] He therefore opposed the specialization urged by the orthodox school, but this did not prevent him from being appointed Chairman of the Kent Agricultural Executive Committee after the Second World War, or a Fellow of Wye Agricultural College in the 1960s. His book also indicated concern for the other issues integral to the organic outlook: health and nutrition, the dangers of free trade, and the need for financial reform. He became clerk to the Kinship in Husbandry when it first met in 1941.[59]

Northbourne was a widely cultured man, a painter and art expert, a student of religions, and a translator of works from French; his son married the grand-daughter of the poet and dramatist Paul Claudel. He published two more books after *Look to the Land: Religion in the Modern World* (1963), and *Looking Back on Progress* (1970). The titles are suggestive, as is the fact that one of the books he translated was René Guénon's *The*

Reign of Quantity and the Signs of the Times. Guénon was a scholar of the esoteric and occult whose work has influenced the contemporary Right in France, and the book contains several ideas common in the organic movement, including concern for the loss of a sense of the sacred and loss of craftsmanship, and the harmful influence of mechanistic and materialist philosophies. Northbourne developed this outlook in his own writings, distinguishing between two mentalities: the 'traditional,' based on revealed religion, and the 'progressive,' based on humanistic philosophy and scientific observation.[60] There are no prizes for guessing which he favoured:

> Anyone who is disposed to emphasize the defects of traditional civilizations would do well to look dispassionately at our modern progressive ... civilization [and] at what it has in fact produced in the way of anxiety, war and rivalry, ugliness (in the despoiling of Nature and in the arts), and subjection ... to the inexhaustible demands of the machine.[61]

Life's meaning could be found only 'in the sacred centre,' in 'a human family with God as its "Father" and Nature as its "Mother".'[62] Loss of a sense of God led to misguided attempts to control Nature, but since humans are partly of Nature and partly of Spirit they mediate between God and Nature: hence the importance of agriculture. For Northbourne, writing in 1970, industrialized agriculture seemed to have brought humanity to the point where it would be forced to face the consequences of defying God. Thirty years earlier, in *Look to the Land,* he had warned against the path being taken: 'We have tried to conquer nature by force and by intellect. It now remains for us to try the way of love.'[63]

* * *

'There are no materialists in the Soil Association,' Lady Balfour is reported to have said,[64] and readers should now be able to see why she was prepared to make such a claim. A religious philosophy of life was integral to the organic outlook as it developed from the 1920s onwards, in both the biodynamic and mainstream movements. Whereas the orthodox school of agriculture argued that greater application of artificials was necessary, the organic school believed that there was already too great a reliance on them and that danger signs, in the form of increased plant and animal diseases, were evident. But even if no connection could be conclusively proved, their belief in a God-given natural order ensured that they mistrusted any agricultural system which ignored the Rule of Return. It is in this sense that the organic pioneers can be said to have responded prophetically to developments in agriculture during the first half of the twentieth century: they read the signs of the times and intuited where these developments must lead, on the basis of axioms derived from their religious faith and of the still-extant examples of traditional methods.

It would be completely wrong, however, to conclude that they were opposed to scientific development *per se,* given the scientific abilities of Howard, McCarrison, Steiner and St Barbe Baker. From the organic perspective, it was the proponents of industrialized farming who were not proper scientists, since they failed to see the ecological connections of natural phenomena. Their knowledge was therefore very limited and much of it inapplicable to the complexities of farming practice. The task of 'true' science was to increase understanding of the laws which God had imposed on nature, and to learn to work with them for optimum productivity. Peasant farmers, whether in the Far East, India or the Dordogne, unconsciously obeyed the principles which a few agricultural scientists like Howard were elucidating through western methods of observation and experiment.

To believe that agriculture was the means by which humanity mediated between God and nature, as Northbourne expressed it, had implications that went beyond agriculture. If a farm should, ideally, be a self-supporting organism, how much more should a nation be so. A farm relying on external inputs for its survival was perilously placed; a nation relying on external inputs of food even more so. Furthermore, if nature was an expression of God, it followed that it must be spiritually beneficial and that a nation which developed its industry at the expense of its agriculture and rural life, as Britain had done for a century, must become unbalanced and spiritually impoverished. But before we examine the work and ideas of those in the organic movement who were particularly concerned about the urban-industrial bias in British life, we need to trace the influence of Howard and Steiner on the organic movement which developed in the United States.

6. Hands across the Water

The organic movement in the United States

If Eastern farming offered the best examples of how to care for the soil, the American mid-West provided the most ominous illustration of what happened when the earth was exploited in complete disregard for the Rule of Return. The Dust Bowl, so powerfully portrayed in John Steinbeck's novel *The Grapes of Wrath* and the film version of it starring Henry Fonda, was a gift to the organic movement. Within a lifetime rich virgin soils had been worn out to the point where they simply blew away. Irresponsible farming had created deserts and caused untold human misery through the resulting social dislocation. What clearer evidence could there be that a healthy soil was the essential basis of a stable society?[1]

The United States Department of Agriculture (USDA) testified to the scale of the challenge by devoting its 1938 Yearbook to the subject of *Soils and Men.* The 300 pages of its first section outlined the problem, analysed its causes and suggested possible remedies. These were not purely agricultural: questions of education, finance and economic stabilization were central to the programme proposed. The following 700 pages covered every aspect of soil science, methods of tillage, erosion prevention, drainage, and soil-plant relationships. Though the Yearbook was not a manifesto for the organic movement, the concluding paragraphs of the introductory summary expressed one of the movement's most dearly-held contentions:

> ... many human activities not ordinarily associated with the soil
> may be traced back to its influence ... Stable civilizations are asso-
> ciated with long familiarity with a given soil; they grow out of it
> and are rooted in it. If disturbances arise that upset the relationship
> of man with the soil ... they may lead to neglect or abuse of the
> land, and this may be followed, under the right conditions, by its
> ultimate ruin and forced abandonment. A stable, healthy and vig-
> orous civilization demands a proper adjustment of men to the soil,
> and opportunities for them to make this adjustment.[2]

The Yearbook does not refer to F.H. King's *Farmers of Forty Centuries,* mentioning him briefly as a soil scientist who used European methods of analysis. His dissatisfaction with American farming must have been firmly established by the end of the nineteenth century, since his 1907 visit to the Far East fulfilled a long-standing ambition. Unfortunately King died in his early sixties, his book being published posthumously, and he was unable to reinforce its message. Not published in Britain until 1927, it became an important text for the organic movement and thereby indirectly re-crossed the Atlantic, for the American organic movement was largely the product of European influence.

This chapter cannot attempt anything like a comprehensive history of that movement, and will concentrate on the various connections between American advocates of the Rule of Return and their British and European counterparts. American agriculturalists were aware of their inexperience in comparison with Asians and Europeans. The pioneers had been rendered irresponsible by the ease with which they could produce crops; now their descendants had to learn some humility. If things were going badly wrong, perhaps the Old World could offer examples of how they could be rectified.

This is not to imply that Americans were dependent on Europeans for their motivation and initiatives. Suzanne Peters has examined the way in which United States food reformers helped prepare for the organic movement, their philosophy similarly being based on 'a respect for Nature and a concern with man's role in Nature's balance.'[3] King undertook his study of Oriental farming in 1907; by the early 1920s Selman Waksman's investigations of humus were under way,[4] and in 1928 he was principal speaker at a Symposium on Soil Organic Matter and Green-Manuring. Dr G.S. Oliver[5] was undertaking his studies of the earthworm at this time, and WESTON PRICE, whose work is discussed in Chapter 8, was travelling the world to study the teeth and diets of primitive peoples.

Nevertheless, the 1920s also saw the European influence make itself felt in a way which was to have far-reaching consequences, when the American organic movement's future propagandist-in-chief JEROME RODALE heard Robert McCarrison address a Pittsburgh audience early in the decade. McCarrison's lecture on 'Faulty Food in Relation to Gastro-Intestinal Disorders,' given to the Society for Biological Sciences, provides the most appropriate starting-point for examining the links between the American and European organic schools.[6]

Jerome Rodale

Rodale was born Jerome Irving Cohen, the son of immigrants from Eastern Europe who settled in New York. His father wanted him to become a rabbi, bringing him up in strict Jewish orthodoxy. Rodale's biographer suggests that this childhood turned him into the 'apostle of nonconformity' who was able to fight so vigorously for unorthodox ideas. Whatever the truth of this, Rodale apparently never abandoned Judaism, and gave considerable financial support to the state of Israel. The change of name, undertaken in 1921, was for purely pragmatic reasons: he wanted to be a novelist, to go into publishing, and to farm, and in these occupations a Jewish name would have disadvantaged him.[7]

Rodale's poor health as a young man working in the notoriously polluted city of Pittsburgh led him to ponder the relationship between health and environment. This, combined with his insatiable curiosity and his passion for public lectures, would explain his attendance at McCarrison's talk, as a result of which he read everything he could find on the Hunzas. The Pittsburgh lecture was the start of Rodale's interest in organic cultivation.

The seed lay dormant for more than a decade, though, until the late 1930s. By this time Rodale had achieved his ambition to become a publisher and was producing *Health Digest* among other journals. While seeking suitable material in an English health magazine he read an article by Sir Albert Howard and was so excited by it that he wrote to him. A close friendship developed through correspondence and Howard came to regard Rodale as chief representative of his ideas in the United States. In 1940 Rodale bought a farm at Emmaus, Pennsylvania, where the Rodale Institute still exists, and began practising Howard's methods. Soon he had sold his interests in all his magazines in order to establish the one that really mattered to him; this was *Organic Farming and Gardening,* founded in May 1942.[8] Its first issue included a description of the Indore Process and an article by Ehrenfried Pfeiffer on biodynamic cultivation. After a few issues Howard became associate editor and remained so until his death, but Rodale continued to collaborate with Pfeiffer and became a leading exoteric exponent of Steiner's methods, attempting to sidestep the internecine quarrel.[9]

Rodale's major statement of organic principles for an American audience, *Pay Dirt,* first published in 1945, actually has very little to say about Steiner's methods. There is an introduction by Howard and a section on him as the 'father of scientific composting.' The book also reprints the *Medical Testament* in full.[10] Several figures in the mainstream British organic movement are mentioned. The publishers' blurb on the dust-jacket described the book as 'the first ... devoted completely to this way of farming and gardening to be written and published in the United States,' so it is significant that much of the evidence adduced by Rodale should have been from British sources. The same company, Devin-Adair, also published Howard's *Farming and Gardening for Health or Disease* (under the title *The Soil and Health),* and Picton's *Thoughts on Feeding* (as *Nutrition and the Soil).*

Rodale also undertook experimental work. In 1947 he established the Soil and Health Foundation, which had a laboratory and offered grants for research programmes, but for several years it was 'an almost total failure.'[11] The laboratory work proceeded too slowly for Rodale's liking and hardly any educational institutions could be persuaded to take up the offer of grants. There were two significant exceptions to this reluctance, although both were predictable: in 1950 the University of Missouri accepted a grant for experimentation with rock fertilizers, under the direction of Professor W.A. ALBRECHT, and Pfeiffer conducted experiments at his farm in New York State with the Foundation's support.

Rodale's interest in gardening and farming was inseparable from his concern for health and nutrition, and in 1950 he founded the magazine *Prevention,*

> to alert the big-city dweller to the possibilities of obtaining wholesome food either through selective buying or through finding a minute plot on which to grow a few vegetables.[12]

A digest of medical information, it became his favourite initiative and went on to have a circulation of over a million. Rodale's views on food were to lead him into open conflict with the American Medical Association, through his opposition to the use of pesticides in food production. From 1941 onwards he was writing against chemical sprays, following Howard's view that a crop's infestation by pests should be regarded as indicating the poor health of plant and soil, and quoting Pfeiffer on the potentialities of companion planting for discouraging pests.[13] In *Pay Dirt,* Rodale cited a number of pieces of medical evidence on the harm caused by arsenic sprays and the dangers posed by the newly-released product DDT, and pointed out the likelihood that insects would in any case develop resistance to chemical means of controlling them.[14] A number of scientists — including Barry Commoner, later a leading environmentalist — were sympathetic to what Rodale was saying, but many were hostile, and the Monsanto Company — the name might ring a bell for those familiar with present-day debates on food technology — produced a package entitled 'Plain talk, Pesticides and the Environment' to rebut the critics of agricultural chemicals. The argument, as disingenuous then as now, was that 'chemicals are indispensable in staving off world hunger, even famine.'[15] From the early 1950s Rodale attacked the power of patronage which chemical companies enjoyed in universities and agricultural colleges, pointing out the conflict of interests involved.

'Genius? or Fraud?' demands the back cover of Jackson's biography of Rodale. Certainly he is a difficult figure to assess. There is no doubt of his central importance to the organic cause in the United States, as spokesman for the ideas of Howard and Pfeiffer, forerunner of Carson's case against pesticides, critic of food additives, inspirer of the next generation of organic farmers and gardeners and popularizer of the organic cause through his magazines, books and plays. Indeed, by 1971 he was being celebrated in the *New York Times Magazine* as 'Guru of the Organic Food Cult,' and the speech he made about this tribute exemplifies his ambiguities. 'My friends,' he announced, 'my time has come.' For thirty years he had been ridiculed as a crackpot, 'the leader of a cult of misguided people relying on half-truths and pseudo-science and emotions.'[16] But now, he claimed, perhaps with a certain amount of exaggeration:

> even the chemical people have become respectful towards me and my manure ideology. I am suddenly becoming a prophet here on earth, and a prophet with profits.[17]

Here was ammunition for those who saw Rodale as having exploited organic ideas to his personal and financial advantage; yet it is improbable that he would have run a farm, set up laboratories, devoted his publishing business to organic causes and endured the years of criticism and mockery if he had not been genuinely committed. Suzanne Peters sees Rodale as someone who sought to Americanize the ideas of Howard and Steiner. She says of him: 'He fused Steiner's esoteric mysticism and Howard's research reforms into a secular and practical mission'[18] and argues that in *Pay Dirt* he ignored the social dimension of farming issues and avoided open confrontation with capitalism. While it is true that *Pay Dirt* concentrates on food and farming issues, the book has obvious social implications, discussing the harm done by tenant farming, the importance of regionalism and the future form of city life. Rodale's confrontations with capitalism came in the following decade.

As for the distancing from spiritual echoes, these had not faded completely out of earshot: the sense of a natural order to be respected is explicit at the end of the book when Rodale itemizes the environmental and social damage done by industrial agriculture and says:

These evils are not inevitable, or natural things. If we, as a nation, permit these practices to go on, we shall richly deserve consequences such as those predicted by the prophet Micah: '... the land shall be desolate because of them that dwell therein, for the fruit of their doings.'[19]

At Rodale's funeral his friend Rabbi Steven Shafer said of him: 'Man works in partnership with God in the process of creation. And that's what Jerry did! He was a partner.' It is interesting to note that Rodale married a Catholic, Anna Andrews, and that during the years he lived in Emmaus he gave a great deal of support to the priest at St Ann's church, Fr Paul Pekarik.[20] It is reasonable to conclude that Rodale's philosophy was not purely secular, though for propagandist purposes he allowed the religious strain in his outlook to be muted.

Louis Bromfield

Among those who read and commented on *Pay Dirt* while it was in manuscript form were Sir Albert Howard, Professor William A. Albrecht, and the man who for a time rivalled Rodale as the leading exponent of organic ideas, LOUIS BROMFIELD. In 1943 Bromfield was one of the celebrities to whom Rodale sent a copy of *Organic Gardening,* and he formed a favourable impression of the journal, which expressed ideas he had held for a long time. A couple of years later he was evidently happy to consider being an honorary director of the then embryonic Soil and Health Foundation. Rodale wanted to publish Bromfield's books on agriculture but this proved legally impossible. Perhaps it is just as well, since by the mid-1950s Rodale considered that Bromfield should no longer be considered an organic farmer. Having supported the organic school during the 1940s, Bromfield seemed in the following decade to regard its members as cultists. Yet in 1955 he travelled to England to give the Albert Howard Memorial Lecture at the Royal Empire Society. Whereas Rodale considered him 'far from an organic farmer,'[21] Bromfield declared himself not *fully* organic.[22] He nevertheless agreed with important aspects of the organic philosophy, and his fame as novelist and farmer establishes him as arguably a more important spokesman for the Rule of Return than Rodale during the decade following the end of the Second World War.

Bromfield's interest in agriculture stemmed from his teenage years, when in 1913 his family moved to a farm. The following year he entered Cornell University to study agriculture, but injury to his grandfather forced him to drop the course and return to help run the homestead. Part-time work on a local newspaper led him to a journalism course, this time at Columbia University, and in 1917 he joined the US Army Ambulance Service as driver and interpreter, attached to the French army. When the war ended he stayed in France, returning to America late in 1919. During the early 1920s his journalistic career took off rapidly, and in 1924 he achieved instant success with his first novel *The Green Bay Tree,* which dealt with the problems caused by the change from an agricultural to an industrial economy. Further successes followed, but Bromfield's love of France drew him back there, and in 1927 he and his family settled at Senlis, north of Paris, where they remained until 1938.

Bromfield's life in France combined cosmopolitanism with peasanthood. He had many contacts in the world of literature and cinema, and mixed with what his biographer presents as a motley group of all races, colours and types.[23] Among them he made the acquaintance of Viscount Lymington.[24] More significantly, Bromfield made four visits to India during the 1930s, and while there visited Indore, where he was impressed by the results of Howard's experiments. The house that he leased in Senlis had with it several acres of land and he became a passionate gardener and vegetable-grower, gaining fame for introducing particular American squashes and tomatoes, and eventually being awarded the diploma and medal of the Workingman's Garden Association of France. He increasingly valued the stability represented by cultivation of the soil. Amid the hectic schedule of his life abroad the thought of returning home and running a farm began to take hold. He is reputed to have said on one occasion: 'I make my reputation with a pen, but my heart is with the spade.'[25]

When it became clear that war was inevitable, Bromfield returned to Ohio and set about warning America of what was happening in Europe. Unlike some of the leading figures in the British organic movement he was implacably opposed to appeasement and even produced a pamphlet criticizing the pro-German clique, which he titled *England — A Dying Oligarchy.*[26] He also invested in farms, but this fulfilment of personal ambition was far from escapism. What he had seen had led him to conclude that the high standard of living in America was illusory and vulnerable to economic fluctuations: 'Any French peasant, any French workingman with his little plot of ground ... had more permanence, more solidity, more security'[27] than the American wage-earner.

By the end of the war Bromfield had become one of the best-known farmers in the United States. The work which he undertook at Malabar Farm in restoring a derelict homestead to productivity helped stimulate changes in the nation's agricultural development, attracting more than 15,000 visitors annually. He wrote four books about his farming work: *Pleasant Valley, Malabar Farm, Out of the Earth* and *From my Experi-*

ence. The first of these, published in 1945, returned him to a position of importance in the literary world, catching the mood of resurgent interest in farming and gardening. Bromfield described it as:

> a personal testament written out of a lifetime by a man who believes that agriculture is the keystone of our economic structure and that the wealth, welfare, prosperity and even the future freedom of this nation are based upon the soil.[28]

It was not aimed at agricultural experts, but so great was the response that a couple of years later Bromfield produced the very substantial *Malabar Farm,* which dealt more specifically with the problems faced by those who wished to take up farming. The book begins and ends with letters to one such person, 'a Sergeant in Okinawa,' representative of the thousands of GIs who had read *Pleasant Valley* and wanted to know more. In the first of these letters Bromfield described true agriculture as a process of understanding 'natural and universal laws,' contrasting it with the exploitative agriculture practised in the United States, which had led to a cultural loss of respect for farmers and to their exploitation by fertilizer firms, the meat-packing industry and other elements of burgeoning agribusiness. Bromfield assessed efficiency in terms of output per acre and pointed out that United States agriculture was increasingly inefficient, with production per acre steadily diminishing. Any worthwhile policy had to concentrate first on soil renewal and preservation: Bromfield was a member of the Soil Conservation Sub-Committee of the Post-War Planning Commission. In the post-war period he established an offshoot of Malabar at Wichita Falls, Texas, which was a pilot farm for various soil-building projects. He argued that a farmer's money came from the soil and its yield per acre, and that increasing productivity per acre would pay the farmer and, by reducing the need for government subsidies, help the national economy. But a productive soil would bring more than just financial benefits: upon agriculture and forestry 'depends another vast source of any nation's power — the health, vigour, intelligence and ingenuity of its citizens.'[29]

Out of the Earth, the third of Bromfield's agricultural books, was the most specialist. In it he widened the scope of his attack on American agriculture to include Howard's old enemy 'the laboratory hermit,' the overspecialization of agricultural education, and the lack of communication between researchers and farmers. Bromfield envisaged a system of pilot farms, run in co-operation with agricultural colleges, where a farmer could visit and:

rub shoulders with the same concrete problems he faces at home, a
place where he could examine the texture of the soil and the health
and vigor of the livestock and look over the fence and know he is
seeing a productive and profitable field and that he can find out
how it was made that way.[30]

Too much of the research carried out by government agencies was lost or
duplicated.

Bromfield also criticized commercial interests: not just fertilizer manufacturers and the food processing industry, but makers of farm machinery. His attitude to machinery in general was ambivalent: its advantages
were counter-balanced by its potential for destruction. As a practical
farmer he resented the waste of time and money incurred when a machine
invented and tested in conditions far removed from those where it would
be used broke down in the awkward conditions of a real field, and advocated smaller implements adapted to a variety of uses. He was wary of
industry's growing hold over farming, and shared Rodale's concern about
the possible harmful effects of poison sprays and chemical additives in
food; in 1951 he testified to a House committee on this latter issue.

Thus far, the case for considering Bromfield a supporter of organic
husbandry is clear. In certain respects, though, his outlook was more akin
to that of the orthodox school. While he supported the ideal of the family
farm, he thought there had to be a move towards specialization, and that
farmers should use machinery in order to do a couple of things well
instead of several indifferently.[31] Like Astor and Rowntree he denied the
central importance of arable crops.[32] He preferred to develop veal and
dairy products, describing Malabar as 'a factory for grass.'[33] Given the
economic and social complexity of the United States self-sufficiency was
impossible, which meant that products had to be sold off the farm. This
in turn necessitated some use of artificials, and on this issue Bromfield
differed from Rodale.

An entire chapter of *Malabar Farm* was devoted to 'The Organic-
Chemical Fertilizer Feud.'[34] Bromfield began by distinguishing Liebig's
broad outlook and sense of wonder from the arrogance of contemporary
chemical specialists, and then proceeded to condemn the narrowness of
the purely organic school, though he admitted that he considered the latter to be nearer the truth than the former. He defended the moderate use
of artificials provided that there was already sufficient humus in the soil.
Contrary to those organicists who claimed that soils could be restored
without any use of chemicals, he said that exhausted minerals had to be
supplied by means of artificials. The yields at Malabar produced by a

mixture of chemical and organic manures were greater than those of an organic purist with whom he was corresponding, and supplied more organic material which could be used further to increase fertility. It was all a question of balance, and once the balance of the soil was restored there was no longer any need to use chemicals.

The debate seems to depend, as debates so often do, on questions of definition. Bromfield regarded as 'fanatics' those who would use no artificials at all, but the term would actually apply to hardly anybody in the organic movement. Whereas Rodale described Bromfield as being far from an organic farmer, Bromfield preferred to describe himself as not fully organic because agriculture is far too complex to be reduced to formulae.[35] Perhaps Rodale was peeved at being regarded as a cultist; it seems unreasonable to deny Bromfield a place among members of the organic school. His organization Friends of the Land (FoL), founded in 1940, was driven by a concern about the waste of natural resources and its social effects, recognizing that preservation of soil, forests and water resources was essential to a nation's survival. Bromfield said that a suitable slogan for FoL might have been: 'The civilization of this nation is founded upon about eight inches of topsoil. When that goes civilization will go with it.' Not very catchy, perhaps, but it exactly expressed the organic school's belief. As it developed, FoL took up a range of causes dear to the British organic movement: diet and nutrition, water pollution, municipal sewage disposal, decentralization of urban life, and self-sufficiency through individual land ownership. Its members included a number of distinguished figures, among them the economist and writer Stuart Chase; Hugh H. Bennett, chief of the US Soil Conservation Department, and the psychiatrist Karl Menninger. Dr Jonathan Forman, an authority on nutrition, was a Vice-President, and two leading soil ecologists, PAUL SEARS and William Albrecht, played prominent parts in the organization.[36] FoL was a forerunner of the 1960s environmental movement, though it did not long survive Bromfield's death in 1956.

What, finally, of Bromfield's religious philosophy? In this matter he was closer to the organic school than Rodale was, frequently referring in his books to the need for recognition of the natural order and acceptance of God's laws. Suzanne Peters says that he 'explicitly disavowed the mysticism of biodynamicists like Pfeiffer,'[37] but he also explicitly maintained that a strain of mysticism was essential for any good farmer. It was a question of degree. Writing about Pierre Sauvegeot, who represented the French Ministry of Agriculture at a San Francisco conference in July 1945, Bromfield judged him to be excessively mystical:

> Every good farmer is a mystic at heart and a religious man, but a
> good farmer's mysticism and faith are founded upon the base of
> the earth itself, and so very different from what to me is that
> implausible mysticism of the detached spirit. I am Protestant
> enough and Anglo-Saxon enough to demand concrete results. That
> is where I am forced to part company with many who practise the
> mysticism of debased Hinduism.[38]

He went on to reject Sauvegeot's plans for a return to nature as irrelevant
to political and economic realities: 'He would have us, in a world of
machines and its teeming ill-fed millions, return to a kind of medieval and
mystical agriculture.'[39] One might point out that this criticism could
equally have been applied to certain elements in the British organic
movement.

The religion of the good farmer was a faith

> in the Great Plan with which he must live daily, as an infinitesimal
> part of the whole divine scheme. He knows that he must adjust
> himself to the immutable laws of that Plan.[40]

Although not a churchman himself, Bromfield felt that the Church could
help this faith, and he wanted the churches to be more closely related to
the lives of rural people. He was sufficiently 'mystical' to believe that
humanity could survive without plumbing but not without the example of
St Francis of Assisi,[41] and to those who might regard such an assertion as
hopelessly impractical he would have retorted that nothing could be more
practical than learning to work with natural law, since to do so would
ensure the abundance which God intended humanity to enjoy.

Edward Faulkner

Bromfield devoted a long chapter of *Pleasant Valley* to the ideas of another
book on agriculture. This was EDWARD FAULKNER'S *Ploughman's Folly*, an
unexpected runaway success when it was published in 1943, which even
received the compliment of a full column in the New York *Daily News*.
When Bromfield wrote a piece on it for a national magazine he was inun-
dated with queries from all over the world as to where it was obtainable.
Faulkner rocketed to celebrity status and reported to Bromfield: 'I have
been forced to increase my lecture fee in order to control the demand.'[42]

One reason for the success of Faulkner's book was its appearance at a
time when America had become acutely conscious of its soil troubles.
Erosion was no longer just a concern of farmers, and *Ploughman's Folly*
appeared to offer a radical solution. Instead of burying organic matter

with the mouldboard plough it was better to leave it on the surface as a form of sheet-composting, or disc it into the topsoil's upper layer; the result would be an ideal surface, granular and water-retaining, for producing crops. '... all that it is necessary to do ...,' Faulkner asserted, 'is to recharge the soil surface with materials that will rot.'[43] Using the mouldboard plough buried those materials too deep, out of the reach of the plants which needed them. There were in fact no convincing reasons for using it, and a number of good reasons for not doing so. Faulkner argued that belief in its value was a prejudice, an untested assumption; in 75 years of experiment stations there had been, before 1937:

> [no tests] designed to compare directly the effects of ploughing, on the one hand, with the surface incorporation of all organic matter on the other. Failure to do this has definitely handicapped the development of basic soil information which might easily have prevented the débâcle toward which American soils have been drifting.[44]

The lands which had eroded had been precisely those which were bare, having been recently disturbed by the plough or other cultivating implements, and the USDA Yearbook *Soils and Men* confirmed the value of forest litter in preventing erosion.[45] Like Howard, Faulkner took the forest floor as the supreme example of how to enrich a soil: 'Principles which are valid in the forest are valid in the field, always.'[46]

The pioneers who first cleared the land found soils which were often black with organic and inorganic materials to the depth of a foot or more — rich soils produced by the rotting of organic matter, which were warmer, and could control water more effectively and prevent erosion. Farmers had come to assume — and Faulkner stressed that it was only an assumption — that the surface had to be cleared for planting, whereas the fact was that:

> a man with a team or a tractor and a good disc harrow can mix into the soil, in a matter of hours, sufficient organic material to accomplish results equal to what is accomplished by Nature in decades.[47]

Like the organic school, Faulkner believed in observing the workings of natural processes and then using science to accelerate them.

According to Donald P. Hopkins,[48] *Ploughman's Folly* was well received by scientists although its argument was nonetheless generally rejected or thought to be of qualified value. The organicists were interested, though not wholly convinced, but there was considerable similarity of outlook between Faulkner and the British organic movement; this was evident in his first book and became even clearer in his second, *Ploughing in Prejudices*. Faulkner believed that the best information on composting methods came from outside the United States, and he was familiar with the writings of Howard, Balfour, McCarrison and Wrench.[49] Influenced by F.H. King, he praised China's agriculture, and he admired 'the often despised peasantry of the so-called backward countries of the world'[50] for their greater productivity per acre than mechanized American farmers. Not that he opposed the use of machinery:

> When we have begun to do by machinery what heretofore we have thought must be done by insects and worms of the soil surface (the intimate intermixing of organic matter with the surface layers) we shall find ourselves automatically leading the world in production per acre as well.[51]

The idea that humans needed to 'feed' the soil was not merely wrong, but verging on the blasphemous. In a later book, *Soil Restoration*, he quoted approvingly a farmer who had said: '"I guess the fertilizer fellows think the good Lord didn't know what he was about when He made this earth".' He himself declared: 'I am willing to trust Nature.'[52] This meant trusting in the God who had created the 'Original Design'[53] of Nature, which provided everything that plants could need.

Ploughman's Folly was first published by the University of Oklahoma Press, a company which Bromfield praised for its commitment to high-quality books on farming.[54] It produced another classic of ecological agriculture in Paul Sears' *Deserts on the March*, first published during the crisis of the Dust Bowl in 1935 and re-issued in 1947, this time with an introduction by Bromfield.

Paul Sears

A botanist, Sears was concerned about the effects of irresponsible resource use on social stability. He perceived a 'general lawlessness'[55] in American culture, a disregard for social obligations which turned liberty into licence and equality into chaos. This perversion of democratic rights caused exploitation and waste, and might even lead to a demand for dictatorship from those affected by the dislocation. To forestall such a situation, Sears wanted to encourage private enterprise to accept its duty to the permanent interests of society and to see government involvement in farming and environmental policy.

Deserts on the March sets the American experience in a historical context, examining the relationship between culture and environment in

China, India and Egypt, discussing European systems of land-management, and surveying the environmental effects of white settlers in the United States, which could be summed up in two words: erosion and dust. Like St Barbe Baker, Sears pointed to the importance of forestry, and like Stapledon, to the importance of grass, in holding the soil together. The organic school were delighted to find Sears emphasizing the central role of humus in preventing erosion.[56]

Like so many of the major texts in the organic canon, *Deserts on the March* is a sermon on the self-destructive nature of hubris, taking as its starting-point the existence of a natural order to which primitive man has to conform if he is to survive. Sears has little to say about God, but has few qualms about personalizing nature:

> a very business-like old lady [who] is not to be conquered save on her own terms. She is not conciliated by cleverness or industry in devising means to defeat the operation of one of her laws through the working of another ... Man is welcome to out-number and dominate the other forms of life, provided he can maintain order among the relentless forces whose balanced operation he has disturbed.[57]

Sears added a note of cautious optimism to the book's second edition in a new final chapter, 'Deserts in Retreat.' The twelve years since the first edition appeared had witnessed a concerted attempt to reclaim exhausted soil, with more than sixty million acres having been brought under proper management by the Soil Conservation Service. Various conservation groups had found themselves led into each other's company, recognizing that their specialist concerns were inseparable from each other. The symptoms were manifold, but the problem was one:

> All renewable natural resources are linked into a common pattern of relationship. We can save any one of them only by measures which save them all. And we are a part of the whole which must be conserved.[58]

Ultimately the issue was moral, not technical, and Sears pointed to the significance for the future of the Amish and Mennonite communities, who had resisted the industrial mentality.

> They generally combine the ancient peasant traditions of stewardship with common religious bonds. This certainly makes sense; obligation to the land is fundamentally a matter of faith, and cooperation has the quality of spiritual fellowship.[59]

* * *

A number of other figures can be briefly mentioned, though their ideas will be thoroughly familiar by now. Also taking an ecological approach was FAIRFIELD OSBORN, whose dramatically-titled *Our Plundered Planet* appeared in Britain in 1948. Like his later work *The Limits of the Earth,* it was published by Faber, and in it he demonstrated familiarity with the humus-vs-artificials debate which had taken place in the House of Lords in the autumn of 1943. The book had more to say specifically about agriculture than Sears' work did, and attacked the increasing reliance on artificials and pesticides and the experiments through hydroponics to dispense with soil altogether, which he saw as dangerous attempts to escape from the 'organic circle'[60] of the natural order; in other words, as disobedience to the Rule of Return. He was typical of American ecological thought in his emphasis on the 'economy of nature.'[61] He also proposed a more poetic metaphor to describe the same principle, opening the book with the image of an 'earth-symphony.'[62] Osborn was typical of the organic school at this period in his conviction that there need be no conflict between science and religion so long as scientists bore in mind that they too were part of the natural order. He explained the scientist's tendency to hubris as follows:

> Can he not turn away from his creator? Who has a better right? He has seemingly 'discovered' the secrets of the universe. What need, then, to live by its principles![63]

In the section on health, Osborn referred to two other important figures in the American organic movement, the dental scientist Weston Price, and William Albrecht. We shall discuss Price's work in Chapter 8. Albrecht was frequently cited as an authoritative sympathizer with the cause of humus. A somewhat controversial figure, he was nevertheless sufficiently highly regarded by the agricultural establishment to contribute an article to the 1938 US Department of Agriculture Yearbook, on the importance of organic matter for soil conservation,[64] and he was sometimes criticized by the extreme fringe of the organic school because he was prepared to compromise where artificials were concerned.[65] Like the organic school, though, he regarded the soil as a live body whose health depended on the cycle of the Rule of Return; life was a biotic pyramid with the soil as its base, and Albrecht argued that the chief value of soil minerals was in enabling plants to construct proteins, which in turn were the key to protection from disease in animals and humans. He extended his thesis into the social realm by suggesting that the growing problem of delinquency might be linked to the poor quality of soils in particular areas.

Albrecht was one of the American agriculturalists who believed that the New World should learn from the Old, and he had close links with the Soil Association; in 1953 he sent the association a paper on fertility decline, and Lady Balfour visited him during her United States tour the same year. On his retirement in 1960 *Mother Earth*[66] summarized some of his ideas and paid tribute to his career as an agricultural gadfly; the following year he spoke at the Natural Food Associates Convention, along with Ehrenfried Pfeiffer.

Biodynamic cultivation had been established in the United States since 1927, when anthroposophists Elise Stolting and Gladys Barnett bought Threefold Farm in Spring Valley, New York State. The movement's importance seems to have depended on the degree to which Steiner's original ideas were secularized, or diluted. We have seen in Chapter 4 how Pfeiffer took biodynamic methods out into the world by concentrating on exoteric practice rather than esoteric theories and, earlier in this chapter, how Rodale took the process of secularization still further. How many of those who sympathized with organic methods went on to investigate the esoteric philosophy is impossible to guess; all one can affirm is that Steiner influenced the American organic movement through Pfeiffer's mediation.

Evidently Pfeiffer did not visit the United States until a few years after Stolting and Barnett settled at Threefold Farm, but by 1938 he had settled in America and was based there until his death in 1961. His doctorate, an honorary one, was awarded by the Hahnemann Medical College of Philadelphia for his work on crystallization, and he was deviser of and scientific advisor to the Oakland plant of the Compost Corporation of America, which by 1951 was producing 100 tons a day of high-quality organic fertilizer from 25 per cent of that city's garbage.[67] Pfeiffer was also a practical farmer in Chester County, New York State, where he grew fine wheat crops developed over the course of a decade from wild strains. His farm was close to Spring Valley, where he ran his laboratory and an anthroposophic agricultural community. It was here that in 1951, at Pfeiffer's request, Lady Balfour spoke about the work of the Soil Association on the first of her American tours.

The records of these tours demonstrate the closeness of the links between the British organic movement and its transatlantic counterpart. In 1951 Lady Balfour met, in addition to Pfeiffer and the anthroposophists, Dr Pottinger, to whose experiments in feeding cats the organic school attached considerable importance;[68] Miss Rooke, who had been Weston Price's secretary; Sears, Osborn, and Rodale. In Philadelphia she learned of plans to establish a family health club on the lines of the Pioneer Health Centre, and in Los Angeles visited the Academy of Applied Nutrition, which she described as America's nearest equivalent to the Soil Association.

Two years later she undertook a second tour, looking particularly at conservation projects, agricultural scientific research, and medical issues. Pfeiffer was again an important contact, and she met Faulkner and Pottinger. The New York doctor W. Coda Martin was at this time gaining a reputation for his work on diet, curing illness through changes in diet and using Pfeiffer's crystallization techniques to determine food quality. The Natural Food Associates (NFA) organization sponsored a third tour in 1958, during which the Living Soil Foundation (USA) was established. The NFA's convention was held at Memphis, the speakers including Pfeiffer and Coda Martin.[69] By this time the Soil Association had about three hundred members in the United States and about eighty in Canada, though these did not include some of the organic movement's leading personalities. The 1957 membership list does not include Albrecht, Faulkner, Osborn or Pottinger.

One section of Lady Balfour's report on her 1958 tour anticipates the controversy soon to be raised by Carson's *Silent Spring:* the account of how the north-eastern seaboard region was sprayed with DDT to combat the spread of the gypsy moth, resulting in contamination of soil, crops and milk, in human poisoning, and in the deaths of all types of resident birds.[70] This was a perfect example of what the organic school had been warning about for many years: that commercial interests will push their products heedless of the unknown results. The natural world required from science a sensitivity to its ecological interdependence, but the USDA had only six scientists working on biological methods of pest control. Although the organic school was investigating these alternatives, they were never likely to make headway against the power of the chemical companies. But when *Silent Spring* drew the world's attention to what was happening, the organic movement was ready to offer a better way.

7. Rural Life: Decline and Revival

The 'myth' of the English countryside

Looking back from the beginning of the twenty-first century, we might be tempted to imagine that the English countryside before the Second World War was experiencing a golden age: no motorways or out-of-town shopping developments; little encroachment by housing estates; no prairie-like fields supplying supermarkets with pesticide-drenched vegetables; villages as yet uncolonized by wealthy professionals; steam-trains still chugging along branch lines ... Contemporary observers, though, saw things differently. In 1939 the former *Times* journalist Douglas Reed published his account of a tour of Sussex in search of:

> 'This England' of the railway companies' and newspaper advertisements, ploughmen homeward plodding their weary way, sheep sleepily ambling through dappled sunlit lanes, cows lowing in the meadows ... I saw, or thought I saw, a ravaged countryside, a land where every prospect displeases ... Bungalows. Thistles. Ye Olde this and that, with men standing outside them in uniforms apparently meant to recall that green and pleasant England which ... has now been spoiled and defaced, as I fear, beyond repair. Villages where ... the children have to be reared on tinned milk because all the fresh milk is bought by the cities. As for the lads and lasses of this England, I found them ... working at filling stations and sports grounds, in tea-rooms and picture theatres.[1]

That same year, George Orwell's novel *Coming Up for Air* presented a similar picture; the novel's central symbol is a sylvan fish pool where the narrator spent the happiest hours of his youth, but which is now drained and turned into a rubbish dump. Other writers of the inter-war period saw the threat to the countryside in sinister terms. For the architect Clough Williams-Ellis the forces at work were the 'octopus' and the 'beast'; while E.M. Forster described the changes to rural life simply as 'havoc.'[2]

D.N. Jeans has suggested that 'The countryside is never so valuable as when it is under threat,' and the inter-war period produced a plethora of writings celebrating England's landscape and rural life, amounting, in his view, to the creation of a 'myth of the English Countryside.'[3] The historians who have examined these writings tend to be suspicious of the ruralists, either because they consider industrial economic development to be paramount, or because they mistrust the right-wing politics often associated with defence of the countryside. If the organic defenders of rural life were generally found on the Right it was in part because:

> the dominant view of the Left at this time was that rural England was best regarded as the granary and dairy of an urban nation and therefore its exploitation ought to be as intensive as feasible.[4]

This utilitarian approach contrasted with the organic school's sense of the countryside as a work of art and as a source of social stability, wisdom and spiritual renewal. The organic movement can be seen as part of a tradition of 'romantic protest'[5] which can be traced back through social and economic commentators like Ruskin and Morris to the Romantic poets. Peter Gould and Jan Marsh have described the history of these initiatives between 1880 and 1914, showing how they tried to provide alternatives to industrialism and to revive craftsmanship, through farm colonies, industrial villages and communities based on political or religious ideals. There were some figures who provided links between this period and the early organic movement. The Tolstoyan anarchist commune at Whiteway in Gloucestershire[6] had as members before 1914 W.T. Symons and C.W. DANIEL, who in 1938 published Wrench's book on the Hunzas, *The Wheel of Health.* At nearby Chipping Campden the designer C.R. Ashbee established in 1902 the Guild of Handicraft; among those who spent time there was Philip Mairet.[7] Another leading figure who bridged the two periods was MONTAGUE FORDHAM, director of the Arts and Crafts Gallery in London from 1899 to 1908, and in 1907 founder of the Land Club Union. We shall return to Fordham shortly, but this chapter's survey of those who advocated rural reconstruction begins with discussion of an Irish mystic.

To start in such a way is not as perverse as it might seem. GEORGE WILLIAM RUSSELL (hereafter referred to by his pseudonym AE, which apparently stood for 'aeon') was also a supporter of agricultural co-operation who worked closely with the agriculturalist Sir Horace Plunkett. There is a direct link between him and the *New English Weekly* through his friendships with A.R. Orage, its first editor, and PAMELA TRAVERS, a member of its editorial board.[8]

Inspired by Theosophy and its socialistic ideals, AE joined the Irish Agricultural Organization Society (IAOS), founded by Plunkett in 1894. Between 1897 and 1905 he travelled Ireland persuading poor farmers to help themselves by organizing credit banks, and drew up plans for land reform. In 1905 he became editor of *Irish Homestead,* weekly newspaper of the IAOS. When the Irish Home Rule Bill was being debated in Parliament in 1913 he visited London and met Orage, whose Guild Socialist propaganda in the *New Age* he much admired; their friendship lasted until Orage's death. To what extent AE's views on agriculture influenced Orage is unclear, but they may well have influenced Mairet, since one finds in AE's writings a number of features of the organic outlook: the sense that human stock degenerates in an urban environment; the belief that agriculture's decay leads civilizations into decline; and the encouragement of rural reconstruction based on a system of co-operative parishes, self-governing, producing most of their own food, manufacturing many of their own goods, and trading collectively.[9] AE contrasted his ideal of the small, organic community, with

> the socialist aim of a single giant organisation ... and with the competitive capitalist society whose irreligious doctrine of every man for himself fostered callousness and greed.[10]

One can also see among his convictions the dislike of the money-lender and middle-man which featured strongly in the organic school.[11] Underlying his outlook was belief in a natural order. AE wrote in the *Irish Homestead:*

> Nature or the powers that be ... never allow life to stray permanently or hopelessly from the natural order, and, if men will not willingly live a natural life, then, with pestilence and famine in the cities, they are scourged back.[12]

Agriculture was therefore the primary industry, and it was essential for social cohesion to redress 'the lopsided balance of power between town and country.'[13]

There is no doubt that AE influenced the leading countryside journalist, WILLIAM BEACH THOMAS. Thomas spent time in Ireland before the First World War and was converted to the cause of agricultural co-operation. During the inter-war period he became the friend of both Sir Daniel Hall and H.J. Massingham, though his writings place him closer to the organic school than to Hall. He contributed to Williams-Ellis' *Britain and the Beast,* and wrote two polemical studies of declining agriculture and the dangers of large-scale mechanized farming, criticizing the Wilson brothers of Wiltshire and George Baylis of Berkshire, heroes of the progressive cause.[14] Beach Thomas called for a 'Green Rising,' contrasting British neglect of agriculture with what was happening in Europe. Farming had been belittled: rural life must be re-vitalized, through a programme of land reform, based on County Councils, which would prevent the creation of *latifundia*.[15] Thomas was prepared to accept a programme of selective nationalization to bring about such reform.

Thomas' proposals bore some similarities to those urged by Montague Fordham, perhaps the most influential of all the advocates of rural reconstruction, and someone whose ideas were unambiguously based on a Christian perception of its importance. A year after founding the Land Club Union in 1907 he published *Mother Earth: A Proposal for the Permanent Reconstruction of our Country Life*. Its ambitious title anticipated the name of the Soil Association journal, and most of the organic movement's concerns can be found in this book.

A friend of the medievalist A.J. PENTY, Fordham regretted the demise of the guild system, much of his discussion concerning the harmful effects of free-market economics, free trade and finance on rural life. He pointed out that Danish products had greatly benefited from security of markets, and urged state intervention to give English producers similar security. Only thus could the countryside be revitalized, rural depopulation reversed and poverty overcome. A margin of profit was essential for the agricultural population; land and capital should be administered for the public good rather than private interest. But there was a cultural and educational task to be undertaken, distaste for rural life being fostered not just by the facts of rural poverty, but by the educational system. Fordham wanted an education:

> specially directed to make [the rising generation] aware of the charm and mystery of nature, and to implant in them a devotion to the soil and all that belongs to it.[16]

Only then could the half-deserted agricultural areas begin to attract the necessary farmers, artisans and craftsmen. Every district needed a model farm, supervised by an agricultural advisor who would work in connection with village Land Clubs and bring in specialists to talk on new farming methods, seeds, plant diseases and other issues. The Clubs would be local co-operative unions to defend the rights of smallholders, organize loan-banks and insurance, provide machinery and transport produce. The task was twofold: to understand and make use of scientific developments, and to encourage reverence for nature. Fordham was sceptical about artificial fertilizers, and, influenced by G.V. Poore, recommended the return of wastes to the soil. He also believed that traditional features of rural life, like country dances and songs, should be taught as part of a movement to make it more attractive.[17] *Mother Earth* is an intriguing mixture of radicalism and traditionalism, whose ambiguities foreshadow the political complexities of the organic school. Opposition to water-borne sewage co-exists with encouragement of scientific agricultural knowledge; nostalgia for a medieval economic system co-exists with sweeping proposals for state intervention in land reform.

After serving in the Red Cross during the First World War, Fordham spent time as a reconstructor of agriculture in East Poland before returning to Britain and establishing in 1926 the Rural Reconstruction Association. In 1925 the Labour Publishing Co. produced Fordham's book *The Rebuilding of Rural England,* but a decade later Fordham was increasingly in right-wing company. In 1935 the Association's Chairman was the pro-Mosley MP Michael Beaumont, and its Council included the by then pro-Fascist A.J. Penty. However, the pamphlet emphasized that the Association had no party bias, including in its membership Conservatives, Liberals and Socialists. The Association wanted to see standard prices, to give farmers security; standard grading of produce; import control, and scientific organization of distribution. Agriculture's development would benefit industry by providing a market for town workers and making food production immune to economic crisis. The proposals had a clear political dimension, being designed to prevent the risk of national disorder consequent upon increased unemployment, and to help ensure 'racial growth.'[18]

The arguments were more fully developed the following year in *The Revival of Agriculture.* Although the book was prepared by a committee of the RRA, Fordham's influence was evident in its positive picture of Tudor economics and its insistence that traders and financiers should be the servants of producers and consumers. It argued for import control, standard prices, agricultural credit banks and a National Food Council, pointing out that the threat of war made increased self-sufficiency a wise policy, as did John Boyd Orr's evidence of widespread malnutrition. Above all, there must be a new conception of economic benefit: not mere financial advantage, but '"wealth," material and spiritual, created and distributed.'[19]

The spiritual dimension was fundamental to Fordham's concern. In his 1938 pamphlet *Christianity and the Countryside* (whose foreword was by his friend William Temple, Archbishop of York) Fordham argued that development of a distinctively Christian economics would facilitate rural revival. By 'Christian economics' he meant establishing a 'Just Price,' abolishing usury, and forbidding profit-making by middlemen at the expense of producer and consumer. National organization of the food industry based on the Just Price, and involving an agricultural credit bank to avoid the power of usury, would enable increased production and absorb a million more workers on the land. Anticipating the work of the COUNCIL FOR THE CHURCH AND COUNTRYSIDE, Fordham said that country parsons needed to be familiar with agricultural problems.[20]

During the Second World War the RRA became closely involved with the ECONOMIC REFORM CLUB AND INSTITUTE, producing in conjunction with it the journal RURAL ECONOMY, which will be considered in Chapter 9. The Association was still arguing for greatly increased home production in the mid-1950s, though by that time its commitment to organic farming was more lukewarm.

For all Fordham's erudition and practical knowledge of rural problems, his hankering after a neo-medieval system tends to mean that he will be dismissed as something of an eccentric. It is much harder to make this charge stick to another advocate of rural reconstruction, R.G. (later Sir George) Stapledon, given his scientific achievements and world-wide reputation as a plant breeder and agronomist.[21] He established the Welsh Plant Breeding Station at Aberystwyth as an international centre of progress, his work on grassland attracting to Wales American soil scientists who sought his advice on fighting the Dust Bowl. He developed the ley-farming system which proved so productive during the Second World War, and during the 1940s was Director of the Grassland Improvement Station in Warwickshire. Early in his career he held a scientifically progressive view of agriculture and mechanization, but by the end of his life was deeply concerned about the dangers of technology and the 'law of operative ignorance.'[22] Of all the figures at the heart of the organic movement he had the closest links with the 'orthodox' establishment, but from the early 1930s onwards associated with figures like Rolf Gardiner and Viscount Lymington. Although not actually a member of either the Kinship in Husbandry or the Soil Association, he influenced both groups.

Stapledon's 1935 book The Land: Now and To-Morrow was a comprehensive and detailed survey of the actual use and possible development of the nation's most fundamental resource, and it appealed to the organicists for various reasons. Stapledon believed that a vigorous agriculture was a prime necessity for national wellbeing, both as protection in wartime and for the sake of the people's health. He regretted the loss of good farming land to urban and industrial development, and devoted a number of chapters to analysing the way in which marginal lands, particularly hill country, could be made more productive. He wanted to see an increased rural population, recognizing that this was impossible until facilities were improved. The aesthetic dimension of rural development was important to him. Like Beach Thomas, he accepted the case for selective land nationalization, and hoped for the creation of National Parks which would combine farming with recreational facilities. The urban population's claims on the countryside were justified; it was no longer the prerogative of the few, and the many had the right to enjoy the physical exercise and spiritual refreshment it offered. If human beings lost touch with the 'animal, vegetable and primitive sides' of their nature they would 'either perish ingloriously, or become completely perverted.' Hence Stapledon's concern to preserve what he termed a 'coefficient of ruralicity,' a rural population unaffected by the urban-industrial mentality: 'The most valuable product of the land ... is the human being.' He praised the countryman's wisdom and the purity of stock he represented, which provided 'an essential reservoir upon which to draw in the improvement and development of a race.'[23]

The cause of yeoman farmers and smallholders was a constant concern of the organic school. Writing fifty years after the 1947 Agriculture Act, Graham Harvey[24] has argued that the emptying of the countryside and the decay of rural life in Britain are the result of large-scale mechanized farming. The year the Act was passed, H.J. Massingham edited *The Small Farmer,* a collection of essays defending the value of smallholders and owner-occupiers for both agricultural productivity and social stability. Massingham went so far as to claim that 'The small mixed farmer has ... been the bedrock of every historical civilisation.' An erudite rural historian with a polemical axe constantly a-grinding, Massingham argued that the Enclosures had initiated a process of rural dereliction by destroying the peasantry, and that the remaining small farmers represented a way of life which, if redeveloped, could save industrial civilization from self-destruction and build 'a new society resting firmly on its native earth.' In the book's closing essay the industrial historian L.T.C. ROLT anticipated E.F. Schumacher's concept of 'intermediate technology,' arguing that small-scale farming need not turn its back on technological advances; appropriate machines could be developed for the tasks required. He believed that if the tenets of the organic school were correct they would 'imply not only an agricultural but a social revolution ... which will undoubtedly favour the small producer.'[25]

To favour the small producer was to help revitalize rural life, but was this revolutionary? In an earlier book Massingham stated explicitly that it was the opposite, referring to:

> Many anti-revolutionary land-reformers of the calibre of Sir
> George Stapledon, Lord Lymington, Lord Northbourne, the late
> Christopher Turnor, Adrian Bell and others [who had] stressed
> decentralization as the first of all needs, and the nursing of
> regional centres and nuclei from a foundation of local practice,
> soil conditions and human intercourse.[26]

For Massingham and his friends in the Kinship in Husbandry, rural reconstruction was a matter of reversing a historical process which he
described as 'War upon the English tradition.' A growth of regionalism
was required, in order to oppose the unholy alliance of big business and
government bureaucracy whose abstract plans were destroying rural life
and 'authentic national character.' Instead of New Towns there should be
reinvigorated market towns, 'once the axles of the villages in their neighbourhood.'[27]

For Massingham, defending the English tradition was essentially a
Christian task. The structure of village life was based on the 'three pri-
maries — God-Man-Earth,'[28] but modern developments were destroying
this pattern. To fight for Christendom was to fight for the pattern, opposed
as it was to both totalitarianism and the capitalist combine.

Massingham, although a rural historian, chronicler of country life, and
dedicated gardener, was never a farmer, but a number of other major figures in the early organic movement were involved in farming in practical
ways. One of Massingham's closest friends was the novelist ADRIAN
BELL, who began farming in Suffolk in 1920, just before the repeal of the
Corn Production Act resulted in severe slump. Farmers who tried to keep
to nineteenth-century high farming methods were ruined, and replaced by
entrepreneurs who instituted monocultures. Bell's autobiographical novel
The Cherry Tree laments the decay of East Anglian rural life, describing
the development of the sugar beet industry, the over-production of corn
with the help of artificials, and the laying down of land to grass. Thriving
towns were eroded back to villages; chain stores took root, their flashy
windows 'filled mainly with tins and cardboard effigies of smiling
health.'[29] In Bell's view, the family farm was the means by which rural life
could be rebuilt. Family farmers were frequently craftsmen, helping to
hold together the rural economy. An organic social structure based on
family work and community skills was secure and greatly preferable to
the atomism of urban life.

Whereas Bell went straight into farming after leaving school, his
friend Henry Williamson made a conscious, willed decision later in life
to undertake the task of rural reconstruction, for reasons both personal

and political.[30] In the mid-1930s he sought escape from his despair and frustration through an active life; he also thought that as a farmer he might 'be of use to a new England.'[31] He became interested in Norfolk through his friend and editor Richard de la Mare, who had a holiday cottage there. Williamson identified with the neglected rural population, and wanted to plead their case. In a world of absentee landlords he could, in a small way, imitate the work of Coke of Holkham, by reclaiming wasted land; to restore a derelict farm was a symbolic gesture, a protest against the malign influence of finance on rural life. As we shall see in Chapter 9, Williamson's views led him to join the British Union of Fascists. There had been no stability in farming since the First World War because the government was in the thrall of international money power; the land was mortgaged, rural culture declined and the nation's health suffered. The teamwork of a small farm was a microcosm of incipient community spirit; the task of sowing oats created 'yeoman-family harmony.' Early in the war Williamson was excited at the regeneration of English farming, but as time passed he feared that the rural revival would once again be forgotten after the war, or would change the countryside in undesirable ways. Farmers were adopting mechanization, often unwillingly, and their farms were becoming mere food-factories. The fertilizer sack was replacing the dung-cart; weeds were disappearing under machines spraying sinister concoctions, and the 'voice of Money, soon to walk again, whispered with a whiff of diesel oil.'[32] At the end of 1945 he gave up the farm: Hitler's defeat had put the pre-war powers back in control.

Williamson refers to 'a young West Country writer, whose farming journal [Phillip Maddison] had read.'[33] This was RONALD DUNCAN, playwright, poet and pacifist, whose column in the *New English Weekly* was published by Faber in 1944 as *Journal of a Husbandman*. Williamson and Duncan became friends, still seeing a good deal of each other in the 1960s. Another friend referred to is 'Christie,' pseudonym for JOHN MIDDLETON MURRY, who, like Duncan, ran a pacifist farming community during the war. Both writers were part of the organic movement and believed in the importance of trying to restore rural life.

Unlike Williamson, Duncan drifted into farming. Anxious for the solitude which would enable him to write a play, he rented a mill in North Devon in 1937. Though only in his early twenties he was already a friend of Ezra Pound, T.S. Eliot and Max Plowman, and had spent time in India with Gandhi. When the war broke out he was sceptical about the British cause, claiming that he knew how 'to distinguish between the Imperial Chemical Industries' interests and [his] own,' and sympathizing with 'the German attempt to establish goods as opposed to gold as a financial base.' Searching one day for his horse he became aware of the decay into which the neighbouring fields had fallen, since the small farm to which they belonged had been abandoned. He decided to found a community based on agriculture, whose members would practise 'economic repentance' and create a 'spiritual communion.' Duncan came to prefer the word 'husbandry' to 'agriculture,' attended meetings of the Kinship in Husbandry and became a good friend of Mairet and Portsmouth.[34]

Most of Duncan's autobiographical account of his community is taken from *Journal of a Husbandman,* but it omits much that is in the earlier book. The journal devoted considerable space to attacking the finance system, the uselessness of urban-biased education, and the 'Planners and Schemers' who ignored rural realities. Duncan wrote sympathetically of feudalism, contrasting its putative bounty with the dereliction of 'our chapel-emancipated freedom ... Perhaps serfdom is as necessary to husbandry as harrows.' The farmer-squires, too, would be preferable to the present situation, since they had cared for maintaining fertility. Duncan was typical of the organic school in emphasizing natural laws which could not be flouted without disaster. He described farming as a 'discipline' of 'submission to the requirements of the cattle, the soil, the weather.' It required a 'religious attitude' every bit as much as a 'sharp hook.' England's fields could not get ploughed until 'we have that reverence for our soil that we are supposed to have for the altar.'[35]

Murry's community in East Anglia was similarly based on a religious and pacifist outlook. Murry, better known as a literary critic than as a farmer, was an intellectual weather-vane, turning at various times in the direction of Marxism, pacifism, anti-pacifism and Christianity.[36] His decision to buy a farm stemmed from his growing scepticism, in the late 1930s, about state socialism. He gradually came to believe that producer co-operatives would avoid the dangers of large-scale bureaucratic interference in a democracy where capitalism had failed, and he wanted his own co-operative to be a farm because 'in the last resort the whole of civilization depends on primary production from the land.'[37] His co-operative venture turned into a pacifist one under the influence of Max Plowman of the Peace Pledge Union.[38] After Plowman's death in 1941 Murry bought a farm the following spring, and was concerned to help establish a Christian social order after the war, believing it possible to do so only if some form of democracy were preserved, which in turn could be a reality only within small communities. His wartime farming community was therefore an experiment in what he termed 'Christocracy': the establishment of a commonwealth in which individual talents would be used for the welfare of the group, not for private advantage. The pursuit of money for its own sake was devilish. Machines likewise became diabolical if uncontrolled by a conscious community.[39] Industry must be decentralized and society reorganized around work and the parish. Murry derived his views from belief in a natural order:

> What is wanted is the will to plan the national economy in accord with a valid social philosophy, of which the end is the good life in the natural order. Those who believe that goodness in the natural order is the necessary basis of goodness in the supernatural order will have no hesitation in believing that the revivification, at a new level of technology, of community life ... is an essential foundation of a Christian society.[40]

Murry also helped propagate the organic cause through his editorship of *THE ADELPHI*. One finds in its pages during the 1940s important names in the movement, including Massingham, Portsmouth, Duncan, McCarrison and Howard. The wartime popularity of farming books was, in Murry's view, evidence of a 'great religious void,' as people sought a faith which was not other-worldly. The 'soil-fertility men' in particular offered an effective 'indictment of the machine civilization' which satisfied 'a deep religious-aesthetic need.'[41] Murry relinquished editorship in 1948, handing *The Adelphi* over to Henry Williamson; after three issues Williamson was replaced by George Godwin. Godwin had written in praise of Roy Wilson's Iceni Nurseries,[42] and he used his 'Man on Earth' column to state the movement's main themes.[43]

Bell, Williamson and Murry undertook small-scale experiments in rural regeneration, but two of the organic movement's most important figures were landowners able to institute more ambitious projects. They were Rolf Gardiner and Gerard Wallop, Viscount Lymington, who became Ninth Earl of Portsmouth in 1943, and who will be referred to in this chapter as Portsmouth.

Anna Bramwell calls Portsmouth an 'extraordinary patriot and adventurer,'[44] but one wonders whether he is not better described as one of the rootless cosmopolitans whom he so much disliked. Born in Chicago of an American mother and brought up in Wyoming, he was part of the hedonistic scene in Paris during the 1920s: the socialite Caresse Crosby remembered this upholder of English-rural-Christian-family values dancing 'savagely, lance in hand' as part of a 'practically undraped' march along the Champs Elysées on its way to a 'wildly ritualistic' art school orgy.[45] (Anyone who has looked at the photograph of Portsmouth in Richard Griffiths' book *Patriotism Perverted* will find it a considerable feat of imagination to envisage the portly peer in such circumstances.)

From the late 1920s to around 1950 he was active on the far Right in British politics, as Chapter 9 will show. Finding the atmosphere of post-war Britain uncongenial he patriotically removed himself to East Africa, where he was involved with the Kenyan white settlers movement.

During the 1930s his estate at Farleigh Wallop in Hampshire became a centre of agricultural experiment. He reclaimed 3,000 acres taken over from mostly bankrupt tenants, laying on water, folding pigs on grass, and using the system of moveable bails pioneered by A.J. Hosier. As a result, arable production doubled and gross output trebled. He experimented in tracing the connection between soil fertility, animal health, and disease-resistance in crops, investigating the world of natural ecology in a way that he subsequently believed had anticipated Rachel Carson's conclusions in *Silent Spring*.[46] He was also interested in agriculture's social ecology, believing that the nation became unbalanced when rural life disintegrated. In the early 1930s he couched the problem in apocalyptic terms, portraying the destruction wreaked by the

> anti-Christ who replaces God with the Conveyor Belt. Since the culture of the mediaeval European town is going down before industrialism the only surviving instinct of lasting civilization is to be found on the land.[47]

It was not for the State to save agriculture; it was for agriculture to save the State. Organic husbandry, with its need for labour, would require a million more people on the land. Britain should 'colonize' her own land; the population thereby created could become the 'parent stock whose surplus ... can provide the immigrants to other unpeopled areas of the Empire.'[48] The multiplication of small farmers would help revive small crafts and industries, with opportunities for rural life and self-sufficiency encouraging the existence of the family unit. In turn, families would co-operate to ensure their parishes and villages were more self-supporting, and towns would be supported by the surrounding countryside. By the early 1940s Portsmouth was advocating a regionalism which might save the nation from the planner's ant-like state, bringing spiritual health through the opportunities it would provide for participation in local affairs. Ultimately, to turn to a way of life based on respect for nature was to help renew Christendom.[49]

The same sense of social imbalance resulting from loss of religious values is found in Rolf Gardiner's life and writings. His estate at Springhead, near Shaftesbury in Dorset, was a centre for attempting to 'remake the pattern of England.'[50] In 1927 Gardiner acquired Gore Farm at Ashmore in Dorset and set about restoring it, a task he undertook in tandem with energetic activity organizing work camps both in Germany and in Cleveland. Six years later he was able to buy an estate in nearby Fontmell Magna, wanting to use it as the centre of an experiment in co-operative work, as he believed that a landowner had a responsibility to his locality. Gardiner wanted to show his own sense of responsibility through turning Springhead into a rural centre which would have 'an irradiating power,' a sort of rural university which would do something like 'the work done by the monasteries in the so-called Dark Ages.' It would address itself to 'the need of the unemployed; the need of the land; the need for government of the region by the region.' The landowner's advantage over the small-holder was that he could 'subordinate all departments to an organic whole.'[51] The activities undertaken on Gardiner's estate between 1933 and 1940 included summer schools, village festivals, Christmas plays, country dances, spring festivals and harvest feasts. He also revived traditional celebrations of Plough Monday through morris-dancing in local towns.

It would be misleading, though, to describe him as a pagan. In Chapter 11 we shall see his part in founding the Council for the Church and Countryside (CCC); here we can note that, like Massingham, he admired the way in which the Christian Church had in the past incorporated a sense of natural rhythms into its pattern of worship. At Springhead he attempted to express the connection between Earth and Spirit, Nature and Culture, Work and Worship:

> The rhythmic order of the cosmos is the pattern of earth-life and of those who husband and cultivate the soil; it is the shape of time expressed in the cycle of the year ... the Mediaeval Church knew this full well when it sanctioned and regulated the magical customs of the seasons and christened the ancient pagan centres of worship. Modern, industrial and urbanized society ... is denying the Natural Order. With a return to these fundamentals there will, therefore, be a need to restore the calendar and its celebrations.[52]

In this way the threat of the bureaucratic Welfare State could be averted, and the nation be revived on the basis of a regionally nourished peasant culture rather than 'modern abstractions and machine-mindedness.'[53] He offered Springhead as an example of the way in which this task might be approached.

Gardiner attached particular importance to forestry. In the early 1930s he trained at Dartington Hall under Wilfred Hiley, and he contributed a chapter on 'Forestry and Husbandry' to Massingham's symposium *The Natural Order.*[54] He noted how the demands of a wartime economy had accelerated the depredations made on woodland and forest, and urged the restoration of tree cover if the Earth were not to become barren. His experience of planting woodlands in Cranborne Chase had led him to appreciate the close connection between forestry and farming, but such work was possible only where the different rural tasks could be co-ordinated into an organic whole.

One of those who worked for Gardiner in Cranborne Chase was JOHN STEWART COLLIS, literary biographer and author of books of 'poetic ecology.'[55] A protégé of A.R. Orage, he used to meet Orage and AE in Chancery Lane in the early 1930s, and was one of the few contributors to the *New English Weekly* whom Orage paid. In 1941 he went to work on Rolf Gardiner's estate, having asked to be excused an office job in the army in favour of agricultural work. He describes Gardiner admiringly in his autobiography, and was evidently sympathetic to the organic cause, regretting the way in which mechanized farming brought a loss of communal celebration and spoiled the beauty of the English countryside.[56] He believed the restoration of woodland vital to rural reconstruction, and in 1950 wrote *The Triumph of the Tree,* a historical, mythological and scientific survey of mankind's relationship with this symbol of life, which concluded that the 'unecological' destruction of forests would lead to disaster: 'For trees always have the last word.'[57]

One day in Cranborne Chase, Collis underwent a mystical experience very similar to Richard St Barbe Baker's childhood vision, realizing that he was sitting in the Garden of Eden, his consciousness united with nature. Having created its own world apart from nature, humanity's next task was 'a further extension of consciousness when we shall realise the unity of life on a higher plane of understanding'[58] and regain Paradise Lost. Humanity must begin to think in terms of the unity of nature, of the necessity of all created things, even the bluebottle and the apparently disgusting processes of decomposition. Collis seems to be offering a theodicy akin to the Leibnizian philosophy pilloried in Voltaire's *Candide:*

> ... if the Beginner of Life could do what He has done, why could
> He not have done better, it may be complained; why could He not
> have eliminated the seamy side? Evidently He couldn't.[59]

Humanity must accept the natural order that God had created: 'The Order of Nature should be a more fruitful conception than the Survival of the Fittest.'[60] The implications of this seem to be: 'fruitful' intellectually, as a means of understanding nature; 'fruitful' in a literal sense, if the Rule of Return were obeyed; and 'fruitful' socially, through establishing a society free from acquisitive competition and the resulting destruction of resources.

The organicists saw no opposition between mystical experiences like
those of St Barbe Baker and Collis, and the practical tasks of rural reconstruction; they suffered from no dualism of 'spirit' and 'matter.' For them,
a sense of the sacred was a prerequisite of genuine materialism — respect
for, and productive use of, the materials God had provided for human survival and creativity. A healthy, stable social order could be established
only on a basis of work undertaken with reverence, and this meant that
agriculture must be central to rural life. The organic pioneers had no time
for the merely picturesque, and little time for shooting and field sports,
which play virtually no part in their vision. They wanted to see a working countryside whose beauty would stem from the ecological fitness of
its woods, fields and buildings. An increased rural population, encouraged by improved housing, transport and facilities, would attract light
industry to the country towns. In this way, the whole organism could be
brought back to health. And if the farming were organic the food produced would benefit the health of the individual cells in the body politic.
To the relation between diet and health we must now return.

8. Organic Food and the Quest for Health

The town of Crewe might be seen as an improbable venue for one of the most significant events in the development of the organic movement. But it was at the Crewe Theatre, on Wednesday 22 March 1939, that the *Medical Testament* on nutrition was launched, a document which suggested that a renewed agriculture on organic lines could transform national health.

Sir Robert McCarrison and Sir Albert Howard were the guest speakers at a meeting attended by doctors, agriculturalists and educationalists, chaired by Dr Kerr of the Cheshire medical committee and reported in full detail by the local paper. McCarrison saw a connection between rural reconstruction and the improvement of health, rejecting the obsession with physical training as futile unless people's physiological needs were being met by a healthy diet, and condemning physical fitness that was:

> ... barren of service [as] a selfish fitness. So long as there are in this country millions of untilled acres deteriorating or over-run with weeds, so long as the need exists for the more abundant home production of vegetable foodstuffs, so long as thousands of our people stand idle in the market-place, so long will there be for many of them abundant opportunities and reason for the pursuit of natural forms of exercise under the open canopy of Heaven.[1]

Howard drew laughter from the audience with characteristically barbed comments at the expense of orthodox research organizations. He summarized his experiences in India, and referred to the work done by Roy Wilson and Sir Bernard Greenwell, provocatively suggesting that the Ministries of Agriculture and Health adopt as their motto: 'A fertile soil mean[s] healthy crops, healthy animals, and ... healthy human beings.'[2] Agriculture should take its rightful place in the national economy as the real foundation of preventive medicine. The day finished on a note of local patriotism, with the farmer T.C. Goodwin praising Cheshire for leading the way in bringing about developments which helped improve the people's health.

The moving spirit behind the *Medical Testament* was the GP at Holmes Chapel, Lionel J. Picton, a keen gardener who had read Howard and McCarrison's work and who, as a younger man, had been influenced by G.V. Poore. Howard likewise knew Poore's writings, which demonstrate that several of the organic movement's important ideas had been formulated by the turn of the twentieth century. In *Essays on Rural Hygiene,* first published in 1893, he made the resounding but debatable claim with which this book opened: 'That organic manures ... are superior to all artificial manures is now generally acknowledged.' The work of Rothamsted Experimental Station was based on a fundamental error, that of supposing 'that farming is in any way comparable to a chemical experiment.' His reflections on soil fertility were linked to his thoughts on human health; he admired Chinese composting, and believed that the soil was 'the only permanent and reliable source of wealth in any country.' He favoured earth closets, urging that some way should be found of reducing the 'waste of valuable matter which takes place in London and our big towns.'[3] This raised the issue of urban-rural balance: such towns were a threat to the countryside, wasting potential manure. Agricultural interests had been sacrificed to those of the manufacturers, who polluted watercourses and allowed chemicals to find their way into town sewage, destroying its manurial value.

Faith in God-given natural laws underlay Poore's outlook: Cowper's line 'God made the country and man made the town' he believed full of meaning 'for those who are interested in the physical and moral welfare of our populations.' Nature would bless us if we worked with her; her forces were inexorable, brooking no disobedience, yet were 'truly beneficent.' 'Without cultivation of the soil,' wrote Poore, 'there can be no high standard of health. The gardener and the farmer are ... the right-hand man of the sanitarian.'[4]

Picton drew together the work of Poore, McCarrison and Howard, successfully practising McCarrison's ideas at his child welfare clinic.[5] In 1938 he read an article by Howard on the Indore Process, which seemed to him to supply the safety factor for implementing Poore's garden sanitation system. At about this time, the Cheshire Medical Committee, to which Picton was honorary secretary, was considering its duty under the National Health Insurance Act to prevent sickness, and concluding that it was failing to do so. Influenced by Picton, the Committee took the view that illness could be prevented by fresh, compost-grown food, and sought advice from McCarrison. The upshot was the *Medical Testament.*

After the meeting the Cheshire doctors waited for the large-scale public debate which they believed would follow, but in vain. 'Only slowly did it dawn on them that nobody, really, was very much interested,' Barbara Griggs bleakly records.[6] Of course, the organicists were very interested, but with the outbreak of the Second World War, agriculture resorted rapidly to artificials, and McCarrison found no more influential post during the war than deputy regional adviser to the Emergency Medical Service, and chairman of his local medical war committee.

The Pioneer Health Centre

The war was also a setback for another important initiative, the Pioneer Health Centre in Peckham, South London. George Scott Williamson, its co-founder, had formed ideas about health similar to McCarrison's in very different circumstances. When a medical student at Edinburgh he had been led by a smallpox outbreak to reflect on the mystery of natural immunity to disease, and an experiment with rats made him wonder whether the social conditions of animals affected their health. He spent much of his career as a pathologist, at the Royal Free Hospital (1920–26) and then, until 1935, at the Ear, Nose and Throat Hospital. During this period he 'continually pondered on the nature of the biological laws that govern *order* in the body — the order and harmony that is [*sic*] characteristic of health.'[7] He examined individuals from a 'holistic' perspective, though as an urban doctor he was more concerned about the social than the natural environment, and about the health-promoting capabilities of family and neighbourhood life. With his wife Dr Innes Pearse he established a family health club in Peckham in the mid-1920s. In 1935 it moved to a large, purpose-built centre with clinics, a swimming-pool and various social and recreational facilities, which became internationally famous.[8] Scott Williamson and Pearse were interested, like McCarrison, in health, which they considered a positive quality, not mere absence of disease; they defined it as 'the physiological condition of an organism living in mutual synthesis with its environment.'[9]

The tone of the Peckham biologists' writing is predominantly scientific, empirical and secular, but, as one would expect with founder members of the Soil Association, there are indications of their belief in a natural order. In 1938 they published an interim report on the new building, which Stapledon reviewed in the *Sunday Times*. He particularly approved the sentence: 'Nature is that which we *obey*,' considering it to embody the 'supreme teaching of the Peckham researches.'[10] Elsewhere, Scott Williamson argued that since nature's powers are benign we should assume that man himself is potentially so, 'were he but obedient to, the natural laws and regularities of cosmos that enfold him.'[11] More specifically theological was the faith of Scott Williamson and Pearse that 'through the process of biological development the Word of God becomes the deed of Man.'[12]

The Pioneer Health Centre identified malnutrition as the cause of many dysfunctions despite the fact that the families were not short of food. During the first year at the purpose-built Centre a Home Farm was acquired at Bromley Common, Kent, to provide fresh food for the young families. It adopted the Indore Process, and Howard and McCarrison became involved. Howard hoped that the farm would produce its own meat and establish a mill and bake-house to produce wholemeal bread from home-grown wheat. He believed that the medical records of families thus fed would make significant reading.

There were many who shared Howard's belief in the Centre's importance. Pearse and Scott Williamson's first book, *The Case for Action* (1931), had prefaces by Lord Moynihan, President of the Royal College of Surgeons, and A.D. Lindsay, Master of Balliol College. Kenneth Barlow recalled meeting 'both the Director of the Federal Health Services of Australia and the Minister of Health for India at Peckham.'[13] However, the Centre was unable to survive financially under the post-war health reforms, which did not favour preventive medicine, and it closed in 1951.[14] The building still stands today, having recently been converted into flats after some years as a college annexe.

The Peckham experiment had enormous significance for the organic movement; apart from anything else, Faber and Faber's work for the movement originated from its pre-war years. Richard de la Mare was the brother-in-law of Jack Donaldson, a wealthy socialist who gave half his inheritance to help the Pioneer Health Centre and who for some time ran its social floor.[15] Through this connection De la Mare was converted to the organic outlook, and was responsible for publishing many key texts in the organic canon in his capacity as Faber's agriculture and horticulture editor. He was a member of the Soil Association Council from its inception until 1951. His son Giles has said of him that he was a man of diffident but definite Christian faith.[16]

Another important medical figure in the organic movement tried to establish a similar project, even more ambitious, near Coventry. This was Kenneth Barlow, whom Scott Williamson treated for appendicitis, suggesting he take up medicine. Through his membership of the SOCIOLOGICAL SOCIETY Barlow became secretary to PATRICK GEDDES, whose support enabled him to train as a doctor. He took up a post as a GP in Coventry in 1935, and contributed to the *New English Weekly, PURPOSE*, and Eliot's *Criterion.* His book *The Discipline of Peace* (1942) was a philosophical work which looked ahead to post-war reconstruction, concerned with

> the permanent conditions of politics — the laws of the relation of man to his environment in nature which political philosophy and social planning have tended to ignore.[17]

The arguments were complex, but the conclusions will by now be familiar: 'the discipline of peace' required western civilization to respect the limits imposed by the laws of nature if social stability were to be achieved. Mechanistic philosophies abstracted from biological reality, resulting in a manipulative, exploitative attitude to the natural world, but life had its own 'architecture,' a 'discipline and organization' which humanity must obey if it wished to survive.[18]

Barlow recorded his post-war struggle to establish the Coventry Family Health Club Housing Association in an unpublished manuscript evidently dating from the 1950s; a brief account can be found in his later book *Recognising Health.* The Pioneer Health Centre had, to an extent, modified the environment of families; the Coventry project was an attempt to enlarge it still further, including a new housing development and a farm. The Association acquired 300 acres of land which, it was intended, could grow fresh food to be made available locally. Barlow's work with Geddes no doubt influenced his attitude to planning the estate, which sought a balance between regulation and a spontaneous impulse to development.[19]

Barlow's extraordinary energy and determination failed to persuade the local Council, and the Association was discontinued. Members of the Peckham staff had frequently lectured there, and LEWIS MUMFORD, a disciple of Geddes, had visited during a trip to England; but by the mid-1950s the Pioneer Health Centre was no more and Scott Williamson was dead. His obituary in the *British Medical Journal,* while admiring the Pioneer Health Centre as an enlightened social experiment, suggested that 'the evidence that the experiment advanced knowledge of the factors that make for health is tenuous.'[20] To the organic movement, Peckham remains a bold attempt at a radically different approach to public health, thwarted by bureaucratic lack of imagination.

The national diet

Kenneth Barlow was particularly interested in the quality of bread. One of the most sinister dates in the organic movement's interpretation of history was 1872, when steel roller-mills began operating in Britain, setting in motion the 'progressive deterioration of our bread until it has reached the status of a mere "filler".'[21] Such debasement symbolized the decline in food standards which had so adversely affected the nation's health. Until the 1870s wheat, offering all sorts of nutritional benefits, had been consumed in its wholeness, but the steel rollers, which disintegrated it into its component parts, offered various commercial advantages.[22] The wheat's remains were the most nutritionally valuable part, and the wheatgerm itself could be sold at a profit to be marketed as a health food. Using white flour also made it easier to introduce:

> chemical bleaching agents and 'improvers,' the object of the latter
> being to 'mature' the flour artificially, thus saving storage space
> and working capital.[23]

Commercial interests were corrupting the nation's food supply: Picton quoted the biblical verse: '"I will break the staff of your bread ... and ye shall eat, and shall not be satisfied".'[24]

During the war Barlow and the Cheshire doctors kept a close eye on events relating to bread, demanding the highest possible 'minimum extraction rate' for flour. (A minimum extraction rate of 85 per cent, for example, meant that one hundred bags of wheat would make 85 bags of flour, the remainder being the nutritionally valuable 'offal.') In 1941 Picton contacted Lord Woolton, the Minister of Food, to urge that flour used for the National Loaf should contain the full wheatgerm, and Woolton replied that millers would be instructed to include the maximum amount. Later, Picton submitted a memorandum setting out the merits of retaining the germ in the flour and found his views confirmed in the report of the 1945 Conference on the Post-War Loaf.[25] Government policy, however, was to reduce the extraction rate, accepting the omission of the oily part of the wheatgerm, that is, all the oil-soluble vitamin E. For Picton, such a decision attacked the very possibility of national survival, since Vitamin E increases female fertility.[26] The organic school were also concerned about what was added to bread, particularly the chalk, bleaching agents and 'improvers,' these last including agene, which caused hysteria in dogs, and chlorine dioxide, used in the First World War as a poison gas.[27]

There were, however, distinct improvements in national diet during the

Second World War, thanks to the influence of the scientist and agriculturalist John (later Lord) Boyd Orr.[28] A qualified doctor, Boyd Orr went
in 1914 to work for the Rowett Institute at Aberdeen, establishing there a
research project into animal nutrition which by 1927 had gained the Institute an international reputation. After the First World War he was joined
by Walter Elliot, who during the 1920s was at the Empire Marketing
Board and responsible for an experiment to determine the effect of
increased milk consumption on children's health; the results encouraged
him to pass legislation allowing local authorities to supply cheap or even
free milk to schools. When Elliot became Minister of Agriculture in 1932
his discussions with Boyd Orr influenced his approach. Both men
believed agriculture and public health were closely connected and that
Britain's widespread malnutrition could be cured by providing 'protective' foods — fresh eggs, fruit, vegetables, and dairy products — which
would also help revive the nation's declining agriculture.

Boyd Orr's classic survey *Food, Health and Income* was published in
1936, an investigation undertaken by the Rowett Institute which revealed
that one-fifth of children were chronically ill-nourished and that half the
population could not afford a nutritionally adequate diet; yet 'foods were
so abundant that the government was taking measures to reduce production so as to raise retail prices.'[29] The outbreak of war enabled Boyd Orr's
ideas to become part of official policy, when Elliot, now Minister of
Health, used him and other nutritionists to improve the national diet. Like
the organic school, Boyd Orr opposed British reliance on cheap imported
goods. After the war he was appointed Director-General of the United
Nations Food and Agriculture Organization, and worked to establish a
World Food Board. In his Sanderson-Wells Lecture *Soil Fertility — The
Wasting Basis of Human Society,* he said that the post-war world's priority must be to produce abundant food, and he drew attention to the need
to preserve top-soil and protect forests.[30]

The fact that Boyd Orr gave a Sanderson-Wells Lecture demonstrates
his connection with the organic movement, though in referring to
SANDERSON-WELLS we begin to approach some of the more sinister
aspects of the organic concern with health. T.H. Sanderson-Wells was a
physician with a particular interest in nutrition, who in 1938 endowed an
annual lectureship at the Middlesex Hospital Medical School. He was
Chairman of the Food Education Society and a founder member of the
Soil Association. The year before Boyd Orr's lecture he collaborated with
Jorian Jenks on an article in the *Medical Press and Circular* entitled 'The
Revival of England,' which argued the case for renewing home agricul-
ture on humus-rich soil, in order to provide high-quality food to counter-

act malnutrition. Sanderson-Wells' earlier book *Sun Diet* (1939) had demonstrated the concern for racial fitness which some other organicists also expressed. 'Inherited racial characteristics,' he wrote, 'are helpless to reproduce their potencies without suitable foodstuffs.' The British were going soft, showing 'a streak of deficiency,' and needed 'a return to the simple, unaltered foods of Nature,' because 'Natural laws are set for the elimination of the unfit, the foolish and the unthinking.'[32]

Similar views were held by a more widely known figure, the French physician ALEXIS CARREL, who was willing to help the unfit on their path to elimination. The Earl of Portsmouth came to know him as a result of writing *Famine in England,* another book which lamented racial degeneration.[33] Carrel won the Nobel Prize for medicine in 1912 for his work on blood vessels and organ transplants; in 1935 he wrote the highly successful *Man the Unknown.* During the Second World War he was appointed Director of the Fondation Française pour l'Étude des Problèmes Humains, in Paris, subsequently being accused of collaboration. He died in 1944. His biographer — perhaps 'hagiographer' is the more accurate term — the Jesuit Joseph Durkin refers to him as politically naive and his ideas as potentially open to abuse by racialists,[34] but one can see why they would have appealed to fascist fellow-travellers like Portsmouth.

Like the organic school, Carrel opposed liberalism and *laissez-faire* philosophies, and condemned western industrialism, whose effects included physical degeneration, debased food, declining birth rate, release from moral restraint, a mistaken favouring of the weak over the strong, the decline of the white races, and an environment alien to human nature. Western thought, he believed, had been shaped by a mechanistic model of man, and only a biological, holistic perspective could point the way to development of the human body and consciousness. Carrel was a Catholic[35] who said that his scientific studies had brought him closer to God, and he saw the idea of a natural order as essential to scientific investigation: natural laws are discovered, not invented, and are 'universal and inexorable.' As humans, we need to be aware of our part in nature, because 'we can never break the bonds which bind us to the earth from which we spring.'[36] Carrel believed that humanity could be transformed if these natural laws were fully understood and obeyed; he combined a conservative with a utopian outlook.

Like Scott Williamson, Pearse and Barlow, Carrel wanted a holistic medicine, embracing the various sciences. However, he went much further than they did in his conception of how medical experts might shape society, outlining plans for what was in effect an élite of Platonic

Guardians who, after years of biological research 'would acquire enough knowledge to prevent the organic and mental deterioration of civilised nations.' One of their chief concerns would be the application of eugenics, to create a hereditary biological aristocracy and prevent insanity and criminality; but certain types of criminal 'should be humanely and economically disposed of in small euthanasic institutions supplied with proper gases.'[37] Carrel's ideas show how an organic interpretation of human life, conflating the biological with the spiritual, leads to a totalitarian model of the state. He believed that climate, soil and food — especially the last of these — all affected individuals, and he recommended the rooting of family life in the life of the soil, with everyone having the right to a garden; but he went well beyond most of the organic school in the importance he attached to eugenics. In this context, it is worth briefly mentioning the Nietzschean ANTHONY LUDOVICI, who will feature again in the following chapter.

Ludovici's book *The Four Pillars of Health* (1945) attacked the organic school for believing that the only necessity for human health was healthy food grown in a healthy soil. Singling out G.T. Wrench in particular, he accused him of ignoring other necessary 'pillars of health': correct use of self; good dietary habits; good habits of hygiene, and good genetic endowment. He wanted an aristocracy of health, whose members would regard it 'as a confession of bestiality, stupidity or ignorance to fall ill.'[38] Wrench's *The Wheel of Health*, which Ludovici had reviewed before the war in *NEW PIONEER*,[39] had misled the organicists into thinking that perfect health might be attained by purely dietetic means, ignoring racial characteristics. Soil care and diet could not counteract the effects of random breeding.

Another blueprint for some sort of Platonic aristocracy was drafted, in a generalized form, by the bacteriologist J.E.R. McDONAGH, who was associated with the Kinship in Husbandry and whom Sir Albert Howard consulted for his views on the nature and causes of disease.[40] Although McDonagh chiefly studied disease rather than health, he began his book *The Universe Through Medicine* (1940) by describing health as 'another word for "harmony".' By the end of the book he was suggesting that the goal of humanity is internationalism, a harmony in which there is a breaking down of 'individual, communal, racial and national barriers.' McDonagh saw two forms of existence at work in the world: there are those beings which *radiate* activity and those who *attract* or *store* it. If these interrelated functions were to be co-ordinated, internationalism would be within reach. Men would be separated into groups according to their work, and linked to the world-state through commissioners. Having attacked financial interests and their harmful effects on agriculture, and having condemned 'the non-productive issuers of paper money,'[41] he proceeded to condemn nations, communities and races which 'radiated' insufficiently, and were therefore:

> not inventive ... Such people ... are more prone ... to suffer from the sub-acute and chronic manifestations of disease. Communities of this kind tend to live in the midst of other communities without becoming part of the latter ... [They] need to segregate and live in a land of their own if they are to exhibit the function of radiation.[42]

Here we have a barely coded reference to the Jews: a plea for Zionism on anti-semitic grounds, with an entire race being characterized as a disease in the world organism.

McDonagh emphasized the necessity of an ecological approach to knowledge, and attacked specialization. Ecological science should be based on what he called 'a conservative agronomy.'[43] Portsmouth described him as very much part of the Kinship, but also as 'unheeded,'[44] not just by the scientific world, it seems, but by the organic movement itself, whose members scarcely referred to him. Nevertheless, a number of his views were compatible with theirs.

There were clearly some very experienced medical practitioners and outstanding medical scientists among those who saw compost-grown food as the way to create a healthy population; but other than certain tribesmen and McCarrison's rats, what evidence existed for their theory?

Some was anecdotal: Lady Balfour and Friend Sykes claimed to have cured poor health by changing to a compost-grown, whole-food diet.[45] In New Zealand Dr Guy Chapman encouraged staff and boys at an Auckland school to grow their own fruit and vegetables on humus-rich soil; as a result there was a decline in colds and influenza, and increased resistance to measles. Dr J.W. Scharff, Chief Officer of Health for Singapore until the fall of Malaya, reported that the health of Tamil labourers improved dramatically after they adopted a diet of compost-grown food.[46]

The organicists attached particular importance to dental evidence. An early edition of *Mother Earth* carried an article by the dental scientist Everard Turner, who concluded, after assessing wide-ranging evidence of dental decay, 'that the common denominator of sound teeth is the natural biological cycle.' Not long afterwards Sir Norman Bennett's death deprived the Soil Association of 'one of its most distinguished members, and the world of dentistry of an elder statesman and brilliant practitioner.'[47] His obituary identified his greatest service to the organic movement as:

the letters on soil and health which he addressed to medical and dental journals. Coming from a man of his standing, they exerted a powerful influence on his colleagues in both professions.[48]

A case which had the support of a man of Bennett's eminence is not to be dismissed lightly. But the strongest and most comprehensive dental evidence for it was provided by an American physician, Dr Weston A. Price, in his book *Nutrition and Physical Degeneration,* first published in 1939 and enlarged in 1945. Price and his wife travelled the world seeking remote communities whose diet was uninfluenced by western trade. He was particularly interested in the incidence of caries and the formation of the dental arches, believing the quality of the dental arch to indicate the quality of a person's complete constitutional development. He studied many thousands of mouths and jaws, and the book is liberally illustrated with photographs, visual evidence for his belief that modern diets led to tooth decay and inherited problems with dental arches. Communities seemed to remain free from many western physical defects

> so long as they were sufficiently isolated from our modern civilization and living in accordance with the nutritional programs which were directed by the accumulated wisdom of the group.[49]

One of the most telling photographs is of brothers in the Hebrides: the elder, who had kept to a native diet, displays a perfect set of teeth; the younger, who had adopted modern foods, suffers from advanced tooth decay and loss.[50] Price believed that western civilization was destroying primitive cultures when it should have been valuing them as examples of a superior wisdom. The communities Price had visited were

> spiritual [with] a devout reverence for an all-powerful, all-pervading power which not only protects and provides for them, but accepts them as a part of that great encompassing soul if they obey Nature's laws.[51]

In contrast:

> Practically all of our modern philosophies ... fail to recognize the nature of the creative forces ... which show how the great Creator made us.[52]

Edgar J. Saxon's *Health and Life*

The issues discussed in this chapter were all taken up by Edgar J. Saxon, editor of *Health and Life* magazine. He has been almost completely forgotten in comparison with McCarrison and the Pioneer Health Centre, and this chapter's final section will amend that injustice.[53]

Saxon was born in 1877 above an East End shop; his family, who were Dissenters, moved to Wimbledon when he was about seven, and he remembered the spread of speculative building there and how his mother wept when some oaks were felled; he said that her grief planted in him the seed which would eventually grow into commitment to the Men of the Trees. As a young man he came into contact with the Tolstoyan anarchist Charles W. Daniel, who ran a bookshop in the City of London. He was writing on Food Reform and Nature Cure in a paper called *The Christian Commonwealth* and was recommended to Daniel as a potential contributor to his journal *The Open Road;* the result was a friendship lasting more than fifty years. In 1911 Daniel founded *The Healthy Life,* of which Saxon became owner and editor in 1920. It was reconstituted as *Health and Life* in 1934. Between the wars Saxon established Vitamin Cafés — the first health food restaurants — and a health centre in Wigmore Street, London, where he had a practice in 'natural health' medicine. His many activities included a School of Reform, a bookstore, amateur theatricals, and lectures at Conway Hall; he also spoke for the Social Credit movement. His friend Dion Byngham,[54] a frequent contributor to *Health and Life,* wrote in his obituary notice that for Saxon to urge 'a saner, more civilised, financial system was all of a piece with his concept of total human health.'[55]

Health and Life is an essential source for students of the alternative health movement in Britain. Among the means of attaining mastery of nature's energies which it advertised were Bach herbal remedies, Social Nudism, the Wessex flesh brush, Psychophonism (one is tempted to add a second 'y'), health teas, homeopathic chemists, eurhythmics, specialist diets, and such nostrums as the 'Diatatic' Electric Condensator, for freedom from neuritis and blindness.

For Saxon, true health was wholeness. Diet was central to its cultivation, and he worked to create a public demand for 'honest food.' By this phrase he meant whole foods, home-grown without artificials and without having been refined, adulterated or processed. He commented on the British people's 'curious notion that purity is the absence of colour,' which led to the popularity of tasteless and devitalized substances like

white bread and sugar. Chemists were the beneficiaries, and the financial
system was the culprit, judging wealth not by a people's health but by 'its
ability and willingness to buy third-rate stuff in shops.' *Health and Life*
praised Boyd Orr's *Food, Health and Income* and summarized his 1939
Economic Reform Club speech. Saxon reviewed the *Medical Testament*
in considerable detail, describing it as 'epoch-making,' and Dion Byngham reviewed Wrench's *The Wheel of Health* in an article somewhat
ominously headed 'Racial Vigour from Whole Food and Sound Soil.'
After the war Byngham reviewed Ludovici's *The Four Pillars of Health,*
evidently sympathizing with Ludovici's criticism of Wrench.[56] In general,
though, the journal emphasized the importance of food and said little
about eugenics.

The Pioneer Health Centre was cited frequently. In 1950 Peter Rad-
brook wrote a two-part article about it, also referring to Kenneth Barlow's
work at Coventry:

> It is interesting and gratifying to find that so many of the ideas and
> ideals for which *Health and Life* has stood for sixteen years are
> incorporated in this fundamental pioneering research.[57]

Saxon shared the view that there was a possible link between chemical fertilizers and the incidence of disease, providing statistics which
sought to draw a parallel between the increased use of artificials and the
increase in deaths from cancer. Full health could be achieved only by
obeying the Rule of Return; as for companies like ICI, he alleged that
'their activities in relation to the sacred soil of Britain make for disease
and death.' Saxon devoted an article to earth-closets, condemning water-
sanitation as 'one of the most gigantic breaks in the natural order which
our race has made.' Later he took up the issue again, in an article which
also noted South African developments in municipal composting. Dion
Byngham complimented Northbourne's *Look to the Land* with a three-
part review, while Philip Kilsby referred to the work of Howard and
Steiner. Readers were encouraged to contact the Soil Association, and
Saxon enthused about the spiritual vitality of the Association's farm at
Haughley, claiming that 'Mealtimes are as festive as the Marriage at
Cana.' The journal also featured the Men of the Trees and published its
creed, while Saxon's article 'Without Trees We Perish' reviewed St Barbe
Baker's *Green Glory* and Collis' *The Triumph of the Tree.*[58]

The organic school believed health to be inseparable from politics and
economics, and Saxon was no exception. In 1947, as the establishment of
the National Health Service approached, he argued that a true health policy would start with the soil, controlling and creating money in order to

create a healthy agriculture. The British were being denied honest food and the flowering of health by a monopoly of power-hungry manipulators, and they would be denied health by the false national policy developing under the influence of the Beveridge Report. *Health and Life* unleashed a tirade of invective against it, because it was based on the assumption that orthodox medical practitioners knew how to care for the nation's health. K.S. Sorabji, the *New English Weekly's* music critic, lambasted the Beveridge Report as a 'Banker-Gangster swindle ... malignant trash ... poisonous'; while Saxon later shrewdly identified the NHS as an instance of 'tigerish totalitarian ideologies dressed up in the lambs-wool of vague humanitarian aspirations.'[59]

Health and Life described its political direction as 'Not Right nor Left, but Straight.'[60] Saxon feared a post-war swing to the Left, with power concentrated in the hands of a bureaucracy; a truly democratic order required devolution. The real choice facing the nation was not between Red and Blue, but Red and Green. The redness of blood could not exist without the primordial greenness of the leaf to feed it. The song 'Greensleeves' expressed:

> [the] wholesome core of the English people, with its ... minor key that hints of the inner strangeness and secret of this Green Isle. Merlin or Marx: which is it to be?[61]

A similarly nationalist tone could be found in the essay on 'Personality' which appeared occasionally on the journal's back cover:

> A man should grow out of the land where he was born, he should have his roots in the soil whence his body is fed, he should bear the lineaments of his locality.[62]

Saxon called for 'a virile, eager and rooted nation — virile because its roots [are] deep in a faithfully husbanded and fertile soil.'[63] Such sentiments seem a fair way down the road to 'Blood and Soil,' but Saxon was unambiguous about the evils of Nazism.[64]

Saxon was committed to Social Credit, speaking at the headquarters of JOHN HARGRAVE'S Green Shirt Movement and addressing the London Social Credit Club on 'Soil, Health and Community.' During the war he went as far as to maintain that practically everything his journal stood for was embodied in the programme of the Social Credit Party,[65] the implication being that the existing financial system was corrupt and diseased. *Health and Life* regularly carried advertisements for another Social Credit journal, the *New English Weekly,* which reciprocated by advertising *Health and Life*.

Saxon's ideas were inseparable from his religous response to the world. He discarded the theology of his Nonconformist upbringing, but retained his reverence for Jesus, whom he presented as the supreme example of radiant health, wholeness and creative energy, and described as 'the God-intoxicated carpenter of Galilee,' the magician 'who with Yoga magic, Merlin magic, turned water into wine,' the poet 'his mind saturated with the agricultural and civic life of Galilee ... the most glorious of all the sons of men.' The earth was God's gift; composting, a form of ritual, and gardening, a means of expressing the Grace of God and spiritual rebirth. Humanity's relationship to the Infinite was itself a source of health.[66]

Saxon devoted a wartime essay to the idea of 'The Natural Order,' an order which meant that any community's primary obligation was to the soil.[67] Spiritual values were best discerned:

> through a faithful, intelligent and reverent approach to and use of material things ... I see human nature as a caged divinity and I believe the Natural Order will do much to destroy the cage.[68]

Obedience to natural law would not bring a planners' Utopia, but something infinitely preferable. Dion Byngham believed that if mankind were to survive:

> tomorrow must see this natural soil-plant-man inter-relationship again recognised and completed, with all its *cultural* and *spiritual* implications. Such a restored plant-man ratio might well lead us back or forward to 'a new and more marvellous Garden of Eden than that of which our ancestors dreamed.'[69]

*   *   *

The organic movement's analysis of the health and nutrition issue can be seen, at one level, as mythological: Paradise Lost, with the hope of it being regained. It was the story of a Fall whose extent could still be measured by the examples of a vestigial Eden to be found in as-yet-untouched communities in remote parts of the world. Health was the original wholeness of living in harmony with the God-given natural order. Everything was interconnected: healthy soil meant healthy animals, plants and humans, and a healthy social order. But the serpent of western commercialism and materialism had entered the Garden. A financial and trading system whose only concern was short-term monetary gain had exploited and exhausted the earth. Urbanism had created a population divorced from the land and spiritually undernourished. The denaturing of bread symbolized this process, but was only one example of how fertilizer companies, industrial farming and food-processing devitalized the nation's foodstuffs. In Britain the result was a C3 nation, poverty in the midst of plenty, and a people denied their birthright of exuberant vitality by a manipulative financial system and a mechanistic philosophy.

To help the nation renew itself, the new biological sciences must be applied. Scientists like Howard, McCarrison, Price, Scott Williamson and Pearse were pointing the way to recovery of a well-balanced life, to an understanding of the laws governing human social behaviour and organization, and to an economy based on the wealth which living processes offered so abundantly rather than on abstract, deracinated calculation.

We can now begin to understand why the organic movement grew within a context of predominantly right-wing, and at times quasi-Fascist, politics. Concern about malnutrition might stem from a sense of injustice, or it might be based on the desire to breed a stronger racial stock. Also, a biological, 'organic' view of society can lend itself to totalitarianism.[70] If the system which is perceived as debauching the nation's food is seen as dominated by forces owing no loyalty to that, or any, nation, then the way is prepared for hostility to supposed contaminants or disease-carriers. It is now time to turn to the political and economic connections of the organic movement.

9. Organic Politics and Economics

The radical right

The close links between the early organic movement and right-wing politics would probably surprise the present-day British public, who are more likely to associate environmentalism with the Left. As the journalist Paul Johnson moved steadily rightwards during the 1970s he devoted a chapter of his jeremiad *Enemies of Society* to 'Ecological Panic,' describing it as:

> characterized by a marked distrust of the free-enterprise economy, and indeed incorporat[ing] many aspects of Marxist mythology, especially the idea that capitalist society creates, then satisfies, artificial and wasteful appetites, and is ultimately self-destructive.[1]

The historian Peter C. Gould believes it is obvious that:

> Greens are better placed on the Left. They have been understandably associated with socialism, the most powerful ideological force opposed to liberal-capitalist industrialisation.[2]

But not to industrialism *per se,* one might add. Anyone familiar with the works of Anna Bramwell (1989), Richard Griffiths (1983, 1998), G.C. Webber (1986) or Patrick Wright (1996) will know that many of the organic movement's leading figures were politically active on the Right during the 1930s and '40s. Nevertheless, Gould's study of late nineteenth-century environmentalism demonstrates that the organic movement's forerunners were to be found in socialist and anarchist groups. The relationship between the organic school and politics is complex both theoretically and historically.

However, there is no doubt where the loyalties of Jorian Jenks lay: in his person Fascism and organic husbandry merged most completely. He was the Soil Association's editorial secretary from 1946 until his death in 1963; during the 1940s and '50s he edited *Rural Economy* and publications of the Council for the Church and Countryside; he was a leading light in the Rural Reconstruction Association; he frequently contributed to the *New English Weekly,* and he wrote major studies of the principles and history of the organic movement.[3] His obituary in *Mother Earth*[4] ignored his active involvement in the British Union of Fascists (BUF). A.W.B. Simpson's study of wartime detention without trial refers to him as 'probably holder of one of Mosley's letters of authority' and as 'one of those authorized to carry on if Mosley was arrested.'[5] John Charnley, a fellow Blackshirt, has described Jenks as 'an outstanding personality in the Movement, our Agricultural expert, who ... was in the main the author of our policy in this field.'[6] Jenks' connection with Mosley continued in the late 1940s, when Mosley attempted a comeback.[7]

Jenks entered agriculture at the end of the First World War as manager of a Berkshire farm, soon becoming a victim of the slump. He emigrated to New Zealand and held special duties under the Deteriorated Lands Act when it was passed in 1925, returning to England in 1928 to do two years' postgraduate work at Oxford's Research Institute of Agricultural Economics. He was a member of Balliol College, and it is intriguing to note the connections with C.S. Orwin at both these institutions. During the 1930s Jenks farmed in Sussex and joined Mosley's movement.

His early experience of losing his job may have created his distrust of the financial system. In an article in *Fascist Quarterly*[8] he expressed his desire for a government 'which thinks in terms of human welfare rather than in terms of sound finance and good economics.' Dislike of the financial system slid easily into anti-semitism, and Jenks was not averse to racial abuse, as when he described:

> a Jew-boy camper whom I found helping himself to my growing crop [and who] was indignant at having been called a thief. I suppose he was working on the manna theory.[9]

Jenks had recently collaborated on a book called *Farming and Money* with J. Taylor Peddie, a scholar who tried to deduce from the Bible a righteous form of economics. The finance system, they argued, was based on a false standard of wealth; agriculture, not money, was the true standard, because it did not consume materials. But British agriculture was suffering because the finance system benefited from its decline. Farming required the creation of an Agricultural Discount Bank, to advance money for strictly productive purposes. Above all, agricultural land must cease to be regarded as a commodity.[10]

Jenks expressed the same ideas more forcefully in his pamphlet *The Land and the People.* The BUF aimed to double agricultural output, which would improve health, create employment and reduce dependence on imports. An economic system which:

> denies honest people the right to enjoy the fruits of their own soil is fundamentally rotten. There is an ample market for all that our land can produce, as soon as the financial machine is diverted from selfish and speculative use.[11]

Usury must be abolished; land had gone to waste because bigger dividends could be made elsewhere. If this situation persisted Britain risked degenerating into:

> a community of town-bred, under-nourished weaklings ... dependent ... upon the charity of international financiers, upon the goodwill and forbearance of other and more virile countries.[12]

Only Mosley could 'restore the Land to the service of the People.'[13]

Another BUF member in the organic movement was Henry Williamson.[14] His biographer and daughter-in-law Anne Williamson has disputed the accuracy of calling him a Fascist, preferring to see him as a twentieth-century Romantic. As a Romantic he was:obsessed with his vision of what the world could and should be [and had] a Romantic vision of an ideal world with a perfect social and political system ... He had just visited Germany where he had seen with his own eyes the great happiness of the young people of the German Youth Movement. Of course, that was what he was meant to see.[15]

Whether or not one accepts Anne Williamson's argument, there is no doubt that Henry was strongly sympathetic to the ideas of the Fascist movement and its fellow-travellers.

Williamson's articles on agriculture attracted the attention of Viscountess Downe, a prominent BUF member in Norfolk,[16] not far from where he was farming, and through her he joined the movement, met Mosley, and heard Jenks address meetings. Williamson himself spoke for the BUF, and *The Story of a Norfolk Farm* originally contained passages so pro-Fascist that his editor Richard de la Mare insisted on their excision.[17] More than twenty years later he dedicated *A Solitary War* to Oswald and Diana Mosley.

Williamson's association with Mosley stemmed from his concern for the state of national agriculture and health. Power had passed from landlords to banks, and land was merely a means to profit; fertility was declining and the corn country was going to ruin. He wanted 'to see a change ... so that whole-wheat bread should be made and sold again to the people; to hell with "big business".' The present system was a 'price-cutting, get-profit-anywhere-anyhow system made by the townsmen, which cared little or nothing for the soil and the people.'[18]

The novels *A Solitary War* and *Lucifer Before Sunrise* are scarcely disguised autobiography, describing Phillip Maddison's wartime experiences of farming in Norfolk, and providing many examples of Williamson's sympathy for Britain's enemy and scepticism about Britain's cause. 'It was ... a Jewish-money war, just as Haw-Haw said!'[19] His sympathy went out to Goebbels, Hess, Pétain and the imprisoned Birkin [Mosley], while he deprecated the British for moaning about the blitzing of Coventry. When the war ended it was as if 'Night had come to the western hemisphere.'[20]

Williamson remained faithful to Mosley, though a passage in *The Phoenix Generation* reveals that in the 1930s he met members of the circle for whom Mosley was too moderate. Maddison is taken to a meeting by someone formerly in the 'Iron Ring' around Birkin/Mosley, at which are 'Lord Eggesford,' an authority on soil conservation, writer of a 'very fine book,'[21] and presumably Viscount Lymington; and the 'Duke of Gaultshire,' recognizable as Hastings, MARQUIS OF TAVISTOCK. These men led initiatives in which anti-semitism and support for organic husbandry were intertwined.

Lymington, whom we have already met as a proponent of rural reconstruction, was Conservative MP for Basingstoke from 1929 to 1934, when he resigned his seat in disgust at the inability of parliamentary democracy to deal with the nation's problems. During this period he joined the ENGLISH MISTERY, a nationalist organization founded by the anti-semite William Sanderson, who advocated selective breeding for the 'maintenance and development of racial traits,' and the elimination of 'alien control' of finance.[22] He wanted to make usury a capital offence and believed that control of finance and commerce was essential if national culture and a peasantry were to survive. Lymington wrote that the Mistery affected all his speeches and actions after 1930, but denied that its members saw themselves as *Herrenvolk:* 'we wanted our revival to be Anglo-Saxon in the sense that Alfred the Great was Anglo-Saxon.'[23] Other members included the half-Italian Anthony Ludovici, Rolf Gardiner, Reginald Dorman-Smith (Minister of Agriculture from 1939 to 1940), and Michael Beaumont, MP, who defended the BUF after its notorious Olympia rally of 1934 and was later prominent in the RRA.

Lymington split from Sanderson in 1936 to form the English Array.[24] Evidently a rumour circulated that the Array plotted to murder British Jews, but Lymington denied any Fascist element to the movement.[25]

Ludovici was a member, as were the Dorset organic farmer RALPH COW-ARD and the market-gardener Roy Wilson.

In December 1938 Lymington launched the *New Pioneer,* a journal whose pages contained many names on the far Right, including former Mosleyites John Beckett and A.K. Chesterton, G.K.'s second cousin.[26] Other contributors included Major-General J.F.C. Fuller, Anthony Ludovici and Rolf Gardiner. The journal enthusiastically reviewed *Mein Kampf* and did all it could to prevent war with Germany. It also devoted considerable space to organic husbandry, contributors on this issue including Sir Albert Howard, Lord Northbourne, Philip Mairet and the Conservative MP, P.C. LOFTUS.

Interlocking with Lymington's circle was another extreme national-ist group favouring organic husbandry. This was the BRITISH PEOPLE'S PARTY (BPP), an anti-war party founded by the Marquis of Tavistock. Ludovici, Lymington and Mairet were members.[27] Tavistock was a for-mer Christian Socialist who became a passionate adherent of Social Credit, an economic reform movement discussed more fully later (see p. 161 and Appendix B). His dislike of the financial system led him to anti-semitism, and he was strong on conspiracy theory, attributing Social Credit's lack of headway to the hidden hand of Jewish influ-ence.[28] He admired Mussolini and Hitler, and claimed that Mosley's movement was more genuinely democratic than the Conservative or Labour parties. The BPP's proposed programme might reasonably be described as national-socialist, its aims including the right to security and social justice, freedom of education, abolition of class differences, freedom of religion, abolition of land speculation, and, the sting in the tail, a reassessment of the 'privilege of British Nationality,' including possible revoking of naturalization 'where it is established that such nationals have indulged in criminal or anti-social practices.'[29] The Party's articles also included these items dear to the heart of the organic movement:

> The abolition of a financial system based upon usury ... and the establishment of a system whereby British credit is made avail-able for the welfare of the British people on the highest possible level of consumption [and] the realization that land should be cul-tivated to the highest possible degree as our greatest material asset.[30]

After the war, the BPP's paper *PEOPLES POST* included a column by Dion Byngham, 'Countryside Causerie,' written under the pseudonym 'Miles Yarrow.' These 'causeries' referred at various times to Lady Balfour, Kenneth Barlow, Sir Albert Howard and G.T. Wrench; to L.T.C. Rolt's *High Horse Riderless,* a statement of the organic movement's principles; and to Richard St Barbe Baker, whose Dorset farm Byngham visited. Byngham was on the BPP's National Council, which also included the virulently anti-semitic A.T.O. Lees.[31]

The close connections between the organic movement and the radical Right should by now be clear, but there are some other figures worth considering. The Conservative MP for Lowestoft, P.C. Loftus, was a sympathizer whose views were, in their implications, sufficiently extreme to explain his associations with Lymington's circle. In 1926 he published *The Creed of a Tory,* a book which defended Europe's medieval heritage and the 'mystical spiritual equality' of Christianity. Loftus was quick to explain that this spiritual equality had nothing in common with the abhorrent idea of social equality. Loftus favoured a hierarchical state in which agriculture would be the most important activity, partly for reasons of defence and economy, but chiefly because it would provide 'the human material to re-vitalise our exhausted city-bred people' so that the nation would not increasingly breed 'from the unfit and the alien and from the lowest types.' The physical deterioration of the British was due in large measure to the decline in the quality of bread; Loftus urged a return to wholemeal as essential for racial reinvigoration. Urban life was another threat to the nation, since it was in cities, with their admixture of aliens, that radicalism and socialism flourished.[32]

Central to the organic movement during the 1940s was the 'Kinship in Husbandry' — a name in which one might discern faint echoes of 'Blood and Soil.' Lymington, Gardiner, Mairet, Northbourne and Massingham were members, and a number of other important figures attended its meetings, including Adrian Bell,[33] Jorian Jenks, Laurence Easterbrook and Ronald Duncan. It first met in the Oxford rooms of the poet EDMUND BLUNDEN, one of only five writers to express support for General Franco in response to a 1937 *Left Review* questionnaire.[34] In an article in the *Anglo-German Review* he rhapsodized on the 'freshness of life' in Nazi Germany, and he is reputed to have hoped that Göring would become Protector of England and restore the blacksmith's trade.[35] Blunden's biographer marginalizes this aspect of his life, contenting himself with a passing reference to the 'rather eccentric enthusiasm'[36] which led him to edit the 1943 pamphlet *A Return to Husbandry.*

Another Kinship member has in recent years been revealed as a Nazi enthusiast: the patriotic historian SIR ARTHUR BRYANT. Andrew Roberts, in *Eminent Churchillians,* exhilaratingly demonstrates him to have been a Fascist fellow-traveller who narrowly escaped internment in 1940.[37]

Bryant's political philosophy was of a rural Golden Age of yeomen and craftsmen, destroyed by capitalists, Jews, liberals and socialists. As late as 1939 he chose *Mein Kampf* as Book of the Month for his National Book Association, and in July that year visited Germany through his friendship with FRANCIS YEATS-BROWN. In the spring of 1940 he produced an *apologia* for Nazi policies, his book *Unfinished Victory,* which presented Hitler as a fairytale hero rescuing traditional German culture from Jewish debauchery. Sickened by the corruption of cosmpolitan urban life, with its poor racial specimens and its contempt for solid peasant virtues, the Führer struck 'boldly out up the perilous paths of urgent action to the summit of his dream.'[38]

Bryant's own dream became something of a nightmare once friends like Admiral Sir Barry Domvile (who kept a photograph of Hitler in his office) were arrested. He bought up all the copies of *Unfinished Victory* he could lay hands on and by the end of the year had produced *English Saga,* the first stage in his reinvention of himself as a popular national historian.[39]

Perhaps rather strangely, given that the organic movement was concerned with the care of the earth, one of its strongest supporters in the House of Lords was Lord Sempill, a famous aviator of the inter-war period. He belonged to the Anglo-German Fellowship and the pro-Nazi 'Link,' was a friend of Ribbentrop, and in 1939 was 'one of the hard core of German enthusiasts who argued publicly for peace with Germany from the Lords.'[40] It has even been suggested that he leaked British naval secrets to the Japanese.[41] After the war he was on the Soil Association Council from 1946 to 1953.

The Association could claim another figure from the same stable as its President in the early years. This was LORD TEVIOT, who as C.I. Kerr, Liberal National MP for Montrose during the 1930s, had belonged to the Right Club and shared the anti-semitic views of the Club's founder, Captain Ramsay. Teviot made a speech at Glasgow in 1938 in which he tried to alert his audience to the Jewish conspiracy which was undermining western civilization.[42]

On the fringes of the organic movement were two other fellow-travellers of the far Right, Anthony Ludovici and Francis Yeats-Brown. Ludovici's racist views on health were noted in the previous chapter, and his membership of the BPP has been noted earlier in this. According to Anna Bramwell[43] he worked for Rudolf Hess during the 1930s. In Britain he wrote a pamphlet entitled *Jews and the Jews in Britain* as 'Cobbett': a somewhat impertinent pseudonym for a cosmopolitan half-Italian who had been Rodin's secretary and translator of Nietzsche. After starting the essay with the stated intention of studying the Jewish problem in an 'impartial spirit,' Ludovici proceeded to condemn the Jews for their 'congenital disinclination towards productive labour,' their 'native hardness,' their emphasis on profit rather than service, their fostering of the capitalist spirit, and the fact that they were nomads rather than peasants. Jews were the perennial middle-men, tending 'to impoverish and weaken all local tradition, national character and national identity.'[44] Ludovici was implacably hostile to Christianity as well, which distinguished him from the great majority of the other figures in this study; he regarded with contempt and disgust a creed which encouraged compassion for the weak or sick.[45]

Ironically, Francis Yeats-Brown's great literary success *Bengal Lancer* was published by the Soviet fellow-travelling Jew Victor Gollancz. Strongly sympathetic to Fascism's aims, Yeats-Brown studied Italy's system at first hand in the early 1930s but reservations about Mosley kept him out of the BUF. Henry Williamson refers to him in *Lucifer Before Sunrise* as 'Francis,' who writes to Phillip Maddison [i.e. Williamson] saying that he wants to farm.[46] Yeats-Brown's biographer refers to letters he wrote praising Adrian Bell and Rolf Gardiner; he was also associated with Lymington's *New Pioneer.*[47]

If one accepts the thesis that the organic movement is a part of the wider Green movement, then Gould's assertion quoted at the beginning of the chapter, that Greens are best placed on the Left, must by now appear in need of qualification. The German youth movements, with which Gardiner was so closely involved, offer a point of comparison: Wohl's study of *The Generation of 1914* summarizes their outlook in terms also applicable to the British organic movement. There was the same sense of the menace of industrialism, which drove people into impersonal cities and gave free rein to rootless speculators, and a fear of a 'rising tide of materialism, modernity, and cosmopolitanism.' There was a dream of cultural renewal and national community, and a sense of the adult world's lies and hypocrisy; a desire for ethical purity and spiritual growth. The radical Right were hostile to parliamentary democracy, wanting an authoritarian state and a folk community, and favouring 'organic' political organizations.[48] During the Weimar era they believed they saw plutocrats dominating the republic, and hungered for a noble socialism where democracy was complemented by the aristocratic principle.[49] They wanted a broad peasantry, and a revolution which would subject both the power of money and the threat of the mob 'to the rule of spirit.'[50]

The British organic movement contained most of these features, but it also owed a considerable debt to the socialist movement, as we can see if we widen our focus to include a political initiative which began before the First World War.

Guild Socialism and monetary reform

Guild Socialism originated in the work of the architect A.J. Penty, a close friend of A.R. Orage, and in article written for the *New Age* by S.G. HOB-SON in 1911–12. Penty's career provides an excellent example of the stages by which a man of the radical Left might end up on the far Right. Originally a disciple of William Morris, Penty wrote *The Restoration of the Gild [sic] System* in 1906, criticizing machine civilization and urging trade unions to turn themselves into modern equivalents of the medieval guilds. He resigned from the Fabian Society in protest at its purely secular and utilitarian attitudes, and by the 1930s was writing, as a Catholic, in praise of Mussolini for having created a corporate state which was in essence 'the Regulative Guild State' and demonstrated 'that Mediaeval ideas still have practical validity.' Penty went through intellectual contortions to distinguish the corporate state from totalitarianism, arguing that Fascism sought 'a wider distribution of property'[51] and regarded a prosperous peasantry as:

> the necessary foundation of a true social order, as a reservoir from which the towns replenish their stock; and persuaded that man does not live by bread alone, they [the Italian government] consider it their duty to protect people from the corroding effects of materialism.[52]

Penty died in 1937, just as the organic movement was beginning to coalesce, but his closeness to its values is clear in his 1932 book *Means and Ends*. It attacked free trade, argued for restricting mechanization of farming, advocated a society based on agriculture as the only possible stable one, warned against cosmopolitanism, urged a system of fixed prices and local markets, and appealed to 'the eternal validity of the theory of Natural Law.' Socialism, once a moral force, was now a menace, and any hope for the future lay with traditionalists, younger members of the Conservative Party, 'followers of Disraeli, who might be described as Tory Socialists.'[53] The German scholar Karl Munkes identified Penty himself as having more in common with the Führer than Disraeli, entitling the final section of his doctoral thesis *'Penty und Hitler weisen den Weg in die Zukunft* [Penty and Hitler point the way to the future.'[54]

S.G. Hobson, also an ex-Fabian, provided an ironic tail-piece to Penty's pilgrimage. He recorded that he had spoken to him by phone a month before Penty's death. Penty told him that he had joined the Fascists, adding that he had never thought much of Hobson's Guilds.[55] Another Guild Socialist, Rowland Kenney, also rejected Penty's later views, writing that Mussolini had 'warped and perverted [Guild ideas] beyond anything we could have imagined possible.'[56]

Hobson, a life-long socialist, denied any necessary connection between his theory of Guild Socialism and Fascism. In his original *New Age* articles he had sought a *via media* between syndicalism and state socialism, believing that a non-feudal conception of guilds might be the answer. In 1915 the National Guilds League was founded, members of its first executive including G.D.H. Cole, the artist Will Dyson, the Anglo-Catholic socialist Conrad Noel, and Maurice Reckitt; other such notables as George Lansbury, Bertrand Russell and R.H. TAWNEY were involved in the movement.[57] For a time it looked as though the Guilds League might challenge Fabian dominance of the Labour movement, but it was divided in its response to the Bolshevik regime and, in 1920, to Orage's espousal of Social Credit. By 1923 it was a spent force. Orage was in France and most Guild Socialists had either defected to Communism or, like Reckitt, converted to Social Credit. Of the various objections which might be brought against Guild Socialism, the most significant in relation to the organic movement is that the direct democracy it desired could have existed only in Penty's ideal world of small producers; it was in essence a protest against the scale of modern industry. (Penty would have argued that this was precisely why we should abolish large-scale machinery and return to a world of small craftsmen.) 'In their innermost hearts,' says Philip Glass, 'many of the guild socialists disliked modern industry and modern life.'[58] Such an attitude could be found in certain members of the organic movement who had been Guild Socialists, notably Massingham; Mairet had been a member of the Arts and Crafts movement but later in life became more sympathetic to the potential of what his friend Lewis Mumford called 'technics.'

Another set of ideas which fed into the organic movement, even more explicitly medieval and Catholic than Guild Socialism, was the Distributism inspired by Hilaire Belloc and G.K. Chesterton.[59] The Distributists wanted to see:

> a balanced or mixed economy of independent farmers and small industries owned by the workers themselves. This would constitute a peasant state, in that small independent farming would be the

mainstay of the nation's economy. By insisting on the efficacy of local power, decentralized control, self-sufficiency, and rural reconstruction, and in their distaste for the machinations of state bureaucracy and industrialism, the authors of Distributism came close to that ideal community of anarchism described in the writings of Kropotkin.[60]

They believed that farming had been ruined because rural areas had been turned into a sort of agricultural factory, forcing farmers to produce for a market economy rather than for consumption, and ensuring that they were trapped by 'the machinations of the market, the transportation network that served it, and the financier who provided the credit.' Distributism had a strong 'back to the land' strain, believing city life to be 'too far removed from the lifeblood of the soil,' and it established agricultural training courses for urban youngsters, and associations for farming and homecrafts.[61] Chesterton wanted sufficient small proprietors to be a political force separate from large-scale Capital and organized Labour, but the back-to-the-land element in Distributism attracted precisely the sort of cranks he dreaded. Not himself a machine-hater, he welcomed any invention which encouraged people's independence.[62]

Distributism was essentially a Catholic movement, its members believing that 'modern society had to return to basic spiritual principles that were fundamentally Catholic (Thomist) in nature.'[63] Chesterton was involved in the Anglo-Catholic Summer Schools which aimed to establish the principles of a 'Christian Sociology.' Father Vincent McNabb was a prime mover among those who wanted to revive agriculture,[64] and one of the journals advocating Distributist policies was *The Cross and the Plough,* mouthpiece of the Catholic Land Association.

There were some close links between Distributism and the organic school. Belloc and Chesterton had written for Orage's *New Age* and shared that paper's distrust of Fabianism. Maurice Reckitt was strongly influenced by Belloc's *The Servile State* and by Chesterton, ensuring that various Anglo-Catholic associations adopted Distributist positions. Reckitt was never fully convinced by the claims of Distributism, but he considered it a major part of his social theory and was on the board of Chesterton's newspaper *G.K.'s Weekly.*[65] There were also close links between the movement and Social Credit: Reckitt, Mairet, Fordham and the sculptor ERIC GILL shifted in and out of both circles.

Both movements displayed a contempt for finance, parliamentary politics, bureaucracy of all sorts, and industrialism ... Social crediters and Distributists ... tended to recognize the importance of similar things, namely guilds, arts and crafts, the Middle Ages, and Catholic social philosophy.[66]

Belloc was one of the people who helped Orage establish the *New English Weekly.*[67]

Social Credit was of central importance to the coalescence of the organic movement, but before we see why this was so we need to look at the work of the Economic Reform Club, which brought together the various putative cures for a sick financial system. Guild Socialism broke up over two main issues: Bolshevism, and Orage's conversion to Major Douglas' Social Credit economics, to which he remained committed for the rest of his life. However, Douglas was not the first person to suggest that the money system lay at the root of social problems; Orage had already been influenced by Arthur Kitson, a prolific inventor and a businessman who believed that finance stifled the productive potential of the machine age. His experiences led him steadily towards a conspiracy theory of money-power. At first a contributor to Blatchford's socialist paper *The Clarion* from around 1900, and then to the *New Age,* he tried to persuade the Labour movement to look at the finance problem; its refusal to do so drove him to the Right, and he became part of the anti-semitic 'Britons' group in the 1920s.[68] He wrote of the 'sacrifice of the public interests on behalf of the money-lending profession' and of the debt-slavery whose methods were outlined in *The Protocols of the Elders of Zion.*[69]

The Economic Reform Club and Institute (ERCI), to give it its full title, developed as a result of the 1931 economic crisis; here was the clearest proof that the financial system was hopelessly inefficient and unjust, and the best possible opportunity for mobilizing the forces of radical change. Edward Holloway, one of the Club's founders, read in 1932 *Life and Money* by Eimar O'Duffy, a book described on its fly-sheet as:

> a critical examination of the principles and practice of orthodox economics with a practical scheme to end the muddle it has made to our civilisation.[70]

Like the Social Crediters, O'Duffy saw the problem as one of industrial and agricultural supply outstripping people's capacity to buy, whereas the monetary system had originated at a time when demand exceeded supply. Holloway organized a meeting attended by Vincent Vickers, a former director of the Bank of England, and followed it up with a petition campaign which drew widespread support, particularly from the churches. The variety of monetary reform groups was an obstacle to serious consideration of financial issues, and the Petition's purpose was to bring them together in a common task: an enquiry into the workings of the monetary system. In 1936 a Petition Club was formed, changing its name the following year to the Economic Reform Club. Its first President was Lord Northbourne; other notable members included the aircraft manufacturer Sir Alliott Verdon-Roe, and Sir Reginald Rowe, assistant treasurer of Lincoln's Inn.[71] In a wartime lecture Rowe condemned the power of bank-created credit to deny plenty to the many, and of interest charges to increase the evils of inequality; he welcomed the Beveridge Report, urged a redistribution of wealth, and described the fight against the finance system as 'a Holy War against evil.'[72]

In 1939 the ERCI organized a dinner in honour of John Boyd Orr, whose guests included Ernest Bevin, Lord Horder, Julian Huxley, Compton Mackenzie, and the chemist Professor Soddy. There were also several figures from the organic movement: Loftus, Lymington, Northbourne and Sempill, and one of the country's top agriculturalists, an organic sympathizer, Viscount Bledisloe. Boyd Orr, Horder and Sempill spoke on 'Health, Agriculture and the Standard of Living.' Boyd Orr said of the current situation:

> We need the food. We have the land to produce it. We have two million unemployed wanting work. If we say we cannot produce the food which the nation needs because we cannot find the money, what we are really saying is that we cannot produce it under the present economic and financial system.[73]

Sempill told the diners: 'We can take a leaf out of Germany's book in the enterprise she is showing with a view to attaining self-sufficiency in agricultural produce.'[74]

The following year, Loftus, Lymington and Northbourne gave *Three Addresses on Food Production*. Northbourne concentrated on the threat of environmental damage posed by increased mechanization; Lymington called for a strong yeoman population and interest-free credit for farmers; Loftus condemned the vested interests which were working against agriculture, describing the Treasury as a bastion of nineteenth-century economic orthodoxy. Monetary profit had become the only criterion of value, but the nation's land was 'not an absolute property of this generation to be used or abused as we desire.'[75]

As its contribution to the debate on post-war reconstruction, the ERCI organized a conference in conjunction with the INDUSTRIAL CHRISTIAN FELLOWSHIP, *The World We Want*. Held in 1942, its aim was:

> To discuss practical proposals for the future guidance of British
> Policy ... so that after this war we may take our full share in ban-
> ishing the twin evils of Fear and Want.[76]

Contributors included Robert Boothby, MP, Norman Mansbridge of the
Workers' Educational Association, Sir Richard Gregory, President of the
British Association (who was invited to the meeting convened by Lady
Balfour in June 1945 which marked the beginning of the Soil Association), Boyd Orr, Loftus, Lymington, Sempill and Stapledon. Gregory
chaired the session on health and agriculture, urging a food policy based
on human needs rather than financial interests, and planned on an international basis as part of a world fellowship. Stapledon spoke for the integration of rural and urban, and wanted agricultural policy to aim at
maximum self-sufficiency by intensifying output per acre. Boyd Orr concentrated on the need to plan post-war food production internationally.
Lymington spoke on land settlement, Sempill chaired a session on monetary and economic reform, and Loftus attacked the international money-
lenders who had exploited the world's soils. He proposed nationalizing
the Bank of England, and said that social security was essential when so
many people lacked purchasing power. The conference's closing resolu-
tion was for the government to set up:

> a monetary system which will allow continuous use of full
> national productive power in peace as in war; the equation of con-
> sumptive power with productive capacity; and the restoration to
> the State of the creation, expansion, and contraction of all types of
> money, thereby enabling the establishment in this country of a
> truly Christian Social Order.[77]

Given the strong presence of members of the organic school in the
ERCI it is not surprising to learn that a special Agricultural Section was
established. Its *Agricultural Bulletin,* which in 1946 became *Rural Economy,* was edited by Jorian Jenks and issued jointly with the support of the
Rural Reconstruction Association. Jenks defined the journal's aim as to
present 'the relationship of rural life and work to the social economy as a
whole.'[78]

Rural Economy was another medium for organic ideas and many
familiar names and topics appeared in its pages. There was Massingham,
on the true nature of 'economy,' a word derived from the Greek *oikono-
mia,* meaning management of a household and, by implication, of natural
resources including the soil; he referred to the Soil Association as a reaction against human mismanagement of nature. Stapledon wrote on the

social value of hill farmers. The 1949 Summer School of the Men of the Trees was reviewed, and in 1950 the journal published St Barbe Baker's New Earth Charter. Lady Howard wrote a two-part article on urban composting. Ralph Coward and W.T. Symons contributed pieces, and in the summer of 1949 Jenks devoted an article specifically to the organic movement.[79]

The journal's pages also reveal links with ST ANNE'S HOUSE, SOHO and the Council for the Church and Countryside (CCC).[80] ERCI members were invited to the St Anne's luncheon club, and a public meeting held at St Anne's House on 'The Survival of England' featured as speakers Jorian Jenks and John Betjeman. *Rural Economy* carried advertisements for the CCC, and W.G. PECK'S *An Outline of Christian Sociology* was reviewed.[81] When Howard died, the ERCI's *Monthly Bulletin* carried an obituary of the man whose 'notable contribution to an understanding of the true values of soil and plant health is well known to Club members.'[82]

The Agricultural Section's Research Committee had Jenks, Massingham and Symons as members, and prepared a memorandum on agricultural credit;[83] its work led to publication in 1955 of the comprehensive report *Feeding the Fifty Million,* which argued that Britain could produce from 75 to 85 per cent of her own food. It was drafted by Jenks, Loftus, and the scientist and Soil Association member Hugh Martin-Leake, and had an introduction by Easterbrook. Despite this strong organic presence the report was ambivalent about the value of a national organic farming policy.[84] Ironically, the increasing agricultural self-sufficiency which marked the post-war decades resulted from rapidly increasing application of artificials.

Holloway became joint editor, with Jenks, of *Rural Economy* in 1954, two years before the journal closed. This association demonstrated the parallel necessities:

> in the national interest, to restore money to its rightful place as the servant (not the dictator) of the social economy [and] to restore agriculture to its rightful place in our national life.[85]

Social Credit

Among the various alternative financial systems represented at the ERCI, the Social Credit ideas of Major C.H. Douglas attracted the organic school's overwhelming support. They are highly complex and it is doubtful if many of its adherents really understood them — or, its critics would say, whether they were coherent enough to be understood.[86] The important point here is that Social Credit sought to relate the issuing of money to the nation's real wealth, and 'to supply [the] shortage of purchasing power which is holding up industry.'[87] The organic school believed the financial system to be harming national health and agriculture through preventing people from buying fresh farm produce. Social Crediters advocated a National Dividend, issued directly to consumers, whether or not they were employed; and, to deflect the objection that such a policy would be inflationary, they introduced the medieval idea of a 'Just Price,' which would ensure that middlemen could not rake off excessive profits. It would also be essential to remove from banks the power to issue credit, and to invest that power in a nationally representative body.

Douglas had made his most important convert, A.R. Orage, by 1920, and we have already seen how this helped split and destroy the Guild Socialist movement. The *New Age,* edited by Arthur Brenton, supported Social Credit throughout the 1920s and into the following decade, but the paper was a shadow of its earlier self. Nevertheless, many branches of the Independent Labour Party (ILP) were interested in Social Credit, and Douglas worked hard to convince the Labour movement of the necessity of tackling the power of finance. Hutchinson and Burkitt, in their detailed re-examination of Social Credit's history and contemporary relevance, emphasize the socialist strand in Douglas' ideas. Certainly Social Credit attracted the support of two well-known leftists, the Marxist poet Hugh McDiarmid and the 'Red Dean' of Canterbury, Hewlett Johnson. However, Douglas' belief that the financial system was run by 'power-seekers' who wanted to 'arrange the people into a perfect hierarchy of obedience'[88] ensured that Social Credit tended towards anti-Jewish conspiracy theory. Lewis Mumford records that as early as 1920 a long conversation between Orage and Douglas about Social Credit proposals featured

> the weirdest nonsense (coming from Orage) on the world contest now taking place between the bureaucracy of Jesuitism, acting through the League of Nations, and the financial manipulations of the Jews, acting through the banking system.[89]

With Douglas failing to convert the Labour Party and the ILP losing interest in his ideas in 1931, Social Credit's appeal moved distinctly to the Right, although it could still try to present itself as something of a 'Fourth Way,' an alternative to capitalism, Fascism and Communism. Mosley's party disliked Douglas' distinctly anti-puritanical attitude to work and the social equality implied by the idea of a National Dividend.[90]

By the mid-1930s Social Credit was almost entirely ignored by politicians, and the *New English Weekly* was the only Social Credit publication to command any respect.[91] Some blamed Douglas' authoritarian personality; others believed he had failed to give practical support to the Social Credit government in Alberta, Canada (though it survived until the early 1970s). Social Credit split into rival factions, the most important rift being between those who followed Douglas, and those who followed John Hargrave.

Hargrave was an important figure in the background of the organic movement, without being directly involved in it.[92] Influenced by E.T. Seton's Woodcraft Movement, and a keen Scout, Hargrave founded in 1920 the KINDRED OF THE KIBBO KIFT (KKK); 'Kibbo Kift' apparently meant 'proof of great strength.' The movement was explicitly religious, seeking spiritual fulfilment through understanding natural law and living in harmony with it,[93] and it influenced the German youth movements of the Weimar Republic. Rolf Gardiner at one time belonged to the KKK; other distinguished members included Havelock Ellis, Patrick Geddes, Julian Huxley and H.G. Wells. Gardiner was particularly important, as it was he who sowed in Hargrave's mind the commitment to Social Credit. When, in 1924, the Kin was losing impetus and direction, Hargrave seized on Social Credit as the means of regenerating it: 'The psychological complex of industrial mankind can only be released by solving the economic impasse.'[94] By 1933 Hargrave had established himself as leader of the Green Shirt Movement, the activist wing of Social Credit which organized demonstrations. Douglas at first approved of this branch, but the two men fell out, and in any case the Green Shirts fell victim to the 1936 Public Order Act, which outlawed the wearing of uniforms for political purposes.

By the late 1930s Social Credit was a spent force. Mairet and the *New English Weekly* nevertheless remained committed to it during the following decade, and Douglas' theories have retained supporters to this day, with Hutchinson and Burkitt attempting to recapture Social Credit for socialism, and showing its relevance to contemporary economic and environmental issues. There is currently a revival of interest in monetary reform as a response to globalization, and in Britain the Christian Council for Monetary Justice stands in a line of descent which can be traced back more than six decades.[95]

Church social reform movements were important in the early days of Social Credit. Maurice Reckitt, the Anglo-Catholic historian, had been active in the Church Socialist League (CSL) from before 1914, an organization attracted by medievalism and which threw in its lot with Guild Socialism. Reckitt was among those who followed Orage into the Social Credit movement, abandoning socialism. The CSL re-named itself the League of the Kingdom of God (LKG) in 1924; from it, developed the Anglo-Catholic Summer Schools of Sociology and the CHRISTENDOM GROUP, which will be discussed in Chapter 11.[96] In 1928 the Christian Social Council was established, its Department of Research being directed by V.A. Demant, a Social Crediter whose salary Reckitt, a wealthy man, paid for three years. The Council published *The Just Price,* which hinted at support for Social Credit, and *This Unemployment,* which openly favoured it.

Finlay suggests various reasons for Anglo-Catholic sympathy with Social Credit, the most important being the perceived connection between Protestantism and capitalism, as argued by Reckitt's friend R.H. Tawney.[97] This view was supported by Demant, who:

> also pointed out that classical liberalism was only possible while people believed in an infinite world so that exports and the balance of power could be extended without limit.[98]

Here again one sees the organic school's mistrust of free trade, and awareness of the need to respect God-given limits to resources. Demant also argued for control of economic activities and values by means of a social philosophy which would set them in their justified but purely functional sphere.[99] Social Credit appealed to critics of capitalism who were not prepared to embrace secular or totalitarian ideologies as alternatives. Since members of the organic school believed that the economic orthodoxy of *laissez-faire* capitalism had sacrificed Britain's agriculture, denying much of its population access to the food and material goods so abundantly produced; and since they believed that successful farming could be based only on a respect for the natural order, Social Credit fitted in comfortably with their philosophy. The following chapter will show how close the relationship was.

10. Philip Mairet and the *New English Weekly*

The reader may feel that the tapestry of groups already discussed is sufficiently complex, and quail at the prospect of still more strands being introduced. Be introduced they must, though, since they will ensure that the whole pattern can be clearly seen, and that we can come to the heart of the organic movement, the *New English Weekly (NEW)*.

The first part of this chapter will examine the matrix from which the *NEW* emerged and in particular the influence on Philip Mairet of the intellectual and political gurus Patrick Geddes and Dmitri Mitrinovic. The latter was responsible for convening the original meeting of Social Crediters who became known as the Chandos Group, and was the driving force behind various political initiatives in which Chandos members were involved. A third influence on Mairet was A.R. Orage, whose renewed commitment to Social Credit in the wake of the Wall Street Crash led to the founding of the *New English Weekly*.

The second part of the chapter is a case study of the *NEW*'s role as a forum for organic philosophy and practice, demonstrating that nearly all the important names in the organic movement appeared in its pages. Here we can see that the *NEW* was of unique importance in the breadth and depth of its advocacy of the organic cause, analysing and developing as it did the various themes dealt with in earlier chapters of this book.

Mairet's mentors

Patrick Geddes

First we must return to the period before the First World War: in the Cotswold town of Chipping Campden, Philip Mairet was working for the Arts and Crafts Guild established there by C.R. Ashbee, and heard speak a man who was to become one of his gurus, Patrick Geddes, whose great achievement Ashbee described as 'the making of a bridge between Biology and Social Science.'[1] Geddes had studied Biology under T.H. Huxley

and had worked with D'Arcy Thompson, famous for his study of biological forms. For thirty years, from 1888, he was Professor of Botany at
Dundee, although he appears to have spent little time there. Sir William
Holford, in his foreword to Mairet's biography of Geddes, quotes Geddes
as saying: 'Our greatest need today ... is to grasp life as a whole, to see
its many sides in their proper relations.' Geddes' social thought was influ-
enced by John Ruskin, Auguste Comte and Frédéric Le Play: from
Ruskin he took the critique of Victorian economic values, and from Le
Play an emphasis on the regional and ecological aspects of civilization.
He saw Le Play's thought as the basis for 'the realization of the Comtean
vision: scientific method could be applied to the natural social organism.'[2]
(The Rural Reconstruction Association was based at Le Play House in
London.) Conditions in Edinburgh made Geddes concerned about working-class health, and led him to a study of town planning; he was active
in the Garden Cities movement. In 1914 he went to India and spent much
of the following ten years there, five of them as Professor of Civics and
Sociology at Bombay. He also established a college at Montpellier in
southern France, which he hoped would form the basis of a rural university and be the centre of a village revival. In 1904 he had founded the
Sociological Society with Victor Branford, its sponsors including H.G.
Wells and the economist J.A. Hobson. Lewis Mumford edited its journal
the *Sociological Review* in 1920; Kenneth Barlow studied at Montpellier
and was for a time Geddes' secretary.[3]

Geddes was a major influence on Mairet and thereby indirectly on the
organic movement. Early in the First World War Mairet met Geddes a
second time, and told him how fascinated he had been by the sociological perspective revealed at Chipping Campden; as a result he became for
a time Geddes' assistant, producing the charts and diagrams which illustrated his lectures at King's College, London. In Mairet's view:

> The exclusive emphasis on technical studies that we have seen
> since the second great war, and the relative neglect of the art and
> science of husbandry, is one of the social distortions he feared and
> foresaw, and laboured to prevent ... It is the supposedly inferior
> functions of industry, those of forestry, fishing, mining, and agri-
> culture that are in most danger of disregard, though materially the
> most indispensable: and it was these he most wanted to dignify by
> taking them up into the educational synthesis of the university of
> the future.[4]

And again:

Only an 'organic' conception of society, such as Geddes had
developed from his standpoint as a biologist, could give a sound
approach to the problems of society when all its interrelated functions were being dynamized by the new powers and techniques.
Henceforth any true politics or economics demanded social vision
with a sense of that 'balance of nature' which is the discovery of
the naturalist and ecologist, but which still operates in the development of technical civilization — to its disaster if not understood.[5]

When Geddes visited London in 1932 to receive his knighthood he
became President of the NEW EUROPE GROUP recently founded by Dmitri
Mitrinovic, another of Mairet's gurus. Indeed, Mairet said that Mitrinovic, whom he first met in 1914, determined the subsequent course of
his life.[6] Given Mairet's central place in the organic movement, this alone
would be sufficient to establish Mitrinovic's importance to this study of
its origins.[7]

Dmitri Mitrinovic

Mitrinovic was born in 1887 in what was then Hercegovina, became
active in the revolutionary movement opposed to Austrian domination,
and was well known in literary circles. In 1913 he moved to Munich,
becoming part of the *Blaue Reiter* group of artists and a friend of Kandin-
sky and Klee. When war broke out he fled to England and did all he could
to help Serbia's cause, organizing an exhibition of the sculptor Mestro-
vic's work at the Victoria and Albert Museum in 1915. Through the translator Paul Selver he came into contact with Orage and the *New Age* circle,
writing for the paper under the pseudonym 'M.M. Cosmoi,' and after the
war dominating it in a way that alienated many readers, his style being
baffling to the point of obscurity.[8]

Andrew Rigby has clarified the main features of Mitrinovic's philosophy as developed in the *New Age;* two of them are particularly relevant to
the organic movement. Influenced by Comte and by the Russian mystic
Vladimir Solovyov, Mitrinovic 'put forward as a hypothesis the idea of
the world and humanity as a developing organism' A new kind of consciousness had to be established, of the world and humanity as one and
indivisible, with each individual aware of his or her part in establishing a
socialism in which identification with nation, class or tribe was overcome
in favour of identification with universal humanity. The second important
feature of his thought was the significance he attached to Christianity in
the development of human consciousness. His theology may have been
obscure and unorthodox, but he was explicit that the person of Jesus

Christ was 'the greatest event in psychology as well as in history,' and he 'regarded the doctrine of the Trinity in the Athanasian Creed as the most precise expression of the dynamic principles and morphology of an organism.'[9] According to Mitrinovic, God the Father represented the World Unconscious; Jesus Christ represented individual self-consciousness, and the Holy Spirit represented

> the establishment of the 'Kingdom of God' on earth, the creation of Universal Humanity. The Holy Spirit would be incarnated as the organic ordering of the whole world, in which races, nations and groupings of all kinds would be functionally related to one another.[10]

But this could happen only if there were 'a community of free, self-conscious individuals [who] had transcended the individualistic ethic to a new "supra-human" consciousness.'[11]

Mitrinovic devoted most of his time during the 1920s and '30s to working with others on ways to develop such a consciousness. His most ambitious initiatives were the New Europe group, founded in 1931, and NEW BRITAIN, founded the following year.[12] Among the chief objectives were monetary reform, the creation of a European federation, and workers' control of industry through National Guilds; and among the contributors to the journal *New Britain,* which enjoyed considerable though short-lived success, were several writers who played a part in the organic movement.

Mairet wrote on Ruskin, while John Stewart Collis offered a piece on another Victorian sage, Thomas Carlyle, and a young Lawrence Hills drew attention to the centenary of William Morris' birth. John Middleton Murry, discussing 'Social Credit and Fascism,' pointed out the latent antisemitism in the former; Rolf Gardiner requested 'Fair Play for Germany,' explaining that Germany was the adolescent of Europe and that 'The clue to German socialism ... is in the new *agrarian* order'; and Montague Fordham wrote on 'Rural Reconstruction in the New Britain.' There was considerable coverage of agricultural issues, with the rural writer S.L. Bensusan producing a series of articles which discussed bread's declining nutritional value, the need for national self-sufficiency, the value of smallholdings, and the decline of corn-growing.[13] In the associated quarterly publication one finds Scott Williamson on 'The Scientist's Outlook,' and Aubrey Westlake demanding that we 'Educate for Wisdom.'[14]

Christianity's importance was emphasized in a piece bearing all the hallmarks of Mitrinovic's style, entitled 'Duty and Right of the Imperium Albion.' After referring to the 'satanical' role of Germany it declared in the following style:

> TO REALIZE CHRISTIANITY AND SOCIALISM, IMPERIALLY AND
> SOCIALLY, IS THE WORLD-TASK OF BRITAIN AND THE BRITISH WORLD
> ... *Prevent the Catastrophe of Christendom and the Decline of*
> *Western Civilization for the sake of Man's glorification of the*
> *Christ-Principle and of the Love of God ... Forward, Upward*
> *towards the Social State!*[15]

The front cover of *New Britain* for 1 August 1934 called upon the Christian world to overthrow the old order and build a new system in accordance with the Sermon on the Mount.

Mitrinovic remained politically active during the late 1930s, with initiatives for an Atlantic Alliance between the Commonwealth, the United States and Soviet Russia, and an alliance between Britain and France. These were attempted steps towards a new world order, aimed at preventing another war. These initiatives tended to be politically eclectic, or ambivalent: New Britain and New Europe included among their members pro-Fascists like Odon Por and J.F.C. Fuller, as well as leftists such as S.G. Hobson and the Communist J.T. Murphy. But Mitrinovic always took a special interest in the political potential of trade unionism, and it was this concern which had drawn together, in May 1926, the group of people introduced in this book's opening chapter, who were destined to play a crucial part in the development of the organic movement.

We are now almost ready to look at the *New English Weekly's* role as a forum for organic husbandry, but must look first at another of the groups which Mitrinovic spawned. This was the ADLER SOCIETY, whose journal *Purpose* also promoted the organic outlook, and in effect merged with the *NEW* in 1940.

The psychoanalyst Alfred Adler visited Britain in 1926 and aroused considerable interest, not least in Mitrinovic and his associates. The following year they founded a society devoted to propagating Adler's ideas: Mitrinovic, Mairet and the poet Alan Porter were its leading lights, and they were soon joined by W.T. Symons and V.A. Demant.[16] Mitrinovic had visited Adler in Vienna and obtained his permission to found a London branch of the Society of Individual Psychology. Mairet's *ABC of Adler's Psychology* (1928) expounded the connection between Adler's ideas and Social Credit; in particular, Mairet found that Adler's theory of compensation for inferiority explained financiers' search for power and the 'extraordinary self-assertiveness in affairs' of Jews,[17] who suffered from having been outcasts.

Douglas sympathized with Adler's view that a craving for power was the chief cause of the world's parlous state, and considered that those who ran the financial system were exhibiting the neurotic's need for security. In the Social Crediters' view, health, personal and social, was achieved by rejecting the profit motive and its attendant violence. Mairet saw an 'organic' significance in Adler's thought, with the living organism exhibiting 'the primary urge of the vital intelligence adjusting the organism as a whole to its environment'; and he considered that 'the Adlerian insights into human nature are assimilable to a Christian moral theology.'[18]

The chief medium for this exotic blend of psychology and economics was the quarterly journal *Purpose,* which first appeared in 1929 and was published by C.W. Daniel. John Marlow was its first editor; in 1930 Mairet and Symons edited it jointly, and Symons became sole editor when Mairet took over the *NEW* following Orage's death in 1934. *Purpose* was a revival of *Focus,* a nature movement magazine with a vaguely theosophical tone, but was more specifically Christian than theosophical or pantheist, and generally more left-wing than the *NEW* or *Health and Life.* Like the *NEW* in its early days, it had great faith in the power of machine civilization to abolish poverty. There was no problem of overproduction, only of distribution. Nature and industry could supply all human needs, but finance imposed poverty. The explanation of this was psychological, a craving for power and devotion to money which were a form of madness and sentenced the many to slow death. The will-to-power was the antithesis of Christ's teaching: 'The spirit of anti-Christ has found in money the perfect means to its inhuman aims.'[19]

Social Credit aimed to *give* money and physical wellbeing to people, not to use it to deny and control them, just as Adlerian psychology aimed to free neurotics from their compulsive need to dominate, enabling them to create a sense of community. Psychological hoarding — the refusal to give to others in a living relationship — was to the individual what financial hoarding was to the economy. Lord Northbourne warned that:

> Nature punishes hoarding with death. Even wheat cannot be stored for more than a few years. Preserved foods can be stored, but they have lost their vitality. We have preferred to hoard our money and so to get interest on it.[20]

The financial system encouraged malnutrition and the destruction of food. F. Le Gros Clark, Honorary Secretary of the Committee Against Malnutrition, described how the poor were condemned to a sub-standard diet, and urged a rise in working-class incomes.[21]

Given the journal's encouragement of increased agricultural production it is no surprise to find some familiar names from the organic

movement in its pages; as well as Northbourne there was Kenneth Barlow, who contributed several articles and reviews. P.M. — presumably
Mairet — reviewed Fordham's book *Britain's Trade and Agriculture,* and
Dr F.G. Crookshank recommended that the new psychology be taught in
places like 'those suggested by Scott Williamson and Innes Pearse.'[22]

Anthony Ludovici contributed an article criticizing the Adlerians'
ideas, but was out of place in *Purpose,* which was consistently anti-Fascist and published some telling attacks on anti-semitism and biological
interpetations of human history and society. The editorial notes described
attacks on Jews as repugnant to a Christian community, since Christianity was rooted in Judaism, and they condemned race and nationalism as
idols. Dr Erich Gutkind pointed out that reactionary movements were
'fixed on ideas such as attachment to the soil, nationality, peasantry,
race'; these were 'infantile,'[23] attempting to make Man the servant of
Nature, whereas Nature should yield to Man; without Man at the centre
Nature became a threat.

Purpose consistently advocated the renewal of agriculture and
reminded readers of their dependence on the soil, but it did not go down
the road of Fascism, because it believed that humans are spiritual as well
as biological. The editorial notes of the final issue, presumably written by
Symons, sum up this view. After saying that there can be no return to
nature myths, which are idolatry for totalitarians, they continue:

> Man, the child of Nature, has now to leave the mother, and attain
> man's estate. His feet must be planted firmly upon the earth, in
> new-found obedience to the natural laws which he has learned
> only to flout ... in knowledge that to obtain obedience is to win
> mastery, with all its responsibilities, and so pass to man's estate
> and 'walk with God.' Men are not permitted to discard their power
> because it has been abused.[24]

By the end of 1939 *Purpose* was in difficulties and announced that it
might accept the *NEW*'s hospitality and appear as an occasional special
supplement to that paper. However, the merger was complete a year later,
and Symons wrote frequently for the *NEW* as 'Pontifex III'[25] as well as
being a member of its editorial board. A member of the Chandos Group,
Symons would have had no difficulty in adjusting; the *NEW* was in effect
the organ of the Group. This had come about as follows.

The Group's aim, following the humiliating defeat of the trade unions
in the General Strike, was to try to develop Social Credit doctrines 'as an
economic technique to serve as the basis of a new and eclectic social criticism and synthesis.'[26] At one point, the Group was almost identical with

the Sociological section of the Adler Society, its aim being to try to establish 'certain absolute and eternal principles of true sociology,'[27] which it
believed were to be most clearly discerned in ancient cultures. The more
immediate concern, though, was with the urgent topic of the mining
industry, and their first corporate production was a book called *Coal: A
Challenge to the National Conscience* (1927), published by the Woolfs'
Hogarth Press. It was strongly sympathetic to the workers, arguing that
the return to normal after the Strike was in fact a return to an unhealthy
social order.[28] In a competitive society there was no sense of a common
purpose, and if men were unhappy with their work it was because that
work did not issue in a satisfying communal life. A society in which
money was the chief value was spiritually empty, yet Church leaders
seemed to have little idea of what a Christian society would be like, having forgotten that the medieval Church had provided axioms for control
of economic behaviour. The authors wanted to see a body of churchmen

> commissioned to enquire into the economic axioms of the indus-
> trial world, with a view to their validity in themselves and their
> Christian implications.[29]

A 'Christian sociology' was needed, and we shall see in the following
chapter that the organic school's respect for the natural order was integral
to the social ideas implied by that phrase.

In 1929 the group published a more wide-ranging survey of social issues,
Politics: A Discussion of Realities, published by C.W. Daniel and edited by
the socialist army officer Col. James Delahaye,[30] 'in company with' Mairet,
Porter, Reckitt, Symons and Albert Newsome. Linda Merricks sees the
book as a forerunner of the New Britain movement, politically ambivalent
in its attempt to harmonize aristocracy and socialism.[31] It attached importance to an 'organic' conception of society, guaranteeing everyone a sense
of meaning from their function in the social order; people could fulfil their
destiny only in co-operation with others. There was an increased emphasis
on monetary reform, and a whole chapter on agriculture and rural life,
which expressed ideas later more fully developed in the *NEW.*

Mitrinovic left the Chandos Group after helping write *Coal,* as did
Alan Porter. Reckitt, Symons, Mairet and Demant were the nucleus; later
members included the journalist Basil Boothroyd, Geoffrey Davies of the
Sociological Society, T.S. Eliot and TOM HERON. Lewis Mumford,
G.D.H. Cole and Karl Mannheim were among the guests over the years.[32]
The Group's involvement with the *NEW,* though, resulted from the activ-
ities of someone who was not a member, Alfred Richard Orage, to whose
brilliant and strange career we must now turn.[33]

A.R. Orage

Orage's name is hardly known today, though the list of writers whom he encouraged, and published in the *New Age,* includes Katherine Mansfield, John Middleton Murry, Herbert Read, T.E. Hulme and Edwin Muir. The giver of opportunities to others, Orage was able to develop his talent as the result of an opportunity he had himself been given by the squire's family in his boyhood village of Fenstanton, Cambridgeshire. They enabled him to enter training college and escape a farm labourer's fate; ironically, the *NEW*'s founder 'never succumbed to the nostalgia for a pre-industrial organic community.'[34] He taught in Leeds, joined the Independent Labour Party and became a skilled socialist orator; but he was never a materialist, and he also joined the Theosophical Society.

Orage made two important friendships in Leeds, one with Holbrook Jackson, a Fabian with contacts in London, and the other with A.J. Penty. In 1902 they founded the Leeds Art Club, to which Herbert Read and Tom Heron would later belong. Orage's work for the club, which attracted speakers of the calibre of G.K. Chesterton, stimulated his ambition and in 1905 he settled in London to take his chances as a freelance journalist. Two years later the *New Age,* a failing independent journal, came up for sale, and with the help of fellow-Fabian Bernard Shaw, Orage was able to buy it and create the platform he wanted. He subtitled the paper 'An Independent Socialist Review' and was soon attacking the Webbs' obsession with statistics. Like Penty and S.G. Hobson, Orage split from the Fabians and made the *New Age* the vehicle of Guild Socialism. The period up to 1914 was that of Orage's greatest success: not only did his paper challenge the bureaucratic tendencies of socialism, but its coverage of literary and artistic topics was of the highest calibre. Arnold Bennett spread awareness of European writing; Hulme and Sickert clashed over modern painters; Marinetti expounded his Futurist aesthetics; Bergson, Nietzsche and psychoanalysis were discussed.

From 1915 onwards Orage fell under the spell first, of Mitrinovic, then of Major Douglas, and then, most heavily, of the mysterious George Gurdjieff.[35] In 1922 he abandoned the *New Age* in order to study Gurdjieff's esoteric system.

> 'It would be saying too much to affirm,' said Orage later, 'that I resigned from the *New Age* and from active participation in social reform in order to find God. I only wish that my motives could be as clearly conscious as that would imply.[36]

After a year or so at Gurdjieff's Institute at Fontainebleau, Orage went to New York to teach 'The Work' — as Gurdjieff's system was, and is, called — and was based there for six years. Gradually his interest in journalism and economics reasserted itself and by 1930 he was strong enough to break from Gurdjieff, telling him that he wanted 'to produce and edit the best weekly journal in England.'[37] In 1931 he returned to England for good, convinced that the economic crisis would be the supreme opportunity for propagating the ideas of Social Credit.

When Orage founded the *New English Weekly* in April 1932 Mairet and Newsome at once joined him and Reckitt reported that all those in the Group felt

> that what we had been working for since 1926 had now its opportunity of expression in surroundings which could never compromise whatever of truth might be expressed.[38]

Orage's reappearance in English journalism was widely welcomed: the *NEW*'s first issue contained goodwill messages from a host of writers, among them AE, Richard Aldington, G.D.H. Cole, Havelock Ellis, Eric Gill, S.G. Hobson, Storm Jameson, H.J. Massingham, Edwin Muir and Herbert Read. Massingham regarded the *NEW* as the *New Age*'s reincarnation, despite the latter's continued existence,[39] and although the two papers ran parallel to each other for much of the 1930s, the more youthful of the two was the senior partner.

Orage's death in November 1934 occurred during the night after he had given his only radio talk. This sudden and unexpected bereavement came as a profound blow to his associates, movingly described by Paul Selver.[40]

To keep the *NEW* going a committee was constituted, with Symons, Reckitt, and shortly afterwards Tom Heron, joining Mairet and Newsome. They approached Eliot, who made himself available for consultation about the technicalities of running a periodical. Thus, as Reckitt described it, '"the journal might have been said to have been deposited into the lap of the Chandos Group".'[41] Mairet took on the role of editor at the beginning of 1935.

Webber has described the *NEW* as having a poorly defined corporate identity,[42] but this is not accurate: the paper's aim in the 1930s was explicitly to put the case for Social Credit. In the 1940s the emphasis was on organic husbandry, though as we have seen the two causes were closely connected. Underlying both concerns was the attempt to articulate a Christian perspective on economic and social problems.[43] Indeed, one historian has gone as far as to say that: 'the *New English Weekly* under

Mairet [became] an instrument of God's righteousness,' and Reckitt regarded the paper's task as challenging secularist interpretations of current affairs.[44] The philosophy of organic husbandry was articulated and elaborated within a specifically Christian intellectual context, and the remainder of this chapter will demonstrate that the *NEW* drew together all the strands of the organic movement, looking in turn at the coverage given to farming policy and food production; the mechanization of agriculture; soil erosion and lost fertility; forestry; restoring and maintaining fertility; health and nutrition; rural reconstruction, and the organic interpretation of society.

A forum for organic husbandry

Farming policy and food production

The *New English Weekly* first appeared when *laissez-faire* agricultural policies were being tentatively abandoned after nearly a century, with the government implementing tariffs and quotas, subsidies and reorganization schemes. 1932 saw the Imperial Conference at Ottawa, the Wheat Act, and the appointment of the corporatist Walter Elliot as Minister of Agriculture. A major Agricultural Marketing Act had been passed the previous year and a second was to come the following year, but it is doubtful whether these measures amounted to a coherent policy. The *NEW* saw them as expedients for a crisis while the basic principles of free trade — cheap food and the supreme importance of industry — remained. Adopting Douglas' policies, with government control of credit creation, would make the nation agriculturally self-supporting, with enormous benefits for both health and prosperity. Lymington's book *Horn, Hoof and Corn* was praised for offering not just a policy, but a vision of agriculture's fundamental importance to national life, and in the same issue A.J. Penty introduced another organic theme, the threat of food shortages: Britain should not go on assuming that it could survive by exporting manufactured goods in return for imported foodstuffs. P.C. Loftus saw the situation as financial imperialism, with Britain exacting a tribute of cheap food in order to pacify the increasing urban population, and he drew a parallel with Ancient Rome.[45] Nothing less than a financial revolution was needed, though how this could be achieved without a social or political revolution was unclear.[46] The present system denied people the earth's abundance, exploiting foreign soils and even destroying food for reasons of 'sound economics.' There was more than a whiff of conspiracy theory in the paper's interpretation of Elliot's opposition to a plan for settling thousands of workers on the land: their output would destroy England's dependence on imported food, which benefited trade and finance.[47]

As the decade went on, the likelihood of war provided another reason for encouraging home agriculture, a point made by Loftus in a letter to the Suffolk branch of the National Farmers' Union, and in Lymington's *Famine in England,* reviewed by P.M. — presumably Philip Mairet. Since intensified production brought the risk of lost fertility, a mixed-farming policy was essential; R.C. Price, a former pioneer in North America, described his experience of how monoculture damaged soils. When Sir Reginald Dorman-Smith became Minister of Agriculture in 1939 the *NEW* saw his chief task as achieving maximum output with minimum loss of fertility.[48]

War presented both opportunities and dangers for national agriculture. The *NEW* hoped that there would be a fairer deal for farmers and agricultural workers, and recognition 'that a fertile soil is the nation's greatest possession,' while Lord Bledisloe wrote a long letter suggesting a complete reconstruction of the farming industry. But the interest in reconstruction might have its dangers: H.J. Massingham mauled Sir Daniel Hall's book on the subject, condemning its values as indistinguishable from profit-seeking industrialism, and pointing out that although Hall rejected mixed farming his book included a statistical table showing that highest output per acre was found in countries where it was most common. The editorial 'Notes of the Week' feared that post-war planning might urge that 'inefficient' farmers should be superseded by '"scientific" commissars running big collective farms with more machinery and chemicals.'[49]

The approaching end of the war brought anxieties about whether there would be another 'betrayal' of agriculture as there had been after the First World War. Reviewing Massingham's *Men of Earth,* S. Sagar asked:

> What is going to happen to rural England? ... I do not think we shall be able to let England return again to weeds and scrub ... The land of England will have to be worked. The question is how. Will it be by mechanized scamping?[50]

'Notes of the Week' raised the same spectre a couple of years later. Referring to the Ministers of State responsible for agricultural policy, the 'Notes' wondered:

> Will they be possessed by the technological mania, and try to 'industrialize nature' — flatten the hedgerows, multiply tractors, try to mechanize and chemicalize everything and to multiply yield per man hour regardless?[51]

Discussing the 1947 Agriculture Bill, the 'Notes' were scathing about:

> [the] confidence of our economists that industrial civilisation will always be able to get cheap foodstuffs by ravaging the fertility of one area and then of another.[52]

In a world of food shortages all Europe should be growing as much food as possible; in any case, overseas countries were themselves starting to industrialize and would be less interested in importing manufactured goods. Philip Oyler argued that everything possible should be done to increase both fertility and manpower, with towns obliged to return wastes to the land for the sake of intensive cultivation. Citing the example of the French Revolution, he suggested giving workers land rather than higher wages. Exactly how such measures were to be imposed without the central authority and revolutionary upheaval which the organic school wanted to avoid was unclear. The *NEW* feared State farms run upon industrial lines but was equally mistrustful of Big Business. A review of Carey McWilliams' book on United States migrant labour, *Ill Fares the Land,* condemned Business' ignorance in pursuing a monoculture which could only result in the 'debilitation and erosion of good farm land.'[53]

Massingham's first contribution to the *NEW*[54] had referred to a 'diseased economic system'; as the paper's life drew to a close he applied the same epithet to Britain's farming:

> No agriculture can possibly be other than diseased when it
> employs only 6 per cent of the population, when it is the catspaw
> of a foreign importing and the victim of a home exporting policy
> and when it moves or stagnates at the whim and dictate of a cen-
> tralized industrialism.[55]

To the last, the *NEW* attributed farming's problems to the power of industry and finance, rejected purely economic assessments of agricultural efficiency, and argued for an increased rural population practising intensive husbandry for the sake of national self-sufficiency.

Mechanization

Since the *NEW* was concerned about the decline of rural life, it tended to be hostile to the accelerating process of agricultural mechanization and the assessment of efficiency by measuring output per man. This issue began to emerge seriously in the late 1930s, a time when there was a rapid uptake of tractors. One correspondent drew readers' attention to a speech by the agricultural engineer D.R. Bomford recommending increased use of diesel tractors and inorganic manures. This drew a reply from B.A. Keen, Assistant Director of Rothamsted,[56] who said that the general trend in industry was to have fewer workers, and that agriculture would not be exempt. Such an argument could only serve to strengthen the organicists' conviction that agriculture must not be regarded as a branch of industry.

Roy Wilson's pamphlet *I Believe: An Appeal for the Land,* which was sceptical about the drive to mechanization, was reviewed anonymously at first, and then more fully by Rolf Gardiner. His views on mechanization provoked debate with a Mrs Gladys Bing, a monetary reform enthusiast with thirty years' experience of rural work. Gardiner condemned mechanization as wasteful, arguing that machines were merely tools and should therefore be subject to wider considerations. Mrs Bing dismissed his vision of communal manual labour: '... pretty pictures of happy families singing as they sweat are mere wishful thinking.'[57]

The issue at stake was whether farming was a form of *culture* or of *industrial production;* if the latter, the logical conclusion was indeed to apply industrial standards of efficiency to the methods employed, increase use of machinery at the expense of animals and men, and replace extracted fertility with chemical manures. For the organic school such a policy was based on a philosophical error, that of conceiving nature mechanistically. Jenks termed the error 'Mechanitis,' one of the 'Diseases of Our Time' which he analysed in the *NEW.* 'Notes of the Week' saw the problem as how to subordinate physical science 'to the natural creation on the one hand, and on the other to the soul and spirit of Man.' Profligate use of natural resources had occurred in all ages, but 'the results of it have been magnified out of all proportion by modern power-techniques.'[58] As the 1947 Agriculture Act took its place on the statute book, the *NEW* warned that Britain was in danger of developing mechanized food production

> driven on at a breakneck pace, with tractors, bull-dozers, combine-harvesters and every outrage that mass-mechanism can perpetrate upon normal husbandry.[59]

The *NEW*'s final phase was marked by a prolonged debate on the machine's role in agriculture, as Massingham and Murry clashed in the correspondence columns. Some comments by Massingham provoked Murry to complain of 'arbitrary anathemas against the "artificial" — machine or manure,' to which Massingham responded by arguing that machines were standardized and inflexible, leading to a loss of the creative satisfaction in work that craftsmanship offered; their effect was to encourage large-scale, extensive farming. Rolf Gardiner and Ralph

Coward weighed in on Massingham's side, while Murry in turn referred to the use of machinery by Sir George Stapledon and Friend Sykes: the countryside certainly required fertile land and satisfied workers, but an experimental approach to farming techniques would lead to appropriate use of machinery, which *had* brought benefits.[60]

Soil erosion and lost fertility

One of the most influential texts in the organic canon was the study of worldwide soil erosion by G.V. JACKS and R.O. WHYTE, *The Rape of the Earth,* but the *NEW* had expressed concern about the problem before the book appeared in 1939. Two years earlier 'Notes of the Week' had drawn attention to a statement on Empire soil erosion by E.J. Russell, commenting that a cheap food policy must finally result in wilderness or desert; the same issue carried an article on North American dust storms, 'Where Nature Rebels.' Kenneth Barlow saw the land's fertility as a social responsibility, its loss bringing more than purely agricultural repercussions: 'To injure the fertility of the soil is to start a rot in the heart of a people which no industry can check'; and G.T. Wrench, whose book on the Hunzas Barlow reviewed, contributed a two-part article on 'Philosophy of the Soil,' regretting that no clear policy of soil protection had ever been developed in England. Shortly after Wrench's article appeared, Sir Albert Howard contributed a two-part piece on soil fertility as the basis of a national health policy, arguing that traditional Chinese wisdom in observing the Rule of Return could no longer be ignored 'by people who have brought themselves and the world they live in to the verge of the abyss.' 'Notes of the Week' were similarly apocalyptic, identifying the financial system as chief culprit in the crime of soil erosion, whose inevitable result would be a world wheat shortage. The 'Dust Bowl' provided a fearful example of the potential danger; G.V. Jacks said that Canada and Australia were moving in the same direction and that Britain herself was living off reserves of fertility built up over centuries.[61]

Proposals by the 1943 Conference on Food and Agriculture were likely, in the *NEW*'s opinion, to exacerbate the threat of erosion. Its report stated that industrial expansion must precede the long-term rehabilitation of agriculture; in other words, commented Jorian Jenks, the Conference wanted to flog the earth still further and to remove barriers to international trade, those barriers being 'one of the very few forms of protection which the soil has had.' Portsmouth's book *Alternative to Death* identified soil erosion as the result of 'the centralized power of international finance' — a thinly coded reference to Jewish conspiracies — but Kenneth Barlow saw the problem as essentially religious: 'The dismal story of soil erosion is a reminder of the sanctions which Natural Law can and does impose upon the law breaker.'[62]

In the post-war period the journal took considerable interest in Africa. As we have seen, South Africa instituted large-scale municipal composting, and there was the fiasco of the Groundnuts Scheme, with the *NEW* predictably sceptical about such imposed monoculture.[63] Rolf Gardiner, who knew Africa well, reported severe soil erosion in Uganda and Nyasaland. Tribesmen were suffering from hunger and malnutrition, and a Nyasaland report identified improved nutrition as correlated with increased soil fertility. Africa's situation was desperate 'unless and until her peoples learn to care for and cherish her poor soil as devotedly as they now grub beneath it for gold and diamonds.' 'Notes of the Week' identified the rape of the earth as a world disease, and praised the late President Roosevelt for initiating flood and erosion control. W.T. Symons, under his pseudonym 'Pontifex III,' commented favourably on Russia's agro-biological plans, which aimed to conserve fertility through ley farming, extended forestry, and protection of water supplies.[64] In this case, at least, the organic school's claim to be non-political had some justification.

Forestry

The Russian plans to increase tree-cover identified an important aspect of the problem of soil erosion, and one which the *NEW* had noted several times. Before the war, Henry G. Finlayson of the Men of the Trees had referred to an unnamed ecologist who believed that civilizations which felled their virgin forests and organized the transportation of water would inevitably fade out. Rolf Gardiner pointed to Nazi Germany's supposed success in regenerating civilization through its care of forests and development of mixed woodlands. G.C. Watson's book *The Soil and Social Reclamation,* reviewed immediately before war broke out, stressed the importance of planting trees in the catchment area of rivers. The commercial imperative of short-term profit lay behind much of the destruction, and it was ironic that a capitalist system should be so sanguine about the squandering of true capital, with timber being wasted on 'needless newsprint.' A correspondent drew attention to the rapid decline in soil fertility when tropical forests were felled and replaced by monocultural crop production, and Ronald Duncan, echoing Sir Albert Howard's views in the opening pages of *An Agricultural Testament,* believed that the fertility of forest soils provided strong evidence for the value of compost.[65]

A year or so before the paper ceased publication, Michael Brant's article on German forestry sparked off a lengthy debate. Brant completely rejected the idea that the Nazis had protected German forests: on the contrary, they had reduced their acreage to three-quarters of the 1933 figure, with results which would affect climate and impoverish agriculture. A correspondent who wrote in to dispute that deforestation affected climate found ranged against him Richard St Barbe Baker (whose book *Green Glory* the *NEW* reviewed) and John Stewart Collis.[66]

If the *NEW* was prophetic about the effects of deforestation, it was equally percipient in warning against some of the proposed remedies. Massingham, reviewing the Scott Report on rural land use, found it too favourable to the Forestry Commission, which regarded woodlands as 'timber-factories' rather than as an integral part of farm husbandry. Howard wrote in to say that re-forestation required land that was in good heart, but the Forestry Commission worked without the livestock whose manure would have fed the soil, while Gardiner condemned the dissociation of forestry from farming as bureaucratic compartmentalism. The problem was not just fragmentation, but monoculture. Massingham drew attention to the extensive plantation at Bala in North Wales, where family farmers had been dispossessed to make way for spruce trees. 'Notes of the Week' referred to the most authoritative voice of all, Sir George Stapledon, whose *Rural Economy* article on regeneration of hill lands had called for co-ordination of agriculture, forestry and industry.[67]

The *NEW* carried advertisements for the Men of the Trees, and the paper had a personal link with that organization: Philip Mairet spoke at its Summer School in 1947, his address on 'The Ecological Basis of Civilization' offering one of the clearest statements of the organic philosophy.[68]

Restoring and maintaining fertility

In an obituary notice for Sir Albert Howard, 'Pontifex III' described him as the man who 'led the world in the constructive alternative to artificial fertilisers,' and revealed that he had from 1936 onwards 'often and generously contributed to this journal, as a specialist writer, reviewer and adviser.' Certainly his influence was being strongly felt by the summer of 1940, when a correspondent complained about the *NEW*'s 'manure-complex.'[69]

The first signs of the manure-complex were evident in 1937, when a pseudonymous contributor, 'Gens,' wrote that soil erosion resulted from ignoring the science of manuring, and that exploiters of colonial lands were acting 'in defiant ignorance of soil chemistry, agro-biology or anything whatever but bank-loans and the prices rigged in the capitals of the world.'[70]

Early in 1939 Howard contributed a two-part article on 'Soil Fertility: A National Health Policy,' in which he held up Chinese cultivation as the supreme example of husbandry and referred to Sir Bernard Greenwell's use of municipal composting. In the letters column he disputed the validity of the Rothamsted experiments and suggested that the Rothamsted soils were exhausted by mismanagement, an imputation rejected in the following issue by Rothamsted's Assistant Director B.A. Keen.[71]

During the war the case for humus was pressed with increasing frequency. Rothamsted's centenary year, 1943, was particularly lively. Jenks seized the opportunity to survey 'The Great Humus Controversy,' and was willing to concede that chemical fertilizers could be valuable as supplements to muck and compost. What he disliked was the attempt to force up output without increasing expenditure on manpower. He claimed that many farmers were unhappy about 'the double boost given to the use of nitrogenous stimulants by the chemical combine and the Ministry of Agriculture.' Howard shared this anxiety, again casting doubt on Rothamsted's scientific methods. That autumn, the 'great humus controversy' reached the House of Lords, when noble sympathizers with the organic cause — Bledisloe, Glentanar, Portsmouth, Teviot and Warwick — criticized the Ministry of Agriculture's policy on artificials; the *NEW* referred to the debate, with sardonic comments about the influence of ICI. A fortnight later 'Notes of the Week' discerned collusion between the government and fertilizer manufacturers, suggesting that a large-scale chemical fertilizer industry would be an advantage for future military purposes, and that a government with no clear idea of what agriculture was would be vulnerable to vested interests.[72]

The year 1943 was also important for the publication of Lady Balfour's *The Living Soil.* Stapledon reviewed the book for the *NEW,* with sympathy but not uncritically. He found it rather too lyrical about the balance of nature, and noted that Lady Balfour attached more weight to writers like Howard, Rayner and Wrench than to more orthodox soil chemists and biochemists.[73] Nevertheless, it would have been unscientific to assume she was wrong; Stapledon stressed scientists' ignorance of all the environmental factors which affect human health.

Several major texts in the organic canon appeared during the war and were duly noted by the *NEW*: Symons reviewed Northbourne's *Look to the Land;* Anthony Ludovici gave Massingham's *England and the Farmer* a mixed review which sparked off a vitriolic exchange of letters between the two men, and S. Sagar reviewed Portsmouth's *Alternative to Death.*[74]

The campaign for organic farming continued unabated after the war, with reviews of Howard's edition of Darwin's study of earthworms and his major survey of the organic farming movement, *Farming and Gardening for Health or Disease.* J.J. — presumably Jenks — reviewed Sykes' *Humus and the Farmer* and, to show that the paper was fair-minded, or to help further increase Faber's sales, Stapledon reviewed Donald Hopkins' attack on the organic case, *Chemicals, Humus, and the Soil.* The case for municipal composting was taken up after Howard's death by Cecil Bachelor, who argued optimistically that there would be no need to import artificial fertilizers if more councils followed the lead of Leatherhead and Maidenhead. Above all, there was the founding of the Soil Association, noted by 'Pontifex III'; he outlined the Association's aims and referred to its forthcoming journal.[75] When the *NEW* folded, in September 1949, the Soil Association Council included among its members four frequent contributors to the *NEW:* Barlow, Gardiner, Massingham and Portsmouth, while a fifth, Jorian Jenks, was Editorial Secretary.

Health and nutrition

The *NEW*'s importance in the history of the organic movement is demonstrated by its publication of the Cheshire doctors' *Medical Testament.* Some years later, though, the reviewer of Doris Grant's *Your Daily Bread,* which included the *Testament* in full, regretted that 'the author fails to mention that this journal first gave it publicity.'[76] It was fair comment: the Testament originally appeared as a special supplement stapled into the *NEW*'s 6 April 1939 issue.

We have already seen that the organic school's concern for humus-rich soils was inseparable from a concern for health, and readers will not be surprised to learn that the *NEW* gave considerable coverage to health issues. Interest in the work of Scott Williamson and Pearse was evident even before Mairet became editor, with their book *The Case for Action* being reviewed.[77] A couple of years later Kenneth Barlow wrote a feature article on the new purpose-built Pioneer Health Centre and he also reviewed the Centre's interim report *Biologists in Search of Material.* In other pre-war pieces he condemned the financial system for denying large sections of the community the right to nourishment, and in a review of Boyd Orr's *Food, Health and Income* urged a conscious policy to meet people's nutritional needs. The prolific agricultural writer A.G. Street also supported Boyd Orr's view that agriculture and health policies should be integrated. As well as the *Medical Testament,* the *NEW* published another important supplement in the spring of 1939, printing the speeches made by Boyd Orr, Lord Horder and Lord Sempill at the Economic Reform Club, on 'Health and Agriculture.'[78]

Early in the war P.M. — presumably Mairet — reviewed two of Edgar Saxon's books, describing him as 'one of the first to relate the science of nutrition to its natural basis in the living earth.' The *NEW* regularly carried advertisements for *Health and Life,* and itself at times presented the positive ideal of health which Saxon's journal strove for. Mere absence of disease did not count as health, and Saxon argued that the official idea of health as represented in the White Paper on the medical services was nothing more than palliation of debility.[79]

The *NEW* became increasingly alarmist as the war neared its end. According to Friend Sykes, agriculture was militating against health and making possible another Black Death. This drew a scathing response from Chandos Group member Hilderic Cousens, who said that it was fortunate that the case for organic methods rested on 'the results achieved by its practitioners and not ... on the fantastic reasoning some of them see fit to adopt.' Cousens drew a fusillade of hostility from Barlow, Howard and Massingham, while a more balanced assessment came from G.E. Breen, editor of the *Medical Press and Circular,* who supported Howard's efforts to base national nutrition on a healthy soil but was not prepared 'to promise everybody that human disease will vanish as soon as this has been achieved.' Stapledon also distanced himself from the full humus-school enthusiasts. Reviewing Hopkins' book, he said it had not been proved that plants grown with chemicals could not be healthy; nevertheless, he was willing to believe that 'the master key that will open the important doors to super-health is a complete understanding of the conditions governing soil fertility.'[80]

The proposals for a National Health Service came under scrutiny at this time. Howard wanted a preventive policy, arguing that for a fraction of the sums to be spent on treatment, restoration of soil fertility could ensure that fresh healthy produce was provided for the people's mealtables. Sir Ernest Graham-Little pointed out that Health Centres would disappear. On the other hand, 'Pontifex III' was enthusiastic about some features of the emerging Welfare State, referring particularly to the improvement of children's nutrition resulting from orange juice, school milk and school meals.[81]

The question of bread's nutritional value received prominent coverage. During the war white bread's apparent lack of value became a matter of national concern, and the *NEW* was, as ever, quick to spot commercial forces at work, revealing that the committee appointed to investigate the matter included three representatives of powerful milling interests. J.L. Benvenisti produced a three-part article on the quality of flour, a thorough piece of investigative journalism which lent weight to the *NEW*'s conspiracy theory by showing, among other things, that the cereals division of the Ministry of Food was staffed largely by members of the milling trade, and that the nutritionally valuable wheatgerm missing from bread was going at preferential rates to particular firms. Nourishing items were being filched and sold for commercial profit; the public needed protection from such parasitic dishonesty. Problems with bread continued after the war: Sir Ernest Graham-Little revealed[82] that the Ministry of Food had secretly ordered millers to double the quota of chalk in the National Loaf. In a letter to the *NEW* he claimed:

> It is an open secret that the Milling Combine is constantly trying to revert to the halcyon period when they could supply to the public flour of 70 per cent extraction, and sell at a fantastic profit, to makers of patent foods and medicines, the residue of the grain, which in fact contains its most valuable constituents.[83]

The organic school favoured wholemeal bread, but where could it be found when local mills had been replaced by combines? For Ralph Coward the existence of local milling was a sign of a healthy body politic.[84] The bread question raised other questions about the state of rural life in general.

Rural reconstruction

An early issue of the *NEW* noted Montague Fordham's election as President of the Rural Reconstruction Association, but otherwise rural matters were scarcely touched on before the Second World War. The issue became more prominent once war had broken out, with Rolf Gardiner seeing an opportunity for England to 'rise from the ashes of her commercialism'; in a sermon at Sherborne School he told the boys that they would 'all become English yeomen and husbandmen again.' He saw the vogue for books on agriculture as a reaction against the 'criminal neglect' of the countryside, praising Stapledon's *The Land* for its 'fecund and intensely practical guide to regeneration.' The same issue carried an advertisement for a harvest camp at Gardiner's estate, a place which brought the young 'in touch with the living earth and the primal tasks of existence.' As the war continued, Gardiner's ambitions grew: he started thinking of rural life in terms of regions, their history, culture and resources. These regions would require their own aristocracy: men like — well, like Gardiner himself, but 'Dukes Not Gauleiters' he explained, lest readers drew the wrong conclusions. His regionalism attracted support from Barlow and Portsmouth, the former seeing it as a counterbalance to the Mass Market and the latter recommending that:

free rein should be given to individual experiments in education,
and the formation of units which are based on the resources and
needs of the soil.[85]

No doubt such experiments would have included the camps Portsmouth
ran on his Hampshire estate.

Other aspects of rural life referred to included Village Colleges and
agricultural education in general. The Luxmoore Report recognized the
need for its extension, a view supported by a correspondent who saw
urban values dominating the educational system and pointed to the success of Young Farmers' Clubs. Rural England had blossomed because of
the war, but the *NEW* was anxious about what would happen afterwards.
S. Sagar identified Massingham's *Men of Earth* as 'a guide to ... the stable and permanent way, the organic way of life.' The journal also considered the Church's role in rural society, with pamphlets written for the
Council for the Church and Countryside by Massingham, DAVID PECK
and Jorian Jenks being reviewed by J.J. — which, assuming that these initials indicated Jenks himself, was a remarkably incestuous piece of journalism even by the organic school's standards.[86]

Interest in rural problems remained prominent in the post-war period,
with the *NEW* arguing that agriculture was of central importance to a
revived countryside. A highly mechanized agriculture, though, was undesirable because it would further diminish the rural population. Perhaps
redundant industrial workers could be moved to rural occupations, or
young men and women could replace the German land-workers who
would soon be repatriated.[87] Rural life was in many ways unappealing,
though, caught in a vicious circle of low wages, depopulation and lack of
facilities. 'Notes of the Week,' referring to the Labour Government's
urban bias, wished:

> that our 'ruralist' writers ... had concentrated their propaganda
> more specifically on the demand for a high priority for rural hous-
> ing, for few or none of the reforms they desiderate can be carried
> out until this need is met.[88]

Massingham responded to this lofty rebuke by pointing out (with justice)
that the 'ruralist' writers had written frequently about the state of housing.[89]

Middleton Murry envisaged a countryside with an electricity supply,
good cottages, producer co-operatives and lively parish councils. None of
these would be possible, though, unless organic husbandry was the basis
of the revived social order.[90]

Earth, nature, and the organic analogy

In 1950 Jorian Jenks published his book *From the Ground Up,* which expressed the organic school's conviction that no civilization or culture could be stable unless rooted in the earth. He had adumbrated the same principle in the *NEW* some years earlier, when reporting on the United States Conference on Food and Agriculture: '... all enduring civilisation is built upwards from the soil, and downward from human desires.'[91] No nation, therefore, could survive without a strong rural component, since the earth was the mother of all life.

An outlook which attaches such importance to the earth and to the organic components of human life is likely to tend in religion to paganism and in politics to Fascism. The *NEW*'s religious stance was in fact distinctly Christian, as the next chapter will demonstrate, though some contributions to it smacked of nature-worship. Its politics are harder to define: George Orwell, a keen Fascist-spotter who worked closely with Mairet in the late 1930s, declared unequivocally that the *NEW* was not pro-Fascist; G.C. Webber, and, more hesitantly, Desmond Hawkins, place the journal on the Right.[92] Certainly there were several 'fellow-travellers of the Right' among its regular contributors, and although it was always anti-Nazi it occasionally exhibited in its early days a certain sympathy for Italy. While regarding Nazism as demonic, it wanted to emphasize the importance of the biological realm and of the soil for human life and society. 'Pontifex,' the pseudonym of Chandos Group member Albert Newsome, wrote in 1938:

> Blood and soil, race and earth, may not be evil gods — so long as they are not the supreme gods. As the only gods, they are devils and possession by them means madness.[93]

This was the tightrope which the *NEW* tried to walk, and over the years it printed a fair amount of debate on the extent to which human life and society should be interpreted organically.

The idea of the earth as Mother was expounded in a three-part article by 'Collum,' who said that it had been largely filtered out of Nordic and Jewish thought, though once it had been world-wide.[94] The ancient religions held a moral warning for twentieth-century civilization, since the earth's barrenness taught humanity 'to treat her honourably by the sheer logic of the consequences of our neglect.' The Earth's needs were prior to humanity's, a moral reinforced in G.T. Wrench's attempt to articulate a 'Philosophy of the Soil.' A nation's survival depended on recognizing its dependence on its soil. Kenneth Barlow took up this point again during the war, saying that the *NEW* had consistently maintained 'that the devel-

opment of the inner quality of a people requires that its roots in the soil
... shall be preserved.' Rolf Gardiner considered the existence of a peasantry fundamental to civilization, it being 'the matrix of culture, the
humus from which all talents are fed.'[95]

Gardiner and his associates teetered on the brink of 'Blood and Soil' in
this way because they believed that an organic interpretation of the world
was more adequate and inclusive than a mechanistic one. Not merely the
soil, but the whole pattern of nature had to be respected. Charles F. Bennett described 'Mother Nature' as 'an infinitely more complex and ingen-
ious chemist than her "insurgent son" Man,' and, in distinctly Steinerian
terminology, said that in the relation of animal and vegetable life to cosmic and solar radiation was to be found 'a highly complex inter-relation-
ship of all forms of matter and energy, physical and psychical.' Lord
Northbourne, who was sympathetic to Steiner's ideas, expressed a similar
view in a letter about hydroponics (soil-less culture), saying that: 'There
is no living thing which is not affected in some way ... by every other living thing';[96] the whole universe, in other words, was an organism.

Order and balance are key concepts in organic thought: 'Notes of the
Week' believed that if the order and balance of nature were respected
through 'true culture and harmonious co-operation, it is hard to say
whether Man or Nature is more the master or the beneficiary.' According
to the organic school, nature was a malign force only if mistreated. Barlow's *The Discipline of Peace,* with its call to respect the 'architecture' of
the natural world, was hailed as the starting-point for a philosophy of rec-
onciliation between modern man and the universe he inhabited.[97]

Some of the *NEW*'s contributors were wary of the organic analogy's
political implications. 'Gens' noted that totalitarians 'all want their own
nations centralised, functionalised on the pattern of a biological organism,' and subsequently produced a more detailed study of the concept of
an 'Organic Society.' While to some extent accepting the validity of the
organic analogy he firmly rejected its identification in Fascist states with
political activity alone, but argued that it was preferable to a mechanistic
conception because it made people 'less likely to ignore the environmental relations of Society.' One correspondent saw the organic as a threat to
the human: 'If a fully inclusive, totalitarian polity, that is, an organism,
could emerge, men as men would perish.' But the most sustained attack
on the organic analogy came from S.G. Hobson, in a scathing review of
Bio-Politics by Morley Roberts, a book which used the idea of a social
organism to justify slavery, anti-semitism and aristocratic oligarchies.
Hobson believed that thought and spiritual progress had to some extent
removed humanity from the thraldom of the purely biological. 'Notes of

the Week' made essentially the same point later the same year, 1938, in a paragraph entitled 'The Phantasy of the "Organic" State.' The writer rejected the 'phantasy' as incompatible with the entire Classical and Christian tradition, which was 'implacably opposed to such a Leviathan.'[98] Society was not the result of an organic process, but was:

> something we make together ... a creation objective to us, something of a totally different order from the biological works of nature, although constructed in relation with them.[99]

A decade later, though, the *NEW* was still arguing for a more organic, less mechanistic, view of society, defining it as a conception

> founded upon observation of the real motives of human beings, of the forces and ideas which in fact make them co-operate with each other and with other beings of Nature.[100]

Such a conception was preferable to the chaos of *laissez-faire,* but the *NEW* did not, in the end, accept nature as the ultimate reality. Nature was itself an expression of the divine spirit which had created it and given it form. Human beings were spiritual as well as biological, and the best way of life was one which could do justice to both these aspects. As 'Notes of the Week' expressed it at Christmas 1947: 'We have nothing else, ultimately, to rely upon but this, the Divine image in man, and faith that it will never be effaced.'[101]

* * *

The instances offered in this chapter only scratch the surface of the *NEW*'s commitment to the organic cause: a wealth of material can be found in its pages, particularly from 1939 onwards. Nevertheless, the case for the paper's unique importance in the organic movement's development should by now have been substantiated. The *NEW* drew together all the main strands into a coherent, if controversial, view of society and man's place in the natural order, consistently arguing that no proposals for social or economic reform could be of value unless they recognized humanity's dependence upon the biological constraints of its creatureliness.

Mairet wrote in the *NEW*'s final issue on 8 September 1949:

> Our work has been of wider effect than the provision of a place for intelligent comment and controversy, or of a seed-bed for ideas. Some of the causes we have espoused have drawn a vital strength from our weekly insistence, which has promoted action upon them elsewhere.[102]

This was particularly true of the *NEW*'s most significant legacy, the organic movement, which, as will by now be clear, was about much more than agriculture: it was a critique of the underlying assumptions and values of industrial society and of the culture of secular modernity, urging a re-think of Western civilization's relationship to the natural world. As such, it helped prepare the way for the environmentalism which has developed since the 1960s, but in contrast with more recent trends, Eastern and pagan religious philosophies played a much less significant part in the organic school's enviromental thought than might be imagined. Its context was a set of ideas termed 'Christian sociology,' and it is to this theological matrix that we must finally turn.

11. The Christian Context of Organic Husbandry

In the late 1980s I attended the annual Schumacher Lectures at Bristol's imposing Colston Hall — evidently Small was no longer Beautiful — and was invited to lunch at a nearby health food restaurant with some luminaries of the New Age. During the meal discussion turned to E.F. Schumacher himself and his conversion to Roman Catholicism. That such a prominent environmentalist should have been a Catholic was evidently a deep embarrassment to these admirers. The received wisdom of the New Age is that the Judaeo-Christian tradition is incompatible with reverence for the environment, and that only through renewal of pantheistic or pagan religion will industrial societies find their way back to a harmonious relationship with nature.

A key text in this orthodoxy is Lynn White Jr.'s 1967 article in *Science,* 'The Historic Roots of Our Ecologic [*sic*] Crisis.' White attributed the environmental crisis to the belief that nature exists only to serve man, condemning this idea as arrogant and blaming it for technology's destructive impact on the natural world. He declared that the Judaeo-Christian tradition's emphasis on God's transcendence, and its destruction of pagan animism, enabled it 'to exploit nature in a mood of indifference to the feeling of natural objects.' After momentarily realizing that 'When one speaks in such sweeping terms, a note of caution is in order,' White was immediately off again, painting a picture of missionaries spending two thousand years chopping down sacred groves, since 'To a Christian a tree can be no more than a physical fact.' (One wonders what St Barbe Baker would have made of such an assertion.) As authority for this statement he adduced the newly-elected Governor of California, who 'spoke for the Christian tradition when he said (as is alleged), "when you've seen one redwood tree you've seen them all".'[1] It is as well to pause here to consider the logic of White's argument: he presents Ronald Reagan as representative of the Christian attitude to nature on the basis of something Reagan is *alleged* to have said about redwoods. Suddenly the line of thought appears less than compelling.

White's essay holds other surprises: the fact that he reveals himself to be a churchman, albeit 'troubled,'[2] is one of them; furthermore, he rejects Zen as a possible alternative to Christianity and proposes as patron saint of environmentalism St Francis of Assisi who, as he makes clear, was not a pantheist.

A decade or so later the American farmer-writer Wendell Berry produced a thoughtful article in reply to White's outburst,[3] but in fact a full and detailed response to its themes already existed when it appeared. This was a long essay by Philip Mairet, *Bailiff for God's Estate on Earth,* written in the mid-1960s for the Council for the Church and Countryside and fated, despite its importance, to complete obscurity.[4] It was the fruit of many years of reading and thinking about the attitude which Christians should adopt towards the natural world.

During the First World War Mairet, a conscientious objector, went to live and work at the Ditchling community of the sculptor Eric Gill. He did not follow Gill into the Roman Catholic Church, but his membership of the Chandos Group led him eventually to join the Anglican communion, into which he was formally received in 1943.[5] This was no sudden conversion; in 1939 he had written to his friend Neil Montgomery:

> But as to having to admit all that the Church claims in its Christology, I came to that conclusion very many years ago ... It is not an exaggeration to say that it has dominated my thoughts for the last twenty years.[6]

The natural law

Mairet was widely read in Eastern and Western religious thought, translated books by the French philosophers Jean-Paul Sartre and Emmanuel Mounier, and was closely associated with Dr J.H. Oldham, one of the Christian world's most influential figures during the first half of the twentieth century. Oldham founded the Christian Frontier Council and Mairet edited, with Alec Vidler, its journal *Frontier* during the 1950s.[7] The two men had also collaborated on *Natural Law: A Christian Re-consideration,* a study which Vidler edited in the mid-1940s, and in which can be seen the outlines of a Christian environmental philosophy.

The book began by observing that the idea of Natural Law was reappearing in discussion of social ethics and political philosophy but that there was a lack of contemporary literature on the topic. Vidler had convened a working group to see what value the idea might have for the post-war world, since economists were being asked to take account of the ends for which economic activity is carried on. 'But what are these ends, and how might reference to them ... affect judgment about the use of e.g. machinery, money, the soil, animals?' The concept of Natural Law pre-supposed God as Creator and Preserver and was a law in the sense that it delineated 'the pattern of the creature's activity by which its true end will be attained.'[8] Since the natural end of Man was God, economic activity could not be an end in itself. The section of the book dealing with eco-nomics bears all the hallmarks of Mairet's writing, encapsulating the essence of the organic philosophy and linking it to the Christian interpre-tation of Natural Law.[9]

It begins by referring to the way in which humans are able partly to transcend their life's given material conditions, and deduces that technol-ogy is an expression of man's spirit, since man is:

> a being who is in nature but also transcends nature, and who finds
> a certain spiritual satisfaction and fulfilment in expressing the
> fact.[10]

But the wealth produced by power technics (the phrase indicates the influence of Mairet's friend Lewis Mumford) had been accompanied by destruction of natural resources, raising the urgent question of whether some balance should be observed between manipulation of nature on one hand and obedience to natural conditions on the other: the former could result in arrogance, the latter in unimaginative subservience. Technologi-cal developments had altered humanity's attitude:

> not only to the materials used in techno-facture, but also to the
> vegetable and animal life upon which man's own subsistence
> depends. In the absence of theonomic [sic] criteria about these
> things, we have no directives as to the limits (if any) within which
> this kind of thinking is valid in the sphere of man's relation with
> nature.[11]

Consequently, a widened conception of cultivation was required:

> *In economic terms we seek to maintain the 'capital values' inher-*
> *ent in natural resources, as, e.g. all-round husbandry.*
>   These 'natural resources' include human members of a society,
> with their morals, traditions, inherited abilities and capacities for
> new creation. Hence the economic problem is not patient of a
> merely conservative solution. It is clear that an organic solution
> does, however, imply the moderation of man's growing ability to
> bend natural processes to his will, by a redefinition of the ends to

which he directs it. The faculty in which he feels a somewhat illusory 'power over' nature, needs to be tempered at the source by a
humility before nature. This is unlikely to occur unless we can formulate certain right principles, right attitudes, and even some precise limiting factors and sanctions inherent in the situation, of
which formulations there is as yet a plentiful lack.[12]

Only a return to belief in Natural Law, the writer concluded, could offer
a means by which the increased power of technology might be restrained.
All political systems in the western world relied on technological solutions to economic problems, and could not survive a breakdown of
humanity's relations with nature.

Vidler's book was reviewed in the *NEW* by the Rev Joseph Dalby.[13]

Mairet contributed a chapter on the same themes to Maurice Reckitt's
symposium *Prospect for Christendom.* Despite his reservations about
technology he did not oppose its uses or try to turn the clock back; he saw
technological achievements as being as great in their way as the Egyptian
pyramids or medieval cathedrals. The problem was how to use technology in a way compatible with human and biological nature; for this reason he was interested in the great experiment of the Tennessee Valley
Authority, in which a technological nation attempted to restore 'the natural, territorial organism upon which it is grafted.'[14] Mairet concluded that:

in religion alone, is the primary and continual source of the cultural spirit ... Out of Nature are our societies born, in their technics
they die, but through Religion they are regenerated. A re-born society can go on developing ever greater technical powers, so long as
it uses, and is not used by them. But when it succumbs to the fasci-
nation and the power of technics, it loses not only its sense of the
supernatural order, but also its foothold upon natural life.[15]

Bailiff for God's Estate on Earth, written about twenty years after the
essay for the Christendom Group, was Mairet's attempt to persuade the
Church to re-define, or re-examine, Christian teaching on man's place in
nature.[16] Like Lynn White Jr., he was disappointed at the lack of any
movement of theological thought towards a recovery of respect for
nature.

The only powerful theological writer who seems fully aware of
what is at stake — and his Divinity is more unorthodox than representative — is Dr Albert Schweitzer, with his almost Buddhistic
doctrine of 'Reverence for Life.'[17]

Mairet believed that humanity could not be reconciled with nature unless it was first reconciled with God, but:

> that does not mean that we can put off our work upon Nature till we have worked out our spiritual salvation. The two things are one and the same, inside and outside of the one great redemptive work. The transfiguration of the realm of Nature will be — and even is — the outward aspect of the restoration by grace of our human nature. If there is to be any goal of collective salvation on earth for us to work for, it must include the perfecting of all the other life upon which Man's life depends and by which it is enriched ... And a people is seen to be on the road towards this goal if and when its powers are directed more and more to such things as the reclamation of wastes and deserts, the beautifying of landscapes, purifying of waters, perfecting of species of plants and animals. And, last but not least, when it employs not as few as possible but as many as possible of its people in this sanest, healthiest and happiest of all human occupations — that of improving, ordering and beautifying the surface of this planet, the Earth, which is the particular garden of God entrusted to our care. Here is infinite scope for all the analytical lore and technical mastery acquired since the scientific revolution. To what other end could they be sensibly employed?[18]

These, then, were the beliefs of the man who, as editor of the *NEW,* enabled the organic movement to develop its ecological philosophy. Who now remembers Mairet? The poet C.H. Sisson, who contributed to the *NEW* in the 1940s, has with justice said that Mairet's name has been all but expunged from the record of the Church of England's twentieth-century social thought.[19] For that matter, he has been expunged from accounts of the life of T.S. Eliot, who dedicated *Notes Towards the Definition of Culture* to him 'in gratitude and admiration,'[20] worked with him on the editorial board of the *NEW,* in which three of the *Four Quartets* first appeared, as special supplements, and was a fellow-member of the Chandos Group for many years. Yet Eliot's recent biographer Lyndall Gordon makes no reference to Mairet.[21]

Eliot's commitment to Anglo-Catholicism is of course well known; less well known is his connection with the organic movement.[22] In fact it should not come as a surprise, given his role as a director of Faber and Faber. Two of Eliot's books express ideas important to the organic school.

A sympathizer with Social Credit, Eliot wrote in *The Idea of a Christian Society* of the need for 'changes in our organisation of industry and commerce and financial credit' because industrialism was incompatible with Christian living and created people who were 'detached from tradition, alienated from religion, and susceptible to mass suggestion.'[23] The profit motive had become a social ideal, with the result that various problems had to be tackled, including:

> the distinction between the *use* of natural resources and their exploitation, the use of labour and its exploitation, the advantages accruing to the trader in contrast to the primary producer, the misdirection of the financial machine [and] the iniquity of usury.[24]

Eliot believed that religious faith implied a life in conformity with nature, 'natural life and the supernatural life hav[ing] a conformity to each other which neither has with the mechanistic life.' A wrong attitude to nature implied a wrong attitude to God, and a society which believed in nothing but commercial, mechanized values would do well 'to face the permanent conditions upon which God allows us to live upon this planet.'[25]

Eliot devoted a chapter of *Notes Towards the Definition of Culture* to the importance of the region, recommending — somewhat ironically, in view of his own transatlantic origins — the desirability of people remaining in the region where they were born.[26] The organic analogy is evident in his picture of:

> a national culture which will draw its vitality from the cultures of its several areas, within each of which again there will be smaller units of culture having their own local peculiarities.[27]

In other words, within the cultural organism are cells whose health is vital to the health of the whole. Eliot believed families to be the most important means of transmitting a culture, and praised the Pioneer Health Centre for its encouragement of family life.[28]

During the 1940s the other members of the *NEW*'s editorial board were Orage's widow Jessie and, later in the decade, his son Richard; Maurice Reckitt; Tom Heron; W.T. Symons, and P.L. Travers. Jessie and Richard Orage appear to have played no significant part, if any at all, in contributing to the content. Pamela Travers, best known as the author of *Mary Poppins,* was chiefly concerned with the literary and artistic columns; her work for the journal resulted from friendship with Orage which in turn derived from her devotion to AE.[29] She was an expert on mythology and symbolism who would perhaps have been more in tune with New Age ideas than with Anglo-Catholicism; she was also involved in the 'esoteric Christianity' of Gurdjieff's disciples. Not a member of the board, but a long-term fixture as music critic, was the venomous right-wing composer K.S. Sorabji, who believed that the Roman Catholic Church was to be thanked for whatever of value remained in European culture.[30] Of the other three members of the board Reckitt is most important, but before we examine his role in developing Christian Sociology, Heron and Symons deserve mention.

Tom Heron has received some attention in recent years as a consequence of his son Patrick's eminent position in twentieth-century British art.[31] Another of his sons, Giles, married Mary Barran, who was personal assistant to Lady Balfour in the late 1950s and early '60s.[32]

Brought up in Yorkshire, Heron came to know the art critic Herbert Read through the Leeds Art Club, and in the 1920s spent some time in Cornwall, where he knew the potter Bernard Leach. An early Fabian, Heron was active in Labour politics, subscribed to the *New Age,* and, through involvement with that paper, became a supporter of Major Douglas; he did not, however, end up on the Right. With his friend Alec Walker he ran Crysede Silks, later establishing his own company, the highly successful Cresta Silks, in Welwyn Garden City. He was the moving force behind wartime Utility Clothing, working with the Board of Trade. His younger sister Kathleen was apprentice to Mairet's wife, the noted weaver Ethel Mairet.

In 1921 Heron converted to Anglo-Catholicism, influenced by the Mirfield Fathers, and five years later wrote a pamphlet called *Christian Vocation in Industry and Marketing.* Although about commerce, not agriculture, it reveals a number of familiar concerns, regretting the lack of any Christian social philosophy for an industrial society, and offering a wider conception of economy than mere monetary gain. The chief purpose of work was to express creativity through craftsmanship and join with others in fellowship. All property was but stewardship of God's gifts, and using them purely for profit led to waste and to defacement of the natural world.[33] Heron regularly attended Chandos Group meetings, was involved with the St Anne's House debating centre in Soho, and in later years attended meetings of the 'Epiphany Philosophers' at Cambridge, a high-powered group of Christian academics.[34] Towards the end of his life he produced a volume of poems, *Call It a Day,* illustrated by Patrick Heron; some of these exemplify the religious outlook which inspired the *NEW,* and one is called 'The Natural Law.'[35]

William Travers Symons was one of those invited by Mitrinovic in May 1926 to the meeting which inaugurated the Chandos Group. He had lived in the Tolstoyan colony at Whiteway in Gloucestershire[36] from 1905 to 1910, and was a member of the ILP and friend of Keir Hardie. He followed a familiar trajectory: from Labour politics, to the *New Age,* to

Social Credit, to the *NEW,* though, like Heron, he did not end up on the Right. In 1931 he produced a dithyrambic analysis of Social Credit called *The Coming of Community,* published by C.W. Daniel and dedicated to Major Douglas. For Symons, Social Credit synthesized socialism and individual freedom. His analysis was frequently couched in religious diction. Douglas' ideas were 'the affirmation of human dignity and a living faith in God' which could lead to a 'Resurrection morning celebrated in a new ritual of Communion.' He wrote of his 'visionary connections of "Social Credit" with the Sacrament of the Mass, with Art, with Socialism, with the craving of the human heart for Community.'[37] There was much more in the same vein.

Unlike Heron, Symons was not a churchman. In a letter to Reckitt dated 12 May 1948, he accused the Church of misrepresenting Jesus Christ and degrading the Gospel:

> to worship Jesus in the manner that the Church prescribes, is to
> put between the soul and God a barrier which Jesus' life and death
> were spent to remove ... None the less, I find in the Church the
> finest men it has been my good fortune to meet, and ... I can see
> no substitute for the Church's civilising influence.

Symons respected Reckitt's passionate adherence to the Church and his extensive historical and theological knowledge, but stated uncompromisingly: 'I am not a Churchman precisely because I *am* a Christian.' Tolstoy's influence evidently remained strong.

Apart from Mairet, Maurice Reckitt was the most influential figure on the *NEW*'s editorial board, sharing with him the writing of the editorial 'Notes of the Week' from 1938 onwards.[38] In a recent history of Christian Socialism, Canon Alan Wilkinson has given a scathingly sarcastic sketch of Reckitt, presenting him as an insular dilettante.[39] *The Church Times* obituary was more generous, describing him as:

> perhaps the most eminent layman among that noble army of
> Churchmen in the Anglican field who strove ... to reassert the
> largely submerged tradition of the Church's own prophetic witness
> to society.[40]

Although not a member of the Kinship in Husbandry, Reckitt shared Mairet's concern about Western civilization's treatment of the natural world. In a contribution to a Gollancz symposium of 1933, *Christianity and the Crisis,* he wrote of the harm done by the canonization of economic activity which involved setting aside all the traditional restraints characteristic of a Christian economic order. Thrift was perverted into avarice, industrial products were unjustly distributed, and the result was a world in which:

> not only are man's engines falling silent ... but even Nature's workings are suspended over fields in which wheat and barley grow no more.[41]

Reckitt attributed the destruction of natural resources to the fact that:

> Modern development, unchecked by reason, pietas, or spiritual standards of judgment, has unrolled itself not in accordance with, but in defiance of, the requirements of a natural order.[42]

The Christendom Group

As editor of CHRISTENDOM: A Journal of Christian Sociology, which ran from 1931 until 1950, Reckitt provided another forum for the organic movement. The journal was the organ of the Anglo-Catholic Christendom Group, perhaps the most influential school of thinkers in the Church of England during the period 1920–50 and was, in its own words:

> a sustained attempt to present and elaborate a Catholic view of social issues and the construction of a valid alternative to the pagan developments of contemporary Plutocracy.[43]

During its early years Christendom did not have a great deal to say about husbandry, but as with the NEW, rural and agricultural issues became more dominant from 1938 onwards. That summer, Reckitt's editorial 'Down to Earth' referred to Lymington's Famine in England and to an article by G.T. Wrench, concluding with a thought which seems far ahead of its time, that 'our churchmanship ... needs to renew itself by a fresh and conscious contact with the perennial realities of Mother Earth.' The same issue featured the Rev P.E.T. Widdrington on 'The Rural Community,' in which several strands of the organic social philosophy could be seen: Britain's industrial bias; the need to restore agriculture; the danger of relying on imported food; and the threat of technics. The article referred to Lymington, Stapledon and the Rural Reconstruction Association,[44] and helped convert H.J. Massingham to Anglo-Catholicism. Massingham referred to it in his own article, 'The Church Across the Fields,' which described how he came to the Kingdom of Heaven through his love of the earth.[45] Christendom reviewed a number of Massingham's books: W.G. Peck wrote on The Tree of Life, and his son David, also a clergyman, reviewed *The English Countryman* and *This Plot of Earth. The Natural Order* also received coverage.[46]

Several leading organicists either contributed to the journal or were referred to in it. Jenks attacked free trade policies. Barlow's paper to the Christendom Group's 1941 Summer School of Sociology was printed, and W.G. Peck praised *The Discipline of Peace* for the importance it attached to the idea of a natural order. The Pioneer Health Centre was celebrated as 'Xanadu in Peckham.' David Peck edited the journal's book section from 1943 onwards, giving good coverage to Faber's agriculture list and praising the firm for rendering 'a signal service to the great cause of the rehabilitation of rural England'[47] in a general review which covered books by Duncan, Gardiner, Portsmouth and Stapledon.

Philip Mairet was inevitably present in *Christendom*. In June 1940, as Britain faced the most ruthless enemy she had ever had to contend with, he condemned England for the destructive path the whole world was now taking, for it was England which first developed those technological forces which set about conquering nature. The piece was entitled 'England and the Natural Order.' He addressed the 1943 Summer School of Sociology, extracts from the speech appearing in *Christendom* the following spring. They showed him to be still attracted by some form of Guild Socialism; he wanted to see a 'modern mediaevalism — a political order to be based upon social function as well as on territorial responsibility.'[48]

Such a comment supports the view of the ecclesiastical historian Adrian Hastings that the Christendom Group was 'an expression of Catholic neo-mediaevalism'[49]; in fact, no-one really has had much good to say of the Group. The Christian Socialist Sidney Dark condemned its members as a 'small body of occidental Gandhis' who met annually at Oxford 'to denounce industrialism with an apparent yearning for the return of the hand loom and spade agriculture.'[50] Martin Wiener and Alan Wilkinson, from different political perspectives, have mocked the Group's social philosophy, though Wilkinson does admit that the Group was far-sighted in ecological issues. Even the sympathetic chronicler Fr Mayhew accepts the charge of nostalgia and impracticability.[51]

William Temple's Malvern Conference

Wiener identifies R.H. Tawney as largely responsible for the nostalgic, ruralist outlook of the reports produced by William Temple's 1924 Conference of the Church's Council on Politics, Economics and Citizenship, and the 1941 Malvern Conference on Christian social values and post-war reconstruction. Tawney, although a staunch Labour Party man, was approvingly quoted by members of the organic school, was a friend of Eliot and Reckitt, and spoke at Anglo-Catholic Summer Schools. His view of the relationship between Protestantism and capitalism appealed to the organic school's view of history, and the 'functional socialism' of *The Acquisitive Society* was closely related to Guild Socialism.

The idea of a natural order was prominent in the conclusions of the Malvern Conference[52] which, given the strong Christendom presence there, is not surprising. Reckitt, W.G. Peck, Demant, Eliot and Murry all submitted papers, and among those present were Tom Heron and Canon Widdrington, the latter a close friend of Reckitt and David Peck. In Wiener's view the report on the Conference looked 'nostalgically to Old England, when religion was strong and industry yet unborn,' and called for a revival of agriculture in order to recreate the kind of community possible only in villages. He concludes: 'The church remained a reservoir of rural romanticism, and of uneasiness with industrial development and economic growth.'[53]

William Temple's book *Christianity and the Social Order* draws conclusions about the best path for reconstruction from a belief in a God-given natural order which embodies natural law, so that every social activity could be considered 'in its context in the whole economy of life.' This idea reflects the organicists' view that a true 'economy' is concerned with a much wider view of human activity than purely financial calculations. Temple believed that capitalism's sole concern with monetary profit was leading to its collapse, which he believed was 'strong evidence both that there is a Natural Order and that our system in part violates it.'[54] At Malvern, W.G. Peck launched the attack on the idea of an autonomous economic purpose in the opening discussion document. He said that the economic system had resulted in unemployment, war, the degradation of work, and an imbalance between town and countryside. These were the consequences of failure to recognize that:

> the life of man in the natural order, with all its economic requirements, is intended to minister to his life as a spiritual being, created for the end of divine communion.[55]

It was therefore necessary, urged V.A. Demant, to dethrone 'Trader Man,' who lived by exchanging and manipulating, and to oppose the power of banking, speculation, bureaucracy and salesmanship:

> These things have a highly moderate place in any complex society, but if it is a directive instead of a humble place, the Natural Law of economic life is violated.[56]

Humanity would perish, Demant prophesied, unless its enhanced technical powers were devoted to 'respectful culture of the earth and nurture of populations to tend it.' Quoting Jacks and Whyte, Loftus and Lymington on the environmental damage done by finance and industry, Demant condemned the secular philosophy which had led man to treat the earth 'just as he behaved towards Almighty God; he has lived on it without recognizing his dependence.'[57]

The Conference's findings contained two passages on agriculture and the environment; they express unambiguously the view of the organic movement:

> we must recover reverence for the earth and its resources, treating it no longer as a reservoir of potential wealth to be exploited, but as a storehouse of divine beauty on which we utterly depend. This will carry with it a deliberate revival of agriculture, both by securing to the agricultural labourer good wages and to the farmer a secure and just price. We regard this as indispensable to the true balance of the national life ... the restoration of agriculture must be utilised for the revival of true community, which is possible in a village as it is not in great cities.[58]

The Council for the Church and Countryside

A couple of years later this impetus towards a Christian revival of the countryside found expression in the Council for the Church and Countryside (CCC), an advisory body under the auspices of the Archbishops of Canterbury and York on matters relating to agriculture and rural life. Its aims were threefold:

(1) To promote a better understanding of agriculture and rural life through a study of its relations to theology and sociology.
(2) To foster a new awareness of religion through the life of husbandry, in which man learns in a quite distinctive manner his dependence upon nature and upon co-operation with his fellow-creatures.
(3) To enhance that awareness of natural values which is essential for the recovery of social balance and sanity, and for the development, in both town and country, of a religious attitude to the conditions upon which life is, and is not, granted to human societies.[59]

One of the CCC's leading figures was David Peck, who during the war was in the rural parish of Little Bedwyn, near Hungerford, and was disturbed by the poverty he saw and the exodus of the rural population. He wanted to revive both the life of the countryside and the life of the Church, and was supported in this aim by Rolf Gardiner and Ralph Coward. Neville Lovett, the Bishop of Salisbury, gave ecclesiastical blessing; Gardiner recalled how, at a meeting to discuss revival of church festivals, Lovett had said that if Gardiner would tell him 'the pagan bits' of a proposed Plough Sunday service, he would christen them.[60]

Peck, Gardiner and Lovett were the driving forces in establishing the CCC, but its wider context was:

> the association of a number of Christian social thinkers whose concern for many years ha[d] been with the Christian concept of man in society, with a number of farmers, landowners, countrymen and men of letters whose concern is for the cultural and spiritual values enshrined in the life of the countryside.[61]

The Council was in effect a front organization for the organic movement. Based at the St Anne's House centre in Soho, it published a steady stream of booklets and Occasional Papers from the mid-1940s onwards into the 1950s, many of them edited by Jorian Jenks. The first Occasional Paper, issued for Rogationtide 1945, reported on the previous Autumn Meeting and revealed that Barlow, Mairet, Pearse and Portsmouth were all involved in the Council's activities. The Book Section, 'Understanding the Soil,' advertised the organic movement by recommending several of its major texts, including Howard's *An Agricultural Testament* and Balfour's *The Living Soil*.[62]

There was a very extensive overlap with the Soil Association, the Rural Reconstruction Association and the Kinship in Husbandry. When a major debate was held at St Anne's House in 1945 between supporters of 'Agri-Culture' on the one hand and of 'Agri-Industry' on the other, the speakers in the former cause — Gardiner, Portsmouth and J.E. Hosking — were all Kinship members. Gardiner, Mairet and Massingham participated in a discussion on artificial insemination of animals to which Howard also contributed. The Harvest 1946 Paper carried a contribution from Montague Fordham. It is interesting to note that Lord Bledisloe was one of the Council's Vice-Presidents, and that John Betjeman was a member.[63]

Despite the 'Encounter,' little attempt was made to present an impartial view of agricultural debate. True, the Council reviewed books by Orwin, Astor and Rowntree, and F.W. Bateson, but only under the heading 'The Manipulative School of Thought'; the following page made it clear that Massingham's *The Wisdom of the Fields* and Howard's journal *Soil and Health* provided the antidote to such writings.[64]

Two of the Council's publications are of particular interest. *Man and Nature* (1950) printed St Barbe Baker's 'New Earth Charter,' a major statement of environmental philosophy and policy, and gave notice of a London meeting at which Ehrenfried Pfeiffer would speak. Reckitt wrote the leading article and Jenks, in his article 'The New Look at Agriculture,' referred to Sir Albert Howard as one of the CCC's original Vice-Principals.[65]

Earth and Heaven, written by David Peck, attempted to develop an environmental theology. Peck began by giving an account of the CCC's origins, which resulted from the converging views of two sets of people:

> The group of country-minded lay folk, arguing inductively, found themselves increasingly led towards a conception of Natural Law; the theologians, arguing deductively from the Christian doctrine of the Natural Law, found themselves in close agreement with the others about the place of country life in social order.[66]

Since Man participated in both the realm of nature and the realm of spirit, any stable and fulfilling social order had both to respect the physical conditions of his bodily life and to acknowledge the priority of his spiritual destiny. Despoliation of the natural world followed logically from the elevation into ends in themselves of aspects of life which were only means to a greater end; aspects which Peck identified as industrial production and the conception of an 'economy' as something to be measured in purely financial terms. For Peck, whose views in this were representative of the organic movement:

> modern Western life, lacking a conception of purpose and reality which can come only from supernatural insight, becomes unnatural, divorces itself from the natural rhythm and pattern to which human life must conform, is unaware of the very terms upon which it is allowed to continue ... In the malaise of modern social order, the life and work of the countryside occupies a highly significant place. 'The land' has become the dominant illustration of the thesis that man must live in obedience to a certain law or pattern — or not at all.[67]

Humanity had to live in conscious co-operation with the natural order. The organic philosophers sought a balance between nature and spirit: care for the earth was a spiritual discipline, and the Divine nature could be grasped through observing natural processes. There was no return to some pagan *participation mystique* with natural cycles, but neither must humans forget, through technological arrogance, that they depended on nature for survival. To use more theological language, the organic philosophers held God to be both *immanent* and *transcendent:* present in His creation but not to be identified with it.[68] They did not deny that humans are in some sense separate from nature; indeed, they saw this as the source of humanity's problems. Man could study nature and use his discoveries as a means of reducing his dependence on it, but danger occurred when he succumbed to the Faustian spirit of wishing to exert control. Peck distinguished between true and false transcendence. The former involved consciously accepting man's place in the scheme of things; it was part of the natural order that man should use and change the environment, but 'the change he makes will not disrupt the natural sym-biosis of creation ... He will understand ... the laws of ecology.' Peck termed refusal to accept these limitations a 'denial of creatureliness.'[69] If man sought to dominate nature:

> without any reference to the terms on which life exists ... he will deny the divine process by which cosmos (order) was created out of chaos (disorder) — the law of creation — and reverse that process.[70]

Peck believed that man's treatment of the land would prove that con-tention. An attitude of 'demonic' transcendence would destroy the land and the basis of human survival. There was thus a close link between farming and theology: through farming man could become aware of the God-given natural order.

The CCC's publications repeatedly expressed the view that the earth's resources must be treated with an acceptance of limits, with a sense of the sacred, of humility. Against a clerical critic Jorian Jenks argued that Howard's work was greatly significant for Christians, since the rules of good husbandry derived from Natural Law.[71] Jenks summarized the rela-tionship between the Church and the organic movement after surveying the two antithetical approaches to agriculture, husbandry and mastery:

> What has all this to do with Christianity? The answer is that it marks a definite turning towards a more religious concept of the terms on which we enjoy life on this earth and of our relations with our fellow-creatures. It would of course be rash to claim that the Organic Movement, which has many ramifications, is as a movement conscious of Christian inspiration, though many of its members are devout Christians and to some at least the miracle of the constant renewal of physical life through natural processes is symbolical of that eternal spiritual life which was promised us through Christ's Resurrection.[72]

Clearly there was a very close connection between the organic movement and advocates of a 'Christian Sociology.' What did this phrase,
which today sounds downright paradoxical, actually mean?

W.G. Peck provided a survey of the ideas in his 1948 book *An Outline
of Christian Sociology.*[73] Originally a Methodist minister, Peck was
ordained an Anglican priest by William Temple in 1925. Although not a
Labour Party member, he spoke on socialist platforms and strongly disliked orthodox economics. This led him to support Social Credit, and he
became a central figure in the Christendom Group, with its opposition to
capitalist industrialism.

Peck argued that since there existed a Christian doctrine of human
nature, a view of society was implicit in Christian thought and no social
system could be effective unless it ministered to man's whole being and
destiny as 'a creature within a created order which is divinely intended to
provide the mode of a life which has for its End the Vision of God.'[74] The
existing social system inverted the true order: people existed to produce
goods whose purpose was to make a profit. Work, whose true aim was to
satisfy human need, was a form of servitude for employees, and Peck
urged workers' control of industry and a 'functional' finance system, in
which money would be the servant of productive work. Industrial capitalism created a sick society, and although Peck accepted the necessity of
a Welfare State he saw it as no more than an attempt to ameliorate the
symptoms.

One chapter was devoted to the balance of urban and rural in society.
Peck saw the British neglect of agriculture as a departure from the natural order. Western civilization had 'accepted the dark and dreadful heresy
that man ... can successfully do whatever he may want to do with his
world and with himself,' and only a return to husbandry could bring about
a balanced social culture.[75]

Peck was concerned with prevention rather than cure: only that society
could be healthy which was based on principles derived from a Christian
understanding of human nature:

> A Christian social order is one which restores the natural as the
> minister and instrument of the Supernatural, in the knowledge that
> natural and supernatural must dwell together, and that their separa-
> tion either makes the supernatural appear remote and irrelevant, or
> distorts the natural into the unnatural, and may do both things at
> once.[76]

Peck's book, which might seem like a manifesto for subsequent action,
is in fact more in the nature of a coda to the Christendom movement.

Mayhew writes bleakly that by the end of the 1940s it 'had produced no detailed suggestions for a better order of society or for the promotion of better conditions of life.' And for Edward Norman, what began as 'a serious attempt to define distinctly *Christian* principles of society, derived from doctrine' finished as typically Church of England 'moralistic social criticism.'[77] But like the *New English Weekly,* it left a valuable legacy of ecological thought.

Finally in this survey of the links between organic husbandry and High Anglicanism let us look at the interpretation of history which went hand-in-hand with the theology. Despite Reckitt's claim that Christianity is neither nostalgic nor pessimistic,[78] the Christendom Group inevitably inclined to look back to the medieval world for inspiration. This tendency was especially marked in Penty but could also be found in Reckitt, who had been strongly influenced by Belloc and had worked with Chesterton. Reckitt believed that during the Middle Ages one could see an attempt at the embodiment of the idea of a Christian society, but that in the sixteenth century the Church had abandoned its post and had subsequently failed to interpret the significance of the Industrial Revolution or to champion its victims. Tawney's influence is evident here. Reckitt rejected charges of escapism; he wanted to go forward in order to leave behind nineteenth-century values, and believed that medieval Christendom could provide clues to the nature of a revivified social order. Britain had been:

> the initiator of that 'reversal of the natural order' which embodies the Economic Idolatry that has been our particular sin against civilization. The Economic Man was born, bred, and blest in England.[79]

The reversal had ruined agriculture, eroded the soil, proletarianized the peasantry, and created 'an unnatural competition of forced exports' which threatened peace.[80] This interpretation of history served as the basis of L.T.C. Rolt's *High Horse Riderless* and Massingham's *The Tree of Life;* Reckitt in fact advised Massingham on this book.

The Tree of Life surveyed the way in which European, and more particularly English, thought had regarded nature. Massingham saw Protestantism as largely responsible for the loss of a sense of the natural world's sacredness; in its more extreme, Puritan, form it demonized nature. The Church had withdrawn into a spirituality detached from involvement in the material and social world, and could not renew itself unless it reconnected with the natural and social orders. Massingham was fighting on two fronts: against the secularism which regarded nature as material to exploit, and against an idealist Christianity which devalued the created world. In effect anticipating Lynn White Jr.'s article a quarter of a century later, he argued that Christian thought betrayed its own tradition when it ignored or downgraded the natural world. He drew particularly on the rural life and imagery of the Gospels, on the Celtic saints, on the medieval concept of natural law, and on seventeenth-century religious writers.

In the book's second half Massingham sketched the process by which Protestantism abandoned a sacramental view of nature, enabling secularism to conceive of nature as a blind interplay of conflicting forces which could be mastered for the sake of economic profit. The significance of his story — one of those 'grand narratives' unacceptable to our post-modern age — is that it pulls together so many of the threads examined earlier in this study, giving them a longer-term context: mistaken concepts of 'economy'; the dangers of free trade; the destruction of craftsmanship; the threats posed by technology; the cancer of urbanism; and, above all, the exploitation and exhaustion of resources — the nemesis of an attitude which has ceased to revere the natural world. In a splendidly apocalyptic passage Massingham summarized the effects of violating natural law:

> The essence of the Christian idea is the worth of the person and of
> the old natural law embodied in the Guilds, the worth of work.
> Thus, a society which violates the natural law vindicates its truth
> as indefeasibly as one that obeys it. This law is at once Christian
> and natural; it was personalized by the rural Christ, propagated by
> the primitive Church, sewn into the social fabric by the craft-
> guilds and the village community, philosophically and imagina-
> tively interpreted by the early seventeenth century, dramatized by
> Shakespeare and broken by Hobbes and Descartes. That breakage
> has led to results proliferating into every social, economic and
> industrial and agricultural activity; it has denatured nature, man
> and the food he eats and it has brought upon the stage of history a
> being propertyless, homeless, rootless, natureless, peaceless and
> godless, robbed of his self-determination and debauched by propa-
> ganda and parasitic mass-amusement. But because the despair of
> this being is reaching the limits of his suffering and endurance, he
> will rediscover the natural law in which God ordains Nature and
> Man to play a duality of parts, and for the lack of which he per-
> ishes. Tertullian said: 'Nature is the teacher, the soul the pupil.'[81]

The answer to the ecological, agricultural, economic and social crisis was therefore theological: a matter of reconnecting the natural with the supernatural, the Church with the fields. Massingham believed the rediscovery of the idea of natural law to be a hopeful sign, and the work of the organic pioneers to be a rediscovery of that law in practical terms:

> Neither Howard nor McCarrison ... would dream of defining their sciences as expert knowledge of natural processes vindicating the Christian natural law. Nevertheless, they are so without any doubt, and so in new directions we are confronted by its fundamental reality.[82]

The Tree of Life called for a regenerated England, one which would reject the progressive experiment and return to a Christianity synthesizing religion, nature, craft and husbandry. In his autobiography *Remembrance* Massingham declared that the most valuable insight he had been granted was that:

> the law of nature ... expounds the divine law ... It is when man interacts with nature, searching her laws with his brain, gathering their rhythms into his being and translating them into his work, that his spirit can touch the eternal.[83]

Massingham's friend L.T.C. Rolt is best known as an industrial historian, so it may come as a surprise to find him among the organicists, but he wrote a study of English history whose values and conclusions were entirely in tune with their outlook.[84] He began formulating his ideas during the Second World War, reflecting on a civilization which worshipped speed and subordinated human lives to the power of machines. His thoughts on past, present and future formed the notes for his post-war book *High Horse Riderless*.

A trained engineer, Rolt was not at all opposed to machinery in itself, and rejected any putative return to a machineless 'simple life.' The problem was one of values: his examination of industrial capitalism led him to ideas of 'a philosophical pattern which was recognizably Christian.' He then tried to discover why Western society had rejected the philosophy of Christendom for the materialism of Descartes and Hobbes, concluding that the medieval philosophy was not inherently flawed but lacked 'eloquent re-statement in the light of the new knowledge.'[85] The unbridled progress of technology had now led Western civilization to such a pass that:

> we are destined to discover that this wisdom which our fathers brusquely dismissed was actually based upon a more realistic philosophy than our own.[86]

The last three pages of *High Horse Riderless* summarize Rolt's argument in twenty paragraphs, starting with the medieval belief in a natural order. Loss of this belief prepared the way for a will-to-power which led to an acquisitive, exploitative and unjust economic system, and thence into the chaos, barbarism and power-worship of the twentieth-century. Any attempt at a renaissance would have to be based on a prosperous and populous agricultural community, since only through the realism of agriculture could the validity of the natural order be appreciated once more.

But *High Horse Riderless* appeared in 1947, the year of the Agriculture Act, which confirmed agriculture on its industrial, chemically-intensive path and ensured that, however prosperous it might become, it would be ever less populous. The organic school's call to repentance went largely unheeded.

12. The 1950s and Today

In the immediate aftermath of the Second World War the organic movement had some grounds for optimism. The countryside had been restored to the centre of national life, and it was clear that there would be no repeat of the 'betrayal' of farmers which had occurred in the early 1920s; Britain's economic position made it imperative to grow as much food at home as possible; the organic case had been presented in many books during the previous decade and had been argued in the House of Lords; and the Soil Association had been formed in order to draw together the evidence for the benefits of obeying the Rule of Return. There was a widespread sense that the nation could not return to *laissez-faire* muddle, with its unemployment, malnutrition and neglected countryside; post-war reconstruction provided a supreme opportunity for reorganizing British life on different principles. A sound agriculture, employing perhaps a million more people and measuring efficiency according to an output per acre which would increase with the increased amount of humus in the soil, would serve as the basis of a new preventive health service by producing healthy food. The Pioneer Health Centre, used as a factory during the war, reopened in 1946 and attracted interest from various parts of the world. *Health and Life, Trees,* the *New English Weekly, Christendom, Rural Economy* and the Kinship in Husbandry were all propagating organic ideas, and although they represented a minority view their writers were prolific and had many contacts.

The year after the Soil Association was founded, however, British agriculture was confirmed on the path of progressive, orthodox methods by the passing of the great Agriculture Act of 1947, whose keynote was efficiency according to the industrial standard of output per worker. The Act's provisions continued wartime policy in a number of respects and so came as little surprise. The organicists saw their fears realized in the Act's emphasis on good husbandry, by which was meant the application of chemical fertilizers, encouraged by government advisors and the commercial interests which influenced policy. The orthodox school appeared to occupy the moral high ground: increased use of fertilizers and machinery had helped the nation survive in war time and it was logical to enshrine those developments in legislation, especially as there was a threat of food shortages. Nor was the government interested in establishing a research project to test the results of organic methods, and it was left to the Soil Association to develop Lady Balfour's Haughley experiment; the project was hamstrung from the start by its shortage of money in comparison with the large sums available for developing artificials and pesticides. The agricultural population had increased under the special circumstances of the war but resumed its long-term downward trend in the 1950s; use of artificials continued its steep climb, and by the end of the decade machinery had almost totally replaced horse-power. Productivity increased, and the organic school appeared irrelevant given the success of conventional methods.

The movement suffered other blows. Several leading figures died in the post-war years: Howard in 1947; Picton, Fordham and Rayner in 1948; Massingham and Marian in 1952; Hastings, DUKE OF BEDFORD and Scott Williamson in 1953. Stapledon entered a long period of invalidism, and Portsmouth removed himself to East Africa. The *NEW* was unable to survive financially and closed down in 1949; *Christendom* followed it into oblivion a year later. The Social Credit movement had dwindled away, and the Labour Party's electoral success in 1945 ensured the dominance of Fabian state socialism and a government representing largely urban and industrial interests. As the 1950s continued and the Age of Affluence replaced the Age of Austerity, there was little mileage to be had from advocating a simpler, more traditional and land-based life. It is possible also that the organic movement was to some extent discredited by its association with the radical Right. Certainly the presence on the Soil Association Council during the post-war period of Sempill, Portsmouth, Teviot and Gardiner, and Jenks' position as Editorial Secretary, indicates that the radical Right was still a strong influence in organic circles, and one wonders how far this might have harmed the organic cause.

Tracy Clunies-Ross[1] has suggested that the organic school of the 1930s and '40s was something quite distinct from the movement which emerged as part of the wider environmental movement in the 1960s and '70s, following the publication of Rachel Carson's *Silent Spring*. Yet it seems inherently improbable that a well-organized group of energetic, dedicated and fluently articulate propagandists should fade away and have no impact on people concerned with the same issues less than two decades later. Even allowing for the deaths and withdrawals of the figures mentioned above, there were plenty of others who carried the torch through the discouraging years of the 1950s and right through to the 1980s, demonstrating a clear continuity between the organic pioneers and the contemporary movement. In fact Mary Langman, who was personal assistant to Scott Williamson at the Pioneer Health Centre in the 1930s, remains actively involved with the Soil Association at the time of writing. Kenneth Barlow was still working for the McCarrison Society in the 1980s, and co-authored a book with Peter Bunyard, one of the leading writers in the modern environmental movement.[2] Richard St Barbe Baker helped establish the Findhorn Community. Lady Balfour was still sufficiently sharp and vigorous to be interviewed by Derek Cooper on Radio 4's *The Food Programme* in 1988, and the following year Barlow's daughter Joanna produced a television documentary on Ralph Coward.[3] An important link between the organic movement and the wider environmental movement was provided by Fritz Schumacher, who was President of the Soil Association in 1970. Another major figure of the 1970s was the self-sufficiency guru John Seymour, who much admired Rolt's *High Horse Riderless* and wrote an introduction to the 1988 reprint. The instances could be multiplied, but the point should be clear: there was a continuous thread which survived the 1950s and linked the founders of the organic movement to the post-Carson generation.

Above, I described the 1950s as a discouraging decade, but this description needs qualifying. It is true that agriculture and rural life developed rapidly in what the organic school regarded as the wrong direction, but Riccardo Ling, a Soil Association member for half a century, recalls the 1950s as an exciting decade, when all sorts of initiatives were being developed.[4] The Association's membership reached around 3,500 by 1957 and was drawn from all over the world; this enabled the Association to fulfil its purpose of gathering as much evidence as possible on soil fertility and nutrition, and of ensuring that practitioners could be up-to-date with what their fellows were doing.

Looking at copies of *Mother Earth* from this period one can only be impressed by the wealth of detailed information they contain, and by the high level of scientific, agricultural and horticultural expertise. To all intents and purposes it was, despite its sentimental name, a scientific journal, and it is ironic that today's controversy over GM crops appears to establish the organic movement as inherently anti-science. Topics covered during the 1950s included the use of antibiotics in animal husbandry, biological pest control, the effects of DDT, the science of ecology, the use of fertilizers, the increase of disease in sugar-cane, the nitrogen cycle, plant viruses, and of course all aspects of soil science: analysis, erosion, fertility, fungi, temperature and structure. The book reviews section was a substantial feature and ensured that many books on relevant issues, whether or not they were by members of the organic movement, were brought to readers' attention, even when they were on specialist topics such as bacterial plant pathogens or the part played by calcium phosphates in nitrogen fixation. There was faith in the capacity of science and of practical experiments in cultivation to establish the organic case. The enemy was not science, but the power of commercial vested interests to over-ride scientific knowledge, and the reluctance of government and research institutions to investigate the organic argument. The Haughley experiment is considered to be at best inconclusive, but it was scientific, and was taken seriously enough to be discussed in the journal *Nature*.[5] A well-known biochemist, Dr Reginald Milton, was in charge of the sampling and analytical work, and the scientific gravitas of his approach can be seen in the lectures he gave to the Association's conferences in 1958 and 1959. Milton and Balfour gave papers at the 1958 International Conference on Nutrition, which serves to underline the point and, incidentally, provides evidence that the organic pioneers were not ignored, as is sometimes claimed today. In 1952 the Soil Association exhibited at the World Dental Conference in London, and five years later it organized a public declaration reaffirming the principles of the *Medical Testament;* this was published in *The Lancet* and the *British Medical Journal,* and was supported by four hundred dentists and doctors, the majority of them not Association members.[6] Throughout the 1950s Jorian Jenks ensured that *Mother Earth* noted any scientific developments and reports of relevance to the Association's concerns, and demanded a degree of concentration from members which is apparently impossible today but which ensured that the journal was a mine of information.

By the mid-1950s the Soil Association had seen any possible rivals to its dominance of the organic movement disappear. The Albert Howard Foundation survived for a few years, but merged with the Association in 1953. Siegfried Marian's *Soil Magazine* became less scientific and more 'New Age' after Marian's death led to Dion Byngham's increased influence on its content, though it had been marginal even during Marian's life-time. The Biodynamic Agricultural Association was still there, influencing the Soil Association Council through the presence of Maye Bruce and Laurence Easterbrook, who remained members of it as the 1950s came to an end. Lady Balfour ensured the Association a world-wide presence through her overseas travels; in addition to her three American tours during the '50s there were visits to the Channel Islands, France, Italy, Australia and New Zealand.

Inevitably, new figures emerged to take important roles in the Association's work: as well as Milton there were C. Donald Wilson, who became the Resident Development Director of Haughley Research

Farms; the Shropshire farmer Sam Mayall; Dr Kenneth Vickery, Medical Officer of Health at Eastbourne; Reginald Hancock, Chief Veterinary Officer at the RSPCA, and Dr N.P. Burman, senior bacteriologist at the Metropolitan Water Board. But at the end of the 1950s there remained a strong presence from the earlier period: in addition to Bruce and Easterbrook, Council members included Rolf Gardiner, Innes Pearse and Aubrey Westlake, while Friend Sykes and Roy Wilson served on the Advisory Panel. Lady Howard was Honorary Vice-President for life, and Jorian Jenks edited *Mother Earth* until his death in 1963. Jenks himself linked past to present in his 1959 book *The Stuff Man's Made Of,* a valuable survey of the organic movement's history, philosophy and practice. One wonders, though, whether the book was perceived as somewhat elegiac, summing up the work of a movement whose aims since the war had conspicuously not been achieved. Not that this made its work irrelevant: quite the contrary, since the single-minded, commercially-driven adoption of industrial farming methods made it even more imperative, for the organicists, to point out the dangers of that path and indicate alternatives. Sooner or later, they believed, the facts about the intensive use of chemicals would incontrovertibly demonstrate the damage done by neglecting what should be the cultivator's prime concern, the health of the soil, and ignoring the natural laws which required variety of crops and obedience to the Rule of Return. That day came only three years after Jenks' book, though it was heralded by an outsider to the movement and one who did not wish to be associated with it.[7] The appearance of *Silent Spring* was a landmark in the history of organic agriculture; but as I hope this study has demonstrated, it was very far from being its inspiration.

* * *

As an exercise in retrieval this book is exploratory in intention and makes no claims to completeness; it exemplifies in a historical context Sir George Stapledon's 'law of operative ignorance' in that it opens up a range of areas ripe for further investigation. Among them are the life and work of Sir Albert, Gabrielle and Louise Howard, Lady Balfour, Jorian Jenks, and the members of the Kinship in Husbandry; the history of the biodynamic movement in the English-speaking world; the Economic Reform Club; the Rural Reconstruction Association; the Council for the Church and Countryside; the Faber archives; the contribution of dental science to the organic case; the effect of commercial pressure on agricultural policy during the Second World War; the history of alternative medicine, with special reference to Edgar Saxon, and the controversies over the quality of bread during and after the Second World War.

There will inevitably be disagreement over points of emphasis in what has been presented. Supporters of the organic movement may well be surprised to find that it emerged as a coherent opposition to orthodox agriculture within a context that was both right-wing and Christian. To say this is not, of course, to imply that these particular political and religious outlooks dominate today's movement, or that they are necessary concomitants of support for organic cultivation; nor is it to imply that all the movement's early enthusiasts were of these persuasions. Nevertheless, the philosophy of organic husbandry which developed in the 1930s and '40s was an all-embracing theory of agriculture, society and religion, and there was a coherence about it which made sense in the circumstances of the times. Another task for future historians of the organic movement will be to analyse why many on the radical Right should have embraced organic farming so warmly,[8] and why these right-wingers were more perceptive than most leftists about the ecological dangers of industrial farming. There were few exceptions, Jack Donaldson and Edward Hyams being perhaps the two most notable. That such political views are not essential to the case for organic husbandry was demonstrated in the 1960s when Robert Waller and Michael Allaby took over the Soil Association journal, and had already been proved in the United States by Jerome Rodale and Louis Bromfield.

The organic school's Christian context is another feature of the early movement that may not appeal to younger sympathizers today if they have adopted the view that Christianity is indifferent or hostile to the natural world. There should be sufficient evidence, though, to convince the reader that in the 1930s and '40s Christianity was integral to the movement's religious philosophy. Perhaps some westernized form of Buddhism or attempt to recreate paganism would play the same role were the movement starting today; such speculation does not alter the fact that it was Christianity, whether in the esoteric form of Anthroposophy or the orthodox form of Anglo-Catholicism, which provided the early movement with essential support and its central philosophical concept, the natural order.

But does the organic movement need philosophical concepts? It might be argued that nowadays it is concerned with practical issues like monitoring the effects of farming practices on food quality and biodiversity. The founders never had to deal with the problems their successors have to face, like the effects of planting GM crops or the widespread use of food additives, and so perhaps they have little to offer to contemporary activists.

Such a view is mistaken, and ignores the prophetic insight and relevance to be found in what the organicists wrote fifty or sixty years ago. One does not need to be an 'ecological alarmist' to recognize that deforestation, increasing shortages of water, the spread of deserts, famine, pollution and rapid urbanization are all processes which pose serious problems for the world's future, or that in the industrialized nations there are valid grounds for anxiety about methods of food production and their effect on public health. The early organic writers, in their opposition to free trade, anticipated the current battle between proponents of 'globalization' — that is, the imposition of American consumerism on every society — and those who fear for the economic and environmental sustainability of the countries persuaded or forced into competition.[9]

They recognized, too, the cultural implications of such a process: the loss of variety, and its replacement by standardized conformity. Massingham's laments for England's almost extinct folk culture and Philip Oyler's celebration of the Dordogne peasantry were forerunners of contemporary interest in vanishing indigenous cultures and 'vacation' nostalgia for rural Provence and Tuscany; one feels that these writers and their colleagues would have sympathized, if not with the methods of recent protests against the World Trade Organization, at least with the motives behind them and the choice of targets. They would be on the side of what Benjamin Barber has termed 'jihad,' in the battle against 'McWorld'[10] and they would be delighted to see a new generation drawing attention to the role that financial institutions play in perpetuating starvation and exhausting natural resources. Barber's book highlights the dangers of the 'jihad' reaction to 'McWorld,' and some of these, too, were exemplified by certain elements in the early organic movement. The conflict of outlooks, between those who see economics as purely a matter of money, and those who want a wider conception including skills and resources, remains essentially the same as sixty years ago.

The fact that we now face certain issues — notably GM crops — which did not exist in the '30s and '40s does not affect the relevance of the early organic writings; indeed, their warnings about the unknown dangers of manipulating nature seem more pertinent than ever, and remind us that to turn commercial profit into the supreme standard of valuation is in fact to behave irrationally, elevating a means into an end.

Yet to many people it must seem that the organic movement today is no more than a consumer pressure group, fighting a quixotic campaign against the contamination of foodstuffs, the use of agricultural chemicals, and the polluting system of food distribution. Its success will be judged by its effectiveness in ensuring that shoppers have available to them an alternative to the products of the food manufacturing industry.

This view erroneously assumes that the organic movement is essentially negative, whereas in fact it is based on a positive view of the benefits which flow from working with nature, and sees health as a dynamic quality rather than mere absence of illness. Unless this is understood one misses the whole point of the movement, which regards the paraphernalia of genetic modification, pesticides, antibiotics and additives as potentially harmful and downright clumsy, unnecessary, and created for commercial gain. Agriculture on this view is a form of preventive medicine if it begins from the health of the soil, and earlier in the book we saw how the organic pioneers argued that a healthy, humus-rich soil would create healthy, pest-resistant crops which in turn would produce healthy animals and humans. If this appears a simplistic view, the early organicists would have retorted that it was far more simplistic to believe that nature could be subjected to industrial treatment without there being serious problems, and that if even there were any problems they would be amenable to technological solutions; in any case, the practical and scientific skill necessary to understand and apply ecological principles is highly sophisticated.

The virtuous circle of fertility and health was, and is, based on a principle the opposite of negative avoidance: that is, the Rule of Return, which recognizes that humanity must pay its dues to nature. Now, belief in such a principle implies a view of the way the world is — a philosophy, in other words. Most of the people in the early organic movement, on the evidence of their writings, went a little further and saw the Rule of Return as a principle implying a view of how God had created the world, as a part of his natural order. Belief in God is not, of course, essential for acceptance of the Rule of Return, but it was fundamental to the philosophy of husbandry expounded by Mairet, Jenks, Massingham, and other writers discussed earlier. No doubt an organic movement would have come into being one way or another; having studied the intellectual context of the movement which did emerge, one is led to the conclusion that the concept of a natural order, derived from Christian theology, was integral to it.

The issue is in fact still highly topical. At the time of writing, in the summer of 2000, the Prince of Wales has been in the news on account of his comments about the dangers of GM crops, which have had the unfortunate effect of appearing to imply that to oppose GM crops is to be opposed to science. By warning the nation that we should have reverence for the laws of God he has encouraged those who would like to present the developers of GM crops as on the side of Science and Progress, and their opponents as on the side of religion and obscurantism. It is a false dichotomy. Back in the 1950s Jorian Jenks summed up matters as follows:

> It can hardly be against Man's real interests that he should learn to qualify the conception of himself as 'master of all he surveys' with another conception — that of himself as the enlightened steward of the natural order, responsible to its Creator for its continuing wellbeing. This may sound like moralizing. But if the ideal of the Whole Man has any meaning at all, then science and technology can no more be divorced from morality than can reasoning be divorced from feeling. Fragmentation sooner or later means frustration.[11]

The early organic school saw no dichotomy between science and religion: the conflict between them was only apparent, and could be resolved through studying and working responsively with the natural order.

Appendix A
Leading figures in the organic movement and the orthodox school of agriculture

Names of people in SMALL CAPITALS indicate an entry in Appendix A. Names of groups, institutions or journals in SMALL CAPITALS indicate an entry in Appendix B.

ADDISON, LORD (1869–1951). Christopher Addison was a medical scientist who held posts in Anatomy at the Universities of Cambridge, London and Sheffield, and edited the *Quarterly Medical Journal*. He was Labour MP for Swindon from 1929 to 1931 and from 1934 to 1935, and Lord Privy Seal from 1947 to 1951. His importance lies in his 1939 book *A Policy for British Agriculture* and in his period as Minister of Agriculture, 1930–31, during which the first Agricultural Marketing Act was passed. While respected by members of the organic school, he nevertheless represented in their view the forces of agricultural orthodoxy.

AE [George William Russell] (1867–1935) Russell evidently adopted the pseudonym AE, by which he was known as a poet, for reasons connected with his commitment to Theosophy: the letters indicate the word 'aeon.' He was both a mystic and an intensely practical man, whose theosophical faith led him to work for human brotherhood through socialism and Irish nationalism: he was a keen advocate of Home Rule. In the 1890s he travelled all over Ireland for the Irish Agricultural Organization Society, and in 1905 became editor of *The Irish Homestead,* its weekly paper. He admired A.R. ORAGE's propaganda for GUILD SOCIALISM and first met him in London in 1913; the friendship lasted till Orage's death. P.L. TRAVERS was a devotee of AE on account of his poetry, and PHILIP MAIRET also knew him well.

ALBRECHT, WILLIAM A. (active 1916–60). Albrecht was Professor of Soils at the College of Agriculture, University of Missouri. He contributed to the United States Department of Agriculture 1938 Year Book, *Soils and Men,* and to WESTON A. PRICE's *Nutrition and Physical Degeneration.* He had close links with the SOIL ASSOCIATION.

ASTOR, VISCOUNT (1879–1952). Waldorf Astor was Conservative MP for Plymouth from 1910 to 1919, and Parliamentary Secretary to the Prime Minister in 1918. He held posts in the Ministry of Food (1918) and the Ministry of Health (1919–21). In 1936–37 he was Chairman of the League of Nations Committee on Nutrition. The various agricultural surveys he organized with B.S. ROWNTREE assured him a place in the organic school's demonology.

BAKER, C. ALMA (1857–1941). Born in New Zealand, Baker owned cattle stations there and in Australia, and rubber estates and tin mines in Malaya. During the First World War he founded the Australian and Malayan Battleplane Squadrons, which earned him the CBE. In later life he advocated RUDOLF STEINER's methods of cultivation, and his book *The Labouring Earth* featured a foreword by LORD ADDISON.

BAKER, RICHARD ST BARBE (1889–1982). Born in Hampshire, Baker spent time on the Canadian prairies before the First World War, and intended to be a missionary. After war service he took the

University of Cambridge Forestry Diploma and worked in Kenya (1920–23), where he founded the MEN OF THE TREES movement in 1922. From 1924 to 1929 he was Assistant Conservator of Forests in Nigeria; in 1932 he attended the Ottawa Conference on Empire Forestry. The remainder of his life was devoted to travel and the protection of the world's forests. He founded and edited the journal TREES, and was a founder member of the SOIL ASSOCIATION. Later he helped establish the Findhorn Community.

BALFOUR, LADY EVE (1898–1990). Niece of the Prime Minister Sir Arthur Balfour and founder of the SOIL ASSOCIATION, Evelyn Balfour studied agriculture at Reading University and farmed in Suffolk from 1919 onwards. Influenced by VISCOUNT LYMINGTON's 1938 book *Famine in England* she met SIR ALBERT HOWARD and SIR ROBERT MCCARRISON and decided to use her farm as an experiment centre for their ideas. Her 1943 book *The Living Soil* was instrumental in drawing together those who founded the Soil Association. She travelled widely, forging links with organic farmers overseas, espcially in the USA, and remained actively involved in the organic movement until the late 1980s.

BARLOW, KENNETH E. (1906–2000). Kenneth Barlow was a member of the SOCIOLOGICAL SOCIETY and worked as private secretary to SIR PATRICK GEDDES, who helped him train as a doctor. Barlow was a GP in Coventry during the Second World War and in the post-war period attempted, unsuccessfully, to establish an ambitious Family Health and Housing Association, complete with farm, based on the model of the PIONEER HEALTH CENTRE. He frequently wrote for the NEW ENGLISH WEEKLY and *PURPOSE,* and his 1942 book *The Discipline of Peace,* a philosophical study of ecological principles, was highly regarded by the organic school. He was a founder member of the SOIL ASSOCIATION and a leading spirit in establishing the MCCARRISON Society.

BEDFORD, HASTINGS DUKE OF (1888–1953). Hastings W.S. Russell, formerly Marquis of Tavistock, latterly the 12th Duke of Bedford, was a Christian Socialist, a pacifist, and a devotee of SOCIAL CREDIT. Opposition to the power of 'usury' led him into anti-semitic circles, and in 1939 he founded the BRITISH PEOPLE'S PARTY, which was forced to disband in 1940 but re-emerged in 1945. The BPP's membership included extreme right-wingers like ANTHONY LUDOVICI, and A.K. Chesterton [not to be confused with G.K. CHESTERTON], later the founder of the National Front. Its paper the *PEOPLES Post* featured writing on agricultural topics by DION BYNGHAM.

BELL, ADRIAN (1901–80). First compiler of the *Times* crossword, and father of the reporter and Independent MP Martin Bell, as well as the noted translator Anthea Bell; he began farming in Suffolk in 1920 and wrote various semi-autobiographical novels based on his experiences. He was a not very strongly committed member of the KINSHIP IN HUSBANDRY.

BELLOC, HILAIRE (1870–1953). An aggressive Roman Catholic, Belloc was a journalist and man of letters whose name is associated with that of his co-religionist G.K. CHESTERTON. Both wrote for A.R. ORAGE's paper the *NEW AGE* and were sympathetic to GUILD SOCIALISM, but later developed a theory of DISTRIBUTISM. Belloc's book *The Servile State* (1912) was admired by members of the organic school; his suspicion of Jewish financial power was also influential. He helped Orage establish the *NEW ENGLISH WEEKLY.*

BLEDISLOE, LORD (1867–1958). Charles Bathurst, created 1st Viscount Bledisloe in 1935, was one of the most distinguished agriculturalists of his time, and was strongly sympathetic to the views of the organic school. He was Gold Medallist at the Royal Agricultural College, Cirencester; a barrister; Conservative MP for Wilton (1910–18); Parliamentary Secretary to the Ministry of Food (1916–17) and to the Ministry of Agriculture (1924–28); Chairman of the Farmers' Club (1923–24); Governor of New Zealand (1930–35), and President of the Royal Agricultural Society in 1946. Of particular interest, given his support for the organic movement, is the fact that he was Chairman of the Committee of the [J.B.] LAWES Agricultural Trust.

BLUNDEN, EDMUND (1896–1974). A First World War poet, writer on rural topics and cricket, and Professor of Poetry at Oxford University, Blunden was a friend of ADRIAN BELL and H.J. MASSINGHAM. The KINSHIP IN HUSBANDRY first met in his rooms at Merton College. He supported General Franco and was an enthusiast for Nazi Germany.

BROMFIELD, LOUIS (1896–1956). A prolific and successful journalist and novelist, Bromfield had, as a young man, wanted to take up farming. After serving in the First World War he spent much of the 1920s and '30s in France, where he became a prize-winning market-gardener. A sense of rootlessness drew him back to his native Ohio in 1939 and he achieved his earlier ambition by transforming Malabar Farm, which became a showpiece of agricultural regeneration. He was an early supporter of J.I. RODALE's work, though Rodale later denied Bromfield's credentials as an organic farmer. Bromfield was sympathetic to the organic school and gave the ALBERT HOWARD Memorial Lecture in London in 1955. He was a director of FRIENDS OF THE LAND.

BRUCE, MAYE E. (1879–1964). Maye Bruce was a practitioner of RUDOLF STEINER's methods of cultivation and a founder member of the SOIL ASSOCIATION. Her Gloucestershire garden impressed the agricultural journalist LAURENCE EASTERBROOK. She also worked for the Red Cross and the Girl Guide movement.

BRYANT, ARTHUR (1899–1985). Arthur Bryant has recently been exposed by the historian Andrew Roberts as a Nazi fellow-

traveller who was lucky to escape internment in 1940. He served in the Royal Flying Corps during the First World War and came to sympathize with the defeated German people. In 1927 he became educational adviser to Conservative Central Office; in the 1930s he organized the Greenwich naval pageants. His 1940 book *Unfinished Victory* was an apologia for Nazism, and he was a close friend of FRANCIS YEATS-BROWN. He was a member of the KINSHIP IN HUSBANDRY, and H.J. MASSINGHAM dedicated books to him. In the postwar years he became a campaigner for conservationist causes.

BYNGHAM, DION (*c.*1893–1990). Harry John Byngham, who adopted the name 'Dion' in order to express his devotion to the spirit of Dionysus, was to be found on the more eccentric fringes of the organic movement. He was a close friend of C.W. DANIEL and a frequent contributor to *HEALTH AND LIFE* magazine; he wrote for S. MARIAN's *SOIL MAGAZINE*; he was a member of AUBREY WESTLAKE's ORDER OF WOODCRAFT CHIVALRY; he was a member of the BRITISH PEOPLE's PARTY and a regular contributor to *PEOPLES POST;* he worked at the community farm of JOHN MIDDLETON MURRY during the Second World War. He was a pacifist who admired George Lansbury; according to his daughter Julia he ghost-wrote the memoirs of HASTINGS DUKE OF BEDFORD.

CARREL, ALEXIS (1873–1944). Carrel won the Nobel Prize for Medicine, and was known to a wide public for his book *Man the Unknown.* The views expressed in it, on Western decadence and the need to improve the health of the white races, struck a chord with VISCOUNT LYMINGTON, and Carrel was regarded by the organic school as a prophetic voice.

CHESTERTON, G.K. (1874–1936). Novelist, artist, poet, journalist and religious polemicist, Chesterton was closely associated with HILAIRE BELLOC. Both men wrote for A.R. ORAGE's *NEW AGE* before the First

World War, and were sympathetic to GUILD SOCIALISM. They subsequently developed the theory of DISTRIBUTISM. Chesterton influenced MAURICE RECKITT, who wrote for his weekly newspaper, and PHILIP MAIRET. He converted to Roman Catholicism in 1922. Politically he began on the Left, supporting the trade unions during the 1926 General Strike, but thereafter his views tended to be associated more with the Right, who were sympathetic to his ideas on rural reconstruction and identified with the suspicion of Jewish finance evident in some of his work.

COLLIS, JOHN STEWART (1900–1984). Collis was to be found, sympathetic but sceptical, on the fringes of the organic movement. He frequently contributed to the *NEW ENGLISH WEEKLY*, and made a career as a literary biographer. During the Second World War he worked as a forester on ROLF GARDINER's Dorset estate, subsequently writing books of 'poetic ecology' on natural phenomena.

COWARD, RALPH (1902–90). Ralph Coward was a Dorset organic farmer, near-neighbour of ROLF GARDINER and a founder member of the SOIL ASSOCIATION. According to Wright (1996, p.173) he was a member of the ENGLISH ARRAY in the 1930s; in the 1940s he was involved in the COUNCIL FOR THE CHURCH AND COUNTRYSIDE and a friend of DAVID PECK. KENNETH BARLOW's daughter Joanna made a television documentary about him in the 1980s.

DANIEL, CHARLES W. (1871/72–1955). Daniel was a Tolstoyan anarchist who established a publishing company in London which produced some classic texts of the organic canon, such as *The Wheel of Health* (1938) by G.T. WRENCH. He also published books by PHILIP MAIRET, the CHANDOS GROUP and EDGAR J. SAXON. He supported SOCIAL CREDIT and published the journals *HEALTH AND LIFE* and *PURPOSE*.

DE LA MARE, RICHARD (1901–86). The son of the poet Walter de la Mare, Richard de la Mare edited the agriculture and horticulture list at FABER AND FABER from the early 1930s until the early 1970s, and was thereby responsible for the publication of many of the most important texts in the development of the organic movement. His connection with the movement stemmed from the fact that his brother-in-law J.G.S. DONALDSON worked at the PIONEER HEALTH CENTRE. He was a founder member of the SOIL ASSOCIATION and served for several years on its Council. He was a keen gardener and a man of deep religious faith.

DEMANT, V.A. (1893–1983). Vigo Auguste Demant was of Huguenot stock. He took a degree in Engineering and then in 1916 read for the Diploma in Anthropology at Oxford. He was ordained an Anglican priest in 1920, became a Canon of St Paul's in 1942, and in 1949 Canon of Christ Church, Oxford and Professor of Moral and Pastoral Theology in Oxford University. He retired in 1971. Demant was a leading figure in the CHRISTENDOM GROUP, a member of the CHANDOS GROUP, and a supporter of SOCIAL CREDIT. With W.G. PECK and MAURICE RECKITT he sought to articulate a CHRISTIAN SOCIOLOGY based on the principles of Catholic theology. He spoke at WILLIAM TEMPLE's 1941 Malvern Conference, on the threat to the natural environment posed by the unregulated profit-seeking of the capitalist trader.

DONALDSON, FRANCES (1907–94). Frances Donaldson was the wife of J.G.S. DONALDSON, who worked for the PIONEER HEALTH CENTRE. Best-known as a biographer, she wrote two books for FABER AND FABER during the Second World War on her farming experiences. She was a friend of SIR GEORGE STAPLEDON. In politics she was a socialist.

DONALDSON, J.G.S. (1907–98). Jack Donaldson was a wealthy socialist who gave half his inheritance to the PIONEER HEALTH CENTRE and worked there from 1935 to

1938. In 1935 he married Frances Lonsdale (FRANCES DONALDSON). The Donaldsons took up farming during the Second World War and continued to farm in Gloucestershire in the post-war period. RICHARD DE LA MARE was his brother-in-law. He was Minister for the Arts in the 1974–79 Labour Government. According to his son he was a man of deep religious faith. His commitment to the organic movement appears to have faded in the post-war years.

DOUGLAS, MAJOR CLIFFORD H. (1879–1952). An engineer by training, Douglas's importance to the organic movement lay in his monetary reform theory SOCIAL CREDIT, to which many of the movement's leading figures were committed. Douglas converted A.R. ORAGE to his ideas shortly after the First World War and was able to use the *NEW AGE* to propagate them. Orage's adoption of Social Credit led to a fatal split in the movement for GUILD SOCIALISM. Douglas's views tended towards anti-semitic conspiracy theory and to that extent lent themselves to adoption by the political Right, but his chief concern seems to have been to make the Labour movement address the financial obstacles thwarting the establishment of socialism.

DUNCAN, RONALD (1914–82). A precociously talented poet and dramatist, Duncan edited the literary journal *Townsman* from 1938 to 1946. An admirer of Gandhi and a pacifist, he turned his previously derelict North Devon farm into an agricultural community during the Second World War and wrote of his struggles in the 'Husbandry Notes' column of the *NEW ENGLISH WEEKLY*. He was a guest of the KINSHIP IN HUSBANDRY, a friend of the EARL OF PORTSMOUTH and HENRY WILLIAMSON, and in the post-war period contributed regularly to the *Evening Standard,* attacking government agricultural policy as 'Farmer Jan.' He had at one time been attracted by Catholicism, but settled into agnosticism.

EASTERBROOK, LAURENCE (1893–1965). After serving in the First World War Laurence Easterbrook decided that he did not want to return to working in the City, and took up farming. His articles on agriculture attracted the attention of Lloyd George, and he worked on Liberal Party land policy. He was agricultural correspondent for the *Daily Telegraph* and later for the *News Chronicle*. From 1939 to 1941 he was Public Relations Officer at the Ministry of Agriculture. During his journalistic work he met C.A MIER and was converted to the ideas of RUDOLF STEINER. He was a guest of the KINSHIP IN HUSBANDRY, a founder member of the SOIL ASSOCIATION and member of its Council for many years, and a Christian Spiritualist.

ELIOT, T.S. (1888–1965). Eliot's importance to the organic movement was threefold: as a director of FABER AND FABER he took an active interest in RICHARD DE LA MARE's commissioning of books on organic husbandry; as a member of the CHANDOS GROUP he helped formulate the ideas of a CHRISTIAN SOCIOLOGY which were the context of the organic movement's development; and as a member of the editorial board of the *NEW ENGLISH WEEKLY* he helped run the paper which was the major vehicle for organic ideas. The last three of his *Four Quartets* were first published as special supplements in the *NEW.*

ELLIOT, ROBERT H. (1837–1914). Elliot owned land in Southern India, Ireland and Scotland. His book *Agricultural Changes* (1898) was a response to the depression which had affected British agriculture since the 1870s; its fourth edition (1910) bore the title *The Clifton Park System of Farming.* Elliot anticipated many of the organic movement's concerns, disliking Britain's dependence on imported foodstuffs and wondering about the possible effects of artificial fertilizers. His system of ley-farming influenced R.G. STAPLEDON, who wrote the introduction to the fifth edition of *The Clifton Park System of Farming*, published by FABER AND FABER in 1943.

ELLIOT, WALTER (1888–1958). Like LORD ADDISON, Walter Elliot was a Minister of Agriculture (1932–36) who was a distinguished medical scientist: he became a Fellow of the Royal Society in 1935, having worked at the Rowett Institute, Aberdeen, in the 1920s with JOHN BOYD ORR and established a link between provision of school milk and improved children's health. He was a Unionist MP for Scottish constituencies from 1918 to 1945 and Minister of Health from 1938 to 1940. As Minister of Agriculture he took a corporatist approach to policy; there was a gradual shift towards a coherent strategy, with further Marketing Acts being passed to follow Addison's of 1931. He asked VISCOUNT LYMINGTON to be his Parliamentary Private Secretary, but Lymington was shortly to resign his seat. Elliot's importance to the organic movement lay in his work with Boyd Orr on the relationship between diet and health.

FAULKNER, EDWARD (1886–1964). Faulkner was a United States farmer, and the son of a farmer, who became sceptical of the value of the mouldboard plough and during the Second World War gained national celebrity when his book *Ploughman's Folly* was published. Although the organic school regarded his opposition to ploughing as stimulating but extreme, his views on the care of the soil had much in common with theirs, and his subsequent books demonstrated the influence of F.H. KING and an affinity with the ideas of SIR ALBERT HOWARD and SIR ROBERT McCARRISON.

FORDHAM, MONTAGUE (1864–1948). A polymath who was variously a lawyer, a Fellow of the Royal Historical Society, and an agriculturalist. From 1899 to 1908 he was Director of the Arts and Crafts Gallery in London, and in 1907 he founded the Land Club Union. From 1922 to 1926 he worked in East Poland as a reconstructor of agriculture. He was Secretary of the RURAL RECONSTRUCTION ASSOCIATION from 1926 to 1946, and a member of the ECONOMIC REFORM CLUB AND INSTITUTE and the NEW BRITAIN movement. He was a close friend of Archbishop WILLIAM TEMPLE and A.J. PENTY.

GARDINER, ROLF (1902–71). [Henry] Rolf Gardiner was one of the most important figures in the organic movement, and one of the most controversial. He was born and brought up in Berlin, and this led him to seek Anglo-German unity at all costs. His father was a distinguished archaeologist; his uncle, Balfour Gardiner, was a noted composer, and his son Sir John Eliot Gardiner is one of today's foremost orchestral conductors. Gardiner espoused GUILD SOCIALISM briefly during his youth but by the early 1930s was involved in the far-Right organization the ENGLISH MISTERY, along with ANTHONY LUDOVICI and VISCOUNT LYMINGTON. He had close links with the German youth movement and used his Dorset estate as a centre for youth camps and for land-work camps for the unemployed. Gardiner trained as a forester at Dartington and envisaged estates like his own as centres of regional rural reconstruction. A man of extraordinary energy, he was instrumental in establishing the KINSHIP IN HUSBANDRY and the COUNCIL FOR THE CHURCH AND COUNTRYSIDE, and was a founder member of the SOIL ASSOCIATION. He wrote frequently for the *NEW ENGLISH WEEKLY* and was involved with Lymington's journal *NEW PIONEER*. In 1950 he organized a European Husbandry Meeting, which met at his Dorset estate and at London's Caxton Hall. During the last twenty years of his life he remained active in work for the Soil Association and the Council for the Protection of Rural England.

GEDDES, PATRICK (1854–1932). Geddes was a biologist and town-planner. He studied under Thomas Huxley and held posts at University College, London, and at Aberdeen and Edinburgh Universities. He was a pioneer of town planning and city improvements, whose importance to the organic movement lay in his biological conception of society and his influence on PHILIP MAIRET, who worked for a time as his assistant and was later his biographer. Geddes was involved in the KIBBO KIFT KIN and in AUBREY WESTLAKE'S ORDER OF WOODCRAFT CHIVALRY founded by . He was a founder of the SOCIOLOGICAL SOCIETY and was involved with the ADLER SOCIETY and the NEW EUROPE group. KENNETH BARLOW became his secretary shortly before his death.

GILBERT, JOSEPH HENRY (1817–1901). J.H. Gilbert studied Chemistry at Glasgow and University College, London, and in 1840 was a student of JUSTUS VON LIEBIG at Giessen. Returning to UCL he met JOHN BENNET LAWES, and in 1843 went to work with him at ROTHAMSTED EXPERIMENTAL STATION, where he remained until his death, keeping meticulous records of all data relevant to the field experiments. He described the purpose of his work as 'the investigation of the scientific problems involved in agricultural processes' (Russell 1966, p.105).

GILL, ERIC (1882–1940). Eric Gill was a noted sculptor, printer and designer who converted to Roman Catholicism and lived in various communities which attempted to combine art, agriculture, craftsmanship and worship. PHILIP MAIRET spent some time at the Ditchling community in Sussex at the end of the First World War. Like A.J. PENTY, Gill was opposed to industrialism and looked back to the medieval period as providing possible models of good living for a post-industrial future; unlike Penty, he associated politically with the Left, though his social ideas had an affinity with DISTRIBUTISM. He designed the gravestone of A.R. ORAGE and the masthead of the journal CHRISTENDOM.

GREENWELL, BERNARD (1874–1939). Sir Bernard Greenwell owned estates in Suffolk and Surrey, and became an adherent of the INDORE PROCESS of composting developed by SIR ALBERT HOWARD. He made use of town wastes to fertilize his land. His son Sir Peter Greenwell was on the SOIL ASSOCIATION Council for many years.

GURDJIEFF, G.I. (c.1866–1949). George Gurdjieff claimed to have travelled widely in the Middle East and Tibet, gathering esoteric knowledge and learning ancient dances, rituals and methods of self-development. His system, known as 'The Work,' attracted many Western adherents including the psychiatrist Maurice Nicoll, the writer Katherine Mansfield (wife of JOHN MIDDLETON MURRY), and A.R. ORAGE. Orage gave up his post as editor of the NEW AGE to study Gurdjieff's system in France and then teach it in America. Stanley Nott, a SOCIAL CREDIT publisher and friend of Orage, also studied 'The Work,' and his son Adam Nott still teaches it today. P.L. TRAVERS was also involved in it.

HALL, A.D. (1864–1942). Sir Daniel Hall was one of the greatest agriculturalists of his time, and, as an advocate of the large-scale, specialist, 'factory' farm, one of the chief characters in the organic school's demonology. After a period as a schoolmaster and a University Extension Lecturer, Hall became the first Principal of Wye Agricultural College in Kent, where he spent from 1894 to 1902. From 1902 to 1912 he was Director of the ROTHAMSTED EXPERIMENTAL STATION, being succeeded by E.J. RUSSELL. After working for the Development Commission he became Head of the Board of Agriculture from 1917 to 1927, and then took over as Director of the John Innes Horticultural Institute at Merton, Surrey, where he stayed until 1939. He wrote an important book on artificial fertilizers, and was an authority on the tulip and the apple. To mark his 75th birthday he was given an Honorary Fellowship at Balliol College, Oxford, and was presented with a collection of essays: contributors included JOHN BOYD ORR, C.S. ORWIN, E.J. RUSSELL and R.G. STAPLEDON.

HARGRAVE, JOHN (1894–1982). An indirect influence on the organic movement, Hargrave was a Quaker who served as a stretcher-bearer during the First World War. He was a pacifist and socialist, as well as an English nationalist who was concerned about racial degeneration and wanted to establish a new folk-memory to replace that destroyed by *laissez-faire* industrialism. He founded the KIBBO KIFT KIN, with which ROLF GARDINER and PATRICK GEDDES were associated, and adopted SOCIAL CREDIT ideas. In the 1930s he formed his own Green Shirt Movement for Social Credit, but was eventually disowned by C.H. DOUGLAS. He was a friend of EDGAR J. SAXON and wrote for *HEALTH AND LIFE*.

HERON, T.M. (1890–1983). Tom Heron was a member of the editorial board of the *NEW ENGLISH WEEKLY* and father of the painter Patrick Heron. One of his other sons, Giles, married Mary Barran, who had been secretary to LADY EVE BALFOUR. Heron was a designer who as a young man had attended the Leeds Art Club, founded by A.R. ORAGE. He spent some time in Cornwall, where he knew the potter Bernard Leach, and subsequently moved to Welwyn Garden City, running the firm Cresta Silks. During the Second World War he was responsible for the design of Utility Clothing. Heron was a socialist who belonged to the Independent Labour Party and supported SOCIAL CREDIT; he did not end up on the Right. He converted from Nonconformism to Anglo-Catholicism and remained a devout Churchman.

HILLS, LAWRENCE D. (1911–90). Lawrence Hills was a gardener and nurseryman who specialized in alpines and wrote books on them for FABER AND FABER, as a result of which he became a friend of RICHARD DE LA MARE and a publisher's reader for the firm for 25 years. During the Second World War he discovered the ideas of RUDOLF STEINER and also made contact with SIR ALBERT HOWARD. In the late 1940s he discovered the virtues of comfrey and

this led him to research the life of Henry Doubleday, who introduced the plant into England in the 1870s. The HENRY DOUBLEDAY RESEARCH ASSOCIATION (HDRA) was formed in 1954, and has since developed into the national centre for organic gardening at Ryton-on-Dunsmore near Coventry. F. NEWMAN TURNER became President of the HDRA. Hills was a member of the SOIL ASSOCIATION and Gardening Correspondent of *The Observer* (1958–66), and of *Punch* (1966–70). He helped establish *The Ecologist*.

HOBSON, S.G. (1870–1940). Samuel Hobson was significant in the background to the organic movement through his development of the ideas of GUILD SOCIALISM, which were developed in collaboration with A.R. ORAGE in the columns of the *NEW AGE* in 1912–13. During the First World War he worked in the Ministry of Munitions. Hobson was active in the NEW BRITAIN movement in the 1930s and wrote occasionally for the *NEW ENGLISH WEEKLY*. Unlike his former colleague A.J. PENTY, he did not believe the Guilds idea to have been realized in Mussolini's Italy.

HOPKINS, DONALD P. (b.1909). Hopkins worked for the fertilizer trade and was a formidable opponent of the organic movement in the pages of the *Fertilizer Journal* and in his book *Chemicals, Humus, and the Soil*, published by FABER AND FABER in 1945. He challenged the organic movement's suspicion of artificials, while not denying the value of humus. Evidently he regarded the organic school's arguments as potentially threatening to the fertilizer trade and took them seriously. The debate was conducted with respect on both sides.

HOWARD, ALBERT (1873–1947). Through winning open scholarships, Howard made his way to the Royal College of Science, Kensington, in 1893, where he gained an associateship in Chemistry with First Class distinction. In 1896 he went to St John's College, Cambridge as a Foundation Scholar and gained a first in Natural Sciences; in 1897 he was first in all England in the Cambridge Agricultural Diploma, and in 1898 second in all England in the National Diploma in Agriculture. From 1899 to 1902 he lectured in Agricultural Science at Harrison College, Barbados; from 1902 to 1905 he was a botanist at Wye College in Kent, continuing the work of A.D. HALL on the hop industry. In 1905 he went to India to take charge of the Experimental Station at Pusa, newly created by Lord Curzon. In 1914 he was created a Companion of the Indian Empire. From 1924 to 1931 he was Director of the Institute of Plant Industry in the State of Indore, returning to Britain in 1931. He was knighted in 1934 and became an Honorary Fellow of the Imperial College of Science in 1935. In 1905 he married GABRIELLE MATTHAEI, who died in 1930; he then married her sister LOUISE MATTHAEI. Howard wrote frequently for the *NEW ENGLISH WEEKLY*, to which he was an advisor; he was involved in the ECONOMIC REFORM CLUB AND INSTITUTE and the COUNCIL FOR THE CHURCH AND COUNTRYSIDE; he supported the work of the PIONEER HEALTH CENTRE; with SIR ROBERT MCCARRISON he launched the *MEDICAL TESTAMENT* in 1939. However, he did not become a member of the SOIL ASSOCIATION, and his journal *SOIL AND HEALTH* ran as a rival to *MOTHER EARTH* from 1946 to 1948.

HOWARD, GABRIELLE L.C. (1876–1930). Sister of LOUISE HOWARD, Gabrielle Matthaei took a Double First in Natural Sciences at Newnham College, Cambridge and later became a Fellow and Demonstrator there. She undertook research on the transpiration and respiration of plants. In 1905 she married ALBERT HOWARD and worked with him in India until her death in 1930. They were known as 'the Sidney and Beatrice Webb of India,' their research being the product of devoted team-work. In 1913 Gabrielle Howard was appointed Second Imperial Economic Botanist to the Government of India. She helped form the Indian Science Congress and presided over its Agricultural and Botanical Sections.

HOWARD, LOUISE E. (1880–1969). Sister of GABRIELLE HOWARD, Louise Matthaei was a Classical scholar and Fellow of Newnham College, Cambridge. She was among the original staff of the International Labour Office at Geneva and became Chief of the Agricultural Service there, writing a major survey of international labour in agriculture. In 1931 she married ALBERT HOWARD and devoted herself to supporting his work. After his death in 1947 she became active in the SOIL ASSOCIATION and a close friend of LADY EVE BALFOUR. She wrote an account of Howard's achievements in India.

JACKS, G.V. (1901–77). Graham Jacks won a science scholarship to Christ Church, Oxford in 1919, and became a noted soil scientist. From 1929 to 1931 he lectured at the Imperial Forestry Institute, and from 1931 to 1946 he was Deputy Director of the Imperial (later Commonwealth) Bureau of Soil Science, subsequently becoming Director. He edited the *Journal of Soil Science* from 1949 to 1961. Despite his employment by the ROTHAMSTED EXPERIMENTAL STATION he was important to the organic movement on account of his 1939 book, written in conjunction with R.O. WHYTE, *The Rape of the Earth,* which provided worldwide evidence of the spread of soil erosion.

JENKS, JORIAN E.F. (1899–1963). One of the most active figures in the development of the organic movement, and a prolific journalist who was involved in many of the organizations which propagated its cause. The son of a highly distinguished expert on jurisprudence, Jenks obtained the National Diploma in Agriculture in 1920 and worked as a farm manager in Berkshire, but was a casualty of the slump and emigrated to New Zealand where he worked for the Department of Agriculture and later had special responsibility for deteriorated lands. In 1928 he returned to Britain and studied at Balliol College, Oxford, working for the Research Institute of Agricultural Economics. During the 1930s he farmed in Sussex and became active in politics, being one of the leading figures in the British Union of Fascists; this resulted in imprisonment in 1940. According to Matless (1998, p.120) he was still active in Mosleyite causes in the late 1940s. Jenks was associated with the KINSHIP IN HUSBANDRY; he wrote frequently for the *NEW ENGLISH WEEKLY*; he was a member of the ECONOMIC REFORM CLUB AND INSTITUTE, editing its journal *RURAL ECONOMY*; he was an early member of the SOIL ASSOCIATION and edited *MOTHER EARTH* from 1946 to 1963; he drafted *Feeding the Fifty Million* (1955) for the RURAL RECONSTRUCTION ASSOCIATION; he was Secretary to the COUNCIL FOR THE CHURCH AND COUNTRYSIDE. In the post-war period he farmed near Alton in Hampshire.

KING, F.C. (dates unknown). King was head gardener at Levens Hall, near Kendal, and a convert to the ideas of SIR ALBERT HOWARD. He was a member of the SOIL ASSOCIATION. Levens Hall gardens were a showpiece for compost-gardening, and King also experimented with 'no-dig' methods.

KING, FRANKLIN H. (1848–1911). F.H. King worked for the United States Department of Agriculture, becoming increasingly sceptical about American farming methods. He resigned in order to fulfil a long-term ambition of examining the farming methods of the Far East and in 1907 visited Korea, China and Japan. His observations, accompanied by many photographs, were published posthumously as *Farmers of Forty Centuries,* a book which the organic school referred to as clear evidence for the value of observing the rule of return of wastes to the soil.

LAWES, JOHN BENNET (1814–1900). As founder of the ROTHAMSTED EXPERIMENTAL STATION, J.B. Lawes was one of the most important figures in the history of agricultural chemistry. Brought up to the life of a country squire in Hertfordshire, Lawes nevertheless developed a taste for Chem-

istry, and after an undistinguished period at Oxford he attended lectures in the subject at University College, London. His investigations into soil nitrogen and the use of bones as fertilizer led him to establish experiments on his estate, for which the assistance of J.H. GILBERT proved invaluable. Lawes was the first industrial entrepreneur in the field of chemical fertilizers, establishing a factory to make superphosphates at Deptford, South London, in 1843. Although influenced by JUSTUS VON LIEBIG, he challenged a good deal of Liebig's theory.

LIEBIG, JUSTUS VON (1803–73). One of the most important figures in the history of Chemistry, Liebig was Professor at Giessen, Germany, from 1824 to 1852, where he established a laboratory which attracted students from many different countries. He made several visits to Britain, and his 1840 book *Organic Chemistry in its Application to Agriculture and Physiology,* perhaps the most important work ever written on agricultural chemistry, was dedicated to the British Association. His pupil J.H. GILBERT went on to work for J.B. LAWES at ROTHAMSTED EXPERIMENTAL STATION. Liebig's ideas were incorrect in various respects and his attempts to produce patent chemical fertilizers were unsuccessful, but his influence was responsible for a powerful surge of activity in agricultural chemistry. The full record of his many interests, which included nutrition, can be found in Brock (1997).

LOFTUS, PIERSE CREAGH (1877–1956). P.C. Loftus was active in East Anglian business and politics. He was Chairman of the brewing firm Adnam's, a JP in Suffolk, an Alderman on the East Suffolk County Council, and the National Conservative MP for Lowestoft from 1934 to 1945. He was a right-wing Catholic who was concerned about the state of agriculture and of the health and vitality of Britain's racial stock. A proponent of monetary reform, he belonged to the ECONOMIC REFORM

CLUB AND INSTITUTE. He was sympathetic to the general outlook of the organic movement, and was Chairman of the RURAL RECONSTRUCTION ASSOCIATION in the 1950s.

LUDOVICI, ANTHONY M. (1882–1971). Anthony Ludovici was briefly private secretary to Rodin in the first decade of the twentieth century, and became a devotee of Nietzsche, whose works he translated into English; through his propagation of Nietzschean ideas he came into contact with A.R. ORAGE and wrote for the *NEW AGE*. He wrote a major study of the racial and cultural value of aristocracy and was a member of the ENGLISH MISTERY. According to Bramwell (1989, p.197) he worked during the 1930s in the department of Rudolf Hess, on conservation projects. Despite this, he does not appear to have been imprisoned during the Second World War. He was involved with VISCOUNT LYMINGTON's short-lived *NEW PIONEER* and was active in the BRITISH PEOPLE'S PARTY. While sharing the organic pioneers' concern for fertile soil as a factor in human health, he condemned their indifference to genetic inheritance and racial breeding. His 1945 book *The Four Pillars of Health* was admired by DION BYNGHAM. Ludovici's Nietzschean hostility to Christianity, which values human beings regardless of their biological and genetic fitness, remained undiminished in his later years, as did his cold contempt for all forms of physical inadequacy.

LYMINGTON, VISCOUNT (1898–1984). Gerard Vernon Wallop, Viscount Lymington, became the 9th Earl of Portsmouth in 1943. He was born in the United States of an American mother and spent his early years on a Wyoming cattle ranch. Service in the First World War was followed by study at Oxford and bohemian life in Paris. In 1925 he became actively involved in farming the family's Hampshire estates, eventually reclaiming 3,000 acres of land which he took over from tenants, mostly bankrupt. From 1929 to 1934

he was the Conservative MP for Basingstoke, resigning in disgust at the torpor of parliamentary politics. He belonged to the ENGLISH MISTERY, of which ROLF GARDINER and ANTHONY LUDOVICI were also members; he later broke away from it to form the ENGLISH ARRAY. He had close links with Nazi Germany and in 1938 founded the short-lived, far-Right journal *NEW PIONEER*. He was a member of the KINSHIP IN HUSBANDRY and a founder-member of the SOIL ASSOCIATION. In the post-war years he spent more time on his Kenya estates and was involved with the white settlers movement. He was one of the most important figures in the development of organic husbandry, and one of the most right-wing.

McCARRISON, ROBERT (1878–1960). Major-General Sir Robert McCarrison was an Ulsterman who qualified as a doctor in 1900 and joined the Indian Medical Service in 1901. He served as Agency Surgeon at Gilgit from 1904 to 1911, during which period he began to investigate the incidence of goitre. In 1913 he was assigned to special duty for investigating goitre and cretinism in India, and in 1918 his scope was widened to include deficiency diseases in general. He was particularly interested in the health of the Hunza tribesmen on the North-West frontier. From 1929 to 1935 he was Director of Nutrition Research for the India Research Fund Association. He was knighted in 1933. He settled in Oxford after retirement from the Indian Medical Service, and from 1945 to 1955 was Director of Post-Graduate Medical Education at the University. By the late 1920s McCarrison was corresponding with GEORGE SCOTT WILLIAMSON and INNES PEARSE, and his work was to influence JEROME RODALE and LIONEL PICTON. Picton connected the significance of McCarrison's work with the research of SIR ALBERT HOWARD. Howard and McCarrison spoke at the launch in 1939 of the *MEDICAL TESTAMENT*. McCarrison's work had been celebrated the previous year by G.T. WRENCH in his book *The Wheel of Health*. In 1966 the McCarrison Society was formed, in which KENNETH BARLOW played a leading role.

MCDONAGH, J.E.R. (1881–1965). A distinguished bacteriologist, McDonagh was Hunterian Professor at the Royal College of Surgeons in 1916, and founder in 1929 of the Nature of Disease Institute. He was associated with the KINSHIP IN HUSBANDRY, and a friend of the EARL OF PORTSMOUTH.

MAIRET, PHILIP (1886–1975). Philippe Auguste Mairet (he anglicized the first name during the 1930s) was a man of remarkably varied gifts. He trained as a draughtsman and a designer, and in 1906 joined C.R. Ashbee's Guild of Handicraft in Chipping Campden. It was there that he first met PATRICK GEDDES, for whom he later worked as an assistant, and he became secretary to the art historian Ananda Coomaraswamy, whose wife Ethel, the noted weaver, he was himself to marry in 1913. During the First World War he was imprisoned as a conscientious objector, and towards the end of it undertook agricultural work at the Sussex community of ERIC GILL. In the post-war period he was involved with GUILD SOCIALISM, and met A.R. ORAGE; he was influenced by DMITRI MITRINOVIC, whose esoteric system he studied for more than a decade. A convert to SOCIAL CREDIT, he was a member of the CHANDOS GROUP and contributed to the Group's books on social issues. He was actively involved in the cluster of groups which overlapped with Chandos: the ADLER SOCIETY, the SOCIOLOGICAL SOCIETY, the NEW EUROPE group, the NEW BRITAIN movement, and the journal *PURPOSE*. When Orage founded the *NEW ENGLISH WEEKLY* in 1932 he joined him as assistant, becoming editor after Orage's death in 1934. From the late 1930s Mairet began to be more closely connected with right-wing groups, contributed to VISCOUNT LYMINGTON's *NEW PIONEER*, and was a member of the KINSHIP IN HUSBANDRY. He belonged to the COUNCIL FOR THE CHURCH AND COUNTRYSIDE; he edited, with Dr Alec Vidler, the Anglican journal *Frontier* during the 1950s. Mairet was also, at different times, a Shakespearean actor at the Old Vic, and translator of Jean-Paul Sartre and Emmanuel Mounier.

MARIAN, SIEGFRIED (1898–1952). An Austrian analytical chemist, Marian taught at Exeter University and in the 1940s worked at Dartington Hall on a reafforestation project. He developed a product called 'Actumus,' highly concentrated humus blended with charcoal, and propounded its virtues in his publication *SOIL MAGAZINE*. He shared many of the concerns of the SOIL ASSOCIATION, but was at times scathing about it, as he was about ROTHAMSTED EXPERIMENTAL STATION. AUBREY WESTLAKE undertook experiments with 'Actumus,' and DION BYNGHAM worked with Marian on *Soil Magazine*.

MASSINGHAM, H.J. (1888–1952). Harold John Massingham — known to his associates in the KINSHIP IN HUSBANDRY as 'John,' and not to be confused with his brother Hugh, the political journalist — was son of the newspaper editor H.W. Massingham. He contributed to the *NEW AGE* and was sympathetic to GUILD SOCIALISM. He welcomed the return of A.R. ORAGE to English journalism in 1932 and contributed frequently to the *NEW ENGLISH WEEKLY* from 1940 onwards. A prolific writer on rural life and topography, he became a member of the KINSHIP IN HUSBANDRY and was a founder-member of the SOIL ASSOCIATION, serving on its Council for some years. A convert to Anglo-Catholic Christianity, he was also involved with the work of the COUNCIL FOR THE CHURCH AND COUNTRYSIDE. Although he claimed to be non-political, co-writing a book with the socialist Jew Edward Hyams, he was a patron of the Right Book Club during the 1940s.

MATTHAEI, GABRIELLE L.C. *see* HOWARD, GABRIELLE L.C.

MATTHAEI, LOUISE E. *see* HOWARD, LOUISE E.

MIER, C.A. [also known as C.A. MIRBT] (1902–75). A major figure in the development of BIODYNAMIC CULTIVATION in Britain, Carl Alexander Mier was born in Marburg an der Lehn in Germany and studied agriculture from 1920 to 1926. In Silesia he came into contact with the Anthroposophist Count Keyserlingk, on whose estate RUDOLF STEINER gave his lectures on agriculture in 1924. Mier became the Count's agricultural advisor. In 1928 he received his doctorate from Berlin University, and was sent to the Anthroposophical World Conference in London to represent the movement's agricultural section. In 1929 he was invited to initiate Biodynamic methods in Britain, and was joined by his family later that year. After various moves they settled at Clent in Worcestershire, where there already existed — and still exists — a Steiner community. Mier influenced LAURENCE EASTERBROOK and helped R.G.M. WILSON establish his composting system at Iceni Nurseries in the Fenlands. He was an active Secretary of the Biodynamic Agricultural Association until the mid-1950s.

MIRBT, C.A. *see* MIER, C.A.

MITRINOVIC, DMITRI (1887–1953). A remarkable Serbian sage, his importance in the development of the organic movement was indirect but substantial. He influenced the thinking of A.R. ORAGE and wrote under the pseudonym 'M.M. Cosmoi' for the *NEW AGE*. PHILIP MAIRET studied his esoteric system for about a decade and was profoundly influenced by him. Mitrinovic was instrumental in initiating the CHANDOS GROUP, although he left it early on. He was sympathetic to GUILD SOCIALISM and SOCIAL CREDIT, and he admired the work of RUDOLF STEINER. He was a leading figure in the ADLER SOCIETY, the NEW EUROPE group and the NEW BRITAIN movement. A Mitrinovic archive was established at the University of Bradford in 1998. Politically he was somewhat ambivalent in his contacts, but tended more to the Left than to the Right. His religion was a form of esoteric Christianity.

MUMFORD, LEWIS (1895–1990). An American polymath who received innumerable international medals and academic honours. He could be found on the fringes of the organic movement, his ideas on the role of 'technics' in human society influencing his friend PHILIP MAIRET. An admirer of PATRICK GEDDES, he visited Britain in 1919 to work with him, and met Mairet and A.R. ORAGE. He was an occasional presence at meetings of the CHANDOS GROUP and took an interest in the PIONEER HEALTH CENTRE.

MURRY, JOHN MIDDLETON (1889–1957). Murry was a literary critic, a friend of D.H. Lawrence before the First World War, and the husband of Katherine Mansfield, who died during her stay at the Fontainebleau Institute run by G.I. GURDJIEFF. Murry's ideological stance changed frequently: in the 1930s he was a Marxist; by 1940 he was a pacifist, editing *Peace News*. He converted to Christianity; he ran a farming community on organic lines during the war, of which DION BYNGHAM was a member. His journal *THE ADELPHI* lent support to the organic cause. He argued for the regeneration of English society, not through State Socialism, but through encouraging the growth of rural communities. Murry was a friend of leading figures in the organic movement, including PHILIP MAIRET and HENRY WILLIAMSON, and wrote occasionally for the *NEW ENGLISH WEEKLY*.

NORTHBOURNE, LORD (1896–1982). Walter Northbourne studied Agriculture at Oxford and lectured there for a time during the 1920s. He experimented with BIODYNAMIC CULTIVATION on his estate near Deal in Kent. He was a member of the KINSHIP IN HUSBANDRY and of the ECONOMIC REFORM CLUB AND INSTITUTE. S.G. HOBSON mentions him as a friend, though one can only assume that the link was monetary reform, their politics being very different. Northbourne was also a painter, a translator, and a student of religion.

OGG, SIR WILLIAM G. (1891–1979). William Gammie Ogg was the son of an Aberdeenshire farmer. A distinguished soil scientist, he was the first Director of the Macaulay Institute for Soil Research, Aberdeen, from 1930 to 1943, when he succeeded SIR E.J. RUSSELL as Director of ROTHAMSTED EXPERIMENTAL STATION. He retired in 1958. From 1953 to 1955 he was President of the Society of Chemical Industry. A vigorous opponent of the organic school, he was the subject of some satirical doggerel in the NEW ENGLISH WEEKLY (25.10.1945, p.14).

ORAGE, A.R. (1873–1934). Alfred Richard Orage does not appear to have been particularly interested in agriculture, but his indirect influence on the organic movement was very considerable. As a young man he was a schoolmaster in Leeds, where he joined the Theosophical movement, was active in Fabian politics, and founded the Leeds Art Club, of which A.J. PENTY and later, T.M. HERON, were members. After moving to London he took over in 1907 the failing journal the NEW AGE and turned it into one of the best periodicals of the time. Disillusioned with Fabianism, Orage and S.G. HOBSON used it to promote GUILD SOCIALISM. Orage was influenced during the First World War by DMITRI MITRINOVIC and, from 1919, by the SOCIAL CREDIT docrine of C.H. DOUGLAS. In 1920 the Guilds movement split into two factions: those who, like PHILIP MAIRET and MAURICE RECKITT, adopted Orage's commitment to Social Credit, and those who opted for Bolshevism. Orage then confounded his followers by leaving England in order to study the esoteric system of G.I. GURDJIEFF and teach it in America. Returning to England in 1931, Orage founded the NEW ENGLISH WEEKLY in 1932, with Mairet as his assistant, to propound Social Credit as the answer to the economic crisis. He died in November 1934, the night after giving his only radio broadcast.

ORR, JOHN BOYD (1880–1971). Sir John Boyd Orr was often referred to by the organic school in support of their views on the relationship between soil, food and health. In 1914 he was appointed Director of the Rowett Institute, Aberdeen, and drew up a scheme of what he believed necessary for research into nutrition. After the First World War he was joined there by WALTER ELLIOT, and by 1927 the Institute had an international reputation. His dietary experiments established the beneficial effects of milk on children's health, and his concern that poorer families could not afford fresh, protective foods led to his involvement with the ECONOMIC REFORM CLUB AND INSTITUTE. His 1936 book *Food, Health and Income* revealed the extent of malnutrition in Britain, and he argued for an integrated health and agriculture policy. His ideas influenced wartime food policy, ensuring that rationing was based on nutritional needs. From 1945 to 1948, he was Director-General of the Food and Agriculture Organization of the United Nations. He was awarded the Nobel Peace Prize in 1949. Boyd Orr gave the SANDERSON-WELLS Lecture in 1948, on the necessity of maintaining world soil fertility, but he was not opposed to artificials, and was a close friend of SIR WILLIAM OGG, Director of ROTHAMSTED EXPERIMENTAL STATION.

ORWIN, C.S. (1876–1955). Charles Stewart Orwin (not to be confused with his wife Christabel, who had the same initials) was an agricultural economist who, as an advocate of large-scale specialist farming, was a leading figure in the demonology of the organic school. He lectured at Wye College in Kent from 1903 to 1906, then until 1913 was land agent for the estates of Christopher Turnor in Lincolnshire. He also farmed as an owner-occupier. From 1913 to 1945 he was Director of the Agricultural Research Economics Institute at Oxford, and from 1912 to 1927 edited the *Journal of the Royal Agricultural Society of Eng-*

land. From 1925 to 1933 he was a member of the Food Council. He wrote enthusiastically about the pioneers of farming who used machinery, cost-accounting and artificial fertilizers to boost the rate of output per man.

OSBORN, (HENRY) FAIRFIELD (1887–1969). Fairfield Osborn was a noted American ecologist, President of the Conservation Foundation, a member of the Scientific Advisory Committee of the Natural Resources Council of America, and President of the Bronx Park Zoo, New York. He wrote two books on care of the environment for FABER AND FABER. LADY EVE BALFOUR visited him during her American tour of 1951. He was knowledgeable about the British organic movement and shared its underlying religious philosophy.

OYLER, PHILIP (1879–1973). Philip Oyler was born into a Kentish farming family and followed in the family tradition, working at various times as a farm labourer, owner and tenant. He managed the Verney estates both in England and in France, and worked during the 1920s at the Hampshire estate of AUBREY WESTLAKE. He was a member of the KINSHIP IN HUSBANDRY and a founder-member of the SOIL ASSOCIATION.

PEARSE, INNES HOPE (1889–1978). As co-founder, with her husband GEORGE SCOTT WILLIAMSON, of the PIONEER HEALTH CENTRE, Dr Innes Pearse was one of the most influential figures in the development of the organic movement. She qualified as a doctor in 1916 and was one of the first women house physicians at the London Hospital. After wide clinical experience she became Scott Williamson's research assistant at the Royal College of Surgeons. Her work in an Infant Welfare Centre led her to believe that children's health must be dealt with in a family setting, and in 1926 she and Scott-Williamson established the family health club in Peckham, South London, which in 1935 became the Pioneer Health Centre. From the mid-1920s she

was in contact with ROBERT MCCARRISON, whose views on health and diet strongly influenced the work at Peckham. She was a founder member of the SOIL ASSOCIATION and gave it many years of enthusiastic service. In 1948 she lectured in the United States on the Pioneer Health Centre's work. She and her husband supported KENNETH BARLOW in his efforts to establish the Coventry Family Health Club.

PECK, DAVID G. (b.1911). The son of W.G. PECK, David Peck likewise became an Anglican clergyman; as a result of being in a rural parish he became concerned about rural poverty and depopulation. He was a leading figure in the COUNCIL FOR THE CHURCH AND COUNTRYSIDE, and wrote for the *NEW ENGLISH WEEKLY*. From 1941 to 1943 he was Area Director of the INDUSTRIAL CHRISTIAN FELLOWHIP, and from 1943 to 1951 vicar of Little Bedwyn in the Salisbury diocese. Later he lectured in Agricultural History at Oxford University. He was a close friend of RALPH COWARD.

PECK, WILLIAM G. (1883–1962). W.G. Peck trained as a Methodist minister, and served a parish in Blackburn from 1911 to 1918. He spoke on Labour Party platforms with figures such as Philip Snowden and Bernard Shaw. His dislike of orthodox economics led him to support SOCIAL CREDIT. In 1925 he was ordained into the Anglican Church by WILLIAM TEMPLE and was soon a central figure in the CHRISTENDOM GROUP. He was Director of Clergy Schools for the INDUSTRIAL CHRISTIAN FELLOWSHIP. In 1948 he wrote an outline of the ideas of CHRISTIAN SOCIOLOGY. *See also* DAVID G. PECK.

PENTY, ARTHUR J. (1875–1937). A.J. Penty was an architect, a friend of A.R. ORAGE at the Leeds Art Club, and one of the key figures in the establishment of GUILD SOCIALISM. His dislike of industrialism's destructive effect on craftsmanship led him to look back to the medieval guilds as ideals of economic organization, and in

1906 he wrote *The Restoration of the Gild* [*sic*] *System*. The idea of Guilds as an alternative to State Socialism was taken up a few years later by Orage and S.G. HOBSON in the *NEW AGE*, to which Penty also contributed. Like Orage and Hobson, Penty was a Fabian who became disillusioned with Labour politics. In the early 1920s he helped establish the CHRISTENDOM GROUP. He contributed to *CHRISTENDOM* in the 1930s, by which time he had moved well to the Right: he ended up as a member of the British Union of Fascists and an ardent admirer of Mussolini, whom he believed had established the Guild State in Italy. He was a friend of MONTAGUE FORDHAM and MAURICE RECKITT.

PFEIFFER, EHRENFRIED (1899–1961). Ehrenfriend Pfeiffer was the leading advocate of BIODYNAMIC CULTIVATION after the death of RUDOLF STEINER. He was born in Munich, and was training as an electrical engineer when, about 1920, he came into contact with Steiner and began to study Anthroposophy. He turned to the study of inorganic chemistry, and after Steiner's death started in Dornach the Laboratory for Biochemical Research, as well as encouraging the spread of biodynamic cultivation in the Netherlands, Germany, Britain and the United States. In 1927 he took charge of the Loverendale Estate in Holland, which he developed to the point where it supported 700 families. In 1933 he emigrated to the United States, where he farmed and undertook research into cancer diagnosis which earned him an honorary doctorate. In 1948 he became Director of the Biochemical Research Laboratory in Spring Valley, New York State, and was visited there by EVE BALFOUR. During the 1930s in Britain he attended many meetings on organic farming, including one in 1939 at the home of LORD NORTHBOURNE, which was also attended by VISCOUNT LYMINGTON and SIR ALBERT HOWARD. He was a speaker at the 1950 European Husbandry Meeting, organized by the KINSHIP IN HUSBANDRY.

PICTON, LIONEL J. (1874–1948). Dr Lionel Picton, OBE, was one of the most important figures in the founding of the SOIL ASSOCIATION. He studied Medicine at Merton College, Oxford, qualifying as a doctor in 1900. During his studies he was influenced by the work of G.V. POORE. After working at the Liverpool Royal Infirmary he became in 1916 a GP at Holmes Chapel, Cheshire. He was for many years honorary secretary of the Cheshire Local Medical and Panel Committee, which in 1939 produced the *MEDICAL TESTAMENT* launched by SIR ALBERT HOWARD and SIR ROBERT MCCARRISON. He edited *The News Letter on Compost*, and was a member of the COUNCIL FOR THE CHURCH AND COUNTRYSIDE. He was a member of the Soil Association's Advisory Panel, and honorary secretary of the British Medical Association's Medical Sociology Section.

POORE, GEORGE VIVIAN (1843–1904). Dr G.V. Poore was surgeon to the Great Eastern in 1866 when it was laying the Atlantic cable, and in the 1870s served as medical attendant to the Prince of Wales. Later in his career he was Professor of Medicine at University College, London. A keen horticulturalist, Poore opposed water-borne sewage systems, arguing in his book *Rural Hygiene*, first published in 1893, for the agricultural benefits of returning wastes to the soil. His ideas influenced SIR ALBERT HOWARD and LIONEL J. PICTON. Several decades before the existence of the SOIL ASSOCIATION he was pointing out the possible dangers of artificial fertilizers.

PORTSMOUTH, EARL OF see LYMINGTON, VISCOUNT.

PRICE, WESTON A. (d. *c.*1948). Price was an American dental scientist, interested in physical anthropology and nutrition. He was an Honorary Fellow of the International College of Dentists, and a member of the Research Commission of the American Dental Association. The organic school attached considerable weight to the mass of evidence he produced, after worldwide travel, of the harmful effects of western diet on dental health and jaw formation. His book *Nutrition and Physical Degeneration* was first published in 1939 and reissued in 1945 with a Supplement to which Dr WILLIAM ALBRECHT provided a foreword.

RAYNER, MABEL MARY CHEVELEY (d. 1948). Dr M.C. Rayner's importance to the organic movement lay in her work, with her husband W. Neilson-Jones, on the process of mycorrhizal association. She was Head of the Department of Botany at Reading University, then worked with the Research Department of the Forestry Commission at Wareham Forest in Dorset. She lectured extensively in universities and research stations in the United States, and was a member of the Advisory Panel of the SOIL ASSOCIATION.

RECKITT, MAURICE B. (1888–1980). Maurice Reckitt was a wealthy man whose Christian faith led him to spend his life serving a wide variety of Church committees and organizations. He became a member of the Church Socialist League while at Oxford, and, being sceptical about Fabianism and collectivism, supported GUILD SOCIALISM, to which his study of medieval history made him sympathetic. HILAIRE BELLOC'S *The Servile State* (1912) was a major influence on his thought, as were S.G. HOBSON'S articles in the *NEW AGE*. Reckitt became a leading figure in the National Guilds movement, working closely with the economist G.D.H. Cole. However, by 1921 he ceased to consider himself a socialist, and followed A.R. ORAGE into support for SOCIAL CREDIT; he was also involved in G.K. CHESTERTON'S movement DISTRIBUTISM. He was a member of the CHANDOS GROUP, and wrote a history for its fortieth anniversary in 1966. His chief importance to the organic movement was as a member of the editorial board of the *NEW ENGLISH WEEKLY*; for many years he shared with PHILIP MAIRET the task of writing the 'Notes of the Week.' From 1931 to 1950, he edited the Anglo-Catholic journal *CHRISTENDOM*, seeking in that journal and the *NEW* to formulate a CHRISTIAN SOCIOLOGY. He wrote historical studies of the Church of England's social thought.

RODALE, JEROME I. (1898–1971). Jerome Rodale was arguably the most important figure in the organic movement's development in the United States. He was a Jewish businessman who in 1923 started a New York electrical wiring company and became a millionaire. Interested in health issues, he heard ROBERT MCCARRISON lecture in Pittsburgh during the 1920s, but it was an article by ALBERT HOWARD which really sparked his interest in organic cultivation. He was also interested in BIODYNAMIC CULTIVATION, and sought to incorporate the ideas of RUDOLF STEINER and Howard into one organic crusade. Howard used him as his American mouthpiece, and Rodale also collaborated with EHRENFRIED PFEIFFER. Rodale founded a journal, *The Health Digest*, in 1935, and in 1942 initiated the journal *The Organic Farmer*, which in 1943 changed its name to *Organic Gardening*. He set up a farm and a research foundation; the latter was largely ignored and was dissolved in 1955. His 1945 book *Pay Dirt* is perhaps the classic text of the American organic canon, and his publishing company, based at Emmaus, Pa., still actively promotes the organic cause.

ROLT, L.T.C. (1910–74). Lionel Rolt is best known as an industrial historian. He was trained as an engineer, but began to wonder where technology, uncontrolled by ethical or religious sanctions, was likely to lead. His 1944 book on canals had a foreword by H.J. MASSINGHAM, to whose 1947 symposium *The Small Farmer* he contributed. His book *High Horse Riderless*, also published in 1947, was a major statement of the religious and social outlook which underlay so much of the organic school's writing.

ROWNTREE, B. SEEBOHM (1871–1954). B.S. Rowntree was Chairman of the Rowntree confectionery firm from 1925 to 1941, and author of many books on social issues. The reports on agricultural policy which he undertook in collaboration with VISCOUNT ASTOR articulated the progressive orthodoxy so disliked by the organic school, with its advocacy of specialist enterprises and its rejection of mixed farming.

RUSSELL, EDWARD JOHN (1872–1965). Sir John Russell was an immensely distinguished agricultural scientist, who told his life story in *The Land Called Me* (1956). From 1898 to 1901 he was Lecturer and Demonstrator in Chemistry at the Victoria University, Manchester; from 1901 to 1907 he was Head of Chemistry at Wye College in Kent; in 1907 he went as a soil scientist to the ROTHAMSTED EXPERIMENTAL STATION, succeeding A.D. HALL as Director in 1912 and holding that post until the Station's centenary in 1943. In 1941–42 he was Vice-President of the Royal Society, and was President of the British Association in 1949. He rejected the fears of the organic school about possible harmful effects of artificial fertilizers. Like many of the leading figures in the organic school, he was a devoted Christian believer.

RUSSELL, GEORGE WILLIAM see AE

SANDERSON-WELLS, T.H. (1871–1958). Thomas Henry Wells, who assumed the name Sanderson-Wells about 1904, qualified as a doctor in 1895 and served as a surgeon to British forces in the Boer War. In 1901 he became a GP at Weymouth, retiring in 1925 as a result of an operation. He then devoted himself to projects for increasing and propagating scientific knowledge of health promotion through diet: he was active in the Food Education Society and endowed annual lectures to be given at London University and the Middlesex Hospital. SIR ROBERT MCCARRISON and SIR JOHN BOYD ORR were among those who gave Sanderson-Wells Lectures. He was a founder-member of the SOIL ASSOCIATION. His book *Sun Diet* (1939) suggested that he was among those members of the

organic movement whose nutritional concerns were part of a wider political desire for 'racial regeneration.'

SAXON, EDGAR J. (1877–1956). As a young man, Edgar Saxon was a journalist writing on Food Reform and Nature Cure, and was recommended to C.W. DANIEL as a possible contributor to Daniel's journal *The Open Road*. In 1911 Daniel founded *The Healthy Life,* of which Saxon became owner and editor in 1920. It was reconstituted as *HEALTH AND LIFE* in 1934. From 1923 he ran a 'Natural Health' medical practice and a health shop in Wigmore Street, London, and established Vitamin Cafés, the first health food restaurants, during the inter-war period. It was through the health movement that he met DION BYNGHAM, who became a life-long friend and a frequent contributor to his journal. He also had close links with AUBREY WESTLAKE. Saxon was making the connection between the state of the soil, diet and health in the mid-1920s, and *Health and Life* gave its full support to the emerging organic movement during the 1930s and '40s. Saxon also shared the movement's support for SOCIAL CREDIT, and joined JOHN HARGRAVE'S political party, though by 1940 he was completely disillusioned with Hargrave. He also became a member of the MEN OF THE TREES and the SOIL ASSOCIATION.

SEARS, PAUL B. (b.1891). Paul Sears was a biologist whose 1935 book on the Dust Bowl, *Deserts on the March,* attracted considerable interest; it was reissued in 1947 with an introduction by LOUIS BROMFIELD. He was head of the Conservation Department at Yale University. LADY EVE BALFOUR visited him during her American tour of 1951.

SEMPILL, LORD (1893–1965). 19th Baron, Col. William Forbes-Sempill, was a leading aviator who served in the Royal Flying Corps during the First World War, ending as a Colonel in the RAF; during the 1920s he was a salesman for aircraft firms and an adviser to the Greek Naval Air Service. He rejoined the Naval Air Service in 1939 and was suspected of leaking information to the Japanese. He was a senior member of the Air League, the Anglo-German Fellowship, and a pro-German body called The Link. In 1939 he argued in the House of Lords for peace with Germany, having been a close associate of Ribbentrop for several years. His relevance to the organic movement lies in his membership of the ECONOMIC REFORM CLUB AND INSTITUTE and the fact that he was a Council member in the early years of the SOIL ASSOCIATION.

STAPLEDON, REGINALD GEORGE (1882–1960). Sir George Stapledon was admired by both the organic and the orthodox school of agriculture, and belonged to both camps while having reservations about both. After some false starts, Stapledon took the agricultural diploma at Cambridge in 1910 and was appointed assistant to the Principal of the Royal Agricultural College at Cirencester, where he carried out grassland surveys and was influenced by the writings of R.H. ELLIOT. From 1912 to 1940 he was at Aberystwyth, first as an agricultural botanist and then, after a two-year break (1917–19) at the Food Production Department in London, as Director of the Welsh Plant Breeding Station. By the 1930s he had an international reputation as an improver of grasslands. In 1935 he published a major study of land resources, *The Land: Now and To-morrow*. He was knighted in 1939, and in 1940 was appointed Director of the grassland improvement station near Stratford-on-Avon, where he remained until his retirement in 1945. He became Scientific Advisor to Dunns Farm Seeds in 1947. Stapledon began his career as a fairly orthodox supporter of progressive agricultural methods but became sceptical about technological triumphalism. Although much admired by E.J. RUSSELL, he was increasingly at home in the world of VISCOUNT LYMINGTON, whom he influenced, and ROLF GARDINER. He was an inspiration to the KINSHIP IN HUSBANDRY, though not a

member. His books were published by FABER AND FABER, and he wrote for the *NEW ENGLISH WEEKLY*. He did not join the Soil Association, though he gave scientific advice on its experimental work; he did not share the Association's uncompromising opposition to artificials. In religion he appears to have been a reverent-minded agnostic; in politics he admired the older Toryism of Disraeli and showed sympathy for the new Italian corporatism, but also contributed to a left-wing wartime series of books generally titled *The Democratic Order*. His biographer Robert Waller edited *MOTHER EARTH* from 1963 until the early 1970s.

STEINER, RUDOLF (1861–1925). Steiner was a scientist, mystic and educationalist whose methods of BIODYNAMIC CULTIVATION influenced several figures in the British organic movement, including MAYE BRUCE, LAURENCE EASTERBROOK and LORD NORTHBOURNE. Like A.R. ORAGE, Steiner was involved in the Theosophical movement in his earlier years, but broke with it to develop his more specifically Christian esoteric system Anthroposophy. His 1924 lectures on agriculture formulated the ideas and methods of biodynamic cultivation, which were propagated in Britain by C.A. MIER and in the United States by EHRENFRIED PFEIFFER.

SYKES, FRIEND (1888–1965). Friend Sykes should not be confused with Frank Sykes, who also wrote books on agriculture for FABER AND FABER. Friend Sykes was a farmer and animal-breeder who in the mid-1930s took over a run-down farm near Andover and within a few years had transformed it into a showpiece for organic methods, producing outstanding wheat and prize-winning racehorses. SIR ALBERT HOWARD believed Sykes's estate to be a better argument for organic farming than anything that the SOIL ASSOCIATION's experiment in Suffolk would produce. Sykes was a founder member of the Association.

SYMONS, W.T. (1879–1976). William Travers Symons, born in London, was apprenticed to his father's firm of marine insurance brokers, working for it from 1893 to 1903. He spent 1904–5 farming in New Zealand; from 1905 to 1910 he was at the Tolstoyan community at Whiteway in Gloucestershire; from 1910 to 1915 he was in insurance in Calcutta, then returned to England to become a partner in the family firm. He read the *NEW AGE*, joined the Independent Labour Party, and subsequently supported SOCIAL CREDIT. During the 1920s he moved in the circles which formed the context of the organic movement's emergence: he was a member of the CHANDOS GROUP and the ADLER SOCIETY; he edited *PURPOSE*, and was on the editorial board of the *NEW ENGLISH WEEKLY*, which during the Second World War was edited from the basement of his London home. He was an anti-ecclesiastical Christian, and remained sympathetic to the Labour movement after the Second World War.

TAVISTOCK, MARQUIS OF *see* BEDFORD, HASTINGS DUKE OF

TAWNEY, R.H. (1880–1962). Richard Henry Tawney was a historian and socialist whose academic work and political activities brought him into contact with some of the figures important in the context of the organic movement's development. He was involved, though critically, in the movement for GUILD SOCIALISM, and his 1921 book *The Acquisitive Society* argued for a form of 'Functional Socialism' which was akin to the ideas of S.G. HOBSON. His most famous work, *Religion and the Rise of Capitalism* (1926), provided ammunition for those who, like H.J. MASSINGHAM and MAURICE RECKITT, looked back to the Middle Ages as a time when economic considerations were subordinated to ethics. Tawney was involved in the CHRISTENDOM GROUP, and was a friend of T.S. ELIOT and WILLIAM TEMPLE.

TEMPLE, WILLIAM (1881–1944). William Temple, the son of an Archbishop, was appointed Bishop of Manchester in 1921, Archbishop of York in 1929, and Archbishop of Canterbury in 1942. He was a noted philosopher, and a theologian who believed that the Christian Gospel had social implications. For some years a member of the Labour Party, he later expressed sympathy for the ideas of SOCIAL CREDIT. He supported the CHRISTENDOM GROUP, and his ideas of a natural order appealed to members of the organic movement. V.A. DEMANT, T.S. ELIOT, JOHN MIDDLETON MURRY and MAURICE RECKITT contributed to Temple's Conference at Malvern in 1941.

TEVIOT, LORD (1874–1968). Charles Iain Kerr, who became 1st Baron Teviot in 1940, held several senior positions in the worlds of banking and commerce. He was Liberal National MP for Montrose Burghs from 1932 to 1940. From 1940 to 1956 he was Chairman of the Liberal National Party and was instrumental in arranging its merger with the Conservative Party. He was an outspoken anti-semite during the late 1930s. A founder member of the SOIL ASSOCIATION, he served as its President from 1946 to 1950.

THOMAS, WILLIAM BEACH (1868–1957). Sir William Beach Thomas was a journalist with a particular concern for agricultural issues. Before the First World War he had worked in Ireland, where he knew AE. In the 1920s and '30s he drew attention to issues of rural depression and depopulation, and to the dangers of agricultural methods based purely on considerations of mechanical and economic efficiency. He wrote many books on rural life, and was broadly sympathetic to the organic cause while also admiring orthodox figures such as A.D. HALL.

TRAVERS, P.L. (1899–1996). Pamela Travers is best known as the author of *Mary Poppins;* she had a more esoteric reputation as a scholar of mythology and as a poet. Born in Australia, she was so impressed by the poetry of AE that she travelled half-way round the world to pay homage to him; he published her poetry in his weekly paper the *Irish Statesman*. P.L. Travers was on the editorial board of the NEW ENGLISH WEEKLY and contributed to VISCOUNT LYMINGTON'S NEW PIONEER. Later in her life she spent time in the United States living with the Navaho and Pueblo Indians, and holding college posts as writer-in-residence.

TURNER, F. NEWMAN (1913–64). Newman Turner farmed in Somerset and was one of SIR ALBERT HOWARD'S most loyal disciples. He was a herbalist, a member of the SOIL ASSOCIATION's Council, a friend of LAWRENCE D. HILLS, and President of the HENRY DOUBLEDAY RESEARCH ASSOCIATION.

WALLOP, G.V. *see* LYMINGTON, VISCOUNT

WESTLAKE, AUBREY T. (1893–1985). Much of Aubrey Westlake's life has been described by Edgell (1992). His father, Ernest Westlake, was a geologist and anthropologist who admired PATRICK GEDDES. The First World War made Ernest deeply sceptical about ideas of 'Progress,' and in 1916 he established the ORDER OF WOODCRAFT CHIVALRY (OWC) Brought up as a Quaker, Aubrey trained as a doctor, and served in France during the First World War with the Friends War Victims Relief Committee. From 1919 to 1937 he was a GP in Bermondsey, South London, retiring in order to devote his time to his estate in Hampshire, developing it as a holiday centre with an organic farm and market garden. During the 1920s and '30s Aubrey continued the work of the OWC: DION BYNGHAM and ROLF GARDINER were involved with it, and PHILIP OYLER worked on the estate. Aubrey Westlake supported SOCIAL CREDIT and was involved in the NEW BRITAIN movement. Influenced by the work of RUDOLF STEINER, he became a member of the SOIL ASSOCIATION and served on its Council; he also wrote for S. MARIAN'S *SOIL MAGAZINE*. For many years he was a friend of JOHN HARGRAVE. West-

lake's pacifism and Social Credit economics brought him into contact with people well to the right politically, but he appears not to have been either anti-semitic or sympathetic to Fascism. In religion he evidently sought to synthesize a pagan closeness to nature with Christian ethical ideals.

WHYTE, R.O. (1903–1986). Born in Scotland, Robert Whyte did his Ph.D. in plant cytology at Cambridge and worked from 1930 at the Imperial Bureau of Pastures and Forage Crops, Aberystwyth (the town where R.G. STAPLEDON was also based). From 1951 to 1966 he worked for the Food and Agriculture Organization of the United Nations. With G.V. JACKS he wrote in 1939 *The Rape of the Earth,* published by FABER AND FABER. This worldwide survey of soil erosion was a key text for the organic movement.

WILLIAMS, TOM [Baron Williams of Barnburgh] (1888–1967). As Minister of Agriculture in the 1945–51 Labour Government, Tom Williams was responsible for the passing of the 1947 Agriculture Act. From 1922 to 1959 he was MP for Don Valley, and during the Second World War became joint Parliamentary Secretary to Robert Hudson, the Minister of Agriculture. He was evidently respected by members of the organic school such as JORIAN JENKS and the EARL OF PORTSMOUTH. The 1947 Act, which had a strong degree of cross-party support, rewarded farmers with security for their wartime efforts, but confirmed British agriculture on its path of mechanization and high input of artificial fertilizers.

WILLIAMSON, GEORGE SCOTT (1883–1953). Scott Williamson was, with his wife INNES H. PEARSE, one of the most important figures in the development of the organic movement. He qualified as a doctor at Edinburgh University in 1907 and was later a lecturer in pathology at Bristol University. During the 1920s he was Director of pathological studies at the Royal Free Hospital, specializing in research on the thyroid gland. He and Innes Pearse established their friendship with ROBERT MCCARRISON at this time. Scott Williamson continued his studies at the Royal College of Surgeons, but in 1926 also began the experiment in social medicine which was to develop into the PIONEER HEALTH CENTRE. He was unable to find the funds to support the Centre in the post-war years; it closed in 1951. Scott Williamson was involved in the NEW BRITAIN movement, and the work of the Pioneer Health Centre brought him into contact with SIR ALBERT HOWARD and members of the KINSHIP IN HUSBANDRY. He was a founder member of the SOIL ASSOCIATION and a member of its Advisory Panel.

WILLIAMSON, HENRY (1895–1977). Best known as the author of *Tarka the Otter* and other nature books, and as an autobiographical novelist, Henry Williamson became involved in the organic movement largely for political reasons, though the influence of his friend and publisher RICHARD DE LA MARE played a part. Williamson was a devoted admirer of Sir Oswald Mosley and of Hitler, and saw farmimg as a means of regenerating the unhealthy English social organism of the 1930s. He took on a farm at Stiffkey, Norfolk, in 1937; soon afterwards he heard JORIAN JENKS speak at a British Union of Fascists meeting and joined the movement, becoming a speaker himself and undergoing a brief period of arrest in 1940. He was a friend of ADRIAN BELL, ROLF GARDINER and JOHN MIDDLETON MURRY, editing *THE ADELPHI* for a brief period in the late 1940s. He gave up farming when the war ended. His account of the 1930s and '40s can be found in the series of novels featuring Phillip Maddison, with the general title *A Chronicle of Ancient Sunlight.*

WILSON, R.G.M. (d. *c.*1982). Captain Roy Wilson, formerly of the Royal Engineers, worked in the City of London for two years before becoming a farmer. His father-in-law Sir Frederick Hiam owned estates in the Fenland and Wilson farmed near Little-

port from 1927 to 1931, when he moved to the farm at Surfleet, near Spalding, which was to become well-known as Iceni Nurseries. Already sceptical of chemical methods, Wilson consulted C.A. MIER and SIR ALBERT HOWARD, and instituted full-scale composting. By 1939 the business was flourishing and supplied organic produce to London shops. Its praises had been sung by LAURENCE EASTERBROOK in the national press, and in 1939 it was the subject of *The Land Our Larder* by George Godwin, who later edited *THE ADELPHI.* Wilson was a member of the ENGLISH ARRAY during the 1930s, and a founder-member of the SOIL ASSOCIATION in the 1940s, serving on its Advisory Panel for many years.

WOOD, MAURICE (1884–1960). Maurice Wood took up poultry farming in Yorkshire after the First World War. Concerned about the effects of mechanized methods, he turned in 1928 to a BIODYNAMIC approach and developed a balanced system of mixed farming; he also established himself as a successful miller. During the Second World War his farm impressed the visiting LAWRENCE HILLS. Wood was a founder member of the SOIL ASSOCIATION and served on its Council.

WRENCH, G.T. (1877–1954). Dr Guy Theodore Wrench wrote one of the most influential books in the organic canon, *The Wheel of Health,* a study of the work of SIR ROBERT MCCARRISON and of the Hunza tribesmen on India's North-West Frontier, published in 1938 by C.W. DANIEL. He spent many years in India and, after partition, Pakistan, but was in London in 1939 for a meeting of the Farmers' Club, and, as a result of his comments in the discussion, met WALTER ELLIOT, then Minister of Health. His books on the importance of peasantries and of maintaining soil fertility were highly regarded by the organic school.

YEATS-BROWN, FRANCIS (1886–1944). Yeats-Brown served as a Lancer, gaining fame for his account of his experiences in his 1930 book *Bengal Lancer.* From 1924 to 1926 he was Assistant Editor at *The Spectator,* and in 1933 briefly edited the weekly *Everyman,* promoting corporatism based on the Italian model. Until 1939 he admired the achievements of Nazi Germany in fostering health and eradicating unemployment. He was a practising Buddhist who admired the warrior ideal. A friend of ARTHUR BRYANT, Yeats-Brown became interested in the farming experiments of ADRIAN BELL and HENRY WILLIAMSON. On social and political issues his outlook was akin to that of a number of the organic pioneers.

Appendix B
Groups, institutions and journals in the organic movement and the orthodox school of agriculture

Names of people in SMALL CAPITALS indicate an entry in Appendix A. Names of groups, institutions or journals in SMALL CAPITALS indicate an entry in Appendix B.

THE ADELPHI. Journal founded by JOHN MIDDLETON MURRY in 1923. In the 1940s it increasingly gave space to members of the organic movement, including H.J. MASSINGHAM and the EARL OF PORTSMOUTH, and reviewed many books on organic farming. In 1948 HENRY WILLIAMSON became editor, to be replaced in 1949 by George Godwin, who continued to support the organic philosophy.

ADLER SOCIETY. This was the British branch of the International Society for Individual Psychology, which had been founded by the psychoanalyst Alfred Adler. The Adler Society was established, with Adler's blessing, by DMITRI MITRINOVIC, and held its first meeting in March 1927. At its headquarters in Gower Street, London, it held a range of meetings on psychology, politics, medicine and religion, sustaining an intense and varied programme until 1932. Its treasurer was W.T. SYMONS; PHILIP MAIRET was a leading spirit, and in December 1928 it was resolved that the CHANDOS GROUP would 'find its vehicle of expression in the Sociological Group of the Adler Society' (Rigby 1984, p.96). In 1930 the medical section of the Adler Society, unhappy about the shift in focus towards social and political issues, withdrew to hold separate meetings and have separate subscriptions. In 1931 Adler took his name away from the Gower Street group. The journal *PURPOSE* was founded in 1929 to promote an exotic mixture of Adlerian psychology and SOCIAL CREDIT.

The Adler Society also had close links with the NEW EUROPE group and the NEW BRITAIN movement.

BIODYNAMIC CULTIVATION. The name given by EHRENFRIED PFEIFFER to the agricultural and horticultural methods outlined by RUDOLF STEINER and practised by his followers. They are based on the idea that the universe is an evolving organism and that every element in it undergoes purposive development towards realization of its spiritual potential. Science, in Steiner's view, had failed to see agriculture as a totality and the farm as an organism; it saw the soil as inert material rather than a sentient force. As with the INDORE PROCESS of SIR ALBERT HOWARD, composting forms the basis of the system, but there are significant differences. Biodynamic methods use activators formed from homoeopathic preparations and based on traditional peasant knowledge of herbal medicine; and Steiner believed in a correspondence between the earth, its products and elements, on the one hand, and the heavens on the other: a system of planetary influences which required sowing according to lunar phases, for instance. Steiner opposed the use of human excrement in biodynamic composting.

BRITISH PEOPLE'S PARTY. A pacifist, antisemitic, national-socialist fringe organization founded in 1939 by the MARQUIS OF TAVISTOCK and proscribed in 1940. It re-emerged in 1945 and survived during the years of the post-war Labour Government. It published a newspaper, PEOPLES POST. It was strong on the conspiracy theory of finance, and its agricultural policy was strongly sympathetic to the organic movement. Members included ANTHONY LUDOVICI, Colin Jordan, later a National Front activist, and DION BYNGHAM.

CHANDOS GROUP. A group of predominantly Anglican social thinkers who are central to the argument of this book. It took its name from the restaurant in St Martin's Lane, London, where it met fortnightly from 1926 until the restaurant was destroyed in the blitz. Subsequently it dined at various Soho restaurants. Members included V.A. DEMANT, T.S. ELIOT, T.M. HERON, PHILIP MAIRET, MAURICE RECKITT, and W.T. SYMONS. LEWIS MUMFORD was an occasional guest. The group originated in a meeting called by DMITRI MITRINOVIC in May 1926, following the collapse of the General Strike, and produced books on social policy: Coal, in 1927 and Politics in 1929, the latter published by C.W. DANIEL. The members were committed, or sympathetic, to SOCIAL CREDIT, and welcomed the return of A.R. ORAGE to Britain in 1931 and the establishment of the NEW the following year. When Orage died in 1934 the editorial policy of the NEW passed to the Chandos Group, who used the paper as a vehicle for the development of CHRISTIAN SOCIOLOGY. The group also had close links with the ADLER SOCIETY, and the CHRISTENDOM GROUP. In 1966 Maurice Reckitt wrote a personal memoir of the Group's forty years of meetings.

CHRISTENDOM. The quarterly journal of the CHRISTENDOM GROUP, it was edited by MAURICE RECKITT and ran from 1931 to 1950. A vehicle for CHRISTIAN SOCIOLOGY, it gave a platform to writers in the organic movement, including KENNETH BARLOW, JORIAN JENKS, PHILIP MAIRET, H.J. MASSINGHAM and DAVID PECK. Members of the CHANDOS GROUP such as T.M. HERON and W.T. SYMONS also contributed. Its first issue carried a foreword by WILLIAM TEMPLE.

CHRISTENDOM GROUP. An Anglo-Catholic movement whose aim was to apply the social theology of the medieval Church to contemporary problems by developing a CHRISTIAN SOCIOLOGY. The Christendom movement stemmed from the Church Socialist League, producing in 1922 a collection of essays entitled The Return of Christendom, which had A.J. PENTY as a contributor and an epilogue by G.K. CHESTERTON. Summer schools of sociology followed, being regularly held at Oxford from 1925 to 1955; T.S. ELIOT, MAURICE RECKITT and R.H. TAWNEY were among those who attended. In 1931 the quarterly CHRISTENDOM was founded. The group was well in evidence at WILLIAM TEMPLE's 1941 Malvern Conference on the future social order, and in 1945 Reckitt edited Prospect for Christendom, whose contributors included V.A. DEMANT, PHILIP MAIRET and DAVID PECK. This was the Group's final publication, but its members, particularly Reckitt, remained active in Church affairs until well into the 1960s. The Group is the subject of a thesis by Mayhew (1977).

CHRISTIAN SOCIOLOGY. Christian Sociology has nothing to do with Sociology as now practised as an academic subject. It was a normative set of ideas about the social implications of Christian theology, which drew its inspiration from the medieval Church's idea of a natural order. In the view of MAURICE RECKITT, a leading figure in the attempt to articulate Christian social principles, the Church had failed to interpret the significance of the Industrial Revolution or champion its victims; influenced by R.H. TAWNEY, he believed that since the rise of Protestantism economic life was no longer subject to theological or ethical restraint. Since humanity was rooted in a biological and social world, nature must be respected, and social relations were a means of achieving full humanity. A just and stable society could not be achieved unless man's spiritual, social and biological natures were recognized. Christian Sociology was the study which derived from the belief that nature and the purpose of society could be understood only in the light of the Christian doctrine of Creation. It saw totalitarianism as the triumph of secularism, and believed that the principles of medieval social thought could be applied to the dislocations of twentieth-century industrialism. The clearest statement of the ideas is to be found in *An Outline of Christian Sociology* (1948) by W.G. PECK. The *NEW ENGLISH WEEKLY* and *CHRISTENDOM* sought to apply those ideas to the problems of the 1930s and '40s.

COUNCIL FOR THE CHURCH AND COUNTRYSIDE. This was in effect a 'front' for the organic movement, founded during the Second World War by DAVID PECK and the Rev Patrick McLaughlin, with the active support of ROLF GARDINER and the Bishop of Salisbury. It was an offshoot of the attempt of the CHRISTENDOM GROUP to articulate a CHRISTIAN SOCIOLOGY; since God had created humanity dependent on the natural world, it followed that a flourishing rural life was vital to the health and stability of society. The Church had neglected its roots in agriculture, and the CCC attempted to relate the Church's social teaching to the rural community. The belief in a natural order was the key to the teaching, and this in turn implied commitment to organic cultivation, which sought to respect the natural order by obeying the rule of return of wastes to the soil. The CCC was based at ST ANNE'S HOUSE, SOHO, and issued regular pamphlets during the second half of the 1940s and the early 1950s: these were usually edited by JORIAN JENKS, and they included reviews of many of the important texts of the early organic movement. Many of the movement's major figures were members of the CCC or involved with it, including KENNETH BARLOW, H.J. MASSINGHAM, the EARL OF PORTSMOUTH, MAURICE RECKITT and FRIEND SYKES. Its work provides one of the clearest examples of the organic movement's Christian context.

DISTRIBUTISM. A social theory developed by HILAIRE BELLOC and G.K. CHESTERTON, which drew sympathetic interest from MONTAGUE FORDHAM, ERIC GILL, A.J. PENTY and MAURICE RECKITT. While recognizing the evils and injustices of industrial capitalism, it rejected the Communist proposal to abolish private property. Instead, Distributists argued that a more widespread distribution of genuine private property was required: the expropriation of the capitalists would not be followed by nationalization but by the creation of many small property-owners. There was a strong ruralist element to the movement, and a considerable mistrust of machinery (not shared by Chesterton himself). The Distributist League was founded in 1926 and its ideas were propagated in *GK's Weekly*, which Reckitt worked for.

ECONOMIC REFORM CLUB AND INSTITUTE. The story of the ERCI has been told by Holloway (1986). It originated from a 1930s petition movement for monetary reform which drew together various organizations concerned about the harm done by the financial system. SOCIAL CREDIT was just one among several of the movements involved. In 1936 a Petition Club was established, subsequently re-named the Economic Reform Club; one of its guarantors was LORD NORTHBOURNE. In 1939 the Club organized a dinner in honour of SIR JOHN BOYD ORR: among those who supported it were LORD BLEDISLOE, Lord Horder, Julian Huxley, P.C. LOFTUS MP, VISCOUNT LYMINGTON, Compton Mackenzie, LORD SEMPILL and Professor Frederick Soddy. The MARQUIS OF TAVISTOCK and W.G. PECK were also members. In 1942 the ERCI organized a conference entitled 'The World We Want,' in conjunction with the INDUSTRIAL CHRISTIAN FELLOWSHIP: speakers included Robert Boothby MP, Sir John Boyd Orr, P.C. Loftus MP, the EARL OF PORTSMOUTH, Lord Sempill and SIR GEORGE STAPLEDON. The ERCI established a close link with the RURAL RECONSTRUCTION ASSOCIATION, publishing the bulletin *RURAL ECONOMY* from the 1940s until 1956;

its editor was JORIAN JENKS. By 1954 the ERCI's membership had dwindled substantially and it merged with the Economic Research Council, which still exists.

ENGLISH ARRAY. A far-Right, royalist group founded in 1936 by VISCOUNT LYMINGTON on breaking away from the ENGLISH MISTERY. Its purpose was to 'regain, preserve and intensify all those attributes and qualities that appertained to English life and the English type at the most vigorous and flourishing periods of our history' (Wright 1996, p.71). Lymington denied that it was Fascist, arguing that through a network of regional leaders it avoided dictatorship (Portsmouth 1965, p.129). The Array supported organic methods of farming and opposed devitalized foods. RALPH COWARD, ROLF GARDINER, ANTHONY LUDOVICI and R.G.M. WILSON were members.

ENGLISH MISTERY. The Mistery was a secret society founded in 1930 by a Northumbrian called William Sanderson, a Freemason who had helped found the antisemitic Order of the Red Rose in 1917 and who wrote regularly for *The Fascist*. It was a royalist organization which wanted an Anglo-Saxon revival in order to stop outside influences corrupting English cultural standards and national purpose. Members included VISCOUNT LYMINGTON, who was strongly influenced by it, ROLF GARDINER, ANTHONY LUDOVICI, and Reginald Dorman-Smith MP, later Minister of Agriculture.

FABER AND FABER. The publishing house which did more than any other to promote the organic cause. T.S. ELIOT was one of its directors. RICHARD DE LA MARE was the agricultural and horticultural editor from the early 1930s to the early 1970s, and LAWRENCE D. HILLS was a reader for him. Faber published books by EVE BALFOUR, KENNETH BARLOW, ADRIAN BELL, V.A. DEMANT, RONALD DUNCAN, ROLF GARDINER, D.P. HOPKINS, SIR ALBERT HOWARD, LOUISE HOWARD, G.V. JACKS and R.O.

WHYTE, JORIAN JENKS, F.C. KING, INNES PEARSE and G. SCOTT WILLIAMSON, EHRENFRIED PFEIFFER, LIONEL PICTON, the EARL OF PORTSMOUTH, M.C. RAYNER, MAURICE RECKITT, R.G. STAPLEDON, FRIEND SYKES, WILLIAM BEACH THOMAS, NEWMAN TURNER, HENRY WILLIAMSON and G.T. WRENCH.

FRIENDS OF THE LAND. Friends of the Land was founded in 1940 by a group of United States citizens concerned about destruction of natural resources. Its directors and advisers included WILLIAM ALBRECHT, LOUIS BROMFIELD, the writer and economist Stuart Chase, and H.H. Bennett, former chief of the U.S. Soil Conservation Service. The organization worked closely with the Audubon Society, the American Forestry Association, and the Soil Conservation Districts Association. It was wound up in 1960, but anticipated later environmental initiatives.

GUILD SOCIALISM. The history and ideas of Guild Socialism can be found in Glass (1966) and Hutchinson and Burkitt (1997). It emerged in the years just before the First World War as an alternative to bureaucratic Fabian Socialism and was increasingly influential in the Labour movement until the early 1920s, when it collapsed under the dual pressure of Bolshevism and SOCIAL CREDIT. In the pages of the *NEW AGE*, S.G. HOBSON and A.R. ORAGE argued for a de-centralized form of Socialism based on National Guilds; the concept of Guilds was derived in part from the medieval model favoured by A.J. PENTY and in part from the example of French Syndicalism. The establishment of Guilds would avoid the pitfalls of State-based central control and nationalization. Hobson and Orage argued for the abolition of the wage system, for self-government in industry and for the trade unions as the potential guilds of the new order. Industrial organization in self-governing workshops would end capitalism. Guilds would set standards of craftsmanship, regulate pay and conditions, and support members in times of

ists were concerned about the mental, moral and spiritual aspects of work, not simply about remuneration and a larger share in the products of capitalism. Another important figure was the academic G.D.H. Cole, a close colleague of MAURICE RECKITT immediately after the First World War, but Cole retained close links with the Labour Party and the Fabians. Other major figures interested in Guild Socialism included Bertrand Russell and R.H. TAWNEY. When Orage split the Guilds movement by adopting Social Credit ideas, he was followed by T.M. HERON, PHILIP MAIRET, MAURICE RECKITT and W.T. SYMONS. ROLF GARDINER and H.J. MASS-INGHAM were at one time adherents of Guild Socialism.

HEALTH AND LIFE. This journal, edited by EDGAR J. SAXON, formerly *The Healthy Life,* was re-constituted as *Health and Life* in 1934 and became one of the most important platforms for communicating the theory and practice of organic cultivation. It advocated 'natural health': the establishment of physical and mental vigour through correct nutrition (i.e. fresh, home-grown food from humus-rich soil) and a positive outlook on life. A number of contemporary forms of 'alternative medicine,' such as the Bach flower remedies, can be found recommended in its pages. The journal supported the work of the MEN OF THE TREES, the SOIL ASSOCIATION, and the PIONEER HEALTH CENTRE; it also argued for SOCIAL CREDIT as the way to create a healthy financial system. DION BYNGHAM was a regular contributor. Politically, the journal was ambivalent, combining anti-fascist sentiment with manifestos favouring rootedness and racial vigour.

HENRY DOUBLEDAY RESEARCH ASSOCIA-TION. Henry Doubleday was a Victorian Quaker who introduced comfrey into Britain in the 1870s. LAWRENCE D. HILLS so admired the virtues of comfrey that when in 1954 he established a research garden at Bocking in Essex he named it

after Doubleday. NEWMAN TURNER was the HDRA's first President. Its aims were to produce comfrey and to undertake research into organic gardening. Now based at Ryton-on-Dunsmore near Coventry, it is one of the largest and most successful societies of organic growers.

INDORE PROCESS. The Indore Process of composting, named after the state in India where it was developed, was conceived and refined by ALBERT HOWARD during the years 1924–31. Howard, after nineteen years in India, was appointed first Director of a new Institute of Plant Industry at Indore, which he had himself planned and organized. He used the Institute in order to initiate agricultural research which studied plants in relation to agricultural practice and the soil, and to devise a practical method of manufacturing humus. Influenced by F.H. KING'S accounts of Oriental agriculture, he developed a method of composting together vegetable wastes and animal residues which was highly successful. By 1940 the Indore Process was being used worldwide in the production of coffee, tea, rice, sugar-cane, and fruit. In Britain it was used on the estates of SIR BERNARD GREENWELL and FRIEND SYKES, and at the market gardens of R.G.M. WILSON. Critics of the Indore Process considered it dependent on cheap labour, and argued that in western countries there was insufficient waste material to create all the compost needed to substitute for chemical fertilizers. Howard advocated the composting of urban wastes, which was undertaken successfully in South Africa and by certain British municipal boroughs, notably Dumfries.

INDUSTRIAL CHRISTIAN FELLOWSHIP. The ICF was an Anglican organization whose aim was to try and make Christian doctrine relevant to the various social problems raised by industrialism. W.G. PECK, a key figure in the CHRISTENDOM GROUP, was the ICF's Director of Clergy Schools, and his son DAVID PECK was an Area Organizer for the ICF from 1941 to 1943.

Organizer for the ICF from 1941 to 1943. Through W.G. Peck there were close links with the ECONOMIC REFORM CLUB AND INSTITUTE, to which several leading figures in the organic movement belonged; in 1942 the ICF and the ERCI jointly sponsored the conference 'The World We Want.'

KIBBO KIFT KIN. The Kibbo Kift Kin (Kibbo Kift was said to mean 'proof of great strength') was the brainchild of JOHN HARGRAVE, who formed the Kin in 1920 after separating from the Scout movement. Its aim was to establish a counter-culture and create an élite which would influence national policy. It was open-air, pacifist and craft-based, aiming to recover a correct attitude to nature. There was a network of regionally-based leaders, and the movement had its own uniforms and rituals. Its 1926 Advisory Council included Havelock Ellis, PATRICK GEDDES, Julian Huxley, Frederick Soddy, Rabindranath Tagore and H.G. Wells. ROLF GARDINER was for a time the Kin's 'gleemaster.'

KINSHIP IN HUSBANDRY. A group who were at the centre of the developing organic movement, formulating a philosophy of 'husbandry' of the earth in opposition to the exploitation of natural resources by industrialism. They hoped that the Second World War might result in a change of direction in British agricultural policy and in attitudes to nutrition and health, and they worked to spread their ideas through permeating various groups and organizations. The Kinship is discussed in Gardiner (1972, pp.196–99) and Portsmouth (1965, pp.77–96). Its members were EDMUND BLUNDEN, in whose rooms at Merton College, Oxford it first met in 1941; ROLF GARDINER, who first called the group together; ADRIAN BELL; ARTHUR BRYANT; J.E. Hosking, a seed merchant and reviver of the flax industry; Douglas Kennedy, director of the English Folk Dance and Song Society; VISCOUNT LYMINGTON; PHILIP MAIRET;

H.J. MASSINGHAM; LORD NORTHBOURNE; Robert Payne, editor of *The Gloucestershire Countryside;* and the rural writer C. Henry Warren. Meetings were attended by RONALD DUNCAN, LAURENCE EASTERBROOK, Michael Graham, JORIAN JENKS and PHILIP OYLER, among others. The EARL OF PORTSMOUTH (1965, p.86) says that SIR ALBERT HOWARD, SIR ROBERT McCARRISON and J.E.R. McDONAGH were part of the group. Bell (1965, p.9) refers to 'several clerics,' but does not name any. SIR GEORGE STAPLEDON was an influence but not a member. Gardiner (1972, p.196) says that the group existed until 1950, the year in which it organized in Britain a European Husbandry Meeting.

MEDICAL TESTAMENT. The Testament was perhaps the most important document in the development of the organic movement. Under the guiding influence of LIONEL J. PICTON, the Local Medical and Panel Committees of the County Palatine of Chester argued that doctors were failing in their duty, under the 1911 National Health Insurance Act, to prevent sickness. Picton had read the work of SIR ROBERT McCARRISON and SIR ALBERT HOWARD, and the *Testament* argued that the way to prevent sickness was to encourage the consumption of fresh food grown in healthy, humus-rich soil. It was launched at Crewe Town Hall on 22 March 1939 with Howard and McCarrison as speakers, and first published in the NEW ENGLISH WEEKLY on 6 April 1939. In 1957 the SOIL ASSOCIATION reiterated its belief in the ideas of the Testament in a statement to *The Lancet* and the *British Medical Journal* signed by over 400 members of the dental and medical professions.

MEN OF THE TREES. An organization dedicated to the care, protection and maintenance of the world's woodlands and forests, founded in 1922 by RICHARD ST BARBE BAKER. The first 'men of the trees' were Kenyan native volunteers who wished to restore their native forests. The movement grew as Baker travelled during movement's journal *TREES* and in 1938 the first summer school was held, at which SIR ALBERT HOWARD spoke. PHILIP MAIRET and EDGAR J. SAXON were involved with the movement, which still exists, under the more 'politically correct' name the International Tree Foundation.

MOTHER EARTH. The name given to the journal of the SOIL ASSOCIATION during its first 25 years. It first appeared in 1946 and was edited by JORIAN JENKS until his death in 1963, then by Robert Waller, the biographer of SIR GEORGE STAPLEDON. It was a far more detailed and specialist publication than the Association's current quarterly magazine *Living Earth.*

NEW AGE. The journal taken over in 1907 by A.R. ORAGE and turned by him into perhaps the most influential and exciting paper of the years before the First World War. Contributors included Arnold Bennett, Katherine Mansfield, Edwin Muir, Bernard Shaw, H.G. Wells, HILAIRE BELLOC, G.K. CHESTERTON, S.G. HOBSON and ANTHONY LUDOVICI. The *New Age* advocated GUILD SOCIALISM in opposition to Fabianism. During the war it came under the influence of DMITRI MITRINOVIC. Keen readers of the paper included T.M. HERON, H.J. MASSINGHAM and W.T. SYMONS. After the war the paper supported SOCIAL CREDIT, and continued to do so after Orage resigned as editor in 1922 and Arthur Brenton took over. PHILIP MAIRET and JOHN HARGRAVE were contributors in this period. The paper's influence and reputation were greatly diminished by 1930 and the *NEW ENGLISH WEEKLY* became a more respected voice of Social Credit in the 1930s. The *New Age* slipped gently into oblivion in the late 1930s.

NEW BRITAIN. The New Britain movement was a short-lived political initiative established by DMITRI MITRINOVIC in response to the economic crisis of the early 1930s. It was an example of what today would be called a 'Third Way,' attempting to find an alternative to capitalism without embracing either Communism or Fascism. Formed in 1933, it developed from the NEW EUROPE group and published the *New Britain Weekly,* whose contributors included the film-maker John Grierson, the philosopher John Macmurray, financial reformer and chemist Frederick Soddy, JOHN STEWART COLLIS, S.G. HOBSON, and PHILIP MAIRET. The short-lived *New Britain Quarterly* contained pieces by MONTAGUE FORDHAM, G. SCOTT WILLIAMSON and AUBREY WESTLAKE. After rapid growth in 1933 the movement's decline was equally rapid the following year, as different factions within it disagreed over policy.

NEW ENGLISH WEEKLY. The *NEW* is central to the argument of this book. It was founded in April 1932 by A.R. ORAGE as a platform for SOCIAL CREDIT ideas and as a review of politics and the arts. When Orage died in November 1934 the editorship passed to PHILIP MAIRET and editorial policy was in effect decided by members of the CHANDOS GROUP. In addition to Mairet himself, T.S. ELIOT, T.M. HERON, MAURICE RECKITT and W.T. SYMONS served on the editorial committee for many years, as did P.L. TRAVERS. The commitment to Social Credit remained, but from around 1938 there was evident a greater concentration on agricultural, rural and health issues, and in the 1940s the paper provided a forum for the developing organic husbandry movement. SIR ALBERT HOWARD had become an advisor to the paper in 1936, and Mairet was a member of the KINSHIP IN HUSBANDRY. Almost every name of any importance in the organic movement can be found in the pages of the *NEW* during the 1940s: a brief list includes KENNETH BARLOW, JOHN STEWART COLLIS, ROLF GARDINER, JORIAN JENKS, H.J. MASSINGHAM, JOHN MIDDLETON MURRY, the EARL OF PORTSMOUTH, and SIR GEORGE STAPLEDON. The fact that this important paper was run by members of the Chandos Group demonstrates the Christian context of the organic movement; the *NEW* was produced deliberately as a challenge to the prevailing secularism of political debate, and was an attempt to articulate the principles of CHRISTIAN SOCIOLOGY in response to contemporary events. Lack of money forced its closure in 1949.

NEW EUROPE. The New Europe group was a political initiative founded in 1931 by DMITRI MITRINOVIC. One of his longer-lasting movements (its last recorded meeting took place in 1957), it advocated progress towards a World Federation through first establishing a European Federation. Mitrinovic argued that there should be a transformation of the European order based on the twin opposing principles of every human organization: federation, representing cohesion and unity, and devolution, representing individual freedom and diversity. Europe, the continent which had achieved the highest development of individual self-consciousness, must take the initiative in recognizing the inseparability of personality and community. In 1932 the New Europe group ran a series of lectures in London whose speakers included Frederick Soddy, the chemist and financial reformer, the philosopher John Macmurray, Arthur Kitson, the financial reformer, and Gerald Heard. PHILIP MAIRET was actively involved in the movement, and PATRICK GEDDES accepted nomination as its first President.

NEW PIONEER. A journal produced by VISCOUNT LYMINGTON between December 1938 and January 1940, whose chief purposes were to avoid war with Germany and to advocate revival of Britain's health and agriculture through encouragement of humus-based farming. Its contributors included some of the most extreme right-wing and anti-semitic figures outside the Mosley movement: John Beckett, A.K. Chesterton (not to be confused with his cousin G.K. CHESTERTON), Ben Greene, and ANTHONY LUDOVICI. Among members of the organic movement who contributed were ROLF GARDINER, SIR ALBERT HOWARD, P.C. LOFTUS MP, and PHILIP MAIRET. It carried advertisements for the

ECONOMIC REFORM CLUB AND INSTITUTE and the NEW ENGLISH WEEKLY, and reviewed books by G.V. JACKS and R.O. WHYTE, EDGAR J. SAXON and G.T. WRENCH. P.L. TRAVERS also contributed.

ORDER OF WOODCRAFT CHIVALRY. (OWC) The OWC was founded in 1916 by Ernest Westlake, father of AUBREY WESTLAKE, and was based at the Westlakes' Hampshire estate. It was a quasi-pagan open air movement intended to enable young people to find a balance between civilization and the life of the instincts, having in that respect some affinity with the KIBBO KIFT KIN of JOHN HARGRAVE. Those associated with the OWC included DION BYNGHAM, ROLF GARDINER, PATRICK GEDDES, Robert Graves, and the philosopher John Macmurray. A full account of the OWC can be found in Edgell (1992).

PEOPLES [sic] **POST.** Newspaper produced by HASTINGS DUKE OF BEDFORD as the organ of the BRITISH PEOPLE'S PARTY. It appeared in 1939–40 and re-emerged in April 1945, continuing publication until the mid-1950s. DION BYNGHAM wrote regularly for it, and Colin Jordan, later a leading spirit in the National Front, contributed. It carried a countryside column written by Byngham under the pseudonym 'Miles Yarrow,' and referred to many of the leading figures in the organic movement. K. Sorabji, the composer and music critic of the NEW ENGLISH WEEKLY wrote for it. The paper carried scathing attacks on both Mosley and Roosevelt, and a defence of William Joyce ('Lord Haw-Haw') by his brother.

PIONEER HEALTH CENTRE. This major experiment in social health care began in 1926 as a family health club in Peckham, South London, established by INNES H. PEARSE and G. SCOTT WILLIAMSON. Its intention was to discover the conditions making for the health of an individual, which, Pearse and Scott Williamson believed, were likely to be found in the family. By 1929, 112 families had joined and undergone periodic 'overhauls' which revealed a generally low standard of health and vitality. Pearse and Scott-Williamson wanted a larger-scale experiment, and in 1935 the Pioneer Health Centre, a modernistic building designed by Sir Owen Williams, was opened. It offered all sorts of social and sporting facilities for families, including a theatre and swimming-pool, as well as facilities for health care and check-ups. A home farm was established at Bromley Common, Kent, where organic food was grown for the Centre's restaurant. J.G.S. DONALDSON gave half his inheritance to help establish the Centre, and SIR ALBERT HOWARD and SIR ROBERT MCCARRISON took an active interest in the Centre's work. It closed during the war, re-opening in 1946. There was worldwide interest in its work, and KENNETH BARLOW attempted to develop a similar project in Coventry. For the organic movement its importance lay in its attempt to look holistically at the individual's health by considering nutrition, physical and social opportunities, and the family environment. With the establishment of the National Health Service the Centre's future became problematic and in the end Scott Williamson was unable to find the necessary financial support to keep it open. It closed in 1951. The building still exists: having been used as a college annexe it has recently been converted into flats.

PURPOSE. Published by C.W. DANIEL, this quarterly journal was a product of the ADLER SOCIETY, attempting to synthesize Adler's psychology with the ideas of SOCIAL CREDIT. It first appeared in 1929 with John Marlow as editor; from 1930 it was edited by PHILIP MAIRET and W.T. SYMONS, and from 1935 by Symons alone. Its final issue was in 1940 when it in effect merged with the NEW ENGLISH WEEKLY. The journal gave a good deal of space to the ideas of the organic movement, with KENNETH BARLOW a frequent contributor. The April-June 1940 issue was entirely devoted

to 'The Land,' with articles by Barlow and LORD NORTHBOURNE. The tone of Purpose was more left-wing than that of the NEW, and the journal opposed anti-semitism and any return to pagan nature myths. Like the NEW it was essentially anti-secular in its philosophy.

ROTHAMSTED EXPERIMENTAL STATION. Rothamsted, at Harpenden in Hertfordshire, was the object of great hostility on the part of the organic movement, as the institution responsible for encouraging the use of artificial fertilizers and denying the possibility of any harmful effects either on the soil or on the health of those who ate the food grown with chemical inputs. It was founded by JOHN BENNET LAWES and JOSEPH GILBERT. Lawes was a chemist who began to test the efficacy of local fertilizing practices and in 1842 took out a patent on the manufacture of a superphosphate. The following year he established a fertilizer factory at Deptford in London and began the experiments at Rothamsted Manor which have now been running for more than 150 years. A.D. HALL was Director from 1902 to 1912. The Station is now largely funded by the Agricultural and Food Research Council. Its most famous investigation is the Broadbalk field, which was taken out of rotation in 1843, wheat being grown year after year on different plots, one of which has received nothing but artificial fertilizing. On Rothamsted's centenary SIR E.J. RUSSELL, the Station's retiring Director, stated that the Broadbalk experiment demonstrated artificials alone to be adequate for wheat growing, and said that they had no harmful effects on either the soil or the quality of the crops. This view was disputed by SIR ALBERT HOWARD. Rothamsted's investigations also include studies of nitrate leaching, plant viruses, fungi control, straw stubble, and protein production from lupins. Karen Gold (1993) has described Rothamsted as the birthplace of modern agriculture: the organic movement would not see this as a compliment.

RURAL ECONOMY. A journal produced by the ECONOMIC REFORM CLUB AND INSTITUTE in conjunction with the RURAL RECONSTRUCTION ASSOCIATION, and describing itself as 'A Non-Party Commentary devoted to the development of a Sound National Economy rooted in the Soil.' It was edited by JORIAN JENKS. Contributors included RALPH COWARD, H.J. MASSINGHAM, SIR GEORGE STAPLEDON and W.T. SYMONS, but most of it appears to have been written by Jenks. The journal reported on or advertised the activities of the COUNCIL FOR THE CHURCH AND COUNTRYSIDE, MEN OF THE TREES (whose 'New Earth Charter' it published), and the SOIL ASSOCIATION.

RURAL RECONSTRUCTION ASSOCIATION. The RRA was founded in 1926 by MONTAGUE FORDHAM and issued various proposals for regenerating British agriculture and saving rural life from decay. It called for farm price support, and attributed the passing of the 1932 Wheat Act to its efforts. When it issued its 1935 statement of agricultural policy its Council included RICHARD ST BARBE BAKER, R.A. Butler MP, and A.J. PENTY; the Chairman was Michael Beaumont MP, a close friend of VISCOUNT LYMINGTON. In the 1940s and '50s it was closely linked with the ECONOMIC REFORM CLUB AND INSTITUTE and published the journal RURAL ECONOMY. In 1955 it issued the report *Feeding the Fifty Million*, with an introduction by LAURENCE EASTERBROOK. Its Research Committee at that time included Edward Holloway of the ERCI, JORIAN JENKS, P.C. LOFTUS MP (the RRA's Chairman), and Dr H. Martin-Leake of the SOIL ASSOCIATION.

ST ANNE'S HOUSE, SOHO. This was the parish house of a church destroyed in the Blitz, established in 1943 as a kind of 'frontier station' between Christian thought and the world of secular literature, philosophy and sociology. V.A. DEMANT and the Rev Patrick McLaughlin were instrumental in establishing it. Speakers there included T.S. ELIOT, PHILIP MAIRET, MAURICE RECKITT, and the philosophers Nicolas Berdyaev and Gabriel Marcel. Visitors included Rose Macaulay, Norman Nicholson, Fr John Groser and T.M. HERON. The COUNCIL FOR THE CHURCH AND COUNTRYSIDE was based there, and the ECONOMIC REFORM CLUB AND INSTITUTE opened a restaurant there during the war.

SOCIAL CREDIT. A set of economic theories on reform of the financial system, developed by MAJOR C.H. DOUGLAS in the years immediately following the First World War, notably in the pages of A.R. ORAGE's paper the *NEW AGE*. The ideas of Social Credit are notoriously difficult to grasp, and the reader is referred to Holter (1934) or to the recent sympathetic study by Hutchinson and Burkitt (1997). Social Credit was a reaction against deflationary economic policies, which denied to a large proportion of the population a share in the material products which society could produce so abundantly: this was a situation of 'poverty in the midst of plenty.' Social Credit appealed to members of the organic movement because it rejected the narrow identification of 'wealth' with money, arguing that the existing financial system encouraged exploitation of natural resources. It distinguished between Financial Credit — the nation's wealth estimated in money terms — and Real Credit — the nation's wealth based on its ability to produce and deliver goods and services. The National Dividend it proposed would ensure that all members of society would be able to purchase the fresh, protective foods necessary for health. Financiers' dislike of economic nationalism had resulted in the running down of British agriculture in the interests of the import and export trade and the money-lenders. The power of banks to create or withhold credit was another force working against the survival of farmers. Politically, Social Credit was ambivalent. Hutchinson and Burkitt have re-established it clearly in its original socialist context, but its opposition to the financial system predisposed it towards anti-semitic conspiracy theory and the radical Right. Its rejection of nationalization made it attractive to many of those who had supported GUILD SOCIALISM, yet there were those such as the Communist poet Hugh MacDiarmid who believed Social Credit compatible with Marxism and, indeed, impossible to establish without revolution. The fact that the NEW ENGLISH WEEKLY was founded to state the Social Credit case in itself demonstrates the importance of Social Credit to the organic movement. Among those committed or sympathetic to its ideas were V.A. DEMANT, T.S. ELIOT, MONTAGUE FORDHAM, JOHN HARGRAVE, T.M. HERON, PHILIP MAIRET, DMITRI MITRINOVIC, MAURICE RECKITT, EDGAR J. SAXON, W.T. SYMONS, the MARQUIS OF TAVISTOCK, and WILLIAM TEMPLE.

SOCIOLOGICAL SOCIETY. The Sociological Society was founded in 1904 by Victor Branford and PATRICK GEDDES in order to make sociology a truly observational science, looking at the actual processes and functions of regional societies rather than dealing in abstractions. In 1920 LEWIS MUMFORD joined Branford in London, where the latter was establishing the Society's new headquarters, and became editor of the Sociological Review before returning to America in 1922. Branford and Geddes advocated reforestation, better housing and town planning, progressive schooling and socialized credit. In 1930 KENNETH-BARLOW worked for the Sociological Review as a sub-editor. The Society's headquarters, Le Play House in Pimlico, London, was also the base of the RURAL RECONSTRUCTION ASSOCIATION during the 1930s.

SOIL AND HEALTH. This short-lived quarterly journal, edited by SIR ALBERT HOWARD, was in effect a continuation of L.J. PICTON'S News Letter on Compost. It ran from February 1946 to Spring 1948, its final issue being a memorial to Howard, who had died the previous October. It was in many respects similar to the SOIL ASSOCIATION journal MOTHER EARTH in its cover-

age of issues relating to humus farming, municipal composting, nutrition and physical wellbeing. Contributors included LADY EVE BALFOUR, D.P. HOPKINS, J.E.R. McDONAGH, WESTON A. PRICE and NEWMAN TURNER.

SOIL ASSOCIATION. The Association arose as a result of the great interest aroused by LADY EVE BALFOUR'S 1943 book The Living Soil. With the support of G. SCOTT WILLIAMSON and FRIEND SYKES a founders' meeting of about one hundred people was held in June 1945. The Association's aim was 'to create a great body of biological knowledge of the life of the soil, and to distribute that knowledge far and wide to the consumer as it accrues to the cultivator' (ME introductory issue, p.6). There were problems in drafting the constitution, and SIR ALBERT HOWARD and LOUISE HOWARD resigned before the Inaugural Meeting was held in May 1946, objecting to the decision to make the scientific Advisory Panel subject to the policy of the Council. Lady Eve was the first President until LORD TEVIOT was appointed at the first General Meeting in October 1946. From 1950 to 1970 Viscount Newport, later Lord Bradford, was President. The Association's journal MOTHER EARTH was edited by JORIAN JENKS. Members of the first Council included Lady Eve Balfour, RICHARD DE LA MARE, Sir Peter Greenwell (son of SIR BERNARD GREENWELL), INNES H. PEARSE, LORD SEMPILL and G. Scott Williamson. Later Council members included RICHARD ST BARBE BAKER, KENNETH BARLOW, MAYE BRUCE, ROLF GARDINER, H.J. MASSINGHAM and the EARL OF PORTSMOUTH. The first panel of experts included LAURENCE EASTERBROOK, M.C. RAYNER, Friend Sykes and R.G.M. WILSON. By 1953 membership had passed 3,000 and was worldwide. Virginia Payne (1971) has told in detail the history of the Association's first twenty-five years.

SOIL MAGAZINE. A monthly journal produced and edited by SIEGFRIED MARIAN during the late 1940s and early 1950s. After Marian's death in 1952 DION BYNGHAM became Assistant Editor. Its general outlook was similar to that of *Mother Earth,* but Byngham's contributions ensured an element of pagan mysticism. AUBREY WESTLAKE also contributed.

TREES. The journal of the MEN OF THE TREES, issued bi-monthly from the autumn of 1936 and quarterly during the Second World War. Its first number contained a blessing from LORD BLEDISLOE. Contributors included MAYE BRUCE, ROLF GARDINER, Lord Horder, G.V. JACKS, C.A. MIRBT, the EARL OF PORTSMOUTH, Vita Sackville-West, and J.W. Robertson-Scott, editor of *The Countryman.*

Endnotes

Chapter 1

1. Poore 1903, p.283.
2. In 1990 membership was around 3,000, with about 2,000 licensees; by 2000 the figures were 10,000 members and 4,000 licensees.
3. Coe 1994; Smiley 1995.
4. On technological optimism, see Blaxter and Robertson 1995, p.274. On limits, see for instance Meadows 1972; Nicol 1967, and Osborn 1954.
5. See for instance, Easterbrook 1964, p.98.
6. Brock 1997, p.x and pp.149–60.
7. *Ibid.* pp.145f. The word 'organic' in this context means simply 'concerned with the compounds of carbon.'
8. *Ibid.* pp.161f, and p.181.
9. Grigg 1989, p.72.
10. This was the belief that nitrogen, phosphorus and potassium, applied from the fertilizer bag, provided everything the soil needed for fertility.
11. Portsmouth 1965, p.37.
12. See Wright 1996, pp.150–62, 176–202.
13. Edgell 1992.
14. Stapledon 1942. On Stapledon's theory of 'operative ignorance' see Waller 1962, pp. 283f.
15. See Newby 1987, pp.154–56.
16. Williams-Ellis, *England and the Octopus,* 1928. See also *Britain and the Beast,* edited by Williams-Ellis 1937.
17. Tiltman 1935, p.22, 146.
18. Harrison 1964, p.40.
19. The poet C.H. Sisson has recognized its importance: Mairet 1981, pp.x–xxii. See also Conford 1998a.

20. Sisson 1993, pp.122f.
21. Eliot 1948, p.7. Gordon 1998, makes no reference to Mairet, Reckitt, Tom Heron or the Chandos Group, and only one to the *New English Weekly,* in connection with the *Four Quartets.* See also Mairet 1958b.

Chapter 2

1. Dale 1956, p.223.
2. Lord Ernle's dated but magisterial panorama, *English Farming, Past and Present,* takes the story through to the 1930s; a more concise version is given by Orwin 1949; his widow Christabel, also C.S., collaborated with Edith Whetham on *A History of British Agriculture: 1846–1914;* Whetham 1978, covers the period 1914–39; Grigg 1989, sets twentieth-century developments against a backdrop of the previous two or three centuries; Newby 1987, offers a comprehensive review of the agricultural and social history of rural England from the mid-eighteenth century to the 1980s; Brown 1987, surveys the period from 1870 to the 1947 Agriculture Act; Dewey 1989, looks at the First World War; Cooper 1989, looks at Conservative Party agricultural policy; Murray 1955, and Ward 1988, look at the Second World War; Holderness 1985, looks at post-1947 developments; Martin 2000, gives an excellent survey of the period from the 1930s onwards; Blaxter and Robertson 1995, offer a laudatory account of the revolution in agricultural technology since the 1930s. More critical accounts of develop-

ments since 1947 can be found in Body 1991, and Harvey 1997.

3. Ernle 1961, p.382.
4. See Enfield 1924, and Penning-Rowsell 1997.
5. See Harvey 1997, pp.115–17; and Tiltman 1935.
6. On the 1947 Act, see Cripps 1948; for criticisms, see Street 1954.
7. On agricultural policy during the Second World War, see Brown 1987, pp.125–46, and Murray 1955. Gangulee 1943 offers a detailed contemporary account of the success of the food production campaign. On the 'plough-up' campaign, see Stapledon 1939. On the increase in the use of artificial fertilizers during the war, see Brown 1987, p.139; and Grigg 1989, p.72. On the increase in mechanization, see Brown *Ibid.* pp.139f.
8. Astor and Rowntree 1939, p.253.
9. Grigg 1989, pp.143–45.
10. Farming To-Day, 1942, pp.72–76.
11. Addison 1939, pp.112f.
12. Elliot 1943, p.139.
13. Orwin 1942, p.61.
14. Astor and Rowntree 1946, pp.14f.
15. Orwin 1934.
16. Russell 1945, p.116.
17. Cripps 1948, p.1.
18. Williams 1965, p.160.
19. Grigg 1989, p.166.
20. Newby 1987, pp.186f.
21. Grigg 1989. p.120.
22. Watson and Hobbs 1951, pp.86–97.
23. See Massingham 1947.
24. Orwin 1930a, p.81.
25. *Ibid.* pp.85f, and p.99.
26. Orwin 1942, pp.103, and p.104.
27. Hall 1941, p.170.
28. Astor and Rowntree 1946, p.88.
29. Harvey 1997, p.114.
30. Grigg 1989, p.119.
31. Donaldson 1972, pp.147–60.
32. Danziger 1988, p.44.
33. Orwin 1930a, pp.102f.
34. Astor and Murray 1932, p.99.
35. On Baylis and Chamberlain, see Orwin 1930a, pp.104–6; 1930b, and 1930c.

36. Orwin 1930a, p.108.
37. *Ibid.*
38. Hall 1941, p.60; p.166; p.142; p.143.
39. Grigg 1989. p.186; pp.184–90.
40. *Ibid.* pp.184f.
41. *FJ* 3.11.48, p.617; p.615.
42. Hall 1947, p.1; pp.19f.
43. *FJ* 29.8.45, p.515. On this issue see also definitions in Fream 1949, p.154, and Black 1981, p.23.
44. Balfour 1948, p.103.
45. Jenks 1959, p.57.
46. On Liebig, see Brock 1997; Jenks 1959, pp.57–59; Porteous 1950, pp.651–53; Watson and Hobbs 1951, pp.72–76.
47. Hall 1947, p.6.
48. Howard 1945a, p.79.
49. *FJ* 29.3.44, p.143. On Lawes and Gilbert see Russell 1966, pp.143–69.
50. Russell 1943, pp.89f.
51. *FJ* 4.8.43, p.349.
52. See Beckett 1999, pp.51–54, for a discussion of the corruption alleged to have been involved in setting up Mond's business.
53. *JRASE* 1931, p.172.
54. Keeble 1932, pp.5, 17.
55. See *JMA* Vol.41, p.693.
56. Long 1948, p.8.
57. Marks 1989, p.254.
58. Brown 1987, p.139.
59. *FJ* 14.8.46, p.525.
60. *FJ* 11.1.50, p.19; and 22.3.50, p.167.
61. *FJ* 28.2.45, p.122.
62. This series of advertisements appeared in the *Fertiliser Journal* in the autumn of 1945: see pp. 540, 563, 596, 634 and 657.
63. Grigg 1989, p.72.
64. *FJ* 3.11.48, p.620.
65. See for instance Julian Rose in Barnett and Scruton 1998, p.124.
66. *FJ* 30.8.44, p.416; and 28.2.45, pp.119–23.
67. *FJ* 2.2.44, p.51; 10.5.44, p.220; 6.12.44, p.581; 3.11.48, p.615.
68. Hopkins 1945, p.251.
69. Grigg 1989, p.45 and p.128.
70. See Holderness 1985, pp.103–10.
71. Blaxter and Robertson 1995, p.271.

72. *Ibid.* p.274.
73. See for instance Body 1991; Harvey 1997, and the Soil Association journal *Living Earth, passim.*
74. DDT's encouragement of the red spider mite provided an early example of this: see Russell 1966, p.366.
75. Waller 1962, p.276.
76. *Ibid.* pp.276f.
77. Dale 1956, p.225.

Chapter 3

1. Hilton 1973, pp.240, 241. Quotations are from a 1973 reprint of the 1949 Modern Fiction Library edition.
2. The chief work to consult on the Hunzas is *The Wheel of Health* by G.T. Wrench, first published by C.W. Daniel in 1938 and reissued by Schocken Books of New York in 1972.
3. Picton 1946, p.21.
4. Howard 1954, p.52.
5. Hugo 1909, p.548.
6. *Ibid.* p.531.
7. *Ibid.* p.531.
8. King 1949, p.75.
9. *Ibid.* p.19.
10. *Ibid.* p.241.
11. *Ibid.* p.13.
12. See Wrench 1972, p.122.
13. *Ibid.* p.123.
14. *Ibid.* p.22.
15. Accounts of McCarrison's career can be found in Barlow 1988; Griggs 1986; McCarrison 1961; Picton 1946; and Wrench 1972. The McCarrison Society, an offshoot of the Soil Association, was founded in 1966.
16. See McCarrison's obituary in *Nature,* Vol.187, pp.195f.
17. Wrench 1972, p.30.
18. McCarrison 1961, p.94.
19. Wrench 1972, p.59.
20. *Ibid.* p.123.
21. McCarrison 1961, p.101; pp.29f.
22. McCarrison 1961, pp.101f.
23. Wrench 1972, pp.56–59.
24. McCarrison 1961, p.15.
25. *Ibid.* p.7.
26. Howard 1945a, p.15.
27. *SH* Spring 1948, p.4.
28. Obituary of Howard, *Nature,* Vol.160, pp.741f.
29. Howard 1945a, p.16.
30. Picton 1946, p.21.
31. Howard 1945a, p.17.
32. *Ibid.* pp.18f; and p.18.
33. Howard 1954, p.49.
34. *SH* Spring 1948, p.17.
35. Howard 1954, p.47.
36. On Gabrielle Howard see the *Newnham College Roll Letter,* January 1931, pp.52–54, and her obituary in *Nature,* Vol.126, 1930, pp.445f.
37. Howard, L. 1954, pp.38f.
38. *Ibid.* p.162.
39. Sub-titled *Their Utilization as Humus,* this was a detailed account of the Indore Process for the benefit of Indian cultivators. Howard and Wad 1931.
40. See *SH* Spring 1948, pp.27–31 and Howard 1945a, pp.239–43.
41. Howard 1940, p.55; pp.229–34; see also Howard 1945a, pp.244–47.
42. *FJ* 13.9.44, p.445.
43. Howard 1940, p.234.
44. van Vuren 1949, pp.7–10.
45. Howard 1945a, p.172.
46. *SH* Spring 1948, pp.18f.
47. Howard 1940, pp.1–5; 1945a, pp.40f.
48. Howard 1945a, p.40.
49. See St Barbe Baker 1944 and 1979 for autobiographical accounts of his life.
50. St Barbe Baker 1944, p.12.
51. St Barbe Baker 1979, p.11.
52. *Ibid.* pp.22–35.
53. *Ibid.* pp.36f.
54. *Ibid.* p.37; p.40.
55. *Ibid.* p.56.
56. *Ibid.* p.163.
57. *Trees* Aug./Sept. 1938, p.139.
58. St Barbe Baker 1979, p.166; p.167.
59. *Ibid.*
60. See for instance *Le Mariage de Loti* and *Madame Chrysanthème,* about Tahiti and Japan respectively.
61. See Conford 1992, pp.81–89. See also Shiva 1988.
62. *Newnham College Roll Letter,* January 1931, p.54.

Chapter 4

1. Steiner 1993, pp.97f.
2. Howard 1940, p.ix, and 1945a, p.199.
3. In the present writer's view the influence of Howard, McCarrison and Lady Balfour was more significant in the development of the British organic movement than was the work of the Steiner school, and I therefore use the term 'mainstream' with reference to them and their followers, and particularly to the Soil Association.
4. Steiner 1993, p.10.
5. *Ibid.* p.188.
6. On Steiner's life and ideas see Hemleben 1975; Landau 1935, pp.45–83 and 312–41; Seddon 1988; Tompkins and Bird 1992, pp.361–71; Wachsmuth 1955; Washington 1996, pp.145–56, 163–66 and 233–53; Webb 1981, pp.62–72.
7. Hemleben 1975, p.39.
8. Hemleben 1975, p.40; p.56.
9. Washington 1996.
10. For a full and fascinating account of the connnections between the organic school, the monetary reform movement and esoteric philosophies in Britain, see Webb 1971, 1980 and 1981.
11. Hemleben 1975, pp. 80f.
12. On Steiner's social philosophy see Waterman 1946.
13. According to Vivian Griffiths, it seems that the request came to Steiner to give the Agriculture Course out of the problem of human nutrition. The decline of food quality was a key factor in the inability of human beings to have an active inner thought life. Steiner gave indications on these subjects and his counsel was sought by many people unable to meditate properly.
14. Brocklebank 1948, p.30.
15. Hemleben 1975, p.133.
16. Brocklebank 1948, p.31.
17. Wachsmuth 1955, p.549.
18. Steiner 1993, p.137.
19. *Ibid.* p.136.
20. Raffael 1996.
21. Steiner 1993, p.260.
22. *Ibid.* p.262.
23. Raffael 1996.
24. *Mother Earth* July 1962, pp.277–82, contains a memorial article on Pfeiffer by Dr Hans G. Heinze, and a tribute by Rolf Gardiner.
25. For more about crystallization, see Kolisko 1978.
26. Portsmouth 1965, p.84.
27. Portsmouth 1965, p.85.
28. *ME,* July 1962, p.279.
29. Portsmouth 1965, pp.83f.
30. Pfeiffer 1947a, p.111.
31. Pfeiffer 1947b, p.13.
32. Portsmouth 1965, pp.88f.
33. See Gardiner 1972, pp.199f, and *ME* July 1962, p.282.
34. Gardiner 1972, p.200.
35. *ME* July 1962, p.282.
36. Mier, formerly Mirbt, changed his name early in the Second World War. For information on him I have relied on a duplicated memoir by Mark Gartner (1990) for private circulation, given to me by Vivian Griffiths of the Biodynamic Agricultural Association, Clent, Worcestershire.
37. Landau 1935, pp.321f and p.329.
38. *ME* October 1960, p.352.
39. Gartner 1990, p.4.
40. *ME* April 1964, p.95; p.97.
41. Easterbrook (n.d.).
42. Unpublished typescript, Griffiths 1999, p.2.
43. Baker 1940, p.72; p.9.
44. *Ibid.* p.11.
45. *Ibid.* p.53; pp.183f.
46. *Ibid.* p.102.
47. Bruce 1943, p.5; p.8.
48. *ME* second issue, p.30.
49. Hills 1989, p.60.
50. Griffiths, V. 1999, p.3.
51. *ME,* October 1959, p.721.
52. *ME,* July 1956, p.633.
53. Mairet 1981, p.100, p.127, p.134 and p.163. The Mitrinovic archive at the University of Bradford demonstrates that Mitrinovic owned an extensive collection of Steiner's works.

54. Massingham 1944, pp.103f. Ironically, Massingham's description is very similar to that of Dr William Ogg of Rothamsted, in a speech attacking the organic movement, reported in *Farmers' Weekly,* 5 September 1947.

Chapter 5

1. *Journal of the Farmers' Club* February 1937.
2. *Ibid.* p.17; p.11; p.16; p.7.
3. *Ibid.* p.18.
4. For Sykes' account of how he turned the almost derelict estate into a thriving concern, see Howard 1945a, pp.262–74; H.J. Massingham described a visit to the estate in *The Wisdom of the Fields,* 1945, pp.173–76.
5. Howard 1945a, p.266; p.267.
6. Sykes 1951, pp.230–36.
7. Howard 1945a, pp.272f.
8. Sykes 1946, p.7.
9. Sykes 1951, p.198.
10. Sykes 1946, p.126.
11. *Ibid.* p.195 and p.269.
12. Turner 1951, p.39.
13. On Wilson, see Godwin 1939.
14. Godwin 1939, p.17; Griffiths 1983, p.322.
15. Blackburn 1949, p.76.
16. *Ibid.* p.91.
17. Howard 1940, p.107.
18. Blackburn 1949, p.124.
19. *ME* Summer 1949, pp.29f.
20. Wylie 1955, p.38.
21. Howard 1945b, p.10.
22. Barrett 1949, p.151.
23. Rayner and Neilson-Jones 1944, p.178.
24. Howard 1940, p.25.
25. Rayner and Neilson-Jones 1944, p.165.
26. See Conford 1998b.
27. *ME* July 1952, p.36.
28. *Ibid.* p.42.
29. *ME,* introductory issue, 1946, pp.3f.
30. Balfour 1944, p.190.
31. Balfour 1944, p.199.
32. *ME* January 1952, October 1952, January 1954.
33. Payne 1971, p.40.
34. Balfour 1975; Payne 1971, pp.65–68.
35. Hills 1989, p.42.
36. *Ibid.* p.64.
37. Easey 1955, p.28; Chase 1948, pp.26f.
38. King 1944, pp.7–10, and pp.105–8; p.8; pp.13, 11, 91.
39. *Ibid.* p.18.
40. *SH* February 1946: inside front cover.
41. *SH* Summer 1947, p.108; pp.209–14.
42. *SH* February 1946, p.31.
43. *SH* Autumn 1946, p.178.
44. *SH* Spring 1948 p.80.
45. *SM* July 1951, p.160.
46. *ME* Spring 1949, pp.32f.
47. *SM* September 1950, p.205.
48. *SM* July 1949, p.9.
49. *SM* September 1950, p.220; pp.50–52.
50. *SM* January 1950, p.3.
51. *SM* November 1950, p.262.
52. *Ibid.; SM* December 1949, pp.18f.
53. Oyler 1950, p.139.
54. *ME* Winter 1950–51, p.57.
55. Oyler 1950, p.60; p.91; p.211.
56. Oyler 1951, p.154; p.31; p.126; p.37.
57. Scofield 1986, p.1.
58. Northbourne 1940, p.87.
59. Gardiner 1972, p.199.
60. Northbourne 1970, p.7.
61. *Ibid.* p.12.
62. *Ibid.* p.17.
63. Northbourne 1940, p.172.
64. Mary Heron, conversation with the author, 18 February 1998.

Chapter 6

1. For a concise and compelling account of the creation of the Dust Bowl, see Hyams 1976, pp.138–50.
2. US Department of Agriculture 1938, p.44.
3. Peters 1982, p.60.
4. Waksman 1938. Waksman was Professor of Soil Microbiology at Rutgers University.
5. On Oliver, see Barrett 1949.

6. Jackson 1974, pp.53f. Jackson incorrectly refers to 'McGarrison.'
7. *Ibid.* pp.240f; pp.54–56.
8. See Jackson 1974, p.63, on Rodale's false start with *Organic Farmer.*
9. Peters 1982, pp.118f.
10. Rodale 1949, pp.29–33; pp.143–49.
11. Jackson 1974, p.115.
12. *Ibid.* p.64.
13. Rodale's work preceded Rachel Carson's *Silent Spring* by twenty years. Another significant precursor, now largely forgotten, was Leonard Wickenden, author of *Our Daily Poison,* reviewed in *Mother Earth,* July 1956, pp.583–87.
14. Rodale 1949, pp.174–82.
15. Jackson 1974, pp.114f.
16. *Ibid.* pp.219f; p.220.
17. *Ibid.* p.220.
18. Peters 1982, p.116; p.108.
19. Rodale 1949, p.239.
20. Jackson 1974, p.229; p.232.
21. *Ibid.* pp.75f; p.75.
22. *ME* July 1955, pp.223–28.
23. Brown 1956, p.54.
24. Portsmouth 1965, pp.94f.
25. Brown 1956, p.55; p.107.
26. *Ibid.* p.89.
27. Bromfield 1946, p.7.
28. *Ibid.* p.vii.
29. Bromfield 1949, pp.11–17, and 393–99; p.11; p.321.
30. Bromfield 1951, p.258.
31. Bromfield 1949, pp.53–57.
32. Bromfield 1951, pp.166f.
33. Bromfield 1949, p.56.
34. Bromfield 1949, pp.274–93.
35. *ME* July 1955, p.224.
36. Bromfield 1946, pp.260–72; p.268; p.271.
37. Peters 1982, p.129.
38. Bromfield 1949, p.263.
39. *Ibid.*
40. *Ibid.* p.397.
41. *Ibid.* p.372.
42. Bromfield 1946, p.165.
43. Faulkner 1945, p.17.
44. *Ibid.* p.51.
45. US Department of Agriculture 1938, pp.609f.
46. Faulkner 1945, p.53; also see pp.22–26.
47. *Ibid.* p.79.
48. *FJ* 6.10.48, p.567.
49. Faulkner 1948, pp.152–56.
50. Faulkner 1945, p.13.
51. *Ibid.* p.115.
52. Faulkner 1953, p.20; p.119.
53. Faulkner 1948, p.107.
54. Bromfield 1951, p.240.
55. Sears 1947, p.145.
56. *Ibid.* pp.63f.
57. *Ibid.* p.5.
58. *Ibid.* pp.166f.
59. *Ibid.* p.169.
60. Osborn 1948, pp.137f; p.66.
61. See Worster 1985.
62. Osborn 1948, p.7.
63. *Ibid.* p.39.
64. USDA 1938, pp.347–60.
65. *ME* April 1954, p.53.
66. *ME* October 1960, p.353.
67. *ME* October 1951, p.17.
68. On Pottinger's cats, see *ME* Autumn 1949, p.51 and Winter 1949–50, pp.35f.
69. *ME* October 1958, pp.273–92.
70. *ME* January 1959, pp.405f.

Chapter 7

1. Reed 1939, pp.19f.
2. Williams-Ellis 1937, pp.44–47. See also Williams-Ellis 1928.
3. Jeans 1990, p.249. For discussion of such writings, see Miller 1995; Shaw and Chase 1989, pp.128–44; Wiener 1992, pp.41–80; Wright 1985, pp.93–134. Matless 1998, offers a wide-ranging study of the issues.
4. Shaw and Chase 1989, p.136.
5. Veldman 1994, pp.9–36.
6. Shaw 1935; Marsh 1982, pp.107–11.
7. Marsh 1982, pp.145–52; Mairet 1981, pp.30–44 and pp.47–50.
8. AE's life story is told in Summerfield 1975. See also Travers 1993, pp.242–56.
9. Summerfield 1975, p.144.
10. *Ibid.* p.145.
11. Ibid, pp.128f.

12. *Ibid.* p.143.
13. *Ibid.* p.145.
14. Thomas 1927; 1931.
15. Thomas 1927, pp.98f; pp.117–20.
16. Fordham 1908, p.13.
17. *Ibid.* p.138.
18. RRA 1935, p.12; p.13 and p.3.
19. RRA 1936, p.29.
20. Fordham 1938, p.13.
21. On Stapledon, see Moore-Colyer 1999; Russell 1966, pp.386–403; and Waller 1962.
22. Waller 1962, p.276.
23. Stapledon 1942, p.3; p.4; p.226; p.231.
24. Harvey 1997, pp.66–77.
25. Massingham 1947, p.49; p.69; p.247.
26. Massingham 1943a, p.132.
27. *Ibid.* p.130; p.131; p.133.
28. *Ibid.* p.130.
29. Bell 1941, p.119.
30. Two versions exist of Williamson's years farming in Norfolk: *The Story of a Norfolk Farm* deals with the period up to the outbreak of war in 1939, and is directly autobiographical; the entire period is dealt with in detailed, fictionalized form in his novels *The Phoenix Generation, A Solitary War* and *Lucifer Before Sunrise,* though these books are very closely based on the reality of his experiences. *The Phasian Bird* is also relevant.
31. Williamson 1941, p.45.
32. Williamson 1967, p.268; p.389.
33. *Ibid.* p.391.
34. Duncan 1964, p.210; p.211; p.256, p.258, and p.279. See also Duncan 1968, pp.112f and p.116.
35. Duncan 1944, p.41; p.84; p.106; p.75; p.88; p.124.
36. On Murry, see Carswell 1978; Lea 1959; and Mairet 1958a.
37. Murry 1952, p.22.
38. Plowman 1944.
39. Murry 1942, pp.108f; p.133; p.137.
40. *Ibid.* pp.115f.
41. *Adelphi* October-December 1944, p.40; October-December 1945, p.45.
42. See Godwin 1939.
43. *Adelphi* July-September 1949, pp.310–18.
44. Bramwell 1989, p.122.
45. Crosby 1979, pp.141f.
46. Portsmouth 1965, p.37.
47. Lymington 1932, p.136.
48. *Ibid.* p.102.
49. Portsmouth 1943, p.164; p.179.
50. Massingham 1941, p.92. There has been a growth of interest in Gardiner in recent years, as folk-dancer, Anglo-Saxon cultural bridge-builder, opponent of modernity, conservationist, and fellow-traveller of the Right. See Boyes 1993, pp.154–63; Bramwell 1989, pp.112–117; Chase 1992; Griffiths 1983, pp.142–46; Trentmann 1994, and Wright 1996, pp.151–62 and pp.176–202.
51. Gardiner 1972, p.3; pp.88f; p.140.
52. Gardiner 1943, p.127.
53. *Ibid.* p.172.
54. Massingham 1945a, pp.129–40.
55. See Collis 1975a and 1975b.
56. Collis 1991, pp.124–26; p.161; p.178 and p.182.
57. Collis 1950, p.246.
58. Collis 1975b, p.308.
59. *Ibid.* p.335.
60. Collis 1950, p.131.

Chapter 8

1. *The Chronicle,* Crewe, 25.3.39.
2. *Ibid.*
3. Poore 1903, p.283; p.105; pp.120f; p.121.
4. *Ibid.* p.3; p.412; p.204.
5. Griggs 1986, p.137.
6. *Ibid.* p.139.
7. Stallibrass 1989, p.12.
8. On the Pioneer Health Centre see Barlow 1988; Comerford 1947; Pearse and Crocker 1943, and Stallibrass 1989.
9. Pioneer Health Centre 1938, pp.19f.
10. Stallibrass 1989, p.110.
11. Williamson and Pearse 1965, p.21.
12. Pearse and Williamson 1931, p.154.
13. Barlow, Kenneth (n.d.), unpublished manuscript on the Coventry Family Health Club, p.149.

14. Williamson and Pearse 1951.
15. Donaldson 1992, p.34.
16. De la Mare 1998.
17. Dust-jacket of Barlow 1942.
18. Barlow 1942, p.100.
19. Barlow 1988, pp.112–19; p.116.
20. *BMJ* 20.6.1953, p.1395.
21. Jenks 1959, p.189.
22. For a detailed discussion, see Barlow 1978; Jenks 1959, pp. 188–91, and Picton 1946, pp.125–69.
23. Jenks 1959, p.191.
24. Picton 1946, p.140.
25. For details of this story, see Barlow 1978, pp.21–35.
26. Picton 1946, p.161.
27. Jenks 1959, p.191.
28. See his autobiography, *As I Recall,* 1966.
29. Orr 1966, pp.117f.
30. Orr 1948.
31. Sanderson-Wells and Jenks 1947. The article was issued subsequently as a pamphlet.
32. Sanderson-Wells 1939, p.96; p.86, p.87, and p.84.
33. Portsmouth 1965, p.86 and p.122.
34. Durkin 1965, pp.xv–xvi.
35. *Ibid.* pp.125f.
36. Carrel 1952, p.37; p.43.
37. Carrel 1935, p.292; p.319.
38. Ludovici 1945, p.1.
39. *NP,* December 1938, pp.23f.
40. Howard 1945a, pp.179f. On McDonagh's ideas, see Westlake, 1961, pp.114–22.
41. McDonagh 1940, p.5; p.370; p.372.
42. *Ibid.* pp.372f.
43. *Ibid.* p.376.
44. Portsmouth 1965, p.122.
45. Balfour 1948, pp.135–37; Sykes 1946, p.208 and pp.250f.
46. Balfour 1948, pp.132f.
47. *ME* Spring 1947, p.16; Autumn 1947, p.7.
48. *Ibid.*
49. Price 1945, p.1.
50. *Ibid.* p.50.
51. *Ibid.* p.419.
52. *Ibid.* p.433.
53. Edgell 1992, is an exception; see pp.624–28.

54. On Byngham see Edgell 1992, pp.184–214, and pp.612–24.
55. *HL* November 1956, p.473.
56. *HL* January 1935, p.21; June 1939, p.501; *Ibid.* p.504; April 1936, pp.310f, and April 1939, p.309; May 1939, p.403; August 1938, pp.118–22; January 1946, pp.19–22.
57. *HL* February 1950, p.72.
58. *HL* January 1938, pp.29–33; September 1944, p.95; September 1943, p.93; July 1945, p.17; December 1940, pp.281–85; January 1941, pp.19–23; February 1941, pp.66–70; September 1939, pp.213–20; July 1947, p.7; August 1949, p.50; August 1950, pp.51–56.
59. *HL* December 1943, p.236; July 1948, p.6.
60. *HL* June 1942, pp.258f.
61. *HL* January 1947, p.15.
62. *HL* February 1948.
63. *HL* July 1941, p.17.
64. Edgell 1992, pp.627f.
65. *HL* January 1939, p.82; June 1942, p.259.
66. *HL* August 1943, p.57; January 1945, p.17; March 1946, pp.94f; November 1944, p.188.
67. *HL* November 1942, p.204.
68. *Ibid.* p.206.
69. *HL* December 1950, p.253.
70. See Macmurray 1996, pp.105–13. Macmurray had contact with a number of figures in the organic movement during the 1930s and his views on the dangers of what he termed 'the organic analogy' may well have been developed as a reaction against the political careers of some of the movement's members.

Chapter 9

1. Johnson 1977, pp.88f.
2. Gould 1988, p.ix.
3. Jenks 1950; 1959.
4. *ME* January 1964, pp.2–4.
5. Simpson 1992, p.241.
6. Charnley 1990, p.100.
7. Craven 1993, p.212.

8. *FQ* July 1936, p.400.
9. *FQ* October 1936, p.525.
10. Jenks and Peddie 1935, p.13; p.92.
11. Jenks 1938, p.5.
12. *Ibid.* p.2.
13. *Ibid.* p.8.
14. Conford 1999.
15. Williamson, A. 1995 p.199.
16. Griffiths 1983, p.87.
17. Williamson, A. 1995, p.268, p.348.
18. Williamson 1941, p.51; p.187.
19. Williamson 1985b, p.105.
20. Williamson 1967, p.515.
21. Williamson 1985a, p.362.
22. Sanderson 1936, p.68, p.81. On Sanderson and the English Mistery, see Craven 1993, pp.121f; Griffiths 1983, pp.317f; Portsmouth 1965, pp.126–33, and Webber 1986, p.150.
23. Portsmouth 1965, p.128.
24. Griffiths 1983, pp.321f.
25. Portsmouth 1965, p.129.
26. On Beckett, see Beckett 1999. On A.K. Chesterton see Baker, David 1996.
27. Webber 1986, p.146 and pp.155f. On Tavistock, see Bedford 1949; Bedford 1959, pp.154–63; Griffiths 1983, pp.351–53 and pp.370–72; Harris and Trow 2000, pp.91–93 and pp.114–18; Hyde 1952, pp.169–73.
28. Bedford 1949, p.155.
29. *PP* July 1947, p.6.
30. *Ibid.*
31. Simpson 1992, pp.298–303.
32. Loftus 1926, p.142; p.41; pp.173f; p.56.
33. In a letter to the author of 22 July, 1996, Bell's daughter Anthea says that he was not a committed member, and his diaries confirm this view. See also Bell 1965, pp.9–11.
34. Hamilton 1971, p.259.
35. Griffiths 1983, p.362; Bramwell 1989, p.121.
36. Webb 1990, p.242.
37. Roberts 1995, pp.287–322. Contrast Street 1979, pp.109–13.
38. Bryant 1940, p.233.
39. On Domvile see Griffiths 1983, pp.179–82 and pp.315–17; 1998, pp.39–42.
40. Edgerton 1991, p.47.
41. On Sempill, see Edgerton 1991, pp.26f and p.47, and Griffiths 1998, pp.144f.
42. Griffiths 1998, pp.83–86, pp.92f, and pp.149f.
43. Bramwell 1989, p.197.
44. Ludovici 1938, p.1, p.67, and p.77; p.110.
45. Ludovici 1961, pp.84–89 and pp.129f.
46. Williamson 1967, p.262.
47. Wrench 1948, p.260, and p.256.
48. Wohl 1980, p.47; p.62.
49. *Ibid.* pp.70f. Philip Mairet's *Aristocracy and the Meaning of Class Rule,* published in 1931, attempted just such a synthesis of oil and water.
50. *Ibid.* p.232. For a detailed discussion of the British radical Right's attitude to rural issues, see Craven 1993. For a comparable movement in France, see Paxton 1997.
51. Penty 1937, p.50; p.59.
52. *Ibid.* p.57.
53. Penty 1932, p.65; p.115.
54. Munkes 1937, p.106.
55. Hobson 1938, p.176.
56. Kenney 1939, p.205.
57. On Guild Socialism see Glass 1966; Hutchinson and Burkitt 1997; Kenney 1939; Reckitt 1941.
58. Glass 1966, p.65.
59. For accounts of Distributism, see Canovan 1977; Corrin 1981; Finlay 1972 pp.45–59; Sewell 1966, 1990.
60. Corrin 1981, p.xiii.
61. *Ibid.* p.127; p.127, pp.150f, and pp.154f.
62. Canovan 1977, p.91.
63. Corrin 1981, p.102.
64. *Ibid.* p.126; Landau 1939, pp.137–40; Sewell 1982, pp.115f.
65. Corrin 1981, p.89; pp.188f.
66. *Ibid.* p.162.
67. *Ibid.*
68. Griffiths 1983, pp.61f.
69. Kitson 1933, p.38, and p.40.
70. Holloway 1986, p.5.
71. It is interesting to note that both

Verdon-Roe and Vickers supported Mosley. See Thurlow 1998, p.108.

72. Rowe 1943, p.3.
73. ERCI 1939, p.14 (unnumbered).
74. *Ibid.* p.23 (unnumbered).
75. ERCI 1940, p.13 (unnumbered).
76. Holloway 1986, p.40.
77. ERCI 1943, p.12.
78. *RE* January 1949, p.2.
79. *RE* January 1948, p.7; April 1948, pp.43–45; September 1949, p.6; March/April 1950, p.6; July/August 1949, p.5; September 1949, p.10; June 1949, pp.1f.
80. *RE* May 1948, p.57. For background to this connection, see Holloway 1986, pp.62f.
81. *RE* March 1949, p.16; May 1949, p.15.
82. *MB* November 1947, p.6.
83. *MB* January/February 1949, p.8.
84. RRA 1955, pp.55–58.
85. Holloway 1986, pp.60f.
86. For summaries of Social Credit see De Maré 1983; Douglas 1934, 1979; Finlay 1972, pp.87–116; Holter 1934; Hutchinson and Burkitt 1997.
87. Holter 1934, p.11.
88. Finlay 1972, p.102.
89. Mumford 1976, p.56. Also see Bradshaw 1996.
90. Finlay 1972, pp.206–14.
91. *Ibid.* p.140.
92. On Hargrave, see Bramwell 1989, pp.106–11; Edgell 1992, pp.343–49 and pp.356–62; Finlay 1970; Hutton 1999, pp.163f; Webb 1981, pp.86–93; *Health and Life* January 1935, pp.26–29.
93. Webb 1981, p.90; p.91 and p.98.
94. Finlay 1970, p.54; p.59.
95. See Rowbotham 1998.
96. On the CSL and the LKG, see Bryant 1997, pp.128–53, and Wollenberg 1997, p.44 and pp.72f.
97. Finlay 1972, p.224.
98. *Ibid.* p.225.
99. *Ibid.* p.226.

Chapter 10

1. Mairet 1957, p.190. On Mairet's experiences at Chipping Campden, see Mairet 1981, pp.30–44 and pp.47–50. On Ashbee, see Cumming and Kaplan 1995, pp.26–28. On Geddes, see Mairet 1957, and Mumford 1956, pp.99–114.
2. Mairet 1957, p.xii; p.28.
3. Miller 1989, pp.115f and pp.123–33; Ruth Barlow (n.d.), p.51.
4. Mairet 1957, p.62.
5. *Ibid.* pp.77f.
6. Mairet 1981, pp.156f.
7. On Mitrinovic, see Davies 1961, pp.114–47; Mairet 1981, pp.173–93; New Atlantis Foundation 1987; Rigby 1984, and Selver 1959.
8. New Atlantis Foundation 1987, pp.71–258.
9. Rigby 1984, pp.59–83; p.69; p.78 and p.71.
10. *Ibid.* p.72.
11. *Ibid.* p.82.
12. See Davies 1961, pp.114–47; MacDermot 1997, pp.vii–x; Merricks 1996, pp.133–55; Purdom 1951, pp.152–58; Rigby 1984, pp.101–39.
13. *NB* 14.6.33, pp.121f; 2.8.33, p.338; 21.3.34, p.557; 2.8.33, p.326 and p.338; 13.6.34, p.114; 25.7.34, pp.286f; 6.9.33, p.487; 13.9.33, p.523; 20.9.33, p.555; 29.11.33, p.42.
14. *NBQ* Vol.1/2, pp.44–46; 1/3, pp.101–3.
15. *NB* 9.5.34, p.739.
16. See Bottome 1946, pp.287–90; Finlay 1972, pp.168–70 and p.180; Mairet 1981, p.xv, pp.83–86, pp.91–94, pp.100–144, pp.156f, pp.174–90; Rigby 1984, pp.91–99.
17. Mairet 1928, p.58.
18. Mairet 1956, p.54.
19. *Purpose* April/June 1930, p.49; April/June 1931, p.49; July/September 1932, p.94; April/June 1937, p.67.
20. *Purpose* October/December 1939, pp.209f.
21. *Purpose* April/June 1935, p.70; July/December 1940, pp.114f.

22. *Purpose* July/September 1932, pp.135f; ibid, p.127.
23. *Purpose* October/December 1933, pp.158–63; October/December 1935, pp.139f; October/December 1933, p.148.
24. *Purpose* July/December 1940, p.98.
25. Finlay 1972, p.173.
26. Reckitt 1941, p.190.
27. Mairet 1981, p.xvi.
28. Porter 1927, p.27.
29. *Ibid.* p.71.
30. On Delahaye see Davies 1961, p.150.
31. Merricks 1996, p.140. See also Mairet 1931.
32. On the Chandos Group there is an unpublished typescript by Reckitt (1966) celebrating its fortieth anniversary. See also Kojecky 1971, p.81, and Peart-Binns 1988, pp.102–07.
33. On Orage, see the personal memoirs by Mairet 1936; Muir 1987; Nott 1969 and 1978; Reckitt 1941; Selver 1959, and Welch 1982. See also Carswell 1978; Milburn 1996, and Montgomery 1978.
34. Montgomery 1978, p.3.
35. On Orage's relationship with Gurdjieff, see Mairet 1936, pp.78–107; Nott 1969 and 1978; Welch 1982.
36. Mairet 1936, p.90.
37. *Ibid.* p.106.
38. Reckitt 1941, p.195.
39. Massingham 1942, p.31.
40. Selver 1959, pp.82f. See also Carswell 1978, p.219.
41. Peart-Binns 1988, pp.111f. See also Mairet 1958b.
42. Webber 1986, p.120.
43. See Sisson 1993, pp.122f.
44. Mayhew 1977, p.145; Peart-Binns 1988, p.115.
45. *NEW* 26.5.32, p.128; 11.8.32, p.405 and pp.393f; 10.11.32, pp.79–81.
46. See the sympathetic but incisive comment of George Orwell 1970a, p.145, who contributed regularly to the *NEW* during the late 1930s.
47. *NEW* 4.1.34, p.269.
48. *NEW* 3.6.37, pp.148f, and 28.4.38, pp.51f; 12.5.38, p.86; 16.2.39, p.281.

49. *NEW* 25.4.40, p.3; 29.8.40, p.215; 1.1.42, pp.93f; 12.3.42, p.183.
50. *NEW* 30.3.44, p.202.
51. *NEW* 4.7.46, p.115.
52. *NEW* 3.7.47, p.101.
53. *NEW* 25.7.46, pp.144f; 29.11.45, p.66.
54. *NEW* 21.4.32, p.21.
55. *NEW* 19.5.49, p.67.
56. *NEW* 23.2.39, p.308; 2.3.39, pp.323f.
57. *NEW* 1.5.41, p.22; 24.7.41, pp.143f; 4.9.41, p.196.
58. *NEW* 31.8.44, pp.152f; 14.3.46, p.211; 24.4.47, p.10.
59. *NEW* 10.7.47, p.111.
60. *NEW* 2.6.49, p.89; 9.6.49, pp.107f; 28.7.49, pp.190f.
61. *NEW* 16.9.37, p.363 and p.387; 28.4.38, p.56; 27.10.38, pp.38f; 15.12.38, pp.151f; 22.12.38, p.170; 9.3.39, p.331; 27.7.39, p.231; 1.8.40, pp.179f.
62. *NEW* 26.8.43, p.138; 18.11.43, p.41; 8.6.44, p.69.
63. On the Groundnuts Scheme see Wood 1950.
64. *NEW* 11.12.47, p.81; 3.7.47, p.102; 20.11.47, p.52; 4.11.48, pp.39f; 17.2.49, p.221.
65. *NEW* 25.3.37, p.468; 13.4.39, p.411; 31.8.39, p.252; 3.7.41, p.108; 18.9.41, pp.215f; 9.10.41, pp.236f.
66. *NEW* 18.11.48, pp.65f; 9.12.48, p.107; 16.12.48, pp.117f; 9.12.48, p.108.
67. *NEW* 26.11.42, p.50; 1.4.43, pp.210f; 8.4.43, p.219; 18.7.46, p.139; 22.4.48, p.11.
68. *NEW* 26.6.47, p.100.
69. *NEW* 30.10.47, p.20; 27.6.40, p.124.
70. *NEW* 11.11.37, p.88.
71. *NEW* 9.3.39, pp.330f; 16.3.39, pp.345f; 16.3.39, pp.355f; 23.3.39, p.387.
72. *NEW* 25.2.43, p.162; 11.3.43, pp.183f; 4.11.43, p.23; 18.11.43, p.38.
73. *NEW* 9.12.43, p.66.
74. *NEW* 13.6.40, p.94; 16.10.41, p.250; 18.11.43, pp.41f.

75. *NEW* 12.7.45, p.115; 17.1.46,
    pp.133f; 13.6.46, p.90; 14.3.46,
    pp.212f; 26.2.48, pp.192f; 20.6.46,
    p.96.
76. *NEW* 19.4.45, p.11.
77. *NEW* 6.9.34, p.405. The book had
    in fact been published three years
    earlier.
78. *NEW* 14.5.36, pp.88f; 22.9.38,
    pp.360f; 28.11.35, p.126; 16.4.36,
    p.17; 10.3.38, p.426; 9.3.39.
79. *NEW* 8.2.40, p.241; see Barlow, *NEW*
    12.6.41, p.81; 21.12.44, p.88.
80. *NEW* 30.11.44, pp.55f; 14.12.44,
    p.80; 25.1.45, p.112; 14.3.46,
    p.212.
81. *NEW* 27.6.46, p.111; 26.2.48, p.196;
    19.2.48, p.180.
82. *NEW* 9.4.42, p.219; 15.3.45,
    pp.169–71; 12.9.46, p.180.
83. *NEW* 17.10.46, p.12.
84. *NEW* 31.5.45, p.64.
85. *NEW* 26.5.32, p.128; 4.7.40, p.130;
    24.7.41, p.143; 19.12.40, p.101;
    15.7.43, pp.115f; 3.6.43, p.58;
    10.6.43, p.69.
86. *NEW* 1.10.42, p.200; 29.4.43, p.16;
    30.3.44, p.202; 18.1.45, pp.101f.
87. *NEW* 7.3.46, pp.200f; 3.7.47, p.103;
    16.10.47, pp.3f.
88. *NEW* 16.1.47, p.127.
89. *NEW* 30.1.47, p.152. It is worth not-
    ing that Faber published a book on
    the issue: Tilley 1947.
90. *NEW* 2.6.49, p.89; 7.7.49, pp.148f.
91. *NEW* 26.8.43, p.138.
92. Orwell 1970b, p.211; Webber 1986,
    pp.64f and pp.119f; Hawkins 1989,
    p.177.
93. *NEW* 13.10.38, p.4.
94. *NEW* 15.4.37, p.8. The writer may
    have been Vera C. Collum, a Fellow
    of the Royal Anthropological Insti-
    tute of Great Britain and Ireland, who
    wrote *Manifold Unity* (1940) and
    translated *Race and History* by
    Eugène Pittard (1926).
95. *NEW* 29.4.37, p.50; 15.12.38,
    pp.151f; 22.12.38, p.170; 8.7.43,
    p.101; 17.2.44, p.149.
96. *NEW* 21.10.37, p.39; 16.2.39, p.291.

97. *NEW* 9.1.41, p.131; 16.4.42, p.227.
98. *NEW* 31.3.35, p.330; 16.1.36, p.266;
    19.3.36, p.446; 5.3.36, p.407;
    17.2.38, pp.366f; 29.9.38, p.367.
99. *Ibid.*
100. *NEW* 20.1.49, p.170.
101. *NEW* 25.12.47, p.99.
102. *NEW* 8.9.49, p.207.

Chapter 11

1. White 1967, p.1205; pp.1205, 1206;
   p.1206.
2. *Ibid.*
3. Berry 1981, pp.267–81.
4. Mairet (n.d.). *Bailiff* exists as an
   undated typescript, with unnumbered
   pages; internal evidence suggests that
   it was written around 1964. A copy
   of it was passed to the present writer
   by the Church historian John S.
   Peart-Binns, Maurice Reckitt's biographer.
5. Mairet 1981, p.xxi.
6. *Ibid.*
7. *Frontier*'s contributors included
   Murry, Jenks, Coward and Reckitt.
8. Vidler and Whitehouse 1946, p.17;
   p.20.
9. No individual writer was specified as
   contributing to any particular section
   of the book, but this section strongly
   resembled Mairet's chapter in Reckitt
   1945.
10. Vidler and Whitehouse 1946, p.40.
11. *Ibid.* p.41.
12. *Ibid.* pp.42f.
13. *NEW* 18.4.46, pp.4f.
14. Reckitt 1945, p.83.
15. *Ibid.* p.84.
16. Mairet (n.d.), p.22 (unnumbered).
17. *Ibid.*
18. *Ibid.* pp.35f (unnumbered).
19. Sisson 1993, pp.122f.
20. Eliot 1948, p.7.
21. Gordon 1998. For that matter,
    Reckitt, Heron and the Chandos
    Group are also ignored, and the only
    reference to the *NEW* is in connec-
    tion with the *Four Quartets*. See also
    Mairet 1958b.

22. Bradshaw 1996, has said that work needs to be done on investigating Eliot's ideas on environmentalism; this chapter is a small contribution to that task.
23. Eliot 1939, pp.11, 30, 21.
24. *Ibid.* p.33.
25. *Ibid.* p.61; p.62.
26. Eliot 1948, p.52. It is interesting to speculate on the extent to which the emphasis on rootedness found among the organic school might have stemmed from a desire to compensate for the rootlessness of their own lives. Portsmouth was brought up in Wyoming and Gardiner in Berlin, both having parents of different nationalities; Mairet, second generation Swiss immigrant, retained the French spelling of his Christian name until he was nearly fifty; the urban Massingham planted himself in the Buckinghamshire countryside, reinventing himself as a countryman; Jenks emigrated to New Zealand in the 1920s.
27. *Ibid.* p.66.
28. *Ibid.* p.104.
29. Travers 1993, pp.242–56.
30. Sorabji 1947, p.31. On Sorabji, see Rapoport 1992.
31. Gooding 1994, pp.24–30; MacCarthy 1998.
32. Giles Heron and J.S. Peart-Binns have produced a memoir of Tom Heron for publication. There is a useful section on Heron in Mayhew, 1977, pp.44–46.
33. Heron 1926, p.10; p.19.
34. Emmet 1996, pp.103–6.
35. Heron 1977, p.22.
36. Marsh 1982, pp.107–11; Shaw 1935.
37. Symons 1931, p.235 and p.259; p.9.
38. On Reckitt's life, see his autobiography *As It Happened* (1941), Christendom Trust (1978), and Peart-Binns (1988).
39. Wilkinson 1998, p.146.
40. *CT* 18.1.80, p.4.
41. Dearner 1933, p.551.
42. Reckitt 1941, p.199.

43. On the Christendom Group, see Bryant 1997, pp.148–51; Mayhew 1977; Wilkinson 1998, pp.142–47, and Wollenberg 1997, pp.72–76; see *Christendom* March 1931, inside front cover.
44. *Christendom* June 1938, p.89; June 1938, pp.94–103.
45. *Christendom* September 1942, pp.156–59. Massingham attended services at Thame parish church and often read the lessons there, according to his widow Penelope in a letter to the present author dated 28 September, 1988.
46. *Christendom* December 1943, pp.114–17; March 1943, pp.27–30; December 1944, pp.253–54; June 1945, pp.63f.
47. *Christendom* September 1943, pp.83–86; September 1941, pp.141–55; June 1942, pp.123–27; June 1944, pp.177–80; June 1944, p.184.
48. *Christendom* June 1940, pp.118–24; March 1944, pp.141f.
49. Hastings 1987, p.175.
50. *NS* 21.6.47, p.460.
51. Wiener 1992, pp.115–18; Wilkinson 1998, pp.143–47; Mayhew 1977, p.iii.
52. On Malvern see Bryant 1997, pp.192–96; Kent 1992, pp.155–65; Mayhew 1977, pp.170–75; Norman 1976, pp.365–89; Wiener 1992, pp.117f. Rather oddly Reeves 1999, does not discuss Malvern.
53. Wiener 1992, p.117; p.118.
54. Temple 1956, p.83; p.79.
55. York 1941a, p.29.
56. *Ibid.* p.138.
57. *Ibid.* p.146.
58. York 1941b, p.12.
59. Ricketts 1945, inside front cover.
60. Gardiner 1972, p.176.
61. CCC 1946d, inside front cover.
62. CCC 1945a, p.6; pp.20–24.
63. CCC 1946a; 1945b, p.7; 1946c, pp.5f; 1947, p.8; 1946c, pp.11–13.
64. CCC 1946b, pp.23f.
65. CCC 1950, pp.18f; pp.1–4 and p.15.

66. Peck, D. 1947, p.1.
67. *Ibid.* p.4.
68. Termed 'panentheism,' this idea has been developed more recently by the feminist theologian Sallie McFague 1993.
69. Peck, D. 1947, p.14; *Ibid.* p.15.
70. *Ibid.* p.16.
71. CCC 1945b, p.23.
72. CCC 1950, p.16.
73. On W.G. Peck, see Mayhew 1977, pp.76–81 and Norman 1976, p.318 and p.363.
74. Peck, W.G. 1948, p.19.
75. *Ibid.* pp.62f and pp.71f.
76. *Ibid.* p.136.
77. Mayhew 1977, pp.184f; Norman 1976, p.320.
78. Reckitt 1954, p.172.
79. *Ibid.* p.94. On 'Economic Man' see Drucker 1939.
80. Reckitt 1945, p.96.
81. Massingham 1943c, p.158.
82. *Ibid.* pp.171f.
83. Massingham 1942, pp.146f.
84. See Rolt 1977, his contribution to Massingham 1947, and Waller 1990. Matless 1998, pp.149–53, has a valuable section on Rolt.
85. Rolt 1988, p.16; p.18; pp.18f.
86. *Ibid.* p.20.

Chapter 12

1. Clunies–Ross 1990, p.144.
2. Barlow and Bunyard 1981.
3. 'Ralph Coward — A Man for All Seasons,' was broadcast in the TV South series *A Taste of the South.*
4. Ling, 2000.
5. See Balfour 1975, and *Nature,* 9.3.57, p.514.
6. *ME* July 1958, p.203; October 1958, p. 293; October 1959, p. 639; January 1957, pp.745–49.
7. On Carson's attitude, see Jackson 1974, pp.33f.
8. Craven 1993, has done valuable exploratory work in this area.
9. See Korten 1995, and Rowbotham 1998.
10. Barber 1996. Barber admits on p.299 that his use of the term 'jihad' is somewhat misleading.
11. *ME* January 1957, p. 741.

Bibliography

Addison, Lord (1939) *A Policy for British Agriculture,* Gollancz.
Astor, Viscount and Murray, Keith A.H. (1932) *Land and Life: The Economic National Policy for Agriculture,* Gollancz.
—, and Rowntree, B. Seebohm (1939) *British Agriculture: The Principles of Future Policy,* Penguin, Harmondsworth.
—, and Rowntree, B. Seebohm (1946) *Mixed Farming and Muddled Thinking,* Macdonald.
Baker, C. Alma (1940) *The Labouring Earth,* Heath Cranton.
Baker, David (1996) *Ideology of Obsession: A.K. Chesterton and British Fascism,* I.B. Tauris.
Baker, Richard St Barbe (1944) *I Planted Trees,* Lutterworth.
—, (1948) *Green Glory,* Lutterworth.
—, (1979) *My Life, My Trees,* Findhorn Press.
Balfour, E.B. (1944) *The Living Soil* (3rd edition), Faber and Faber.
—, (1948) *The Living Soil* (8th edition), Faber and Faber.
—, (1975) *The Living Soil and the Haughley Experiment* (new and revised edition), Faber and Faber.
Barber, Benjamin (1996) *Jihad vs. McWorld: How Globalism and Tribalism Are Reshaping the World,* Ballantine Books, New York.
Barlow, Kenneth E. (1942) *The Discipline of Peace,* Faber and Faber.
—, (1978) *The Law and the Loaf,* Precision Press, Marlow.
—, (1988) *Recognising Health,* Kenneth Barlow.
—, (n.d.) Unpublished manuscript on the Coventry Family Health Club.
—, and Bunyard, Peter (1981) *Soil, Food and Health in a Changing World,* A.B. Academic Publishers, Berkhamsted.
Barlow, Ruth (n.d.) *Before I Forget* (unpublished manuscript).
Barnett, Anthony and Scruton, Roger (1998) *Town and Country,* Cape.
Barrett, Thomas J. (1949) *Harnessing the Earthworm,* Faber and Faber.
Beckett, Francis (1999) *The Rebel Who Lost His Cause: The Tragedy of John Beckett, MP,* London House.
Bedford, Hastings, Duke of (1949) *The Years of Transition,* Andrew Dakers.
Bedford, John, Duke of (1959) *A Silver-Plated Spoon,* Cassell.
Bell, Adrian (1941) *The Cherry Tree,* Penguin, Harmondsworth.
—, (1961) *My Own Master,* Faber and Faber.
—, (1965) *Apple Acre,* Country Book Club.
Belloc, Hilaire (1927) *The Servile State* (3rd edition), Constable.
Berry, Wendell (1981) *The Gift of Good Land,* North Point Press, San Francisco.
Black, A. & C. (1981) *Black's Agricultural Dictionary,* ed. D.B. Dalal-Clayton, A. &. C. Black.
Blackburn, John S. (1949) *Organic Husbandry: A Symposium,* John S. Blackburn, Ben Rhydding.

Blaxter, Sir Kenneth and Robertson, Noel (1995) *From Dearth to Plenty*, Cambridge University Press, UK.
Blunden, Edmund (1943) *The Return to Husbandry*, Dent.
Body, Richard (1991) *Our Food, Our Land*, Rider.
Bottome, Phyllis (1946) *Alfred Adler: Apostle of Freedom*, Faber and Faber.
Boyes, Georgina (1993) *The Imagined Village: Culture, Ideology and the English Folk Revival*, Manchester University Press, UK.
Bradshaw, David (1996) 'T.S. Eliot and the Major: Sources of Literary Anti-Semitism in the 1930s,' *Times Literary Supplement*, 5.7.1996, pp.14–16.
Bramwell, Anna (1989) *Ecology in the 20th Century*, Yale University Press.
Brock, William H. (1997) *Justus von Liebig: The Chemical Gatekeeper*, Cambridge University Press, UK.
Brocklebank, Kathleen (1948) 'Steiner's Philosophy and Agriculture,' *Mother Earth*, Autumn 1948, pp.30f.
Bromfield, Louis (1924) *The Green Bay Tree*, Cassell
—, (1946) *Pleasant Valley*, Cassell.
—, (1949) *Malabar Farm*, Cassell.
—, (1951) *Out of the Earth*, Cassell.
—, (1956) *From My Experience*, Cassell.
Brown, Jonathan (1987) *Agriculture in England: A Survey of Farming, 1870–1947*, Manchester University Press, UK.
Brown, Morrison (1956) *Louis Bromfield: The Man and His Books*, Cassell.
Bruce, Maye E. (1943) *From Vegetable Waste to Fertile Soil*, Faber and Faber.
Bryant, Arthur (1940) *Unfinished Victory*, Macmillan.
Bryant, Chris (1997) *Possible Dreams*, Hodder & Stoughton.
Canovan, Margaret (1977) *G.K. Chesterton: Radical Populist*, Harcourt Brace Jovanovich.
Carrel, Alexis (1935) *Man the Unknown*, Harper & Bros.
—, (1952) *Reflections on Life*, Hamish Hamilton.
Carson, Rachel (1963) *Silent Spring*, Hamish Hamilton.
Carswell, John (1978) *Lives and Letters*, Faber and Faber.
Charnley, John (1990) *Blackshirts and Roses*, Brockingday.
Chase, J.L.H. (1948) *Cloche Gardening*, Faber and Faber.
Chase, Malcolm (1992) 'Rolf Gardiner: an inter-war cross-cultural case study,' in Barry J. Hake and Stuart Marriott, *Adult Education Between Cultures*, University of Leeds, UK.
Christendom Trust (1978) *M.B.R.*
Chronicle, The [Crewe] (1939) 'Land Fertility and the People's Food: Medical Testament on Nutrition,' 25.3.1939.
Clunies-Ross, Tracey (1990) *Agricultural Change and the Politics of Organic Farming* (Ph.D. thesis), University of Bath, UK.
Coe, Jonathan (1995) *What a Carve Up!*, Penguin.
Collis, John Stewart (1950) *The Triumph of the Tree*, Cape.
—, (1975a) *The Vision of Glory*, Penguin, Harmondsworth.
—, (1975b) *The Worm Forgives the Plough*, Penguin, Harmondsworth.
—, (1991) *Bound Upon a Course*, Alastair Press, Bury St Edmunds.
Collum, Vera C.C. (1940) *Manifold Unity*, John Murray.
Comerford, John (1947) *Health the Unknown*, Hamish Hamilton.
Conford, Philip (1988) *The Organic Tradition*, Green Books, Hartland.
—, (1992) *A Future for the Land*, Green Books, Hartland.
—, (1998a) 'A Forum for Organic Husbandry: The *New English Weekly* and Agricultural Policy, 1939–1949,' *Agricultural History Review* Vol.46, pp.197–210.

—, (1998b) 'Breaking New Ground,' *Living Earth* No.199, pp.23–25.

—, (1999) 'Good Husbandry,' *Henry Williamson Society Journal* No.35, pp.27–34.

—, (2000) *The Natural Order: Organic Husbandry, Society and Religion in Britain, 1924–1953,* (Ph.D. thesis), University of Reading, UK.

Cooper, Andrew Fenton (1989) *British Agricultural Policy, 1912–1936: A Study in Conservative Politics,* Manchester University Press, UK.

Corrin, Jay P. (1981) *G.K. Chesterton and Hilaire Belloc: The Battle Against Modernity,* Ohio University Press.

Council for the Church and Countryside (1945a) *Occasional Paper: Rogationtide 1945,* CCC.

—, (1945b) *Occasional Paper: Harvest 1945,* CCC.

—, (1946a) *Encounter: Agri-Culture or Agri-Industry,* CCC.

—, (1946b) *Occasional Paper: Rogationtide 1946,* CCC.

—, (1946c) *Occasional Paper: Harvest and Other Matters,* CCC.

—, (1946d) *Church and Countryside Associations,* CCC.

—, (1947) *Occasional Paper: Parish and Parson,* CCC.

—, (1950) *Occasional Paper: Man and Nature,* CCC.

Craven, Josef (1993) *'Health, Wholeness, Holiness' — Radical Right and Fascist Attitudes to the British Countryside, 1918–1939* (M.Phil thesis), University of Birmingham, UK.

Cripps, Anthony (1948) *The Agriculture Act 1947,* Butterworth.

Crosby, Caresse (1979) *The Passionate Years,* Ecco Press, New York.

Cumming, Elizabeth and Kaplan, Wendy (1991) *The Arts and Crafts Movement,* Thames and Hudson.

Dale, H.E. (1956) *Daniel Hall: Pioneer in Scientific Agriculture,* John Murray.

Danziger, Renée (1988) *Political Powerlessness: Agricultural Workers in Post-War England,* Manchester University Press, UK.

Davies, D.R. (1961) *In Search of Myself,* Bles.

Dearmer, Percy (1933) *Christianity and the Crisis,* Gollancz.

Delahaye, J.V. (1929) *Politics: A Discussion of Realities,* C.W. Daniel.

De Maré, Eric (1983) *A Matter of Life or Debt,* Veritas, Bullsbrook, WA.

Dewey, P.E. (1989) *British Agriculture in the First World War,* Routledge.

Donaldson, Frances (1992) *A Twentieth-Century Life,* Weidenfeld & Nicolson.

Donaldson, J.G.S. and Donaldson, Frances (1972) *Farming in Britain Today,* Penguin, Harmondsworth.

Douglas, C.H. (1934) *The Douglas Manual,* Stanley Nott.

—, (1979) *The Monopoly of Credit,* Bloomfield Books, Sudbury.

Drucker, Peter F. (1939) *The End of Economic Man,* Heinemann.

Duncan, Ronald (1944) *Journal of a Husbandman,* Faber and Faber.

—, (1964) *All Men Are Islands,* Hart-Davis.

—, (1968) *How to Make Enemies,* Hart-Davis.

Durkin, Joseph T. (1965) *Hope for Our Time: Alexis Carrel on Man and Society,* Harper & Row, New York.

Easey, Ben (1955) *Practical Organic Gardening,* Faber and Faber.

Easterbrook, Laurence F. (1950) *British Agriculture,* British Council/Longmans Green.

—, (1964) 'Why I Believe in the Organic Approach to Farming,' *Mother Earth,* April 1964, pp.95–99.

—, (1970) *How To Be Happy Though Civilised,* Spiritualist Association of Great Britain.

—, (n.d.) *Why I Believe in that Mysterious Thing — Reincarnation,* T.W. Pegg.

Economic Reform Club and Institute (1939) *Health, Agriculture and the Standard of Living,* ERCI.

—, (1940) *Three Addresses on Food Production*, ERCI.
—, (1943) *The World We Want*, ERCI.
Edgell, Derek (1992) *The Order of Woodcraft Chivalry, 1916–1949*, Edwin Mellen Press, Lampeter.
Edgerton, David (1991) *England and the Aeroplane*, Macmillan.
Eliot, T.S. (1939) *The Idea of a Christian Society*, Faber and Faber.
—, (1948) *Notes Towards the Definition of Culture*, Faber and Faber.
Elliot, Walter (1943) *Long Distance*, Constable.
Emmet, Dorothy (1996) *Philosophers and Friends*, Macmillan.
Enfield, R.R. (1924) *The Agricultural Crisis, 1920–1923*, Longmans Green.
Ernle, Lord (1961) *English Farming, Past and Present* (6th edition), Heinemann.
Farming To-Day (1942) *'Farming To-Day' Broadcasts*, Littlebury, Worcester.
Faulkner, Edward (1945) *Ploughman's Folly*, Michael Joseph.
Faulkner, Edward (1948) *Ploughing in Prejudices*, Michael Joseph.
—, (1953) *Soil Restoration*, Michael Joseph.
Finlay, John L. (1970) 'John Hargrave, the Green Shirts, and Social Credit,' *Journal of Contemporary History* Vol.5, pp.53–71.
—, (1972) *Social Credit: The English Origins*, McGill-Queen's University Press.
Fordham, Montague (1908) *Mother Earth*, Chiswick Press.
—, (1925) *The Rebuilding of Rural England*, Labour Publishing Co.
—, (1938) *Christianity and the Countryside*, ICF.
Fream, W. (1949) *Fream's Elements of Agriculture* (13th edition), John Murray.
Gangulee, N. (1943) *The Battle of the Land*, Lindsay Drummond.
Gardiner, Rolf (1943) *England Herself*, Faber and Faber.
—, (1972) *Water Springing From the Ground*, Springhead, Fontmell Magna.
Gartner, Mark (1990) *Carl Alexander Mier; Gertrude Mier*, (privately printed), Clent.
Glass, S.T. (1966) *The Responsible Society: The Ideas of Guild Socialism*, Longmans.
Godwin, George (1939) *The Land Our Larder*, Acorn Press.
Gold, Karen (1993) 'Muck and Brass Research,' *Times Higher Education Supplement*, 31.12.1993.
Gooding, Mel (1994) *Patrick Heron*, Phaidon.
Gordon, Lyndall (1998) *T.S. Eliot: An Imperfect Life*, Vintage.
Gould, Peter C. (1988) *Early Green Politics*, Harvester, Brighton.
Grant, Doris (1962) *Your Daily Bread*, Faber and Faber.
Greenwell, Sir Bernard (1939) 'Soil Fertility — The Farm's Capital,' *Journal of the Farmers' Club*, February 1939.
Griffiths, Richard (1983) *Fellow Travellers of the Right*, Oxford University Press, UK.
—, (1998) *Patriotism Perverted*, Constable.
Griffiths, Vivian (1999) *David Clement: A Life Near the History of the Organic Movement* (typewritten manuscript).
Grigg, David (1989) *English Agriculture: An Historical Perspective*, Basil Blackwell.
Griggs, Barbara (1986) *The Food Factor: Why We Are What We Eat*, Penguin/Viking, Harmondsworth.
Group of Churchmen, A (1922) *The Return of Christendom*, Allen & Unwin.
Guénon, René (1953) *The Reign of Quantity and the Signs of the Times*, Luzac & Co.
Hall, A. Daniel (1941) *Reconstruction and the Land*, Macmillan.
—, (1947) *Fertilizers and Manures*, John Murray.
Hamilton, Alastair (1971) *The Appeal of Fascism*, Anthony Blond.
Harris, John and Trow, M.J. (2000) *Hess: The British Conspiracy*, André Deutsch.
Harrison, Ruth (1964) *Animal Machines*, Vincent Stuart.
Harvey, Graham (1997) *The Killing of the Countryside*, Cape.

Hastings, Adrian (1987) *A History of English Christianity, 1920–1985,* Collins.

Hawkins, Desmond (1989) *When I Was: A Memoir of the Years Between the Wars,* Macmillan.

Hemleben, Johannes (1975) *Rudolf Steiner: A Documentary Biography,* Henry Goulden, East Grinstead.

Heron, T.M. (1926) *Christian Vocation in Industry and Marketing,* Society of SS. Peter and Paul.

Heron, Tom (1977) *Call It A Day,* Out of the Ark Press, Zennor.

Hills, Lawrence D. (1989) *Fighting Like the Flowers,* Green Books, Hartland.

Hilton, James (1973) *Lost Horizon,* Macmillan.

Hobson, S.G. (1938) *Pilgrim to the Left,* Edward Arnold.

Holderness, B.A. (1985) *British Agriculture Since 1945,* Manchester University Press, UK.

Holloway, Edward (1986) *Money Matters: A Modern Pilgrim's Economic Progress,* Sherwood Press.

Holter, E.S. (1934) *The A.B.C. of Social Credit,* Stanley Nott.

Hopkins, Donald P. (1945) *Chemicals, Humus, and the Soil,* Faber and Faber.

Howard, Albert (1940) *An Agricultural Testament,* Oxford University Press, UK.

—, (1945a) *Farming and Gardening for Health or Disease,* Faber and Faber.

—, (1945b) *Darwin on Humus and the Earthworm,* Faber and Faber.

—, and Wad, Yeshwant D. (1931) *The Waste Products of Agriculture: Their Utilization as Humus,* Oxford University Press, UK.

Howard, Gabrielle (1931) Obituary in *Newnham College Roll Letter,* January 1931, pp.52–54.

Howard, Louise E. (1954) *Sir Albert Howard in India,* Rodale Press, Emmaus, Pa.

Hugo, Victor (1909) *Les Misérables,* Dent.

Hutchinson, Frances and Burkitt, Brian (1997) *The Political Economy of Social Credit and Guild Socialism,* Routledge.

Hutton, Ronald (1999) *The Triumph of the Moon: A History of Modern Pagan Witchcraft,* Oxford University Press, UK.

Hyams, Edward (1976) *Soil and Civilization,* John Murray.

Hyde, Douglas (1952) *I Believed,* Reprint Society/Heinemann.

Jacks, G.V. and Whyte, R.O. (1939) *The Rape of the Earth,* Faber and Faber.

Jackson, Carlton (1974) *J.I. Rodale: Apostle of Nonconformity,* Pyramid Books, New York.

Jeans, D.N. (1990) 'Planning and the Myth of the English Countryside, in the Interwar Period,' *Rural History* Vol.1, pp.249–64.

Jenks, Jorian (1938) *The Land and the People: British Union Agricultural Policy,* British Union.

—, (1950) *From the Ground Up,* Hollis & Carter.

—, (1959) *The Stuff Man's Made Of,* Faber and Faber.

—, and Peddie, J. Taylor (1935) *Farming and Money,* Williams and Norgate.

Johnson, Paul (1977) *Enemies of Society,* Weidenfeld & Nicolson.

Keeble, Frederick (1932) *Fertilizers and Food Production on Arable and Grass Land,* Oxford University Press, UK.

Kenney, Rowland (1939) *Westering: An Autobiography,* Dent.

Kent, John (1992) *William Temple: Church, State and Society in Britain, 1880–1950,* Cambridge University Press, UK.

King, F.C. (1944) *Gardening with Compost,* Faber and Faber.

King, F.H. (1949) *Farmers of Forty Centuries,* Cape.

Kitson, Arthur (1933) *The Bankers' Conspiracy!,* Elliot Stock.

Kojecky, Roger (1971) *T.S. Eliot's Social Criticism*, Faber and Faber.

Kolisko, E. and Kolisko, L. (1978) *Agriculture of Tomorrow* (2nd edition), Kolisko Archive, Bournemouth.

Korten, David C. (1995) *When Corporations Rule the World*, Earthscan.

Landau, Rom (1935) *God is My Adventure*, Nicholson and Watson.

—, (1939) *Love for a Country*, Nicholson and Watson.

Lea, F.A. (1959) *The Life of John Middleton Murry*, Methuen.

Liebig, Justus von (1840) *Organic Chemistry in its Applications to Agriculture*

Loftus, Pierse (1926) *The Creed of a Tory*, Philip Allan.

Long, H.C. (1948) *Profit From Fertilizers* (3rd edition), Crosby Lockwood.

Loti, Pierre (1916) *Madame Chrysanthème*, T. Werner Laurie.

—, (1925) *The Marriage of Loti (Rarahu)*, T. Werner Laurie.

Ludovici, Anthony M. (1938) (as 'Cobbett') *Jews, and the Jews in England*, Boswell Publishing Co.

—, (1945) *The Four Pillars of Health*, Heath Cranton.

—, (1961) *Religion for Infidels*, Holborn Publishing Co.

Lymington, Viscount (see Portsmouth, Earl of)

McCarrison, Robert (1961) *Nutrition and Health*, Faber and Faber.

MacCarthy, Fiona (1998) 'The Warrior Artist,' *The Guardian* 20.6.1998.

MacDermot, Violet (1997) *Introduction to The New Europe Group and New Britain Movement: Collected Publications, 1932–1957*, New Atlantis Foundation, Ditchling/Bradford. (See also New Atlantis Foundation)

McDonagh, J.E.R. (1940) *The Universe Through Medicine*, Heinemann.

McFague, Sallie (1993) *The Body of God*, SCM.

Macmurray, John (1996) *The Personal World*, ed. P. Conford, Floris, Edinburgh.

McWilliams, Carey (1945) *Ill Fares the Land*, Faber and Faber.

Mairet, Philip (1928) (as Philippe Mairet) *ABC of Adler's Psychology*, Kegan Paul.

—, (1931) (as Philipped Mairet) *Aristocracy and the Meaning of Class Rule*, C.W. Daniel.

—, (1936) *A.R. Orage: A Memoir*, Dent.

—, (1956) *Christian Essays in Psychiatry*, SCM.

—, (1957) *Pioneer of Sociology: The Life and Letters of Patrick Geddes*, Lund Humphries.

—, (1958a) *John Middleton Murry*, British Council/ Longmans.

—, (1958b) 'Memories of T.S.E.,' in *T.S. Eliot: A Symposium for His Seventieth Birthday*, ed. Neville Braybrooke, Hart-Davis.

—, (1981) *Autobiographical and Other Papers*, Carcanet, Manchester.

—, (n.d.) *Bailiff for God's Estate on Earth*, Council for the Church and Countryside.

Marks, H.F. (1989) *A Hundred Years of British Food and Farming: A Statistical Survey*, Taylor & Francis.

Marsh, Jan (1982) *Back to the Land*, Quartet.

Martin, John (2000) *The Development of Modern Agriculture: British Farming since 1931*, Macmillan.

Massingham, H.J. (1926) *Downland Man*, Cape.

—, (1941) *England and the Farmer*, Batsford.

—, (1942) *Remembrance*, Batsford.

—, (1943a) *The English Countryman* (2nd edition), Batsford.

—, (1943b) *Men of Earth*, Chapman & Hall.

—, (1943c) *The Tree of Life*, Chapman & Hall.

—, (1943–44) *Chiltern Country* (2nd edition), Batsford.

—, (1944) *This Plot of Earth*, Collins.

—, (1945a) *The Natural Order,* Dent.

—, (1945b) *The Wisdom of the Fields,* Collins.

—, (1947) *The Small Farmer,* Collins.

Matless, David (1998) *Landscape and Englishness,* Reaktion Books.

Mayhew, Peter (1977) *The Christendom Group: A History and an Assessment* (M.Litt. thesis), University of Oxford, UK.

Meadows, Donella H. (1972) *The Limits to Growth,* Earth Island.

Merricks, Linda (1996) *The World Made New: Frederick Soddy, Science, Politics and Environment,* Oxford University Press, UK.

Milburn, Diane (1996) *The Deutschlandbild of A.R. Orage and the New Age Circle,* Peter Lang, Frankfurt/M.

Miller, Donald L. (1989) *Lewis Mumford: A Life,* Weidenfeld & Nicolson, New York.

Miller, Simon (1995) 'Urban Dreams and Rural Reality: Land and Landscape in English Culture, 1920–45,' *Rural History* Vol.6, pp.89–102.

Montgomery, Lesley (1978) 'The Eye of the Storm' (unpublished manuscript of BBC Radio *Drama Now* broadcast, 7.2.1978, on A.R. Orage), BBC.

Moore-Colyer, R.J. (1999) 'Sir George Stapledon (1882–1960) and the Landscape of Britain,' *Environment and History* Vol.5, pp.221–236.

Muir, Edwin (1987) *An Autobiography,* Hogarth Press.

Mumford, Lewis (1956) *The Human Prospect,* Secker & Warburg.

—, (1976) *Findings and Keepings,* Secker & Warburg.

Munkes, Karl (1937) *Arthur Penty und der Nationalsozialismus,* Buch-und-Kunstdruckerei, Bottrop.

Murray, Keith (1955) *History of the Second World War: Agriculture,* Longman/HMSO.

Murry, John Middleton (1942) *Christocracy,* Andrew Dakers.

—, (1952) *Community Farm,* Peter Nevill.

New Atlantis Foundation (1987) *The New Europe Group and New Britain Movement: Collected Publications, 1932–1957,* New Atlantis Foundation, Ditchling/Bradford. (See also MacDermot, Violet.)

Newby, Howard (1987) *Country Life: A Social History of Rural England,* Weidenfeld & Nicolson.

Nicol, Hugh (1967) *The Limits of Man,* Constable.

Norman, E.R. (1976) *Church and Society in England, 1770–1970,* Clarendon Press, Oxford.

Northbourne, Lord (1940) *Look to the Land,* Dent.

—, (1963) *Religion in the Modern World,* Dent.

—, (1970) *Looking Back on Progress,* Perennial Books, Bedfont.

Nott, C.S. (1969) *Journey Through This World,* RKP.

—, (1978) *Teachings of Gurdjieff,* RKP.

Ogg, William (1947) 'Fertiliser Fears "Unfounded",' *Farmers' Weekly* 5.9.1947, p.28.

Orr, John Boyd (1936) *Food, Health and Income,* Macmillan.

—, (1948) *Soil Fertility: The Wasting Basis of Human Society,* Pilot Press.

—, (as Lord Boyd Orr) (1966) *As I Recall,* Macgibbon and Kee.

Orwell, George (1939) *Coming Up for Air,* Gollancz.

—, (1970a) *The Collected Essays, Journalism and Letters of George Orwell,* Vol.1: *An Age Like This,* Penguin, Harmondsworth.

—, (1970b) *The Collected Essays, Journalism and Letters of George Orwell,* Vol.2: *My Country Right or Left,* Penguin, Harmondsworth.

Orwin, C.S. (1930a) *The Future of Farming,* Clarendon Press, Oxford.

—, (1930b) *A Specialist in Arable Farming,* Clarendon Press, Oxford.

—, (1930c) *Another Departure in Plough Farming,* Clarendon Press, Oxford.

—, (1934) *Pioneers in Power Farming,* Agricultural Economics Research Institute, Oxford.

—, (1942) *Speed the Plough,* Penguin, Harmondsworth.

—, (1949) *A History of English Farming,* Nelson.

Orwin, Christabel S. and Whetham, Edith H. (1964) *A History of British Agriculture, 1846–1914,* Longmans, London.

Osborn, Fairfield (1948) *Our Plundered Planet,* Faber and Faber.

—, (1954) *The Limits of the Earth,* Faber and Faber.

Oyler, Philip (1950) *The Generous Earth,* Hodder and Stoughton.

—, (1951) *Feeding Ourselves,* Hodder and Stoughton.

Paxton, Robert O. (1997) *French Peasant Fascism,* Oxford University Press, UK.

Payne, Virginia (1971) *A History of the Soil Association* (M.Sc. thesis), Victoria University of Manchester.

Pearse, Innes H. and Williamson, G. Scott (1931) *The Case for Action,* Faber and Faber.

—, and Crocker, Lucy H. (1943) *The Peckham Experiment,* Allen & Unwin.

Peart-Binns, John S. (1988) *Maurice B. Reckitt: A Life,* Marshall Pickering, Basingstoke.

Peck, David G. (1947) *Earth and Heaven: A Theology of the Countryside* (2nd edition), CCC.

Peck, William G. (1948) *An Outline of Christian Sociology,* James Clarke.

Penning-Rowsell, Edmund C. (1997) 'Who "Betrayed" Whom? Power and Politics in the 1920/21 Agricultural Crisis,' *Agricultural History Review,* Vol.45, pp.176–94.

Penty, A.J. (1906) *The Restoration of the Gild System,* Swan Sonnenschein.

—, (1932) *Means and Ends,* Faber and Faber.

—, (1937) *Tradition and Modernism in Politics,* Sheed & Ward.

Peters, Suzanne (1982) *The Land in Trust: A Social History of the Organic Farming Movement* (Ph.D. thesis, McGill University), National Library of Canada, Ottawa.

Pfeiffer, Ehrenfried (1947a) *The Earth's Face,* Faber and Faber.

—, (1947b) *Soil Fertility, Renewal and Preservation,* Faber and Faber.

Picton, Lionel J. (1946) *Thoughts on Feeding,* Faber and Faber.

Pioneer Health Centre (1938) *Biologists in Search of Material,* Faber and Faber.

Pittard, E. (1926) *Race and History,* Kegan Paul.

Plowman, Max (1944) *Bridge into the Future,* Andrew Dakers.

Poore, G.V. (1903) *Essays on Rural Hygiene* (3rd edition), Longmans, Green.

Porteous, Crichton (1950) 'Justus von Liebig (1803–1873),' *Fertiliser Journal* 18.10.1950, pp.651–53.

Porter, Alan (1927) *Coal: A Challenge to the National Conscience,* Hogarth Press.

Portsmouth, Earl of (1932) (as Viscount Lymington) *Horn, Hoof and Corn: The Future of British Agriculture,* Faber and Faber.

—, (1938) (as Viscount Lymington) *Famine in England,* Right Book Club.

—, (1943) *Alternative to Death,* Faber and Faber.

—, (1965) *A Knot of Roots,* Bles.

Price, Weston A. (1945) *Nutrition and Physical Degeneration* (revised edition), Weston A. Price, Redlands, Ca.

Purdom, C.B. (1951) *Life Over Again,* Dent.

Raffael, Michael (1996) 'Biodynamic Steak in a Healthy Future,' *Weekend Telegraph,* 30.3.1996.

Rapoport, Paul (1992) *Sorabji: A Critical Celebration,* Scolar Press, Aldershot.

Rayner, M.C. and Neilson-Jones, W. (1944) *Problems in Tree Nutrition,* Faber and Faber.

Reckitt, Maurice B. (1941) *As It Happened,* Dent.

—, (1945) *Prospect for Christendom*, Faber and Faber.

—, (1954) *The World and the Faith: Essays of a Christian Sociologist*, Faith Press.

—, (1966) *The Story of the Chandos Group, 1926–1966* (unpublished manuscript).

Reed, Douglas (1939) *Disgrace Abounding*, Cape.

Reeves, Marjorie (1999) *Christian Thinking and Social Order*, Cassell.

Ricketts, C.M. (1945) *The Rural Ministry: Some Considerations and Suggestions*, SPCK.

Rigby, Andrew (1984) *Initiation and Initiative: An Exploration of the Life and Ideas of Dimitrije Mitrinovic*, East European Monographs, Boulder/Columbia University Press, New York.

Roberts, Andrew (1995) *Eminent Churchillians*, Phoenix.

Roberts, Morley (1938) *Bio-Politics: An Essay in the Physiology, Pathology and Politics of the Social and Somatic Organism*, Dent.

Rodale, J.I. (1949) *Pay Dirt* (9th edition), Devin-Adair, New York.

Rolt, L.T.C. (1977) *Landscape With Canals*, Allen Lane.

—, (1988) *High Horse Riderless*, Green Books, Hartland.

Rowbotham, Michael (1998) *The Grip of Death*, Jon Carpenter, Charlbury.

Rowe, Reginald (1943) *The Economic Crusade*, ERCI.

Rural Reconstruction Association (1935) *The Agricultural Policy of the Rural Reconstruction Association*, RRA.

—, (1936) *The Revival of Agriculture*, Allen & Unwin.

—, (1955) *Feeding the Fifty Million*, Hollis & Carter.

Russell, E. John (1943) 'Broadbalk,' *The Countryman*, Autumn 1943, pp.89–90.

—, (1945) *Agriculture: To-Day and To-Morrow*, Michael Joseph.

—, (1947) Obituary of Sir Albert Howard, *Nature* Vol.160, pp.741f.

—, (1966) *A History of Agricultural Science in Great Britain, 1620–1954*, Allen & Unwin.

Sanderson, William (1936) *Statecraft* (3rd edition), English Mistery.

Sanderson-Wells, T.H. (1939) *Sun Diet, or Live Food for Live Britons*, John Bale.

—, and Jenks, Jorian (1947) *The Revival of England* (pamphlet reprinted from *The Medical Press*, 30.7.1947.).

Scofield, A.M. (1986) 'Organic Farming — The Origin of the Name,' *Biological Agriculture and Horticulture* Vol.4, pp.1–5.

Scott, Lord Justice (1943) *Report of the Committee on Land Utilisation in Rural Areas*, HMSO.

Sears, Paul B. (1947) *Deserts on the March*, University of Oklahoma Press, Norman, Okla.

Seddon, Richard (1988) *Rudolf Steiner: Essential Readings*, Crucible Books.

Selver, Paul (1959) *Orage and the New Age Circle*, Allen & Unwin.

Sewell, Brocard (1966) *My Dear Time's Waste*, St Albert's Press.

—, (1982) *Like Black Swans*, Tabb House, Padstow.

—, (1990) *G.K.'s Weekly: An Appraisal*, Aylesford Press, Upton, Wirral.

Shaw, Christopher and Chase, Malcolm (1989) *The Imagined Past: History and Nostalgia*, Manchester University Press, UK.

Shaw, Nellie (1935) *Whiteway: A Colony on the Cotswolds*, C.W. Daniel.

Shiva, Vandana (1988) *Staying Alive*, Zed Books.

Simpson, A.W. Brian (1992) *In the Highest Degree Odious: Detention Without Trial in Wartime Britain*, Clarendon Press, Oxford.

Sisson, C.H. (1993) *Is There a Church of England?*, Carcanet, Manchester.

Smiley, Jane (1996) *Moo*, Flamingo.

Sorabji, K.S. (1947) *Mi Contra Fa: The Immoralisings of a Machiavellian Musician*, Porcupine Press.

Stallibrass, Alison (1989) *Being Me and Also Us,* Scottish Academic Press, Edinburgh.
Stapledon, R.G. (1939) *The Plough-Up Policy and Ley Farming,* Faber and Faber.
—, 1942) *The Land: Now and To-Morrow,* Faber and Faber.
Steinbeck, John (1939) *The Grapes of Wrath,* Heinemann.
Steiner, Rudolf (1993) *Spiritual Foundations for the Renewal of Agriculture,* Bio-
    Dynamic Farming and Gardening Association, Kimberton, Pa.
Street, A.G. (1954) *Feather-Bedding,* Faber and Faber.
Street, Pamela (1979) *Arthur Bryant,* Collins.
Summerfield, Henry (1975) *That Myriad-Minded Man,* Colin Smythe, Gerrards Cross.
Sykes, Friend (1946) *Humus and the Farmer,* Faber and Faber.
—, (1951) *Food, Farming and the Future,* Faber and Faber.
Symons, W.T. (1931) *The Coming of Community,* C.W. Daniel.
Tawney, R.H. (1961) *The Acquisitive Society,* Fontana.
—, (1972) *Religion and the Rise of Capitalism,* Penguin, Harmondsworth.
Temple, William (1956) *Christianity and the Social Order,* Penguin, Harmondsworth.
Thirsk, Joan (1997) *Alternative Agriculture: A History from the Black Death to the
    Present Day,* Oxford University Press, UK.
Thomas, William Beach (1927) *How England Becomes Prairie,* Ernest Benn.
—, (1931) *Why the Land Dies,* Faber and Faber.
Thurlow, Richard (1987) *Fascism in Britain,* Blackwell, Oxford.
—, (1998) *Fascism in Britain: From Oswald Mosley's Blackshirts to the National Front,*
    I.B. Tauris.
Tilley, Michael F. (1947) *Housing the Country Worker,* Faber and Faber.
Tiltman, Marjorie Hessell (1935) *English Earth,* Harrap.
Tompkins, Peter and Bird, Christopher (1992) *Secrets of the Soil,* Arkana.
Travers, P.L. (1993) *What the Bee Knows,* Penguin.
Trentmann, Frank (1994) 'Civilization and Its Discontents,' *Journal of Contemporary
    History* Vol.29, pp.583–625.
Turner, Newman (1951) *Fertility Farming,* Faber and Faber.
United States Department of Agriculture (1938) *Soils and Men,* USDA, Washington DC.
Van Vuren, J.P.J. (1949) *Soil Fertility and Sewage,* Faber and Faber.
Veldman, Meredith (1994) *Fantasy, the Bomb, and the Greening of Britain: Romantic
    Protest, 1945–1980,* Cambridge University Press, UK.
Vidler, A.R. and Whitehouse, W.A. (1946) *Natural Law: A Christian Re-consideration,*
    SCM.
Wachsmuth, Guenther (1955) *The Life and Work of Rudolf Steiner: From the Turn of the
    Century to His Death,* Whittier Books, New York.
Waksman, S.A. (1938) *Humus,* Baillière, Tindall & Cox.
Waller, Robert (1962) *Prophet of the New Age,* Faber and Faber.
—, (1990) 'Radical Thoughts of L.T.C. Rolt,' *Resurgence* 142, pp.46f.
Ward, Sadie (1988) *War in the Countryside, 1939–45,* Cameron Books.
Washington, Peter (1996) *Madame Blavatsky's Baboon: Theosophy and the Emergence
    of the Western Guru,* Secker & Warburg.
Waterman, Charles (1946) *The Three Spheres of Society,* Faber and Faber.
Watson, James A. Scott and Hobbs, May Elliott (1951) *Great Farmers,* Faber and Faber.
Webb, Barry (1990) *Edmund Blunden: A Biography,* Yale University Press.
Webb, James (1971) *The Flight From Reason,* Macdonald.
—, (1980) *The Harmonious Circle,* Thames and Hudson.
—, (1981) *The Occult Establishment,* Richard Drew, Glasgow.
Webber, G.C. (1986) *The Ideology of the British Right, 1918–1939,* Croom Helm.
Welch, Louise (1982) *Orage with Gurdjieff in America,* RKP.

Westlake, Aubrey (1961) *The Pattern of Health*, Vincent Stuart.

Whetham, Edith H. (1978) *The Agrarian History of England and Wales*, Vol. VIII: 1914–1939, Cambridge University Press, UK.

White, Lynn Jr. (1967) 'The Historic Roots of Our Ecologic Crisis,' *Science* Vol.155, pp.1203–7.

Wickenden, Leonard (1956) *Our Daily Poison*, Devin-Adair, New York.

Wiener, Martin J. (1992) *English Culture and the Decline of the Industrial Spirit, 1850–1980*, Penguin.

Wilkinson, Alan (1998) *Christian Socialism: Scott Holland to Tony Blair*, SCM.

Williams, Lord, of Barnburgh [Tom Williams] (1965) *Digging for Britain*, Hutchinson.

Williams-Ellis, Clough (1928) *England and the Octopus*, Bles.

—, (1937) *Britain and the Beast*, Dent.

Williamson, Anne (1995) *Henry Williamson: Tarka and the Last Romantic*, Alan Sutton, Stroud.

Williamson, G. Scott and Pearse, Innes H. (1951) *The Passing of Peckham, 1951*, Pioneer Health Centre.

—, and Pearse, Innes H. (1965) *Science, Synthesis and Sanity*, Collins.

Williamson, Henry (1941) *The Story of a Norfolk Farm*, Faber and Faber.

—, (1948) *The Phasian Bird*, Faber and Faber.

—, (1967) *Lucifer Before Sunrise*, Macdonald.

—, (1985a) *The Phoenix Generation*, Macdonald.

—, (1985b) *A Solitary War*, Macdonald.

Wilson, R.G.M. (1941) *I Believe: An Appeal for the Land by 'A Farmer,'* Capt. R.G.M. Wilson, Cambridge.

Wohl, Robert (1980) *The Generation of 1914*, Weidenfeld and Nicolson.

Wollenberg, Bruce (1997) *Christian Social Thought in Great Britain Between the Wars*, University Press of America.

Wood, Alan (1950) *The Groundnut Affair*, Bodley Head.

Worster, Donald (1985) *Nature's Economy: A History of Ecological Ideas*, Cambridge University Press, UK.

Wrench, G.T. (1972) *The Wheel of Health*, Schocken Books, New York.

Wrench, J.E. (1948) *Francis Yeats-Brown, 1886–1944*, Eyre & Spottiswoode.

Wright, Patrick (1985) *On Living in an Old Country*, Verso.

—, (1996) *The Village that Died for England*, Vintage.

Wylie, J.C. (1955) *Fertility From Town Wastes*, Faber and Faber.

York, Archbishop of (1941a) (William Temple) *Malvern 1941: The Life of the Church and the Order of Society*, Longmans Green.

—, (1941b) *Malvern: The Life of the Church and the Order of Society* (booklet reprinting the Conference's findings), ICF.

Index

Names of people in SMALL CAPITALS indicate an entry in Appendix A. Names of groups, institutions or journals in SMALL CAPITALS indicate an entry in Appendix B.